SAS Publishing

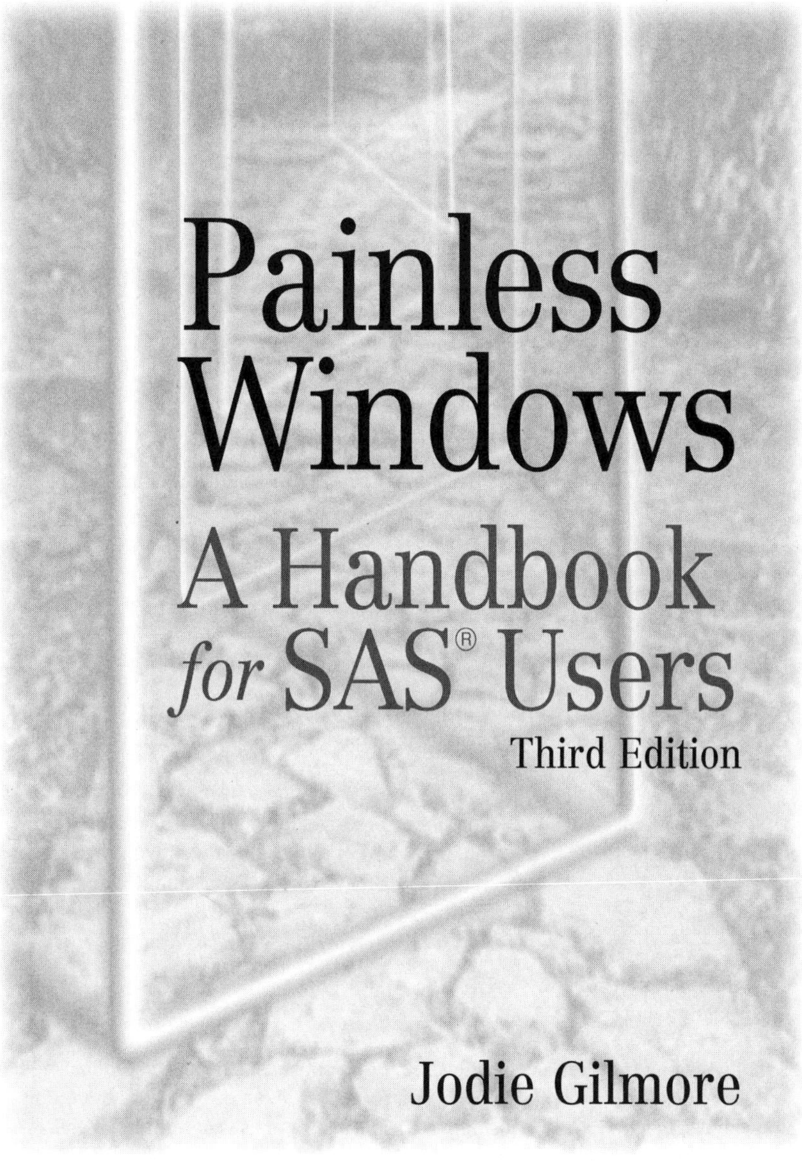

Painless Windows

A Handbook for SAS® Users

Third Edition

Jodie Gilmore

The Power to Know®

The correct bibliographic citation for this manual is as follows: Gilmore, Jodie. 2004. *Pailness Windows: A Handbook for SAS® Users, Third Edition,* Cary, NC: SAS Institute Inc.

Painless Windows: A Handbook for SAS® Users, Third Edition

ISBN 1-59047-399-X

SAS Institute Inc., SAS Campus Drive, Cary, North Carolina 27513.

1st printing, March 2004
2nd printing, January 2005

Table of Contents

1 Learning to Do Windows

2 Performing the Basic SAS Software Tasks under Windows

3 Editing and Working with Files

4 Submitting SAS Code

5 Printing

6 Adjusting Your Windows Environment

7 Using Advanced Features of the Enhanced Editor

8 Using the SAS Output Delivery System

9 Managing SAS Files

10 Using SAS Enterprise Guide: A Primer

11 Customizing Your Start-up Files and SAS System Options

12 Using Batch Mode

13 Using SAS to Execute System Commands and Applications

14 Sharing Data between SAS and Windows Applications

15 Using SAS/CONNECT Software to Connect Your PC to Other Systems

Appendix 1 Troubleshooting

Appendix 2 Using the SAS System Viewer

Appendix 3 Becoming Familiar with the Windows Explorer

Appendix 4 Accessibility and the SAS System

Appendix 5 Exporting and Importing Information from the SAS Registry

Welcome to SAS 9.1 for Windows

What This Book Is

Painless Windows: A Handbook for SAS Users, Third Edition is a task-oriented book about SAS 9.1 (and subsequent releases) under Microsoft Windows. The book does not assume the reader is a Windows expert or a SAS guru, but somewhere in between.

The examples in this book were run under Windows 2000 Professional. However, SAS 9.1 also runs in all of the following environments:

- 32-bit Windows 2000 Server, Windows 2000 Advanced Server, and Windows 2000 Datacenter Server
- 32-bit Windows XP Professional Edition and Windows XP Home Edition
- 32-bit Windows 2003 Server, including the Standard, Datacenter, Enterprise, and Web editions
- 32-bit Windows NT Workstation, Windows NT Server, Windows NT Server Enterprise Edition, and Windows NT Terminal Server Edition
- 64-bit Windows XP Professional Edition
- 64-bit Windows 2003 Server, Enterprise and Datacenter editions.

The information contained herein applies equally well to all these environments, as well as to subsequent releases from Microsoft.

SAS 9.1 does not run on older versions of Microsoft Windows, such as Windows ME, Windows 95, or Windows 98. Also, you cannot run the 32-bit version of SAS 9.1 on a 64-bit operating system, or the 64-bit version of SAS 9.1 on a 32-bit operating system.

Note

> Although SAS 9.1 runs on Windows XP Home Edition, this version of Windows is missing some important security, recovery, and domain authentication features that affect the performance of SAS 9.1 in this environment. Therefore, use of the Windows XP Home Edition is not recommended for SAS users.

This book assumes that you are familiar with some version of the SAS System but not with SAS 9.1 or with Windows. It also acknowledges that you may not even like Windows but that you have to use SAS software under Windows to do part of your job. In this book, you learn to use key features of Base SAS software to accomplish certain tasks under Windows.

Example tasks include

- opening a file that contains SAS code
- using the Enhanced Editor
- submitting SAS code
- using the SAS Output Delivery System (ODS)
- using the SAS Explorer to manage files
- using SAS Enterprise Guide
- saving changes to your SAS code
- printing output from your SAS code
- working in batch mode.

The book also touches briefly on some other components of the SAS System, including DDE, OLE, SAS/AF, and SAS/CONNECT software.

You also learn how to get around in Windows. For example, the first chapter shows you how to slow down your mouse and how to redisplay an application you want to use after it has disappeared behind several other applications. The chapters include many screen shots, showing what your display should look like while you are filling out dialog boxes and using menus.

What Software You Need

The information in this book assumes you have Microsoft Windows 2000, Microsoft Windows XP, Microsoft Windows NT, or a subsequent version of Windows. There are 32-bit and 64-bit versions of SAS. They must be run in the environment that they were written for. Also, the examples and discussion throughout this book assume you have SAS 9.1 for Windows (or a subsequent release).

What This Book Is Not

This book is not a comprehensive guide to using Windows. For example, it does not discuss how to tune Windows performance, configure an eight-server system, or use the Control Panel to add serial ports to your system. Nor is this book a guide to SAS software itself. It assumes you know what a DATA step is, that you have used PROC PRINT, and that you know the difference between a system option and a statement option. If you need a guide to using SAS software in general or need more information on Windows, refer to "Further Reading" later in this chapter.

This book is not meant to replace SAS Institute reference documentation. It does not show you every nuance of the tasks it discusses, nor does it show you every way to perform a task. Also, there are aspects of SAS 9.1 that this book does not cover. For example, it does not cover using e-mail or advanced OLE features. For nitty-gritty details, turn to SAS Institute's reference guides and online documentation.

Finally, this book is not an installation guide. SAS Institute provides comprehensive installation and configuration instructions along with the software. If you need installation assistance, contact your on-site SAS Installation Representative, ask your company's help desk, or review the documentation that came with your SAS software.

Book Overview

This book contains 15 chapters and 5 appendices. The chapters are task-oriented and progress from simple tasks such as opening and closing files to more complicated tasks such as using SAS/CONNECT software to connect your PC to other computers. In addition, this book contains a main table of contents, individual chapter tables of contents, and an index. Use these tools to quickly find what you are looking for. If you encounter a term you are unfamiliar with, check the glossary.

Graphics: This book contains many pictures of menus and screens. Because Windows is a highly customizable operating system, your menus and screens may not look exactly like those shown in this book. However, you should still be able to use the graphics to orient yourself.

Note

> The screen captures in this book are in gray scale. To see color versions of some screens, visit this book's Companion Web Site at http://support.sas.com/publishing/bbu/companion_site/58783.html.

What's New **and** **FasTip** **Sections:** Many sections begin with a What's New section that summarizes the relevant new features of the SAS System (most of these will be SAS 9.1 features; a few are from SAS 8; a few have been around a while but have not been documented in this book before).

FasTips give bare-bones information on performing a task. If you have performed the task before and need a quick reminder, check these first. FasTips do not appear in some chapters that cover complex tasks that cannot be summarized in a few words or in the appendixes.

Third Edition Highlights

Use the following table to scan for the major changes to the SAS System and to this book since the last edition.

Feature	Section and/or Chapter
Tutorial on using the SAS Enhanced Editor	Chapter 7
Enhanced coverage of the SAS Output Delivery System	Chapter 8
Expanded coverage of using DDE with Microsoft Word and Microsoft Excel	"Understanding Dynamic Data Exchange (DDE)" in Chapter 14
Overview of using Enterprise Guide V2.0	Chapter 10
Information on the SAS System and accessibility	Appendix 4
Brief discussion of the SAS Registry	Appendix 5

Typographical Conventions

This book uses several type fonts to convey particular information. For example, menu items are in one font, while SAS code is in another. The following list gives the purpose of each font used:

bold:	Boldface is used to set off elements in menus, windows, and dialog boxes.
`monospace:`	Monospace is used for SAS code and operating system commands.
italics:	Italics are used in SAS code to indicate user-supplied values.
Edit → Clear All	Menu and submenu items are separated by an arrow and appear in the same font as window and dialog box elements.

What You Should Read

If you are a neophyte Windows user, you should read Chapters 1 and 2 thoroughly. They give you a survival kit of information that you need in order to understand the rest of the book. If you have used the SAS System under Windows, but are new to SAS 9.1, read the **What's New** section at the beginning of the sections that describe the tasks you want to do.

Further Reading

Because this book is a beginner's guide, it does not contain information on complex tasks, nor does it cover all features of either the SAS System or Windows. Check the following list for books you may want to have on hand for further research. The list is by subject.

SAS System Documentation: The following books are about the SAS System. This is not a complete list; check the SAS Institute *Publications Catalog* or the SAS Customer Support Center Web site (support.sas.com) for additional titles. Books with "(SUP)" after their titles are published through the SAS User Publishing program.

Note

SAS Institute also provides SAS Help and Documentation with SAS software.

Base SAS Software:

Getting Started with SAS

Output Delivery System: The Basics (SUP)

Professional SAS Programmer's Pocket Reference, Fourth Edition (SUP)

SAS 9.1 Companion for Windows

SAS Companion for the Microsoft Windows NT Environment, Version 6, First Edition

SAS 9.1 Language Reference: Concepts

SAS 9.1 Language Reference: Dictionary, Volumes 1 and 2

SAS 9.1 Procedures Guide, Volumes 1, 2, and 3

Step-by-Step Programming with Base SAS Software

SAS 9.1 Output Delivery System: User's Guide

The Little SAS Book: A Primer, Third Edition (SUP)

What's New for SAS 9 and 9.1

What's New in SAS Software for Version 8

What's New in SAS Software, Release 8.1 and Release 8.2

What's New in SAS Software for Version 7 and the Version 8 Developer's Release

SAS/AF Software:

Getting Started with the FRAME Entry: Developing Object-Oriented Applications, Second Edition

SAS/AF Software Procedure Guide, Version 8

SAS Component Language: Reference, Version 8

Other Useful SAS System Books:

Carpenter's Complete Guide to the SAS Macro Language (SUP)

Communications Access Methods for SAS/CONNECT 9.1 and SAS/SHARE 9.1

Debugging SAS Programs: A Handbook of Tools and Techniques (SUP)

Essential Client/Server Survival Guide, Second Edition

Moving and Accessing SAS 9.1 Files

SAS/CONNECT 9.1 User's Guide

Note

> You can find changes and enhancements documentation for SAS 9.1 in SAS Help and Documentation under the **What's New for SAS 9 and 9.1** topic, and also on the main SAS Web site, www.sas.com.

Microsoft Windows Documentation: The following books, listed in alphabetical order, are about Windows. Check your local bookstore and library for additional titles.

Windows 2000:

Inside Microsoft Windows 2000

Mastering Windows 2000 Professional

Undocumented Windows 2000 Secrets: A Programmer's Cookbook

Windows XP:

Mastering Windows XP Professional

Microsoft Windows XP Inside Out

Windows XP for Dummies

Windows XP in a Nutshell

Windows XP Professional: The Ultimate User's Guide

Windows Server 2003:

Inside Windows Server 2003

Mastering Windows Server 2003

Microsoft Windows Server 2003 Unleashed

Windows Server 2003 for Dummies

Windows Server 2003: The Complete Reference

1 Learning to Do Windows

All GUIs Are Not Created Equal

Fifteen, even ten years ago, personal computers (PCs) were not the norm on everyone's desktop. But today, almost everyone has access to a PC, while improved technology has significantly improved PC performance. Ten years ago, most other operating systems, such as VMS (now OpenVMS) and UNIX, were almost entirely command-line driven. Today, most operating systems feature some sort of graphical user interface (GUI). But far from making a Windows-specific book about SAS obsolete, these changes in technology make such a book even more valuable.

Many people must switch between other operating systems and their PC several times a day. Some things remain constant, such as the basics of using a mouse. But file management, the available SAS system options, printing—all these tasks vary just enough from one GUI to another to confuse and annoy users, especially if they are new to the SAS System. So a handy, task-oriented reference devoted to the Microsoft Windows environment is an important productivity tool.

This chapter serves as an introduction to the Windows environment by defining some common terms, showing you how to take control of your mouse, showing you how to move and resize windows, and explaining how files are stored on the PC.

How Windows Works

Like most GUIs, the Windows graphical user interface includes windows, dialog boxes, icons, buttons, and other items. Usually, you use a mouse to interact with the GUI, although you also use the keyboard.

To work with applications under Windows, you use the Windows desktop, and in particular, the **Start** button. The **Start** button is a Windows component that organizes all your Windows applications into groups and makes interacting with the operating system easier. Some applications, such as Microsoft Paint and Microsoft Wordpad, come with Windows; other applications you install separately, such as the SAS System.

Windows lets you do several things at once. For example, you can print a file at the same time as you invoke an application. In particular, you can have several "instances" of a program open at once. Therefore, you can start multiple SAS sessions, all running at the same time.

Note

> Only the first SAS session started uses the default SASUSER.PROFILE catalog, which is where most customizations to the SAS windowing environment are stored. Unless subsequent SAS sessions are started with a different SASUSER system option that points to a different permanent location, these subsequent sessions will use a temporary profile catalog called WORK.PROFILE and will be unable to access previously saved customizations or save customizations for future use.

Terms You Should Know

Every operating system has its own jargon, and Windows is no exception. If you have used a different GUI on another operating system, some of the terms are familiar. But you should scan this section anyway, to see if there are discrepancies between how you understand a term and how this book uses it.

The glossary at the end of this book provides a more complete list of terms used with the SAS System for Windows. The following alphabetical list gives you a head start so that you can read this chapter without having to refer to the glossary constantly.

active window: the application or part of an application that is ready to accept input.

application: a program with its attendant windows. Examples include the SAS System, Microsoft Word, and Internet Explorer.

click: to press a mouse button once. Unless otherwise stated, click means to press the left mouse button.

Clipboard: a Windows component that is like an online pegboard—a place to store something until you need it again. Typically, the Clipboard is used to store text and graphics that you want to copy somewhere else.

close: to shut an individual window or shut down an entire application.

desktop: your screen, where all applications appear.

dialog box: a type of window that solicits information from you. Usually, you must supply this information before you can continue using an application.

double-click: to quickly press a mouse button twice in a row (usually the left mouse button).

icon: a pictorial representation of something, such as a window, file, or action.

mouse: the handheld device you use to select and manipulate applications and text. The mouse activates the mouse pointer on the screen.

point: to move the mouse pointer over an item on the screen, such as a menu choice, a word, or an icon.

popup menu: a context-sensitive menu that appears when you click the right mouse button.

program group: a collection of applications available from the **Programs** selection of the **Start** button menu. Examples of program groups include Accessories and SAS.

right-click: to press the right mouse button once. Usually, right-clicking displays a context-sensitive menu called a popup menu.

Start button: the button in the bottom-left corner of the screen, labeled "Start. " Clicking this button enables you to launch applications, alter configuration settings, access Windows help files, and perform other tasks.

Taskbar: a list of all open applications, located by default across the bottom of the Windows desktop.

Becoming Familiar with the Windows Desktop

When you start Windows, the Windows desktop appears. That may be all that happens, or other applications may start, depending on how your system is configured. The Windows desktop keeps a list of all open applications. This list is displayed across the bottom of the screen and is called the Windows Taskbar. The active application's name is highlighted; to move to a different application, click the application's name in the Windows Taskbar.

Figure 1.1 shows a sample Windows desktop. The Taskbar indicates that two applications are open: SAS and Microsoft Word. Your desktop may look slightly different from the one in Figure 1.1.

Figure 1.1 Sample Windows Desktop with Taskbar

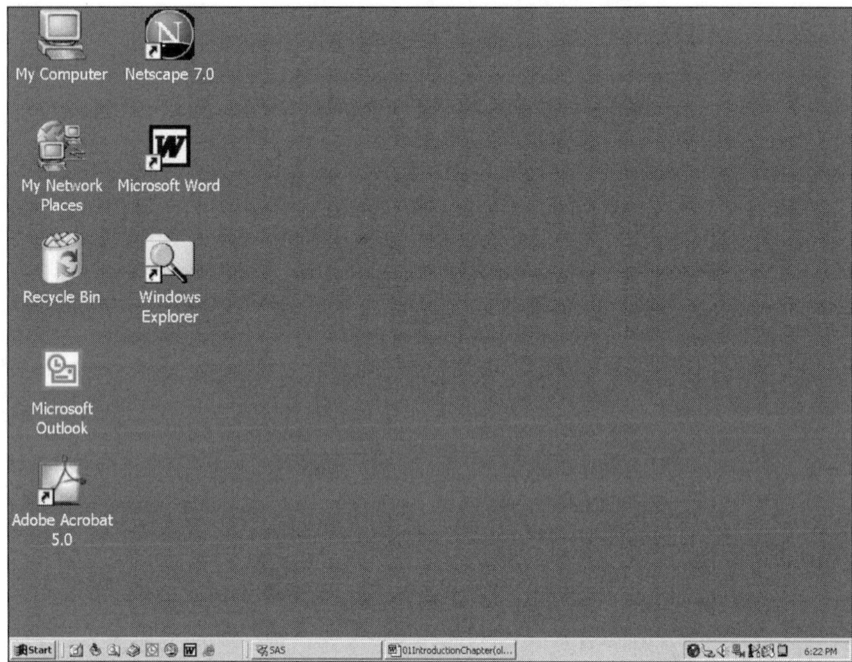

Besides the Taskbar, two more useful components of the Windows desktop are the **Start** button and the **Recycle Bin**.

- 

The **Start** button is located in the bottom-left corner of the Windows desktop. You use it to start applications and manage your Windows session. See "Starting Applications" later in this chapter.

- 

The **Recycle Bin** is a temporary storage area for deleted files (when you use the Windows Explorer or My Computer to delete them). See "Restoring Deleted Files" in Appendix 3 for more information.

Windows Geography

The applications and windows you see as you work with Windows have many things in common. This section familiarizes you with the "lay of the land" under Windows. Figure 1.2 shows some of the standard window elements.

Figure 1.2 Standard Window Elements

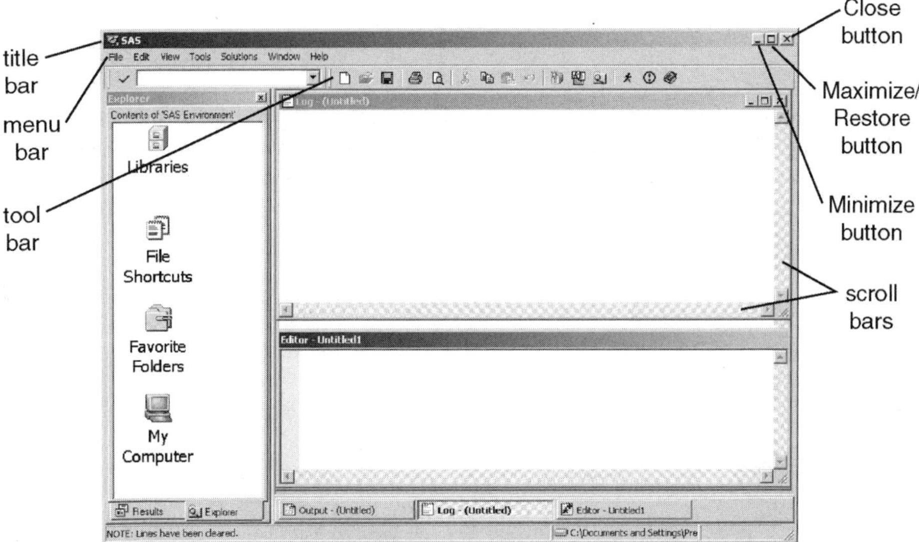

A brief description of each element in Figure 1.2 follows; "Getting to Know the SAS System Interface" in Chapter 2 presents more details on these and other window elements specific to the SAS System.

Title Bar: Each window has a title bar that tells the name of the window. In this case, the title bar at the top tells you the application is SAS. Each individual window, such as the Log window and the Enhanced Editor window, also has a title bar. As well as providing the title of the application, the title bar is also the "handle" for moving windows, as discussed later in this chapter.

Menu Bar: If you are used to nonwindowing environments, you are familiar with giving operating system commands. In Windows, you often use the menu bar to issue these commands. For example, instead of typing "save example1.sas" on a command line, you click **File**, then click **Save**. While this may seem awkward at first, it does provide the advantage of not having to remember command syntax.

Use the following guides as you browse the menus:

- If a menu choice has an arrow after it, that means there is another layer of choices.
- If a menu choice has ellipsis points after it, that means clicking it opens a dialog box.

- If there is no symbol after the menu choice, clicking that choice executes a command, such as SAVE.
- Shortcut keys are listed to the right of menu choices. Instead of using the menus, you can press the shortcut keys to achieve the same result. For example, CTRL-S is the shortcut key for SAVE.

Tool Bar: Another method of issuing commands under Windows is to use the graphical tool bar. For example, to save a file in the SAS System, click the icon that looks like a computer disk. Most applications, including the SAS System, allow you to define your own tools; this enables you to customize your environment and work efficiently.

Scroll Bars: Most windows provide both horizontal and vertical scroll bars. These enable you to move left, right, up, and down in the window. Clicking the up arrow moves the view up, and clicking the down arrow moves the view down. Similarly, clicking the left arrow moves the view to the left, and clicking the right arrow moves the view to the right. To move larger distances, click in the scroll bar area instead of on the arrows. "Scrolling" in Chapter 3 provides more detailed information on using scroll bars.

Minimize Button: Click the Minimize button (the left-most of the three buttons in the top-right corner of a window) to cause the window to shrink to an icon. If you minimize an entire application, the window disappears from the desktop; to restore the application, click its name in the Windows Taskbar. Typically, only the active window shows the Minimize button.

Maximize/Restore Button: The middle button in the top-right corner of the window does double duty. If it appears as a single box (as in Figure 1.2), clicking it causes the window to take up the whole screen (that is, maximize). If it appears as two layered boxes, clicking it causes the window to return to the size it was before it was maximized. Typically, only the active window shows the Maximize button.

Close Button: The Close button is the right-most button in the top-right corner of a window, and it contains an X. Clicking it closes the application or window. Typically, only the active window shows the Close button.

Taking Control of Your Mouse

While using Windows with only a keyboard is possible, it is more efficient to use a mouse. But often, people unfamiliar with the mouse are frustrated by having the pointer move too quickly, not being able to double-click properly, and other problems caused by lack of practice. However, using the mouse does not have to be a rat race! Windows provides a way to slow the mouse down, adjust the double-click rate, and in general let you take control of your mouse.

Using the Mouse Buttons: Most mice have two or three buttons. The left button is used to "click" on things—icons, filenames, options, and so on. The right mouse button is reserved for special tasks, such as opening popup menus. If your mouse has a middle button, you can pretty much ignore it, although some software applications (including the SAS System) let you associate commands with the middle mouse button.

Note

> If you use a left-handed mouse, the left and right buttons are switched. The "left button" is always the button under your index finger.

More advanced types of pointing devices, such as trackballs, can also be used with the SAS System.

Adjusting How Your Mouse Works: To adjust how your mouse works, follow these steps:

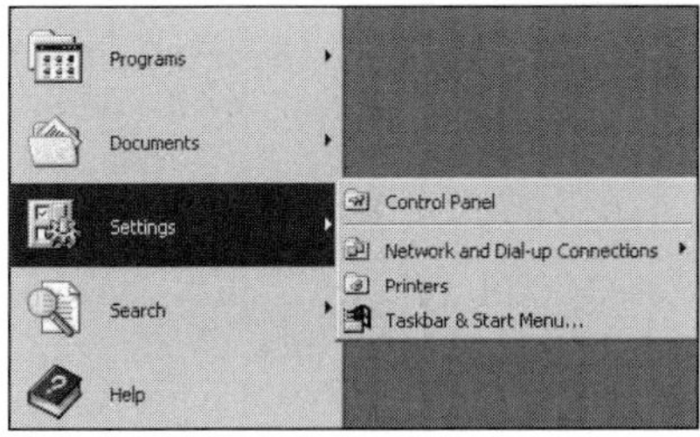

1. Click the **Start** button, then click **Settings**. When the second-level menu appears, click **Control Panel**.
2. When the Control Panel appears, double-click the **Mouse** icon. The Mouse Properties dialog box opens. Figure 1.3 shows a sample Mouse Properties dialog box.

Figure 1.3 Sample Mouse Properties Dialog Box

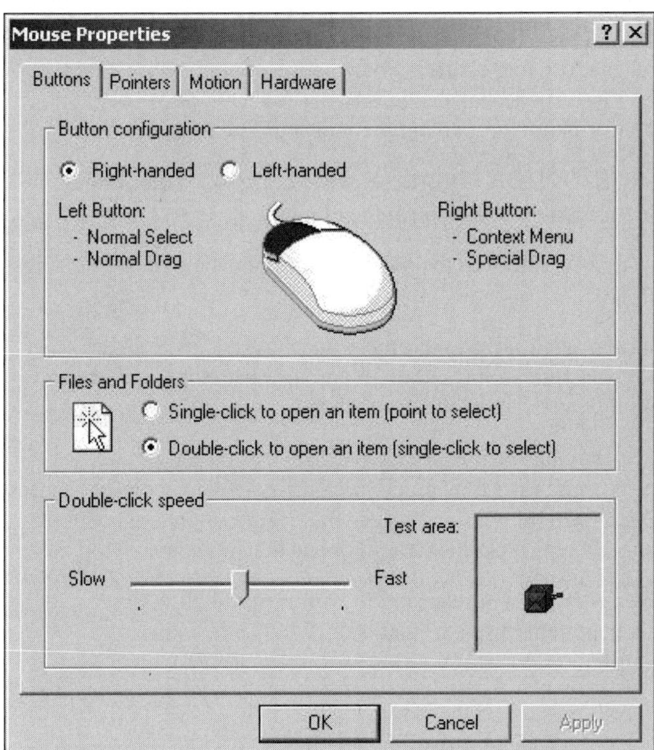

3. There are four tabs in the Mouse Properties dialog box. The top tab is labeled **Buttons**. On this tab, you can adjust the mouse's double-click speed and the left- or right-handed configuration of your mouse.
4. Many Windows users prefer a slower double-click speed. In the **Double-click speed** area, place your mouse pointer over the slider, hold the left mouse button down, and drag the mouse pointer so that the slider moves to the left (toward **Slow**). Release the mouse pointer and double-click the jack-in-the-box icon (or other icon) in the **Test** area to see if you like the new speed. If your double-click is successful, the icon shows a jack-in-the-box pop out. Double-clicking again closes the jack-in-the-box.
5. If you are left-handed, click **Left-handed** in the **Button configuration** area. The text next to the mouse explains what function each mouse button has. If you choose this option, the button under your left index finger (originally the "right" mouse button) becomes the "left" mouse button and vice versa.
6. To slow your mouse down so that you can follow it more easily with your eyes, click the **Motion** tab at the top of the Mouse Properties dialog box. In the **Speed** area, place your mouse pointer over the slider, hold the left mouse button down, and drag the mouse pointer so that the slider moves to the left (toward **Slow**). Release the mouse pointer; now move the mouse pointer, to see if you like the new speed.
7. To make the mouse pointer easier to find on the screen when you move the mouse, you may want to select the **Display pointer trails** option.

Depending on your mouse driver (the software that controls your mouse), you may see other options; explore the other tabs in the Mouse Properties dialog box to see what options are available to you. See Appendix 4 for information on making the mouse pointer bigger.

When you are happy with your selections, click **OK**. This closes the Mouse Properties dialog box. To close the Control Panel, click **File → Close** in the Control Panel menu.

As you become more adept with your mouse, return to the Mouse Properties dialog box and adjust the settings again to fit your new skill level.

Using Your Mouse to Communicate with Applications: Your mouse is the primary method of communicating with Windows applications, although you also use function keys and keyboard sequences. You need to master several skills with the mouse:

Pointing	Pointing involves moving the mouse pointer until it is directly on top of something, such as an icon or a menu choice. In some cases, pointing causes Windows to take an action. For example, in the **Start** button menu, simply pointing (without clicking) to a menu item opens the submenu.
Clicking	Clicking involves pressing and releasing the left mouse button once. Usually, you click an item to select (that is, highlight) the item.

Right-clicking Right-clicking involves pressing and releasing the right mouse button once. Usually, you right-click an item to display a context-sensitive menu.

Double-clicking Double-clicking involves pressing the left mouse button twice in rapid succession. Usually, you double-click an item to activate the item (such as starting an application from an icon).

Dragging Dragging involves holding the mouse button down while you move the mouse around. Usually, you drag an object to move it (such as moving window borders or text in a text editor).

Learning the Basic Survival Kit

There are several things you should know before you start using Windows extensively. For example, how do you start applications? When you are done with them, how do you close them? What if you want to use a new application but do not want to close the others? Learning the answers to these and a few other questions helps you work more efficiently under Windows.

Starting Applications: An easy way to start an application is to use the **Start** button menu. Clicking the **Start** button displays a first-level menu, shown in Figure 1.4.

Figure 1.4 Start Button Menu

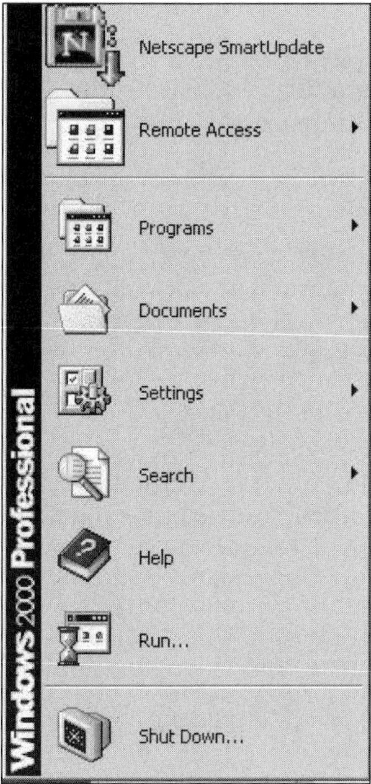

To start an application, such as the SAS System, click the **Programs** item in the **Start** button menu. A second menu appears, a sample of which is shown in Figure 1.5.

Figure 1.5 Programs Menu from the Start Button

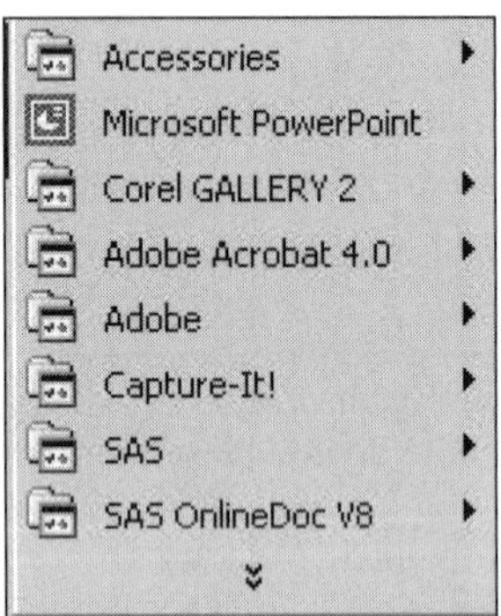

This menu shows the program groups available on your system, such as **Accessories** and **SAS**. Your desktop may show other groups, such as **Microsoft Office Tools**, depending on what software is installed on your PC.

Note

Most of the time, merely placing the mouse pointer over the text is sufficient to select it in a menu, but not always. And clicking doesn't hurt anything. Therefore, in many places, this book says "click **Programs**" or gives other similar instructions.

Program groups in the **Programs** menu that are followed by a right arrow contain subgroups. Clicking the main program group displays the subgroup. Take a moment to investigate all program groups on your desktop, to see what applications are available to you. To close the **Programs** menu without starting an application, click outside the menus (or press ESC).

Closing Applications: The easiest way to close applications is to click the Close button. This is the button marked with an X, in the top-right corner of an application's main window. Sometimes, you also have to confirm that you want to exit the application. (For example, by default the SAS System prompts you with the question "Are you sure you want to end the SAS session?")

Two other methods of closing an application include

- clicking the **File** choice in the application's menu bar, then clicking **Exit** or **Close**
- right-clicking the application's name in the Taskbar and clicking **Close**.

Note

> In the SAS System, an individual window's Close button (along with the Minimize and Maximize/Restore buttons) is not visible until you make the window active by clicking in it.

Managing Several Open Applications at Once: One of the nice things about Windows is that it lets you use several applications at the same time. But you have only one screen, so the open windows are layered. The window that is "on top" is usually the active window. To make another window active, you must somehow get to it.

Suppose you have started the SAS System, and now you want to open Microsoft Word, without ending your SAS session. Follow these steps to open Word:

1. Click the **Start** button.
2. Click **Programs** in the **Start** button menu, then click Microsoft Word. (Your menu path to the Microsoft Word program may be somewhat different, depending on how Word was installed.)

Now two applications are open at once: the SAS System and Word.

Here are some ways you can return to your SAS session:

- Click the **SAS** icon on the Windows Taskbar.
- Press ALT-ESC to toggle through all open applications.

Using Dialog Boxes: To communicate with most Windows applications, you must use dialog boxes. These are interactive ways to give commands and information to an application. When you adjusted your mouse settings, you were using a dialog box. Dialog boxes have many features in common, such as the following:

- Clicking **OK** or **Close** applies your changes and closes the dialog box.
- Clicking **Cancel** closes the dialog box without having any other effect.
- Sometimes you can type a value into a field; this is called a *text-entry field.*
- If there are several choices for a field value, clicking the down arrow next to the field displays a list of choices. Click one of the choices to change the field value. This window component is called a *drop-down list box.*
- Other times, the entire list of choices is displayed in a *list box*; use the scroll bars to navigate the list. Click a choice to select it.

- If there are options that can be turned on or off, clicking the box or button next to the option toggles its value. If a box has an "x" in it, or if a round button is filled in, the option is on. The difference between check boxes (square boxes) and radio buttons (round buttons) is as follows:
  - You can choose several options in a list of check boxes.
  - Options with radio buttons are mutually exclusive. 
- ? Many dialog boxes offer a context-sensitive help button near the top-right corner of the dialog box. Clicking this button changes the mouse pointer to an arrow with a question mark beside it. Now click the part of the dialog box you want more information about. The help information is displayed in a window. Press ESC to close the help window. Occasionally, instead of the context-sensitive help button, you may see a button labeled **Help**.

In dialog boxes that list files, you may see three useful icons (among others). Click the icon to activate it.

-  Move up a level in the folder hierarchy.
-  Create a new folder.
-  Customize the view, such as showing file details or changing to large icons.

Figure 1.6 shows an example dialog box that displays many of these features.

Figure 1.7 shows another dialog box with more features.

Figure 1.6 Standard Dialog Box Features

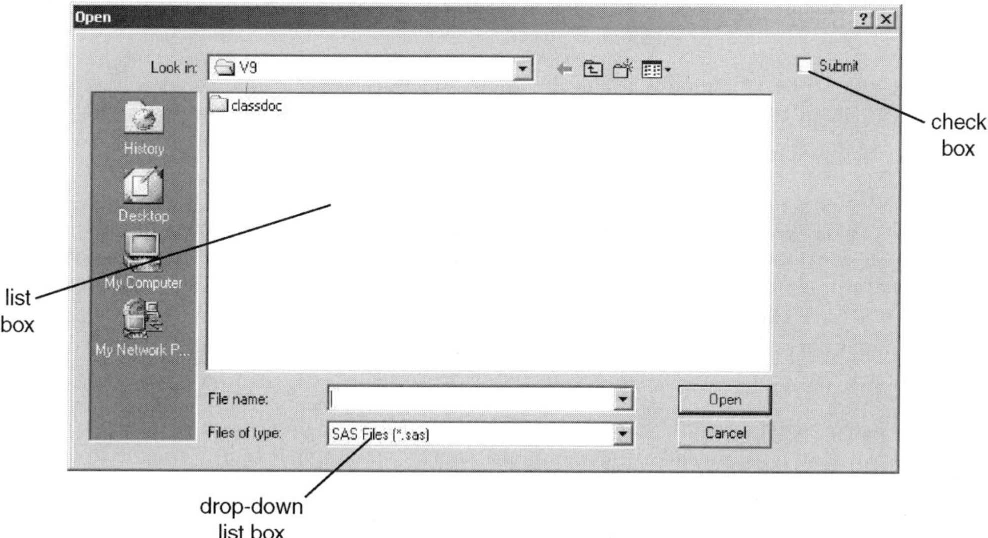

Figure 1.7 More Standard Dialog Box Features

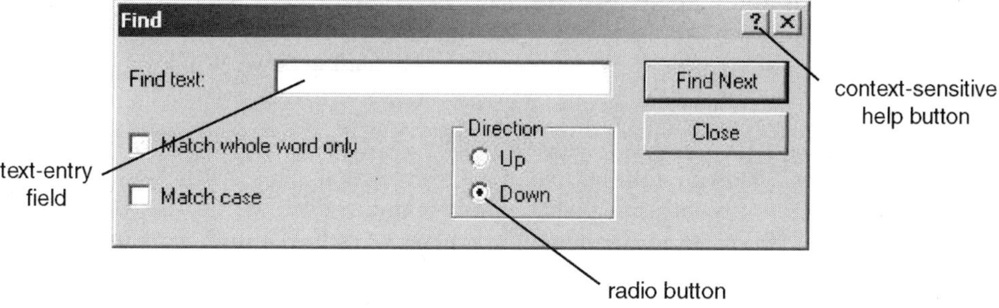

Controlling How Programs Work: The icons you see on the desktop are not magic. They are pictorial representations of operating system commands and command options. When you install an application such as the SAS System, the installation utility adds the icon to the appropriate program group in the **Programs** menu and associates certain commands and options with the icon. These commands control the location of the program's executable file (such as SAS.EXE) and other aspects of running the program. This collection of commands constitutes the application's "properties."

You can change an application's properties by using the Properties dialog box. "Altering the Properties of the SAS System Icon in the Windows Start Menu" in Chapter 11 gives some examples of how to change SAS System properties.

Moving and Resizing Windows: Sometimes the default size or position of a window is not satisfactory. You've already learned about the Minimize and Maximize buttons, but you can also move windows or cause them to shrink and grow.

To move a window, place the mouse pointer in the title bar of the window. Now press the mouse button down and hold it down while dragging the mouse. The entire window follows the mouse pointer. Release the mouse button when the window is where you want it.

To resize the window, place the mouse pointer on the edge of the window. The pointer turns into a horizontal, vertical, or diagonal double-headed arrow (depending on whether the mouse pointer is positioned on a side, the top or bottom, or a corner of the window, respectively). Hold the mouse button down and drag the mouse—the window edge follows the pointer—until the window is the size you want. Resize a window in both the vertical and horizontal directions at once by placing the mouse pointer over a corner of the window. In this case, the pointer turns into a diagonal double-headed arrow.

To practice resizing windows, double-click the **Recycle Bin** icon on the Windows desktop. Now make the Recycle Bin window narrow, then tall, then back to its original size. Close the Recycle Bin by clicking its Close button.

Note

You cannot resize a maximized window except to minimize it.

Shutting Down the Windows Environment: You can choose to leave Windows running all the time, even when you are away from your desk. Or, you may want to turn your computer off. But you should never turn off your computer without properly shutting down Windows.

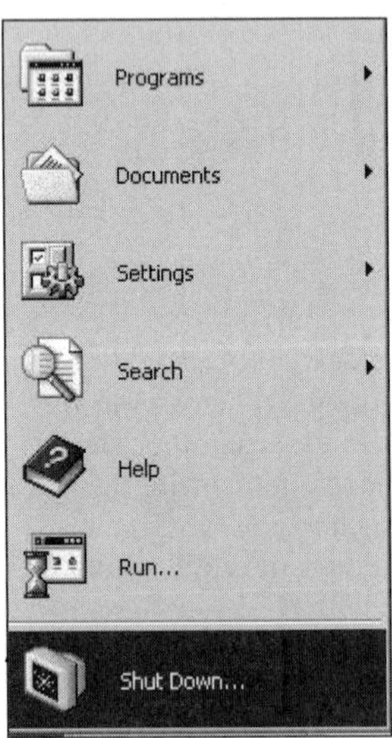

To shut down Windows, click the **Start** button, then click **Shut Down** (at the bottom of the **Start** button menu). A dialog box appears, asking what type of shut-down you want to use. Click the down arrow under **What do you want the computer to do?** and select **Shut down**. Now press ENTER. Windows shuts down and turns your computer off.

Caution

> If you shut the computer down without closing your applications, you could lose work, corrupt your Windows profile, destroy data files, and leave files in an open state that may not allow you to use them next time you start your system. Shutting down the computer without first closing your SAS session prevents the SAS System from closing the WORK files, as well.

Handy Keyboard Shortcuts for Windows

Table 1.1 provides a list of handy keyboard shortcuts for performing tasks in the Windows environment. Refer to this table as you read the rest of the book. If you do not want to use the mouse for a task, use the keyboard shortcut listed in the table.

Table 1.1 Keyboard Shortcuts

Keyboard Shortcut	Action
ALT-ENTER	Opens the Properties dialog box for an icon
CTRL-ESC	Opens the **Start** button menu
ESC	Closes the **Start** button menu
ALT-ESC	Toggles through all open applications
ALT-TAB	Toggles between the two last-used applications
TAB	Moves the cursor from field to field in dialog boxes
SHIFT-TAB	Moves the cursor backward through fields in dialog boxes
BACKSPACE	In file list windows, such as the SAS Explorer, Windows Explorer, or Open dialog box, moves you up one level in the file hierarchy
Windows button + E	Opens the Windows Explorer Note: Not all keyboards have a Windows button.

Menus also provide a type of keyboard shortcut, called hotkeys. These are the underlined letters you see in each of the menu choices. If a menu is open, pressing the hotkey is equivalent to clicking a menu choice.

To open a menu without using the mouse, press the ALT key. This highlights the first item in the menu bar. Once the highlighting appears in the menu bar, use your arrow keys to move to the menu item you want, and press ENTER to execute the command. Or, type the letter that is underlined in the menu.

Note

> The hotkey is not always the first letter of the menu choice. Also, hotkeys are not visible until you press ALT to move the keyboard focus to the menu bar.

At the end of Chapter 7 there are more keyboard shortcuts listed that are specific to the SAS System.

Understanding How Files Are Named and Stored

What's New: By default, the SASUSER data library corresponds to C:\Documents and Settings*Windows-user-name*\My Documents\My SAS Files\9.1 for Windows 2000. In the NT environment, the SASUSER data library corresponds to C:\winnt\profiles*Windows-user-name*\Personal\My SAS Files\9.1.

The WORK data library corresponds to C:\Documents and Settings*Windows-user-name*\Local Settings\Temp\SAS Temporary Files_TD#### for Windows 2000. In the NT environment, the WORK data library corresponds to C:\winnt\profiles*Windows-user-name*\Local Settings\Temp\SAS Temporary Files_TD####.

Many user-supplied SAS names, such as tables, catalog entries, and even informats and formats, can have long names. File references and library references, however, are restricted to eight characters.

If you are coming from a UNIX or OpenVMS background, you are familiar with the hierarchical structure of folders, subfolders, and files under Windows. But if you are more familiar with z/OS, you may be used to a different file structure. It is important to understand how Windows files are stored and named before you begin to use SAS software to create and manage files.

Note

> The terms *folder* and *directory* are synonymous.

Understanding the Windows File Structure: Under Windows, individual files have a filename and an extension. Think of a file as a collection of information, where the filename describes the information and the extension describes the format of the information. For example, MEMO.TXT is a memo and is in plain ASCII text format. HOUSE.TIF is a picture of a house in the TIFF bitmap format.

Windows supports long filenames—that is, you can use a total of 255 characters for the filename. In addition, filenames and extensions can contain spaces, quotation marks, and other characters not allowed in filenames under many other operating systems.

Examples of valid filenames are CONFIG.SYS, DECEMBER'S REPORT.TXT, and JOAN & TOM.DOC. The following characters are not allowed in filenames: / \ : ; ? "< > | *.

Understanding Truncated Filenames: If you intend to use files with Windows applications that do not support long filenames, or with other operating systems that do not support long filenames, be aware that sometimes the long filename may be truncated to eight characters, replacing certain characters (such as commas and spaces) with underscores (_) and extra characters with a tilde (~) and a numeral. Even some Windows dialog boxes and applications still show the truncated name instead of the full name.

Table 1.2 shows four examples of long and truncated filenames (assuming the files are stored in the same folder). For example, if you issue the DIR command in a command-prompt window, the files are listed with their truncated names.

Table 1.2 Long and Truncated Filenames

Long Name	Truncated Name
DECEMBER'S REPORT.TXT	DECEMB~1.TXT
DECEMBER'S BILLS.TXT	DECEMB~2.TXT
THAT'S ALL.TXT	THAT'S~1.TXT
X,Y.TXT	X_Y~1.TXT

The last file, X,Y.TXT, has the ~1 added, even though the filename is short. This is because of the substitution of the underscore for the comma.

Note

Windows supports long file extensions (that is, they are not limited to three characters). However, when a filename is truncated, the long file extension is truncated to the first three characters.

Understanding Files and Folders: Files are grouped together in *folders*. (In DOS and early versions of Windows, the term *directory* was used. Directory and folder are synonymous.) Folders can contain subfolders as well as files. For example, you might have a folder called BILLS, and within that folder you might have some miscellaneous files along with two subfolders, PAID and OVERDUE. In turn, these subfolders might contain files for each individual bill.

The root folder is the top-level folder that contains all other subfolders and files. Usually, this is called C:\ and is the default folder when you boot your PC. The C:\ folder can contain many subfolders, which can contain other subfolders, and so on. Figure 1.8 shows a sample folder hierarchy.

Figure 1.8 Sample Folder Hierarchy

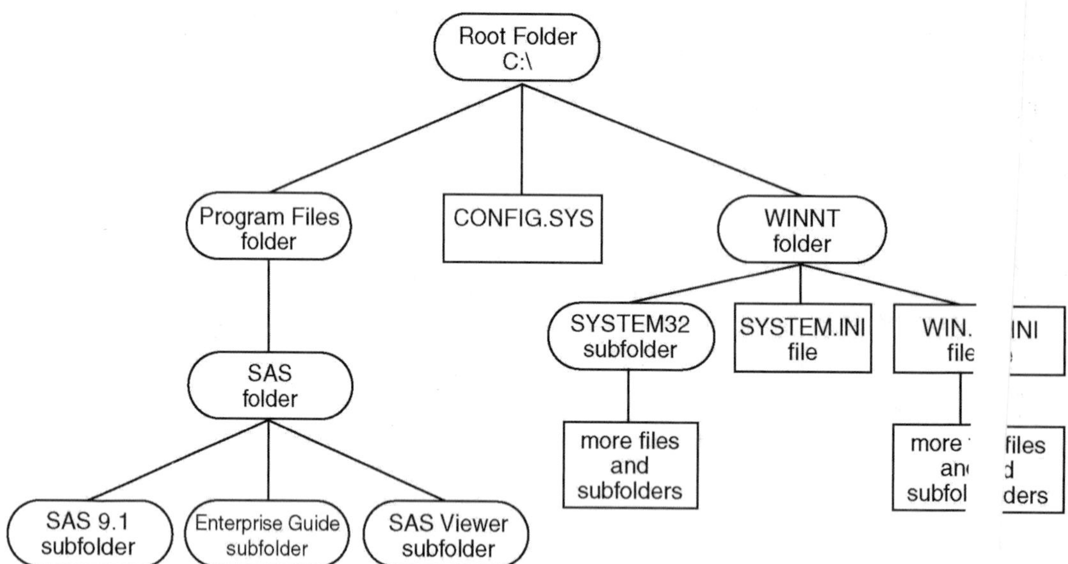

Understanding Drives: Another concept you need to understand is drives. While the root folder is referred to as C:\, the drive is referred to as C:. Your computer may have several drives—the hard drive might be C:, the 3 1/2" floppy drive might be A:, and the CD-ROM drive might be D:. If you are on a network, you probably have access to many drives. To find out how your system is organized, use the Windows Explorer, which is discussed in Appendix 3.

Understanding Common File Extensions: Some file extensions are associated with particular applications. For example, files with an extension of .SAS are SAS programs, while files with a .DOC extension are usually Microsoft Word files. Table 1.3 gives some common file extensions.

Table 1.3 Common File Extensions

External Files		SAS 9.1, SAS 8, or SAS 7 Files	
Extension	**File Type**	**Extension**	**File Type**
CFG	configuration	SC2, SAS7BCAT	SAS catalog
DAT, CSV	raw data	SI2, SAS7BNDX	SAS data file index
HTM, HTML	HTML	SA2, SAS7BACS	SAS access descriptor
LOG	SAS log	SV2, SAS7BVEW	SAS data view
LST	SAS output	SS2, SS7, SAS7BPGM	SAS stored program
PDF	Portable Document Format	SAS7BITM	item store file (SAS Registry)
RTF	Rich Text Format	SAS7BDMD	data mining database file
SAS	SAS code	SD2, SAS7BDAT	SAS table
TXT	ASCII text	SM2, SAS7BMDB	multidimensional database file

Using Wildcard Characters: Like most operating systems, Windows accepts wildcard characters in filenames when you are performing file maintenance (such as deleting, moving, or searching).

Table 1.4 lists the wildcard characters Windows accepts.

Table 1.4 Wildcard Characters

Character	Meaning
*	replaces any number of characters
?	replaces a single character

To show how these wildcard characters work, here are a few examples:

PROG*.SAS finds PROG1.SAS and PROGRAM2.SAS

PROG?B.SAS finds PROG1B.SAS but not PROG11B.SAS

REVENUE.* finds REVENUE.SAS and REVENUE.DAT

Understanding How SAS Files Are Stored under Windows: As a SAS user, you already know about the various types of SAS files and that these files are stored in SAS data libraries. Under Windows, the concept of a SAS data library is loosely analogous to that of a folder containing SAS files, with the addition of the concept of SAS engines. An example will help illustrate this.

Suppose you have two folders, C:\REPORTS and C:\INCOME. In the REPORTS folder, there are some SAS 9.1 SAS tables. In the INCOME folder, you also have SAS 9.1 SAS tables but also some Version 6 SAS tables. To access the two types of SAS files in the INCOME folder, you would submit two SAS LIBNAME statements pointing to this folder. One of the LIBNAME statements would have a V9 engine associated with it, while the other would have a V6 engine associated with it.

Note

In this book, the following terms are used interchangeably: "table" and "data set"; "row" and "observation"; and "column" and "variable."

You can also concatenate several folders into one SAS data library. See Chapter 9 for more information on managing SAS data libraries.

Knowing the Important Files and Folders: Certain files, folders, and subfolders are important to you as a SAS software user. Table 1.5 gives some of these and briefly describes their purpose.

Table 1.5 Important SAS Files and Folders

Default Filename (Windows 2000)	Purpose
SAS.EXE	is the **SAS executable file** (loader program).
SASV9.CFG	contains the **default SAS System options**, including those set by the SAS System INSTALL utility. You can have alternate SAS configuration files with different names and option settings.
AUTOEXEC.SAS	contains **start-up SAS statements** you want to execute when you begin a SAS session.
C:\Documents and Settings*Windows-user-name*	is the default **SAS System current folder**, when started from the **Start** button menu.
C:\Documents and Settings*Windows-user-name*\My Documents\My SAS Files\9.1 subfolder	corresponds to your **SASUSER SAS data library**, and contains your SAS profile catalogs, key definitions, tool definitions, and so on.
C:\Documents and Settings*Windows-user-name*\Local Settings\Temp\SAS Temporary Files subfolder	contains your **WORK SAS data library**. The WORK library for a SAS session is created as a subfolder of this subfolder, in the form _TD#####.

Note

The pathnames in Table 1.5 are the default or most common locations; many can be changed during SAS installation or subsequently. Also, the values shown in Table 1.5 are for the Windows 2000 environment; values for other versions of the Windows operating system may be somewhat different.

Using Filenames in SAS Statements and Commands: When you type the names of folders, subfolders, and files in SAS statements, commands, and dialog boxes, separate the folder name, subfolder name, and filename with a backslash. For example, the following INCLUDE command references a file named MEDICALREPORT.DAT in a folder called MYDATA, which is a subfolder of the root folder on the C: drive:

```
INCLUDE 'C:\MYDATA\MEDICALREPORT.DAT'
```

This is called the full pathname for the file, which states explicitly where the file is stored. When in doubt, specify the full pathname for files; while there are rules for what constitutes the folder and file extension default, it is always safe to specify the full pathname.

Defining File Shortcuts and Library References: One of the most common uses of the full pathname is using the FILENAME and LIBNAME statements to define file shortcuts (also called filerefs) and library references (often referred to as librefs) in your SAS programs. Here is an example of each of these statements, using the full pathname for the file or folder:

```
   /* Points to a specific external file. */
filename misc 'c:\misc\qtr1.dat';

   /* Points to a specific folder containing SAS files. */
libname inv 'c:\sas\invoices';
```

Note

If the filename contains spaces or other punctuation such as a single quotation mark, use double quotation marks in SAS statements such as FILENAME and LIBNAME statements.

Testing Your Survival Kit

Now that you understand a little bit about how Windows works, you are ready to see if you can "do Windows." Try the next chapter, which walks you through most of the fundamental tasks involved in using Base SAS software. After you've done the first two or three exercises, you'll see that "doing Windows" is not so hard after all. And even if you never like Windows, at least you will not feel like you're looking through frosted glass while you work.

2 Performing the Basic SAS Software Tasks under Windows

Getting Ready for the Tutorial

Because of the tutorial nature of this chapter, it does not show you every aspect of every task—there are many ways to edit a file, for example, and this chapter shows only a few techniques. But if you master the techniques in this chapter, you can then learn new techniques as you go along, using the online help, other manuals, and so on.

Now that you understand Windows' file-naming conventions, know how to double-click, and are able to open and close applications, you are ready to apply these skills to using the SAS System. Most of this chapter is a tutorial. You should try each exercise so that you get a feel for how the SAS System works under Windows.

The sections listed below are not tutorial, but they do provide important information. If you are new to SAS 9.1 for Windows, you should read these sections.

- "Getting to Know the SAS System Interface"
- "Getting Help"
- "Becoming Familiar with the SAS Explorer Window"
- "Using the Favorite Folders Feature"

Before you begin the exercises in this chapter, you should close Windows and bring it up again, so that you have a "pristine" environment to work in. (For more information on closing Windows, see "Shutting Down the Windows Environment" in Chapter 1.)

Starting Your SAS Session

FasTip: Click the **Start** button. Click **Programs → SAS → SAS 9.1 (English).**

To start the SAS System, click the **Start** button, then click **Programs**, then click **SAS**.

Now click **SAS 9.1 (English)**, as shown in Figure 2.1. Your display should look similar to this before you start this exercise.

Note

Your display may not be identical to Figure 2.1 because you may have different software installed. Also, if you are using a different language version of the SAS System, the language in the name will be different.

Figure 2.1 Starting the SAS System

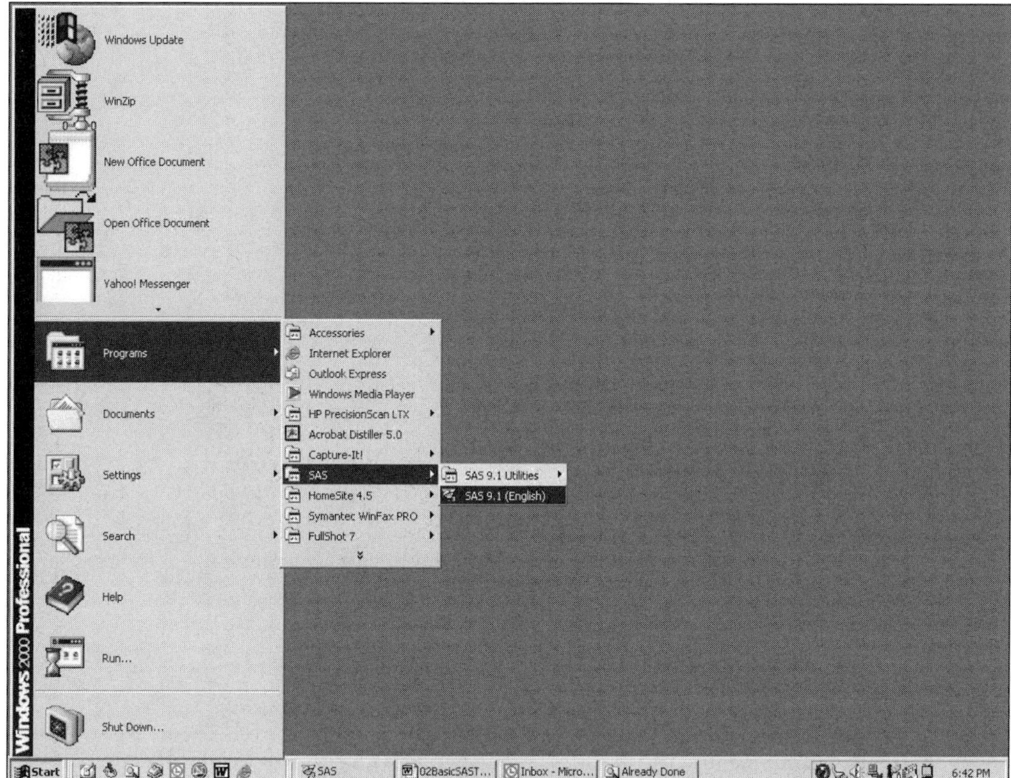

The SAS System logo appears, followed by the default windows: Output, Log, Enhanced Editor, SAS Explorer, and Results windows. Figure 2.2 shows how these SAS windows look. Typically, there are some notes in the Log window that state your site number, version number, and other site-specific information.

Figure 2.2 Initial SAS Windows after Start-up

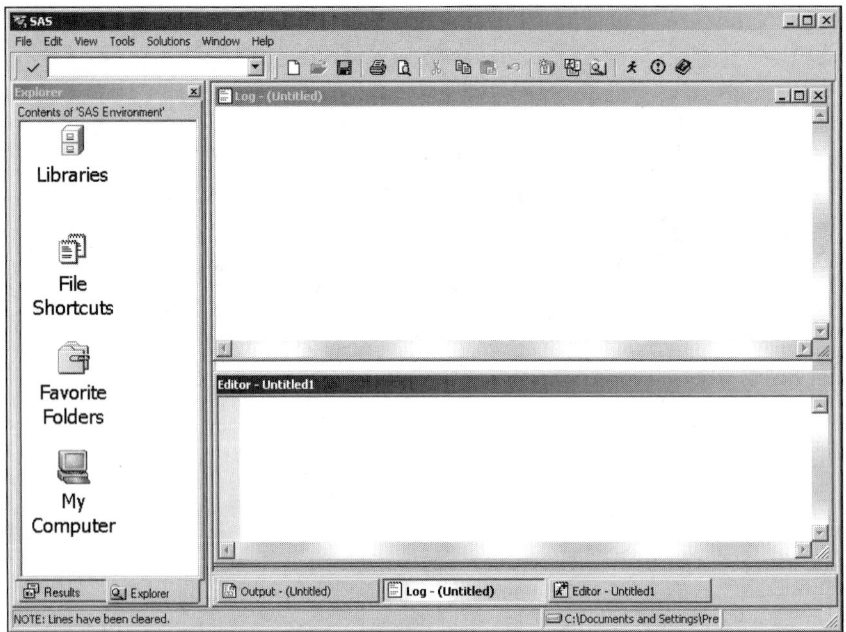

Note

> In the Windows environment, you can have more than one SAS session running at once. The number of sessions is limited only by the amount of RAM (random-access memory) your computer has.

SAS System Tutorial Guides: If this is the first time you have started the SAS System, the dialog box shown in Figure 2.3 appears. Through it, you can access a quick-start guide and a resource guide for new features.

Figure 2.3 Tutorial Dialog Box

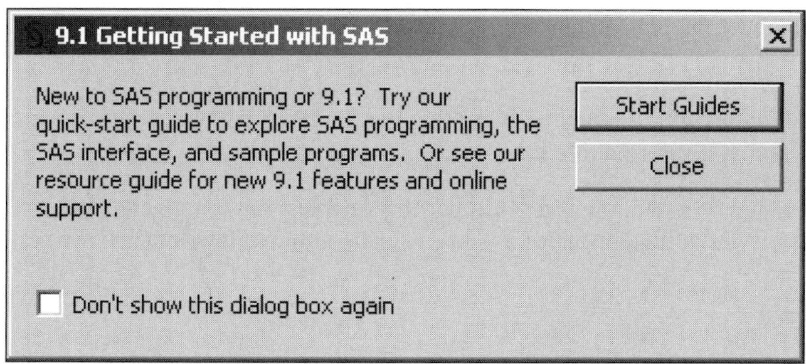

You must close this dialog box before you can use your SAS session. If you want to see the tutorial, click **Start Guides**. If you want to postpone seeing the tutorial, click **Close**.

This dialog box will appear every time you start the SAS System until you click the check box, indicating you don't want to see this dialog box again. You can access the tutorial from the SAS System main menu, by clicking **Help → Getting Started with SAS Software**.

Getting to Know the SAS System Interface

What's New: What used to be called the SAS working folder is now called the SAS current folder.

The default text editor is now the Enhanced Editor, not the Program Editor.

While the basic geography of the SAS System, such as the Log and Output windows, is the same across operating systems and was covered in Chapter 1, this section provides specific information relative to the SAS System windowing interface. Here is a brief orientation session.

Note

Many aspects of the appearance and behavior of the SAS System are configurable. The discussion that follows assumes that you are using the defaults for the various features. If you are using someone else's system, and it has been configured to differ from the defaults, ask the machine's owner to reset the features to the default behavior before you read the rest of this chapter.

Main SAS Window: The large window that has "SAS" across the top and contains all open SAS windows is called the main SAS window (in previous versions of the SAS System, it was referred to as the SAS application workspace, or AWS). The main SAS window acts as a container for your SAS session—in general, everything you do in your SAS session, such as opening new windows, interacting with dialog boxes, and so on, occurs inside the main SAS window.

Note

> SAS Help and Documentation opens outside the main SAS window, in its own window.

Title Bar: Across the top of the main SAS window is the title bar. Every window that you open from inside the main SAS window also has a title bar.

Scroll Bars: Down the right side of a window is a scroll bar that enables you to move up and down in the window. The scroll bar at the bottom of a window lets you move left and right across the window.

Menu Bar: Just under the title bar is the SAS System main menu. Here you find commands to open and save files, print, submit code, change system options, invoke other parts of the SAS System, and ask for help.

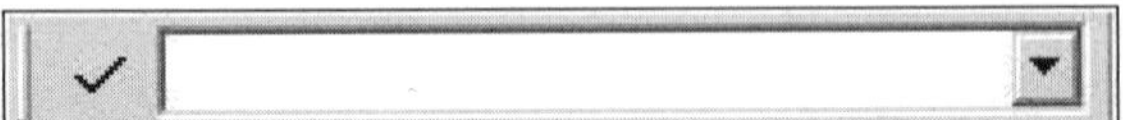

Command Bar: Under the menu bar, on the left, is a white box—this is the command bar, and it is where you type SAS commands. To use the command bar, place the mouse pointer on it and click. To return to a SAS window, click in the window. (Alternatively, you can press F11 to move the cursor to the command bar; press ESC to return the cursor to the active SAS window.)

The command bar remembers the commands that you have issued in your SAS session and keeps a list of them. If you want to repeat a command, click the down arrow next to the command bar to display a list of recently issued commands. Click the command you want. This copies the command to the command bar. Once the command bar contains the command you want to issue, click the check mark to the left of the command bar to execute the command, or press ENTER. The command list is saved from one SAS session to the next.

As you type in the command bar, the SAS System uses an "auto complete" feature to guess what you are going to type, based on commands you have already entered. If the command that appears in the command bar after you type a few letters is correct, simply press ENTER.

You can resize the command bar by placing the mouse pointer over the vertical double-bar that appears to the right of the command bar (the pointer turns into a double-headed arrow). Drag this bar to the left, making the command bar smaller. You may need to do this in order to see all the tools on the tool bar.

See "Customizing the Tool Bar and Command Bar" in Chapter 6 for information on customizing the command bar.

Tool Bar: To the right of the command bar is the tool bar. This is a graphical menu, where clicking an icon executes a command (such as save, print, or help). Each window in the SAS System has its own tool set (except for the Log, Program Editor, and Output windows, which all use the same tools). The tool bar icons change when you make a new window active. By default, there are 15 tools on the tool bar for the main SAS windows, such as the Log and Enhanced Editor windows. If you cannot see all 15 tools, try resizing the command bar to leave more room for tools, as described previously. See "Customizing the Tool Bar and Command Bar" in Chapter 6 for information on customizing the tool bar.

Minimize, Maximize/Restore, and Close Buttons: See "Windows Geography" in Chapter 1 for a description of these window features.

Context-Sensitive Menus: Notice that each SAS window does not have an individual menu bar. That is because the selections available in the main menu change, depending on which window is active. If you click in the Log window, its title bar is highlighted, and it is now the active window. If you click **Edit** in the main menu, you see that, for example, **Replace** is grayed out—this is not a valid command in the Log window. But if you click in the Enhanced Editor window and then look at the **Edit** menu, **Replace** is available.

Popup Menus: Another way to see the menus for a particular window is to right-click in the window. The menu that appears is called a popup menu. For example, Figure 2.4 shows the Log window's popup menu with the **Edit** menu expanded.

Figure 2.4 Popup Menu for the Log Window

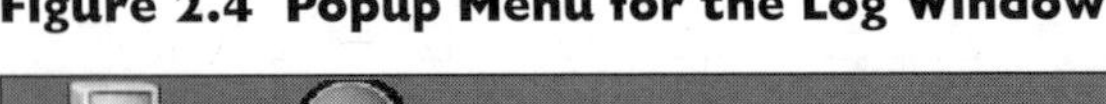

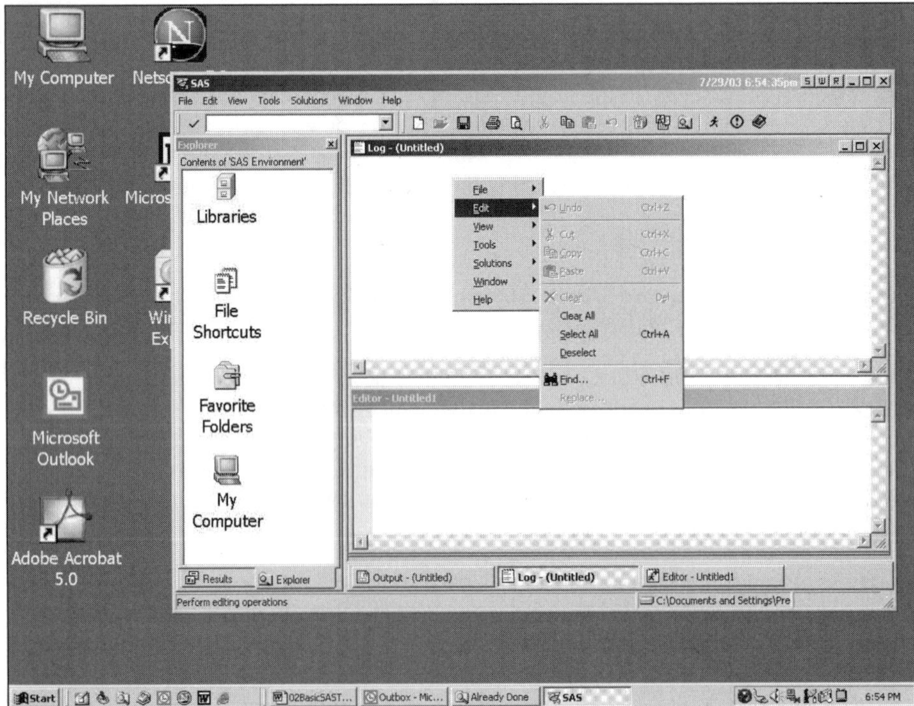

If you activate a menu by mistake, press ESC. Alternatively, click outside the menu, anywhere in the main SAS window. This closes the menu.

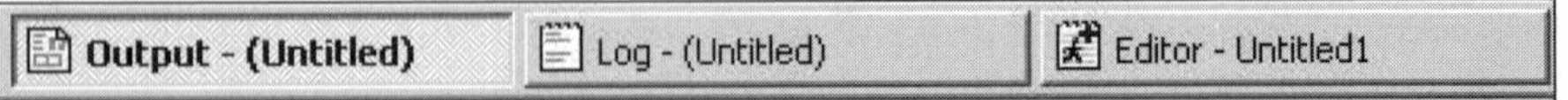

Window Bar: A quick way to access open SAS windows, the window bar (located across the bottom of the main SAS window) works like the Taskbar on the Windows desktop. Click the window's name in the window bar to jump to that window.

Docking Area: By default, the Results and SAS Explorer windows are "docked" (that is, anchored) in the left side of the main SAS window and cannot be moved to other places in the main SAS window. See "Looking at Output" and "Becoming Familiar with the SAS Explorer Window" later in this chapter for descriptions of the Results and SAS Explorer windows, respectively. The callout in Figure 2.5 shows the docking area.

Figure 2.5 Docking Area

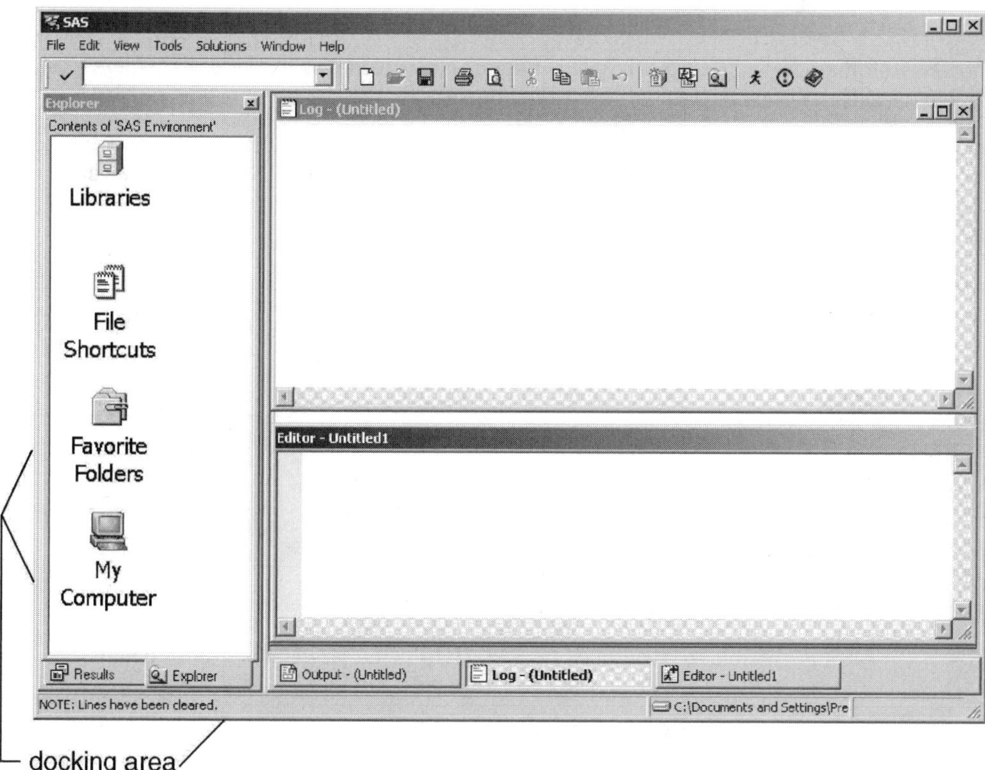

Practice Using the SAS Menus: Use the following exercise to practice using the menus.

1. Make the Enhanced Editor window active by clicking anywhere within it.
2. Click **Window** in the SAS System main menu.
3. Click **Output**. This takes you to the Output window.
4. Right-click in the Output window. The popup menu appears.
5. Click **Window**, then click **Log**. Now both the Output and Log windows are visible.
6. To return to the default appearance, right-click in the Log window, and click **Window** → **Editor**.

Note

The Window menu choice is not available from the popup menu in the Enhanced Editor window.

Other Main SAS Window Features: The main SAS window contains some other useful items:

- At the bottom of the main SAS window is a status bar, which displays brief help messages about various tools and the results of SAS commands.
- Also in the status bar is a folder icon with a folder name after it. This icon tells you which folder the SAS System is using as its current folder. "Changing the SAS System Current Folder" in Chapter 3 provides more information, as does "Determining the SAS System Current Folder" in Chapter 11.
- If you place your mouse pointer over a tool in the tool bar and wait a bit, a "screen tip" appears below the tool that tells you what the tool does.

Getting Help

What's New: SAS Help and Documentation now contains all the SAS books that are available in online format, in addition to help topics.

The **Help** menu has been rearranged; navigational tools inside SAS Help and Documentation have changed.

The "Getting Started with SAS Software" tutorial has been updated.

It is possible to customize the SAS **Help** menu (see Chapter 6 for details).

FasTip: Click the Help icon on the SAS tool bar (accesses the **Using This Window** feature).

While this book only scratches the surface of using the SAS System for Windows, all the information you could possibly want is at your fingertips—or at least at your mouse pointer. So, before continuing with the tutorial, read this section to familiarize yourself with SAS Help and Documentation. Chapter 6 offers some additional information on SAS Help and Documentation.

Note

SAS Help and Documentation is also available online at no cost. For more information visit the SAS Publications Catalog at support.sas.com/pubs.

The fastest way to obtain help while using the SAS System is to click the Help icon on the SAS tool bar. This opens a help topic that provides information about the active window. Or, access more detailed help by using the **Help** menu.

Also, many dialog boxes offer context-sensitive help. To access it, click the Help icon located in the top-right corner of the dialog box, then click a field or button in the dialog box to display an explanation of the dialog box feature. To close the explanation, click anywhere outside the explanation. A few dialog boxes also contain a Help button.

F1 In the Enhanced Editor, you can press F1 while your cursor is over a keyword (such as "print"). If a help topic exists for that keyword, a dialog box appears, allowing you to select the topic you want to see.

Using the Help Menu: If you click **Help** in the SAS System main menu, you see the choices illustrated in Figure 2.6.

Figure 2.6 SAS System Help Menu

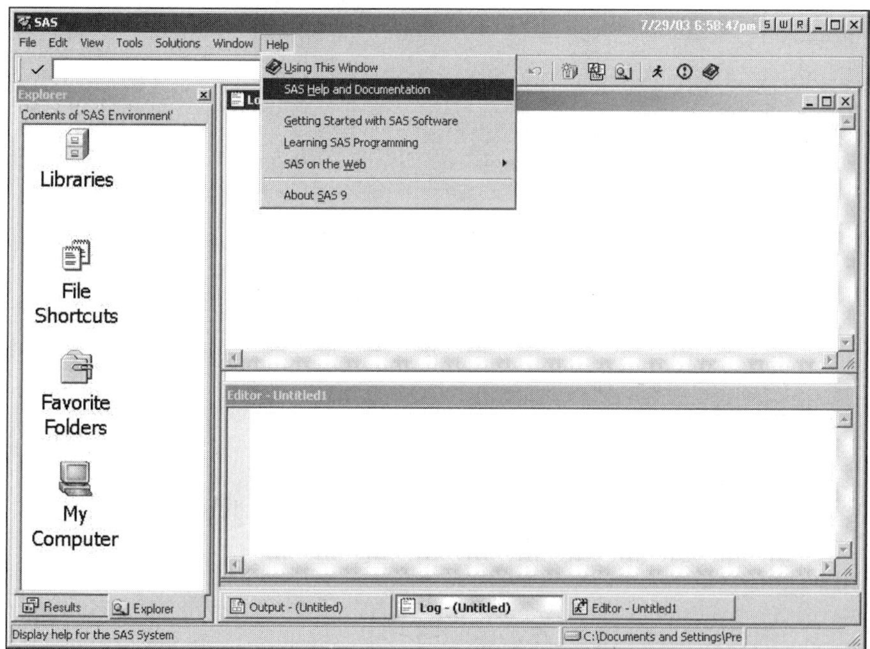

Here is an explanation of the **Help** menu choices:

- **Using This Window** opens the help topic for the active SAS window.

  Note

Some windows do not have Using This Window help available.

- **SAS Help and Documentation** displays the table of contents for all available online help and documentation topics. Also available are tabs for searching, accessing the help index, and displaying a list of favorite topics.

- **Getting Started with SAS Software** accesses a tutorial that you can use to become familiar with the SAS System for Windows.
- **Learning SAS Programming** accesses the SAS OnlineTutor product, if it is installed on your system. You can also access SAS OnlineTutor on the Web at http://support.sas.com/training/elearn/onlinetutor.html.
- **SAS on the Web** gives you the capability to access even more help, assuming you are already connected to the World Wide Web (SAS does not provide the connection).
- **About SAS 9** opens a dialog box that details the version you have installed. From here you can access information about your system and see various legal notices.

Practice opening the various **Help** menu items by clicking them, then close the resulting windows by clicking their Close buttons.

How SAS Help and Documentation Is Organized: The information in SAS Help and Documentation is organized from general to specific. By making choices in SAS Help and Documentation windows, you progress through the layers toward the specific topic or task that you are interested in (this is sometimes referred to as "drilling down").

When you open a SAS Help and Documentation window, the topics are listed in the left pane of the window, and the information is presented in the right pane. Across the top of the window are some navigational and other tools.

Navigating Topic Lists: Topic lists work similarly to the Windows Explorer, in that they use folder icons and + and − signs to indicate which topics have subtopics:

- Topics represented by a folder icon expand and list that topic's subtopics when you double-click them. Alternatively, click the + sign.
- The folder icon you double-clicked "opens." If you double-click the folder icon again (or click the − sign), the folder icon closes and the list of subtopics disappears.
- Clicking a text-file icon displays the topic information.

Figure 2.7 shows a sample help window that illustrates these icons.

Figure 2.7 Sample Topic List

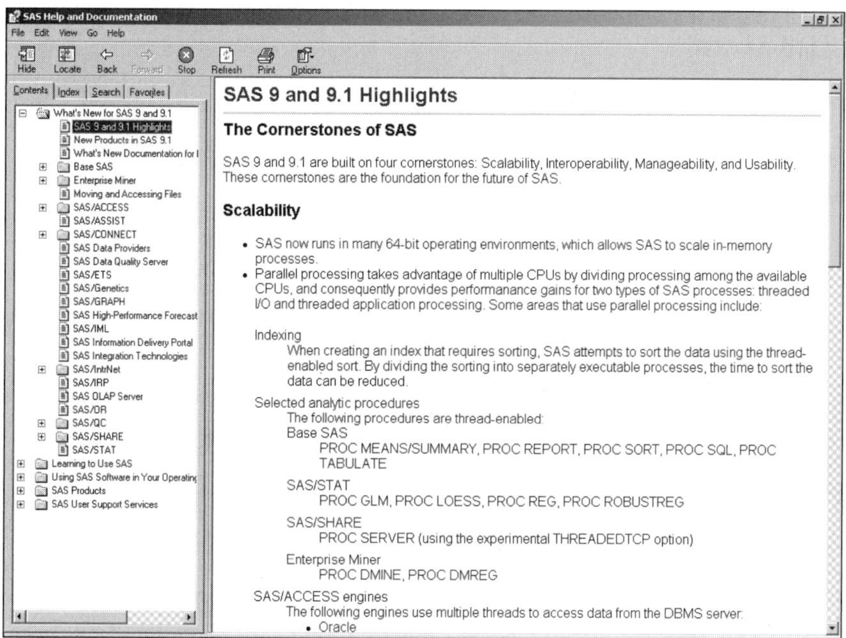

Navigating the Help Topics: In the topic information, you may see highlighted text. These highlighted text strings are called "links." When you move the mouse pointer over a link, the pointer turns into a hand. Clicking a link takes you to more information on that topic.

Use the tools at the top of the SAS Help and Documentation window to navigate. Most of the navigational tools work like Web browser navigational tools. Here is a description of the most commonly used tools:

Hide suppresses the topic list pane (that is, the left pane). When you choose this tool, it changes to **Show**. Clicking **Show** displays the topic list again.

Locate highlights in the contents list (displayed in the left pane) the current topic (displayed in the right pane).

Back takes you back one topic in your topic history list (works just like a Web browser).

Forward takes you forward one topic in your topic history list (works just like a Web browser).

Print prints the current topic on the default printer.

Options displays a list of various options you can use to customize SAS Help and Documentation.

Searching for Specific Text Strings: You can search SAS Help and Documentation for text strings. This is useful if you do not know what the topic is called but you know the information for that topic contains a certain word.

To perform a text search, follow these steps:

1. Click the **Search** tab in the topic list pane of the SAS Help and Documentation window.
2. Type the search string in the text entry field at the top of the **Search** tab.
3. Click **List Topics**.
4. Once the topic list on the **Search** tab shows the topic that you want, double-click the topic to display it. The searched-for word or words are highlighted on the page (assuming you haven't turned this feature off, which you can do, using the **Options** navigation button).

The **Index** tab also allows you to type a text string; as you type, the list of topics scrolls to entries that start with the letters you type. However, the **Index** tab searches only for the "official" keywords associated with the topic, whereas the **Search** tab allows you to search for all text.

If you want to find a specific phrase, use quotation marks. For example, typing proc format (without quotation marks) in the search field returns a lot of pages that contain both the word "proc" and the word "format," but on many of the pages, the words are not consecutive. Typing "proc format" (with quotation marks) in the search field returns only those pages that contain "proc" and "format" next to each other.

Accessing Commonly Used Help Topics Easily: Rather than clicking and double-clicking your way through the topic contents, you can "bookmark" commonly used help topics. These topic names are then listed on the **Favorites** tab.

To bookmark a favorite help topic, follow these steps:

1. Use the topic contents list to display the favorite topic in the right pane of the SAS Help and Documentation window.
2. Click the **Favorites** tab.
3. Right-click in the **Topics** area, and click **Add** in the resulting popup menu.

The topic is now listed. The favorite topics are listed alphabetically. To access a topic listed on the **Favorites** tab, double-click a topic.

By right-clicking in the **Topics** area on the **Favorites** tab, you can also rename an entry or delete it.

Using the Help Command: You can type HELP in the command bar, with or without arguments. Here are a few ways in which this technique can be useful:

- Type HELP in the command bar—equivalent to clicking the Help icon on the SAS System tool bar. This opens the "Using This Window" topic for the active SAS window.
- Type HELP HELP in the command bar—opens a list of topics, the first of which is a help topic that tells you how to use and navigate SAS Help and Documentation. Double-click this topic to open it.
- Type HELP *keyword* in the command bar—opens a topic that corresponds to an index entry on the **Index** tab of the SAS Help and Documentation window. In many cases, the keyword is the same as the index entry, but not always, so you may have to do some trial-and-error experimentation to see which keyword accesses the topic you want. Not all topics may be accessed using this approach. In general, *keyword* should have the "*language-element type*" form, such as

```
HELP LIBNAME statement
```

or

```
HELP FORMAT procedure
```

or

```
HELP FONT system option
```

Note

The **Help** menu can be customized, using the HELPREGISTER system option. See Chapter 6 for details.

Accessing the SAS Sample Library

To use the tutorial in this chapter, you must first have a SAS program to work with. One easy way to start a program is to choose a similar program from the SAS Sample Library. Follow these steps to copy a SAS program from the SAS Sample Library:

1. In the main SAS System menu, click **Help** → **SAS Help and Documentation**.
2. In the topic list in the left pane of the SAS Help and Documentation window, double-click **Learning to Use SAS**. When the topic expands, click **Sample SAS Programs**.
3. Click the **Base SAS** link.
4. Scroll down to the **Miscellaneous** category of sample programs, then click **Basic Data Set Manipulations**.
5. To place the program on the Windows Clipboard, click **Edit** → **Select All** in the main menu of the SAS Help and Documentation window. The program is highlighted.
6. Now right-click in the topic window and click **Copy** in the resulting popup menu.
7. Close the SAS Help and Documentation window by clicking its Close button.
8. Click in the Enhanced Editor window to make it active.

9. Make sure the cursor is at the beginning of the first line of the Enhanced Editor window; now click **Edit** → **Paste** in the main SAS System menu. The sample program appears in the Enhanced Editor window.

10. Your cursor ends up at the bottom of the file. To quickly move to the top, press CTRL-HOME.

Editing a File

What's New: This tutorial uses the Enhanced Editor instead of the Program Editor.

Now that you have your SAS program in the Enhanced Editor window, you can make changes. For example, there are some help-navigation text lines that are not valid SAS code that must be deleted. You may also want to delete the large comment section and add your own comments.

Highlighting a Large Chunk of Text: Sometimes you may want to work with a large chunk of text. An easy way to do this is to highlight it using the mouse and Shift key. For example, you can highlight the help-navigational text and large comment section at the beginning of the file, then delete it. Click at the beginning of the first line. Now scroll until you can see the end of the comment and the first line of code. Hold the Shift key down, and click at the end of the last comment line. The entire comment should be highlighted, as shown in Figure 2.8. (In this figure, both the main SAS window and the Enhanced Editor window have been maximized.)

Figure 2.8 Highlighting a Large Chunk of Text

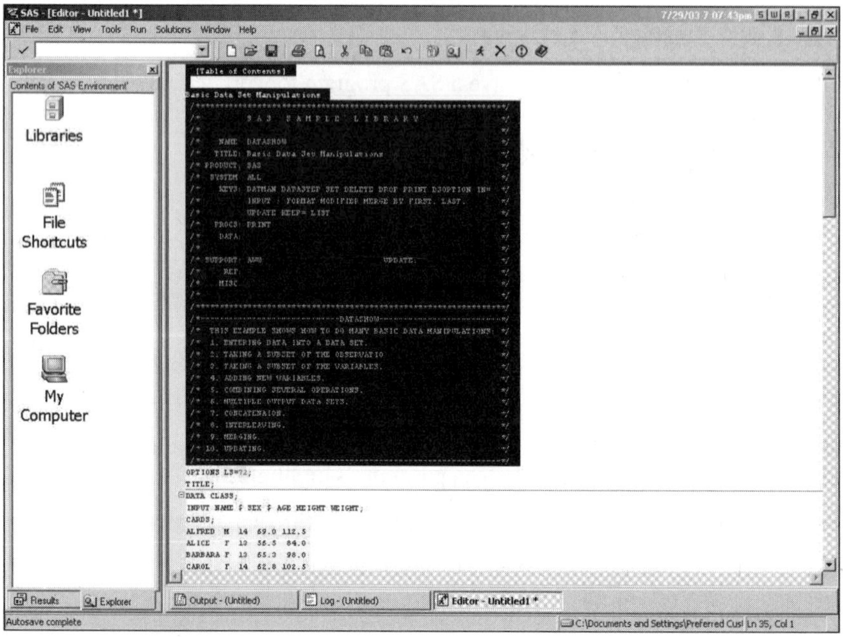

To delete the highlighted text, click **Edit** → **Clear** (or press the Delete key) in the SAS System main menu. The highlighted text disappears.

The sample program also has some unwanted help-navigational text at the end. To quickly move to the end of the program, press CTRL-END. Click at the beginning of the last line of text, then press SHIFT-END. The line is highlighted, as shown in Figure 2.9.

Figure 2.9 Highlighting a Line of Text

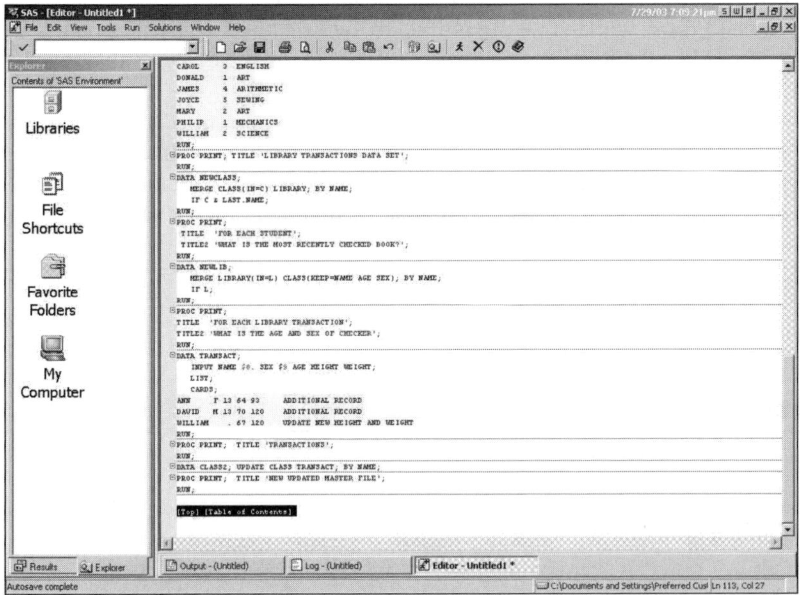

Press the Delete key to delete the text.

Undoing Changes: If you accidentally delete something, don't panic—you can undo it. For example, to regain the text you just deleted, click **Edit** → **Undo** in the SAS System main menu (or press CTRL-Z). The deleted text reappears.

Adding a Line: To add a line, click at the end of the line preceding the new one, then press ENTER. Now type your new text (such as `/* My own data manipulation code */`). There are many other editing features of the Enhanced Editor window you can use, or you may prefer to use the Program Editor window. You can toggle between insert mode (the default) and overstrike mode, search for and replace text, do a spell-check, and so on. Chapter 3 goes into more detail on editing files.

Submitting a File

 **FasTip:** Click **Run** → **Submit** or click the Run tool on the toolbar.

Now that you have the code looking the way you want, submit it. Methods of submitting code abound—you can use a function key, the tool bar, the menus, or commands.

For this exercise, we'll use the menus. To submit the code, be sure the Enhanced Editor window is active. Then, click **Run** → **Submit** in the SAS System main menu. The code is submitted. The code remains in the Enhanced Editor, while notes are written to the Log window, and the output is routed to the Output window. Also, the Results window pops to the top in the docking area.

Note

> If your code contains an error, the Output and Results windows may not appear. If this happens, examine the notes in the Log window to see where the error is. To return to the Enhanced Editor window, click the **Editor** button in the window bar at the bottom of the main SAS window.

Chapter 4 provides more information on submitting SAS code in a variety of ways.

Looking at Output

FasTip: Click the **Results** tab in the docking area of the main SAS window.

By default, when you submit a program that generates output, the SAS System sends program output to the Output window. (You can change this behavior; see Chapters 6 and 8 for more information.) The Results window, in the docked area, lists each procedure that produced output. Figure 2.10 shows the Results window adjacent to the data-manipulation program output in the Output window.

Note

> In Figure 2.10, the Results window has been resized so that more of the text is visible.

Figure 2.10 Last Page of Output from the Data Manipulation Program

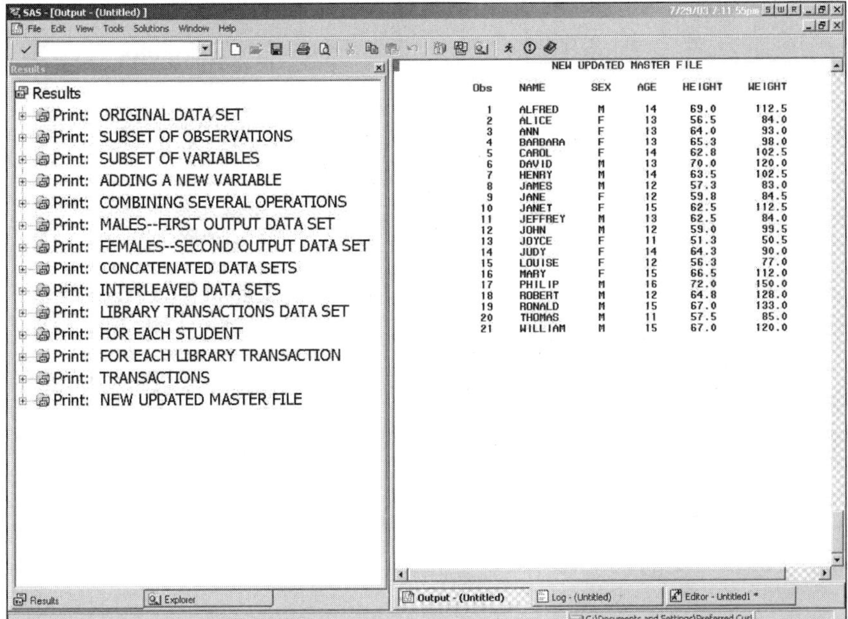

Each procedure in your program that creates output is listed in the Results window. These are sometimes called output nodes. The output is organized into folders, subfolders, and items within those folders that represent individual pieces of the output. Because the example program generated only simple PROC PRINT steps, that is all that is listed.

Navigating in the Results Window: Navigating in the Results window works the same as navigating in other folder-oriented windows:

- Click a plus sign to expand the view of an output node.
- Click a minus sign to collapse the view.
- Double-click an output line to view that piece of the output. The Output window or the Results Viewer window displays the appropriate output.
  - Items preceded by the icon represent pages in the Output window.
  - Items preceded by the icon represent pages in the Results Viewer window. (See Chapter 8 for more information on the Results Viewer window.)
- Press the Backspace key to move up one level in the Results folder hierarchy.

- Right-clicking in the Results window enables you to select either **Expand All** or **Collapse All**, which expands or collapses all output nodes at once.

Figure 2.11 shows the Results window from Figure 2.10, with several folders and subfolders expanded.

Figure 2.11 Results Window with Output Nodes Expanded

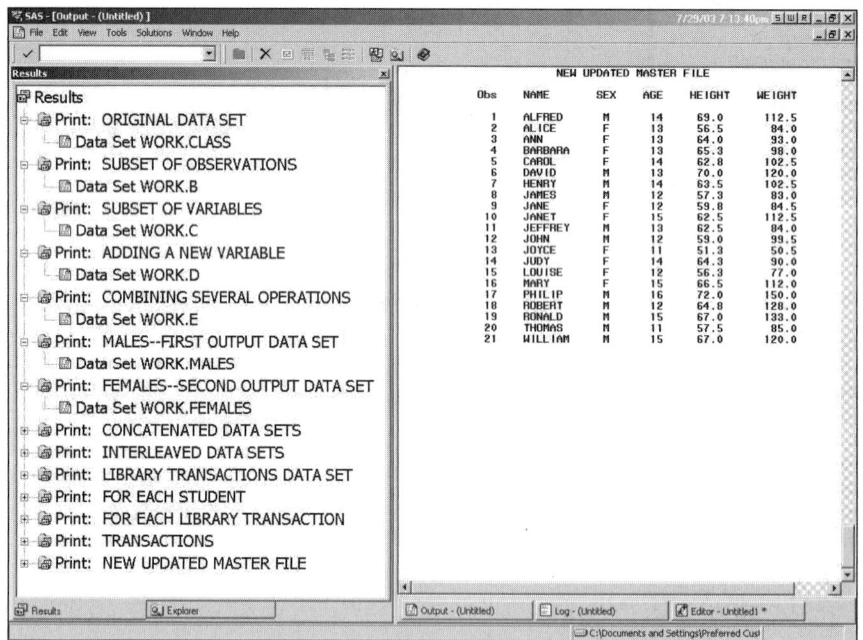

You can use the Results window to manage your output. For example, you can rename, delete, save, and print the output. Each of these tasks is explained in the next few sections.

Renaming Output

It's a simple matter to rename a piece of your output in the Results window. To try this, right-click the item named **Data Set WORK.C**, then click **Rename** in the resulting popup menu. The Rename dialog box appears, as shown in Figure 2.12.

Figure 2.12 Renaming an Output Node

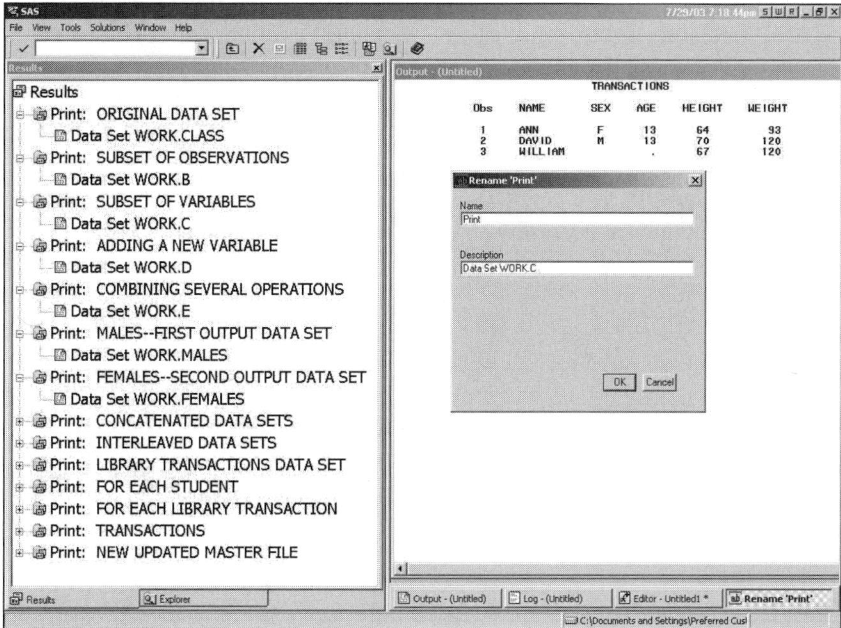

To remind yourself that this data set resides in the WORK SAS data library, and is therefore not permanent, let's add the word "Temporary" to the **Description** field. Click at the beginning of the field and type `Temporary`. Now click **OK** to close the dialog box. The item in the Results window reflects the new name.

Deleting Output

What's New: The syntax for turning the Results window off and on has changed.

Deleting One Output Node: To delete a piece of output, first click the output node you want to delete, to highlight the node. Now right-click in the Results window and click **Delete** in the resulting popup menu. The output is deleted both from the Results window and from the Output and Results Viewer windows. You can delete only the highest level of output; you cannot delete individual output items listed under a higher-level node.

Note

If the output was written to a file as well, as is the case with HTML output, for example, deleting the item from the Results window does not delete the file itself.

Deleting All Output Nodes: To clear the Results window all at once, click the word **Results** at the top of the results list, then right-click. In the resulting popup menu, click **Delete**. When the dialog box asks if you are sure you want to clear the window, click **Yes**. Alternatively, issue the CLEAR command from the command bar. (This action cannot be undone.)

If you clear the Output window by clicking **Edit** → **Clear All** in the SAS System main menu, the Results window is cleared as well.

Turning the Results Window Off: You may want to turn the Results window off for huge jobs where tracking each piece of output is unnecessary. To do this, submit the following SAS statement:

```
dm 'odsresults' cancel;
```

To turn the Results window back on, submit

```
dm 'odsresults';
```

Note

See Chapter 8 for more details on the SAS Output Delivery System (ODS).

Printing Output

Printing Only One Listing-Format Output Item: Output that appears in the Output window is called listing-format output. To print a specific listing-format output item from the Results window, first click the item you want to print, to highlight it. Now right-click, and in the popup menu, click **Print**. The output is sent to your default printer.

Note

When you print a single output item from the Results window, the print dialog box does *not* appear. Therefore, be sure your printer and page setup options are set (as described in Chapter 5) before you choose **Print** in the Results window popup menu.

Printing All the Listing-Format Output: To print all the output at once, make the Output window active, then click **File** → **Print** in the SAS System main menu (or press CTRL-P). The Print dialog box appears. To send the output to the printer, click **OK**.

For more details on printing, see Chapter 5. For information on printing output generated by the Output Delivery System (ODS), see Chapter 8.

Determining Output Properties

Your output has several properties associated with it. Listing-format output properties include date created and beginning and ending Output window line numbers.

To see the properties for a particular piece of output, first click the item for which you want to see properties, to highlight it. Now right-click in the Results window and click **Properties** in the resulting popup menu. This opens the Properties window for that piece of output. Figure 2.13 shows the properties for one of the listing-format items from the sample code.

Figure 2.13 Properties for a Piece of Output

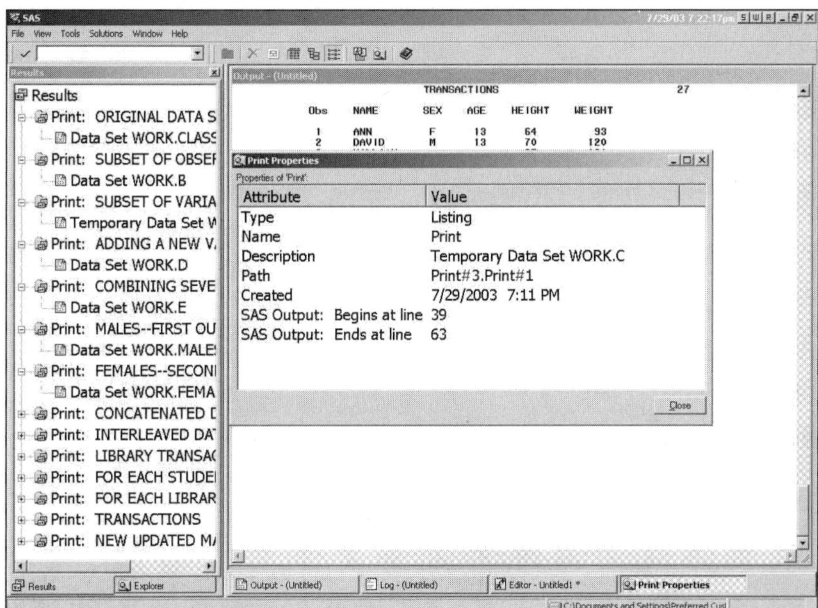

To close the Properties window, click the **Close** button.

Saving Output

FasTip: Click the Save icon on the SAS tool bar.

This section walks you through saving the output from the Output window; the steps for saving the contents of other SAS windows work much the same.

1. Make the Output window active.

2. Now click **File** → **Save As** in the SAS System main menu. The Save As dialog box opens. Figure 2.14 shows a sample Save As dialog box.

Figure 2.14 Sample Save As Dialog Box

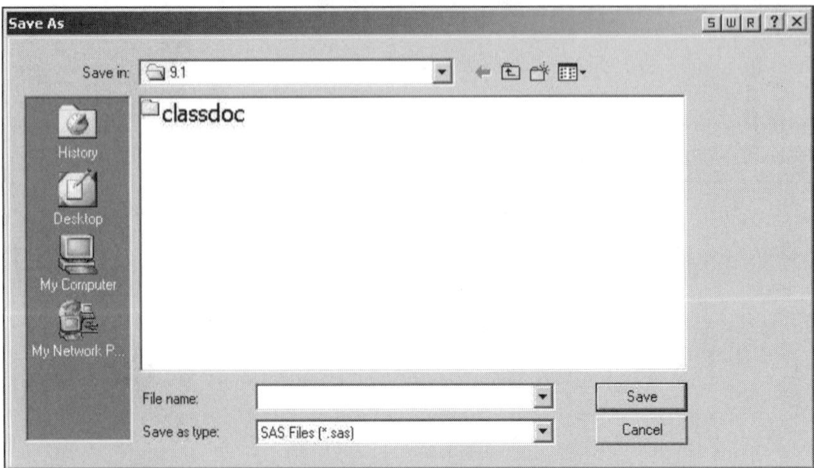

3. Type the name that you want to use for the file in the **File name** field—we'll use DATAMANIP.LST. If you do not specify the full pathname, the file is stored in the SAS current folder.

The first time you access the Save As dialog box from a particular window, as in Figure 2.14, the **Save in** field defaults to the folder associated with your SASUSER SAS data library (by default, C:\Documents and Settings*Windows-user-name*\My Documents\My SAS Files\9.1 for the Windows 2000 environment). For Windows NT users, the SASUSER SAS data library defaults to C:\winnt\profiles*Windows-user-name*\Personal\My SAS Files\9.1.

4. Click the **Save** button; the file is saved and the dialog box closes. "Saving an Existing File" and "Saving a New File" in Chapter 3 explain further how to use the Save As dialog box.

Becoming Familiar with the SAS Explorer Window

What's New: The SAS tool bar now offers a tool to toggle the tree view on and off.

The SAS Explorer window offers a familiar way to organize and access the components of the SAS environment, such as SAS data libraries, SAS program files, SAS catalogs, and SAS tables.

Note

> Windows also offers an Explorer. See Appendix 3 for information on using the Windows Explorer.

The SAS Explorer window is "object-oriented." So, instead of typing a command or traversing a menu path, you click, double-click, and right-click icons that represent various SAS System items. The following sections show you the highlights of using this interface to the SAS System.

Opening the SAS Explorer Window: When SAS starts up, a SAS Explorer window opens by default, in the docking area. By default, the SAS Explorer window shows the components of the SAS environment represented by large icons. For example, Figure 2.15 shows the mouse arrow in the default SAS Explorer window that appears when you start the SAS System.

Note

> By default, the SAS Explorer window is "docked," which means it is locked on the left-hand side of the main SAS window. For information on how to change this default behavior, see "Adjusting the Docking View" in Chapter 6.

To switch to a view that is more like the Windows Explorer (which uses a two-pane approach), click **View** → **List** in the SAS System main menu. Then click **View** → **Show Tree**. Figure 2.16 shows what this view looks like.

Figure 2.15 Initial SAS Explorer Window, Using Large Icons

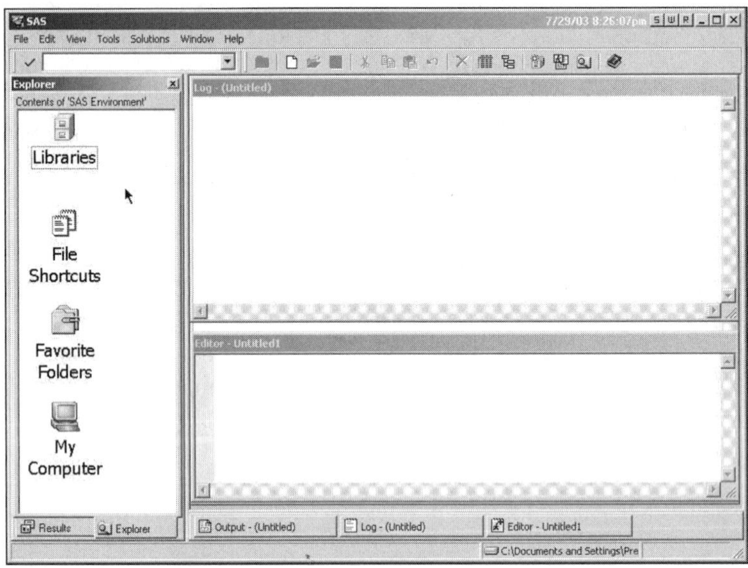

Figure 2.16 SAS Explorer Window, Using the List/Tree View

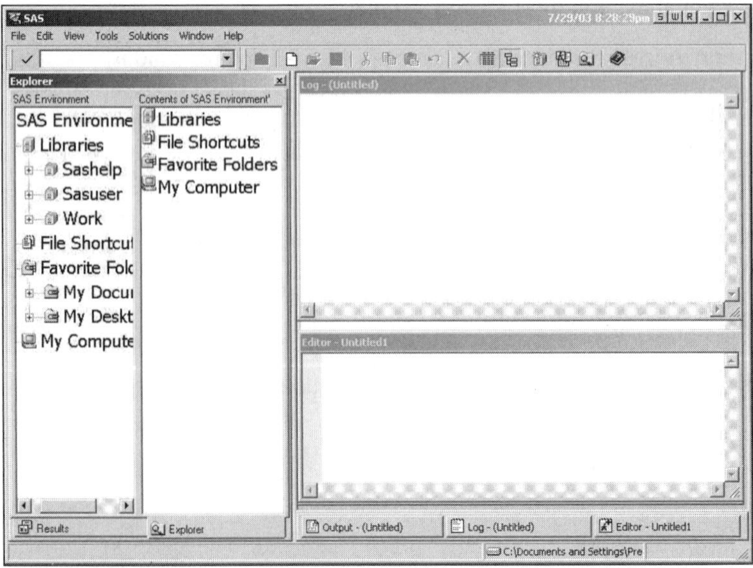

Note

> The left and right panes of the SAS Explorer window in Figure 2.16 have been resized so that all the contents are visible.

The rest of this book assumes that you are using the list/tree display in the SAS Explorer. An easy way to turn on the tree view is to click the Toggle Tree icon on the SAS System tool bar.

You can have multiple instances of the SAS Explorer window open at the same time. To open another SAS Explorer window, click the Explorer icon on the SAS tool bar.

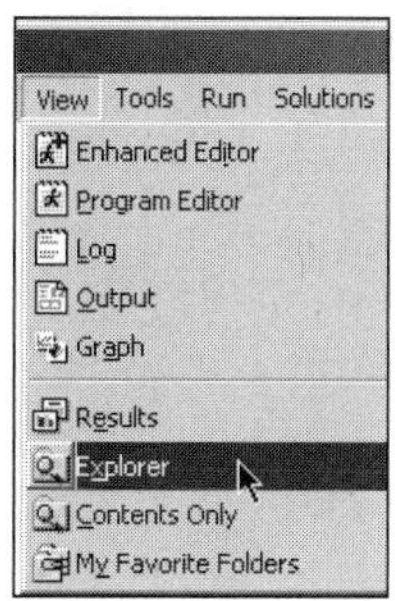

You can also open the SAS Explorer window by clicking **View → Explorer** in the SAS System main menu. The new instances of the Explorer window are not docked. To differentiate between the various instances of SAS Explorer windows, the title bar contains a number, as shown in Figure 2.17.

Figure 2.17 Multiple Instances of the SAS Explorer Window

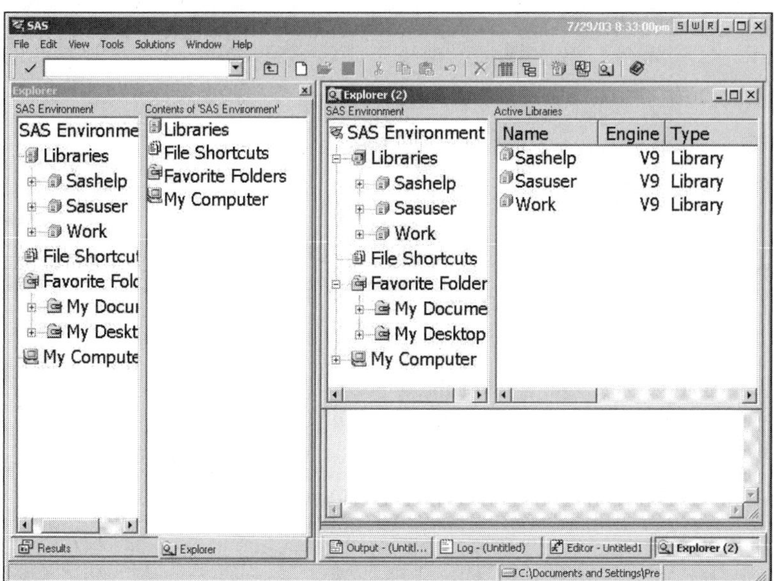

The following sections illustrate some of the tasks that you can perform from the SAS Explorer window.

Navigating in the SAS Explorer Window: When you first open the SAS Explorer window, you see four icons: **Libraries**, **File Shortcuts**, **Favorite Folders**, and **My Computer**. Double-clicking an icon changes the view to show the contents of the icon that you double-clicked.

To see the contents of a subfolder, click it—the contents of the subfolder are listed in the right pane of the SAS Explorer window. For example, Figure 2.18 shows the SAS Explorer window after you click the SASUSER subfolder, which is part of the Libraries folder.

Figure 2.18 SAS Explorer Window with SASUSER Catalog Expanded

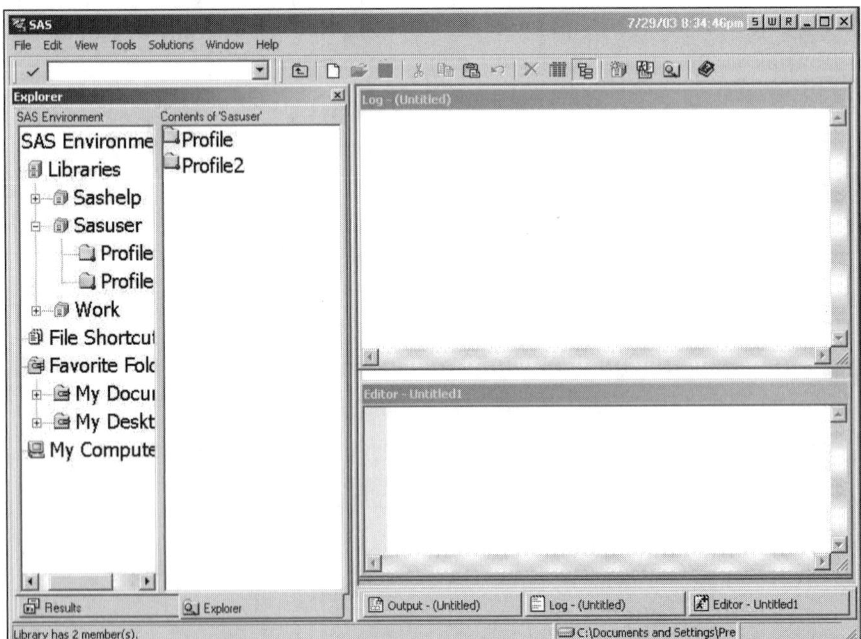

- To access an item that is listed in the right pane of the window, double-click the item. The action taken depends on the item. For example, double-clicking a table name opens the VIEWTABLE window.
- To collapse a folder view, click the minus sign next to the folder.
- To move up a level in the SAS Explorer window folder hierarchy, click the Up One Level icon on the SAS tool bar (or press BACKSPACE).

To familiarize yourself with this interface to the SAS System, take a few moments to explore the various folders to see what is stored where.

Moving and Copying Files: You can use the SAS Explorer window to move or copy files from one place to another. For example, suppose you decide you want the WORK.B table created by the example program to be permanent. It currently is stored in the WORK data library. To see this, expand the Libraries folder in the SAS Explorer window, then click **Work**. In the right pane of the window, you see the B table, as shown in Figure 2.19.

Figure 2.19 Preparing to Copy the B Table in the SAS Explorer Window

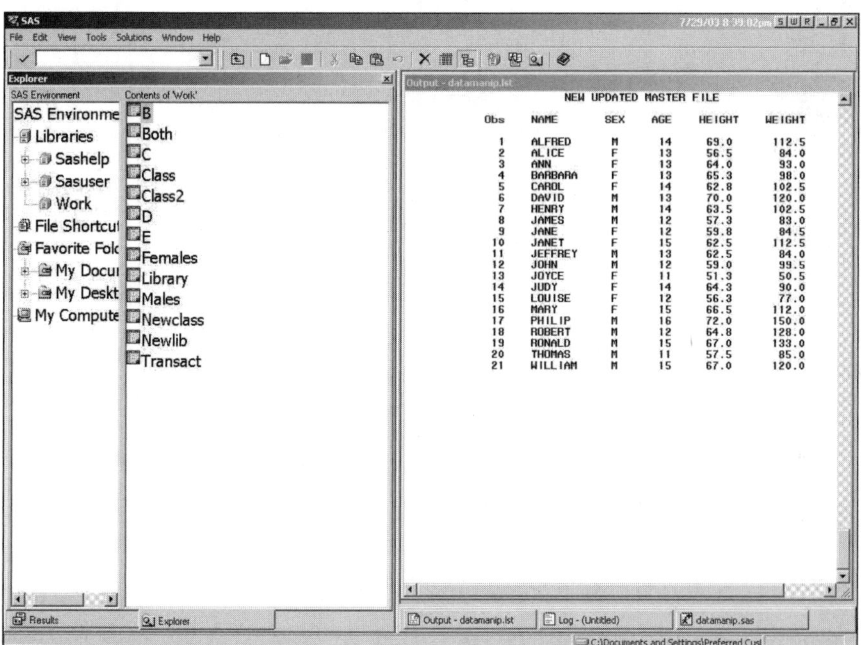

To move this file to the SASUSER data library, click the table in the right pane of the window so that it is highlighted. Now drag the table into the left pane of the window until the mouse pointer is over the SASUSER data library. Release the mouse button, and expand the view of the SASUSER data library. The B table has been moved (deleted) from the WORK data library and inserted into the SASUSER data library.

If you want to copy a table (or other item), use the right mouse button to drag the file. When you release the mouse button, you are asked whether you want to move or copy the item. Select **Copy**.

Renaming Files: Suppose you want to rename the C table to ThirdTable. To do so, display the contents of the Work folder, then right-click C in the right pane of the SAS Explorer window. When the popup menu appears, click **Rename**. A dialog box appears, as shown in Figure 2.20.

Figure 2.20 Rename Dialog Box Accessed from the SAS Explorer Window

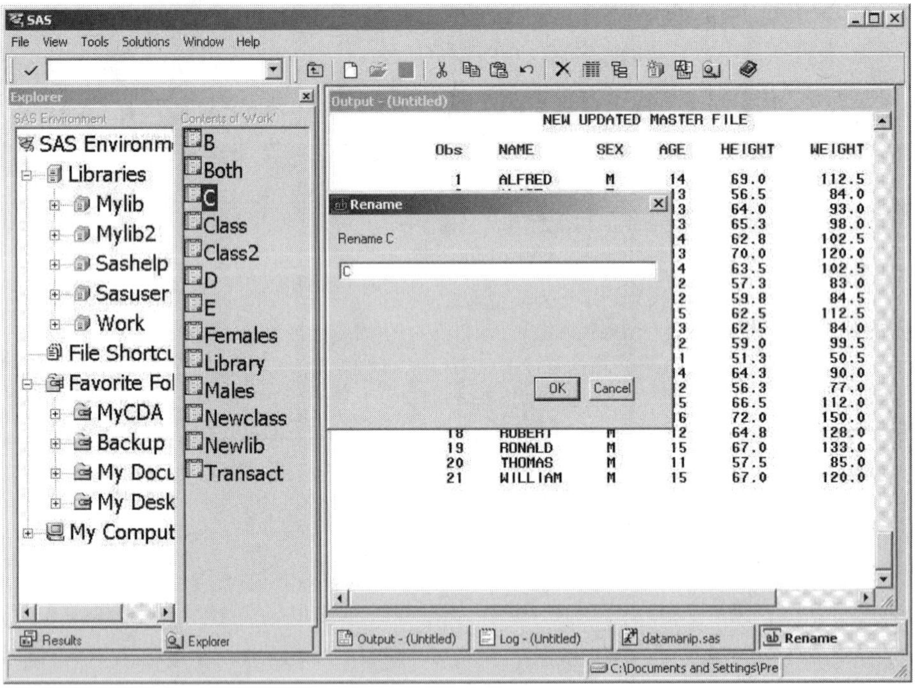

Type the new name in the text entry field and click **OK**.

Deleting Files: Deleting files works similarly to renaming files. To delete the E table, right-click the table name in the right pane of the SAS Explorer window. When the popup menu appears, click **Delete**. To complete the delete, click **OK** in the Delete Confirmation dialog box when it appears. To cancel the delete, click **Cancel**.

Creating a File Shortcut: You can use the SAS Explorer window to create file shortcuts (also known as filerefs). To create a file shortcut, follow these steps:

1. Right-click **File Shortcuts** in the left pane of the SAS Explorer window.
2. In the resulting popup menu, click **New**. The File Shortcut Assignment dialog box appears, as shown in Figure 2.21.

Figure 2.21 File Shortcut Assignment Dialog Box Accessed from the SAS Explorer Window

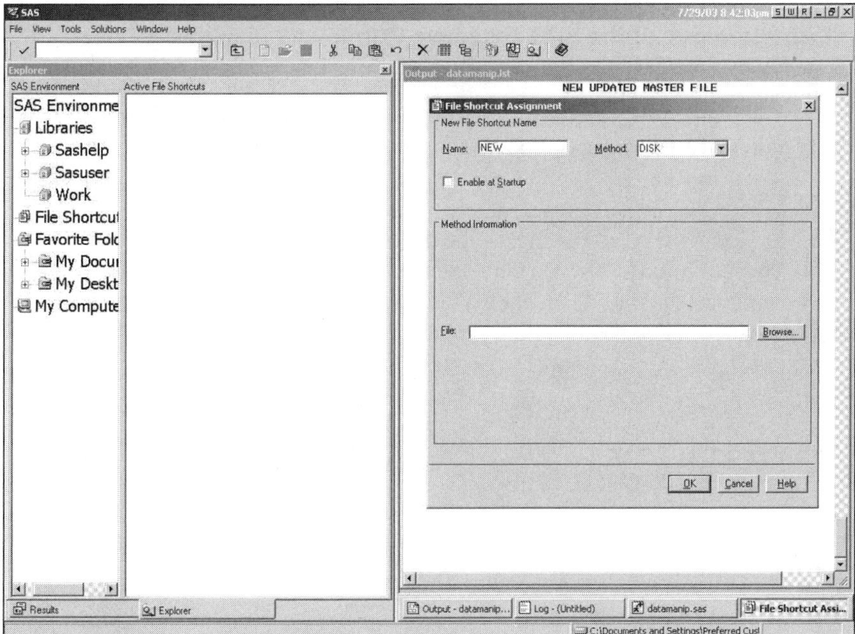

3. Type the file shortcut name in the **Name** field. For this example, type FILEREF1. (Use the Delete or Backspace key to delete the default name of NEW.)

4. Type the full physical pathname for the file in the **File** field. For this example, type C:\My Documents\My SAS Files\datamanip.lst. You can use the **Browse** button to help you find the file if you don't know the pathname.

   If you want the file shortcut to be automatically assigned whenever you start a SAS session, click the check box next to **Enable at Startup**.

5. When the **Name** and **File** fields contain the correct information, click **OK**.

The new file shortcut is now listed in the right pane of the SAS Explorer window. You can now use this file shortcut in your SAS programs.

By default, file shortcuts are temporary, and do not last from one SAS session to the next. However, if you select the **Enable at Startup** option in the File Shortcut Assignment dialog box, the file shortcut is assigned whenever you start a new SAS session.

Refreshing the SAS Explorer Information: If you add or delete files outside the SAS System, or otherwise change the information that is listed by the SAS Explorer window, you may need to "refresh" the SAS Explorer information. To do so, make the SAS Explorer window active. Now, click **View** → **Refresh** in the SAS System main menu.

Getting More Information out of the SAS Explorer Window: You may need more information than is shown by default in the SAS Explorer window. For example, it may be useful to see the file creation date or the file size.

There are two ways of gaining further information.

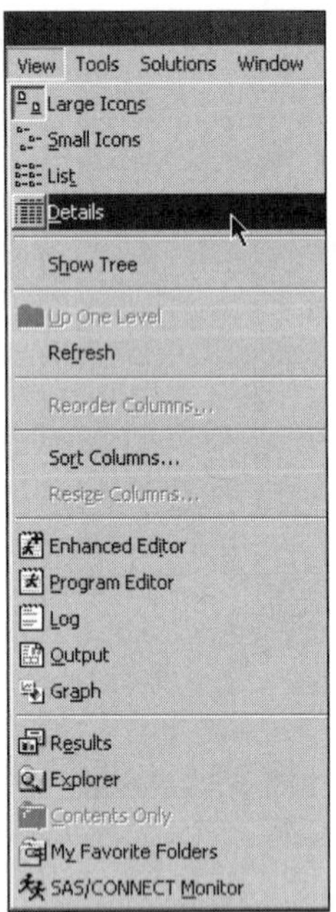

First, you can choose the detailed view instead of the list view. To change from list view to detailed view, make sure the SAS Explorer window is active. Then click **View** → **Details** in the SAS System main menu, or click the Toggle Details icon on the SAS System tool bar.

Now the right pane of the SAS Explorer window shows more information about every file. The details differ, depending on what content the SAS Explorer is showing. Details for SAS files in SAS libraries include **Name**, **Size**, **Type**, **Description**, and **Modified** (the date and time the file was last modified). To see all of this information, you may have to scroll right in the window. Figure 2.22 shows a sample of the detailed view (the SAS Explorer window has been enlarged so that more information is visible).

Figure 2.22 Detailed View in SAS Explorer Window

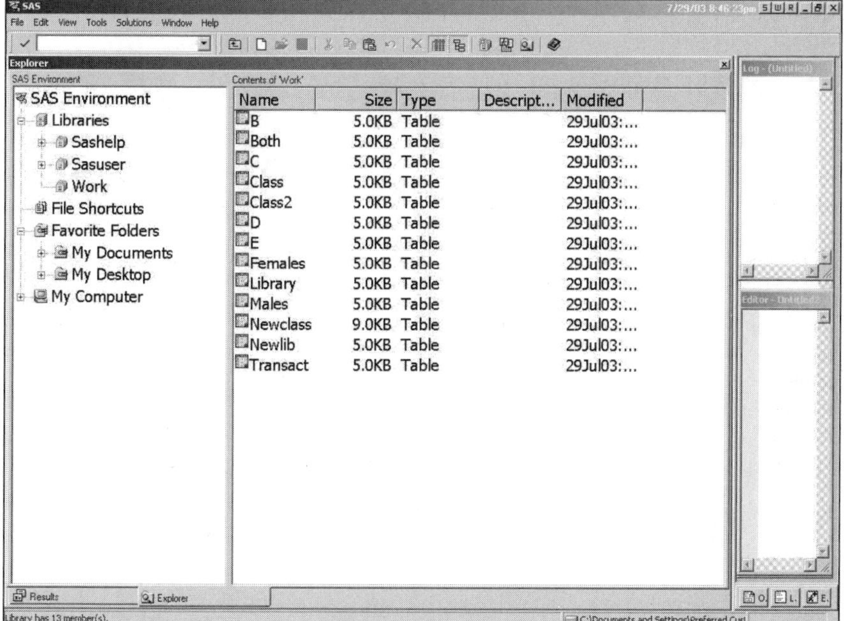

Note

To return to the less-detailed view, again click **View** → **List** in the SAS System main menu or click the Toggle Tree icon on the SAS System tool bar.

The second way of gaining more information about a file or object is to right-click it (in either the right or left pane of the SAS Explorer window), then click **Properties** in the popup menu. The Properties dialog box appears. The information displayed in the Properties dialog box varies, depending on what type of item you selected.

Note

A quick way to open the Properties dialog box for any item is to first select the item by clicking it, then press ALT-ENTER.

For example, display the contents of the WORK data library, and right-click the D table, then click **Properties** in the popup menu. A dialog box similar to the one in Figure 2.23 appears.

Figure 2.23 General Properties for a SAS Table

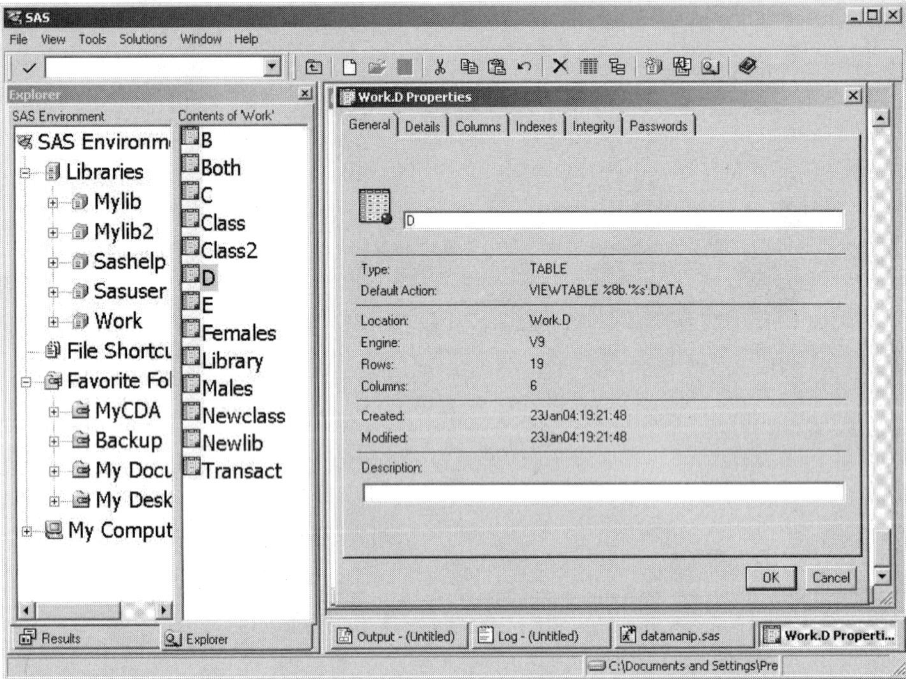

The **General** tab is displayed by default. This tab lets you type a description for the table. The description is listed in the detailed SAS Explorer view, and can help you find SAS data sets easily. Click the other tabs to view other types of properties. For example, Figure 2.24 shows the **Columns** tab for the D table.

Figure 2.24 Column Properties for a SAS Table

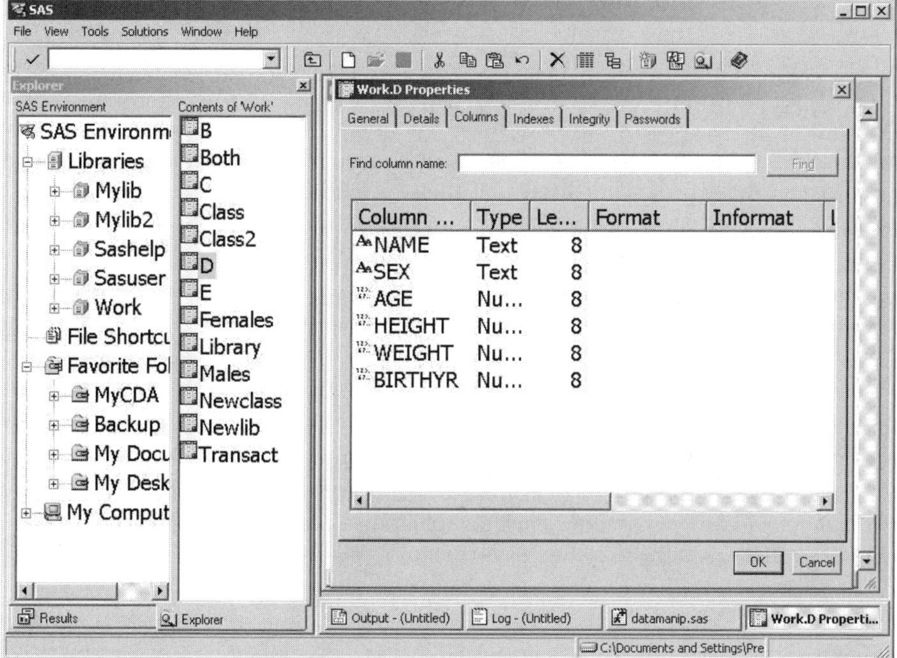

You can display properties for any item displayed in the SAS Explorer window. To close this Properties dialog box, click **OK**.

Sorting Your Files: To sort your files, select the detailed view, as described in the previous section. Now click a column head, such as **Type** or **Name**. The files are sorted in ascending order by the column you selected. To reverse the sort, click the column head again.

Note

You can also use the menus to sort your files. Click **View → Sort Columns** in the SAS System main menu. This opens the Sort Columns dialog box, which is described in more detail in Appendix 4.

Saving the Format of the SAS Explorer Window: If you prefer the detailed view to the list view, for example, it is cumbersome to have to turn on the detailed view every time you open a SAS Explorer window. You can save the view settings. To do so, follow these steps:

1. Get the window looking like you want it and make sure the SAS Explorer window is active.
2. Click **Tools → Options → Preferences** in the SAS System main menu, then click the **General** tab.

3. Select the **Save settings on exit** option.
4. Click **OK**.

Now the appearance of the SAS Explorer (and all other SAS windows) is saved when you close your SAS session, so they look the same the next time you start SAS up.

Customizing the SAS Explorer Window: You can customize the SAS Explorer window. For example, you can change the default action for double-clicking SAS files. See "Customizing the SAS Explorer" in Chapter 6 for more details.

Using the Favorite Folders Feature

Although the **My Computer** icon in the SAS Explorer window offers access to all your external files, you may find it convenient to use the **Favorite Folders** icon to access shortcuts to the folders you use most often. You can define as many favorite folders as you want.

Adding a New Favorite Folder to Your Collection: To add a folder to the Favorite Folders collection, first use the **My Computer** icon to navigate to the commonly used folder. Once the folder is shown in the SAS Explorer window, click the folder to highlight it. Now right-click, and click **Add to Favorite Folders** in the resulting popup menu.

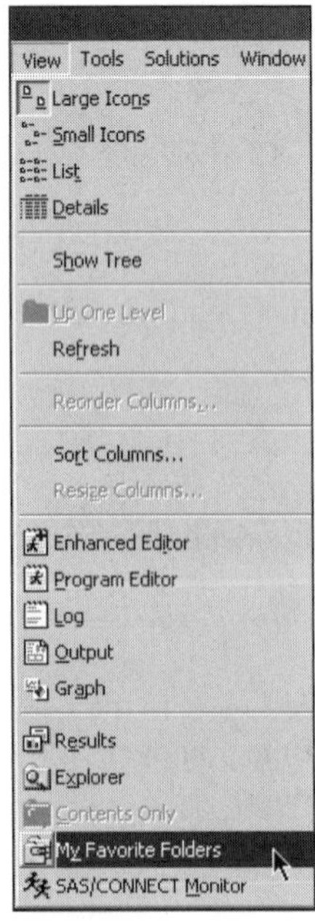

A similar approach is to click **View → My Favorite Folders** in the SAS System main menu. This opens a new window, called My Favorite Folders, which shows both the Favorite Folders folder and the My Computer folder at the same time. You can then navigate to the folder you want to add to the Favorite Folders folder, right-click it, and select **Add to Favorite Folders**. The window is immediately updated.

Figure 2.25 shows a sample My Favorite Folders window with a few favorite folders added.

Figure 2.25 My Favorite Folders Window

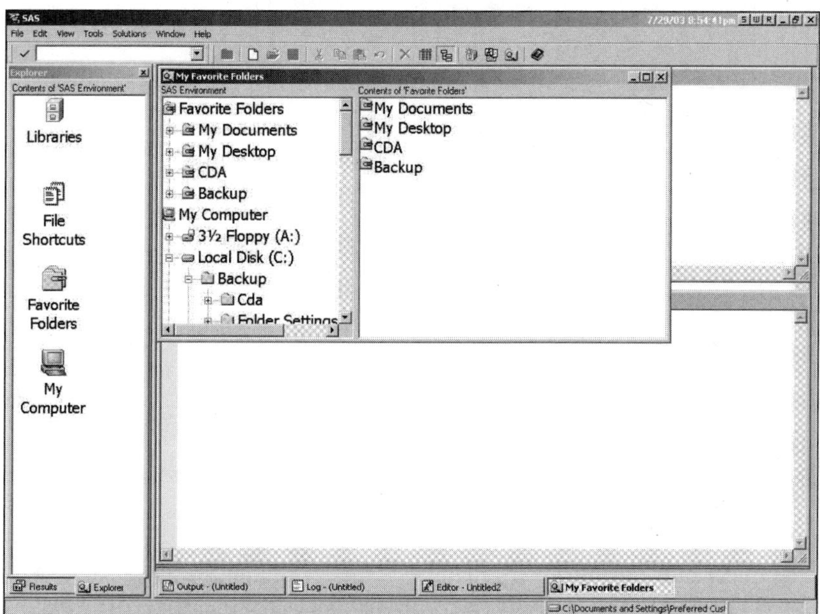

You can also add favorite folders using the following steps:

1. Open the My Favorite Folders window.
2. Right-click in the right pane, and in the resulting popup menu click **New Favorite Folder**. The New Favorite Folder dialog box appears, as shown in Figure 2.26.

Figure 2.26 New Favorite Folder Dialog Box

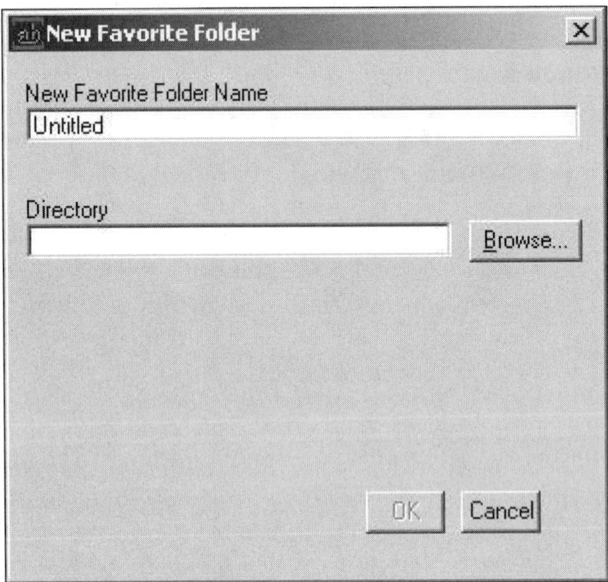

3. Type a name for the folder in the top text entry field, and type the full physical pathname of the folder in the **Directory** field. (If you do not know the full pathname, click the **Browse** button and navigate to the folder you want in the Select dialog box, then click **OK**.) When the text entry fields contain the right information, click **OK** to close the New Favorite Folder dialog box. The new folder is now listed under Favorite Folders in the SAS Explorer window.

Renaming a Favorite Folder Shortcut: The name you give the favorite folder is a logical reference to the actual physical folder, just as a library reference is a logical pointer to the physical location of a SAS data library. You can change the name of the favorite folder (which does not change the actual folder's name) by highlighting it, then right-clicking and selecting **Rename**. This opens the Rename Favorite Folder dialog box. Type the new name for the shortcut, then click **OK**.

Note

Although you can view the contents of your hard drive and floppy drives from the My Favorite Folders window, you should not manage these files (such as copying, deleting, or renaming) from the My Favorite Folders window. See Appendix 3 for information on how to use the Windows Explorer to perform these tasks.

Deleting a Favorite Folder: To delete a favorite folder, right-click the folder name. In the resulting popup menu, click **Delete**. When prompted whether you are sure you want to delete the folder, click **OK**. Remember that deleting a favorite folder from the SAS Explorer window or My

Favorite Folders window does not delete the actual physical folder—it just deletes the logical reference to the folder.

Ending Your SAS Session

FasTip: Click the main SAS window Close button.

To end your SAS session, click the main SAS window Close button. When a dialog box prompts you for whether you really want to end the session, click **OK**. The SAS System shuts down, and you are returned to the Windows desktop.

By default, you are asked if you really want to end the SAS session. Click **OK** to finish shutting the SAS System down. You can turn this prompt off using the Preferences dialog box—see "Setting Session Preferences" in Chapter 6 for more information.

Note

If you had text in SAS Text Editor windows, such as the Enhanced Editor, Program Editor, or NOTEPAD windows, you are prompted to save the text in those windows before your SAS session ends. You can choose not to save the text at that point by clicking **Cancel**, or click **OK** to access the Save As dialog box and save your program or text.

Placing the SAS System on the Desktop

You may find it useful to have a SAS System icon on the desktop. That way, you can simply double-click the icon to start the SAS System instead of having to use the **Start** button menus. A copy of a program icon is called a shortcut.

To place a SAS System shortcut on the desktop, follow these steps:

1. Right-click in a blank area of the desktop.
2. When the popup menu appears, click **New**, then click **Shortcut**.
3. The Create Shortcut Wizard appears. In the text-entry field, type the pathname of the SAS.EXE file, along with any system options. Or, use the **Browse** button to navigate to the SAS.EXE file, highlight it, and click **OK** to close the Browse for Folder dialog box.
4. Once the text-entry field contains the SAS command, click **Next**.
5. In the next dialog box that appears, type a name for the shortcut that you are creating. For example, you could type My SAS System.
6. Click **Finish**. The shortcut is added to your desktop.
7. If necessary, use the mouse to drag the new shortcut's icon around the desktop so that it is positioned where you want it.

Now you can double-click the new shortcut icon on the desktop to start the SAS System, without having to navigate the **Start** button menus.

Note

> Each shortcut that you create has its own properties, such as a command line and current directory. When you change one shortcut's properties, the changes do not apply to other shortcuts to the same program.

Deciding Where to Go from Here

If you use the SAS System for Windows only occasionally and all you do is submit a file, look at the output, and print or save it, you may not need to read much more of this book. However, this chapter has only scratched the surface of SAS 9.1—it is a powerful, flexible tool if you are willing to explore it. You can create your own tool bar icons, use the SAS System to access data in other applications, and so on.

Why not be adventurous? Read Chapter 3, which explains more about using the Enhanced Editor window, and perhaps Chapter 5, about printing. Or, read Chapter 15 if you'd like to download some files from your mainframe. Take another look at the table of contents at the beginning of this book, and see what topics interest you—each chapter opens another panoramic view on SAS 9.1 for Windows.

3 Editing and Working with Files

Introduction

This chapter shows you how to use the Enhanced Editor or Program Editor to perform basic file-editing tasks. While this chapter uses the Enhanced Editor window to illustrate file-editing techniques, you can use these techniques in any SAS Text Editor window (such as the Program Editor, the NOTEPAD window, and the SOURCE window in SAS/AF software). Where there are differences between the Enhanced Editor and the Program Editor behavior, these are noted.

The Enhanced Editor has many additional features not available in other text-editing windows; these more advanced features are covered in Chapter 7.

Note

> You do not have to use the SAS Text Editor to edit your files—you can use a different Windows text editor. See "Using a Different Text Editor" later in this chapter for more information.

Moving the Cursor

The basic tools for moving the cursor are your arrow keys. Keyboards differ, but you should have at least one set of arrow keys—up, down, left, and right. If your keyboard has a numeric keypad, you can use the arrow keys on the pad as well.

Note

> To use the keypad arrow keys, NumLock must be off. Check your keyboard for a NumLock key, and see if the NumLock indicator light is on. If it is, press the NumLock key once to turn it off.

The basic increments of cursor movement are

- by character
- by line
- by word
- by page.

Moving Character by Character: The left and right arrow keys move the cursor one character at a time to the left and right.

Note

> In the Program Editor, you can move the cursor past the end of the line. By default, the Enhanced Editor does not allow this, although you can use the Enhanced Editor Options dialog box to change this behavior. See Chapter 7 for more details.

Moving Line by Line: The up and down arrow keys move the cursor up and down one line. The Home key moves your cursor to the beginning of a line of text; the End key moves your cursor to the end of a line of text.

Note

In the Program Editor, you can move the cursor below the last line of text. The Enhanced Editor does not allow you to do this.

Moving Word by Word: Use the CTRL key with the left and right arrow keys to move the cursor from word to word. CTRL-LeftArrow moves the cursor one word to the left; CTRL-RightArrow moves the cursor one word to the right.

Note

The exact definition of a "word" differs between the Program Editor and the Enhanced Editor. Suppose the cursor is at the beginning of the following line of text:

```
  ll      '''''
```

CTRL-RightArrow in the Program Editor moves the cursor to the first space after the two lowercase L's. In the Enhanced Editor, CTRL-RightArrow moves the cursor just before the first single quotation mark.

Moving Page by Page: The PageUp and PageDown keys scroll the active window one full page up and down, respectively. The size of the page is relative to the size of the window.

Note

In the Program Editor, you can use the PageUp and PageDown keys to scroll below the last line of text. The Enhanced Editor does not allow you to do this.

Moving to the Top and Bottom of a File: Using the CTRL key with the PageUp and PageDown keys moves your cursor to the first and last characters of your file:

- To move to the first character, press CTRL-PageUp.
- To move to the last character, press CTRL-PageDown.

Note

CTRL-HOME is equivalent to CTRL-PageUp, and CTRL-END is equivalent to CTRL-PageDown.

More Shortcut Keys: You can navigate through your text and highlight text using a variety of shortcut keys. See **Help → SAS Help and Documentation → Using SAS Software in Your Operating Environment → Using SAS in Windows → Default Key Settings for Interactive SAS Sessions**, then click the appropriate topic.

Undoing Changes

FasTip: Click the Undo icon on the SAS tool bar.

Before you start editing a file, it is good to know how to undo your changes, especially while you are learning to use the mouse and the editing commands.

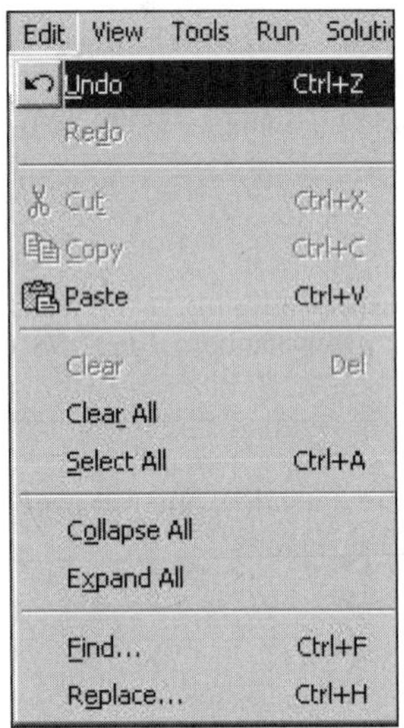

To undo a change, such as a line deletion or insertion of text in the wrong place, click **Edit** → **Undo** in the SAS System main menu (or press CTRL-Z). This undoes the last thing you did (except for irreversible actions, such as saving or printing a file). Choosing **Undo** several times in a row undoes recent changes in reverse order.

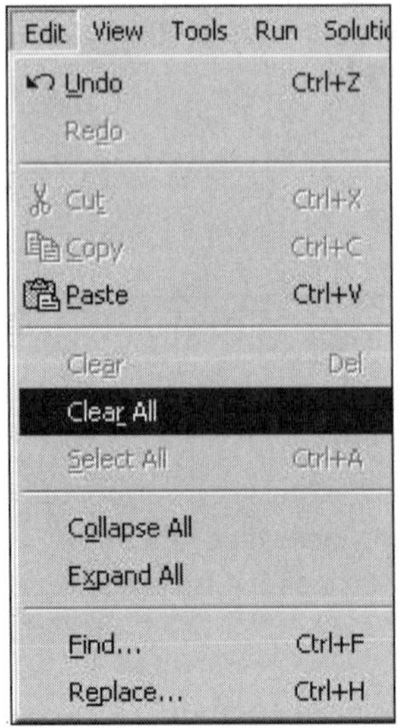

Another way of undoing changes, if you haven't yet saved the file, is to clear the editor (click **Edit** → **Clear All** in the SAS System main menu, or press CTRL-E). Now open the file again—the changes you made were never saved, so the original file is the same as it was.

Note

> The Clear All command is directly available in the Enhanced Editor's popup menu by simply right-clicking; you do not have to click **Edit** first.

You may want to keep backup files, in case you make a mistake that you cannot fix, such as overwriting a file.

Note

> No change that you make to your file is permanent until you save the file. See "Saving Files" later in this chapter for more information on how to save your file.

Marking Text

What's New: You can now clear the mark with the navigation (arrow) keys as well as by clicking.

To mark text means to highlight one or more characters, usually in preparation for moving, copying, or deleting the text.

Clearing a Mark: Before you become adept at marking text, you may highlight too much or too little. To clear the mark, either press an arrow key or click anywhere in the window.

Note

> If pressing an arrow key does not work in the Program Editor, use the Program Editor Options dialog box to activate this feature. See "Using the Program Editor instead of the Enhanced Editor" in Chapter 6 for more information.

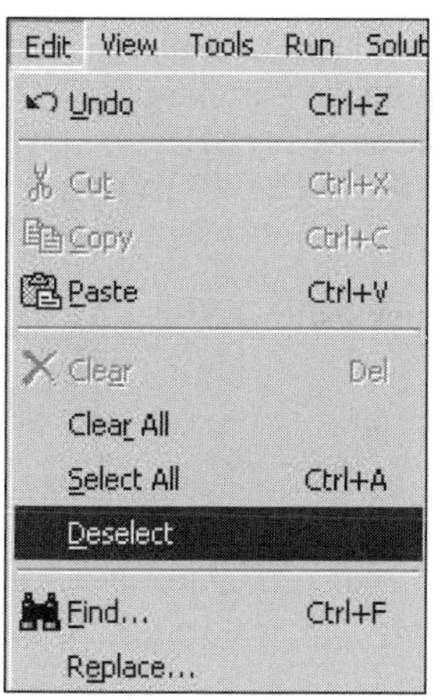

If you are using the Program Editor, you can also use the menus to clear a mark: click **Edit** → **Deselect** in the SAS System main menu. The Enhanced Editor does not offer this menu choice.

Using the Mouse to Mark Text: You can use either your mouse or the keyboard to mark text. Here is the basic procedure for highlighting with the mouse:

1. Click the first character of the section that you want to highlight.
2. Hold down the mouse button and drag the mouse until all the text that you want to include is highlighted.
3. If you need to go beyond the edge of the window, drag the mouse pointer over the edge of the window, and the window scrolls. However, it scrolls quite quickly. You may have to practice a bit before you can get it to stop exactly where you want.
4. Release the mouse button when all the text that you want to mark is highlighted.

More techniques you may find helpful include the following:

- Double-clicking in the middle of a word highlights that word.
- Holding down the Shift key while clicking extends a mark (equivalent to dragging to extend the mark).
- Holding down the CTRL key while clicking a line of text highlights the entire line.

Note

> This technique works only in the Program Editor window. It does not work in the Enhanced Editor window.

- Holding down the ALT key while dragging the mouse pointer highlights a rectangular block (column) of text.
- Place the mouse pointer in the left margin of the Enhanced Editor window to the left of a line of text, then click. The entire line is highlighted. (This is not applicable to the Program Editor.) You can also drag the mouse in the margin to select multiple lines of text.

Using the Keyboard to Mark Text: If you prefer to use the keyboard to mark text, place the cursor over the first character of the section you want to mark. Now hold the Shift key down, and use the cursor movement keys to extend the mark. For example, pressing SHIFT-CTRL-LeftArrow extends the mark one word to the left, and pressing SHIFT-CTRL-PageDown extends the mark to the end of the file.

Marking All Text: If you want to select all of the text in the window, click **Edit → Select All** in the SAS System main menu (or press CTRL-A).

Deleting Text

What's New: By default, selecting **Clear All** from the **Edit** menu does not activate a confirmation prompt. The text is simply cleared.

FasTip: Mark the text, then press the Delete key.

To clear an entire window (even the Log window), click the New icon on the SAS tool bar.

Note

> For all windows except the Enhanced Editor window, clicking the New icon simply clears the text. If the Enhanced Editor window is active, however, clicking the New icon opens a second instance of the Enhanced Editor.

As with moving the cursor, you can delete text by character, by word, or by line. You can also delete all the text in the window. In addition, you can choose to delete text by using keys on the keyboard or by using the menus.

Deleting a Single Character: To delete a single character, press the Backspace or Delete key. Here is the difference between the two:

- The Backspace key deletes the character immediately before the cursor position.
- The Delete key deletes the character under the cursor.

Deleting a Word: To delete a word, double-click the word, then press DELETE. To delete the rest of a word after the cursor, press CTRL-DELETE.

Note

> In the Program Editor, pressing CTRL-DELETE deletes the rest of the word, but not the spaces following the word. In the Enhanced Editor, pressing CTRL-DELETE deletes the rest of the word plus the following spaces.

Deleting Lines of Text: The basic method of deleting text is to first mark the text (see "Marking Text" earlier in this chapter), then press DELETE.

To delete all the characters in the line after the cursor position (except the carriage return), click before the first character you want to delete. Now hold the Shift key down and click at the end of the line.

Note

In the Program Editor, you can also press ALT-DELETE to delete from the cursor position to the end of the line.

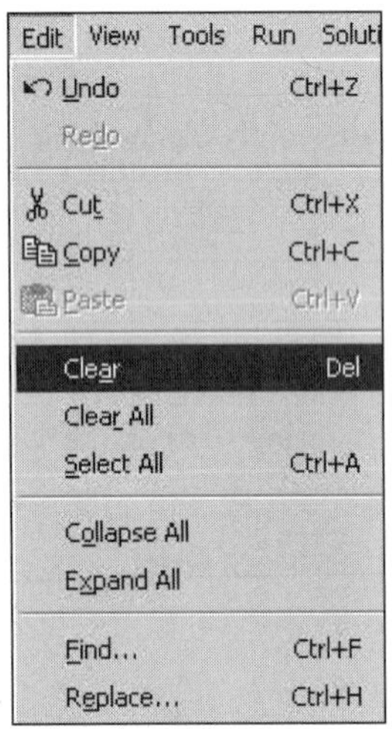

Using the Menus to Delete Text: Instead of pressing DELETE to delete marked text, you can use the menu. Click **Edit** → **Clear** in the SAS System main menu. Be careful—if you select **Clear All** instead, the entire window is cleared. If this happens to you, immediately click **Edit** → **Undo**. The text reappears.

Replacing Old Text with New Text: You can replace old text with new text by first marking the text that you want to replace, then beginning to type the new text. The old text is deleted, and the new text appears as you type.

Clearing an Entire Window: You can clear the text from a window in several ways. Here are two methods:

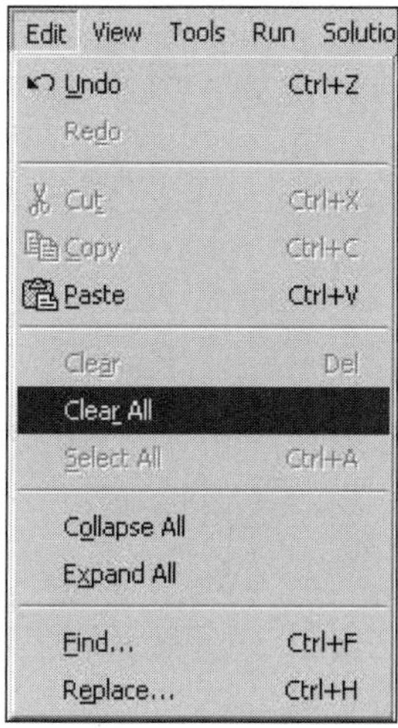

- Click **Edit** → **Clear All** in the main SAS System menu.

- Click the New icon on the SAS System tool bar.

Cutting Text

FasTip: Mark the text, then press CTRL-X.

Cutting text is not the same as deleting it. When you delete text, it is gone. If you cut the text, it is placed on the Windows Clipboard for future use. You can then paste the text somewhere else in a SAS window or in another application such as Excel or Word.

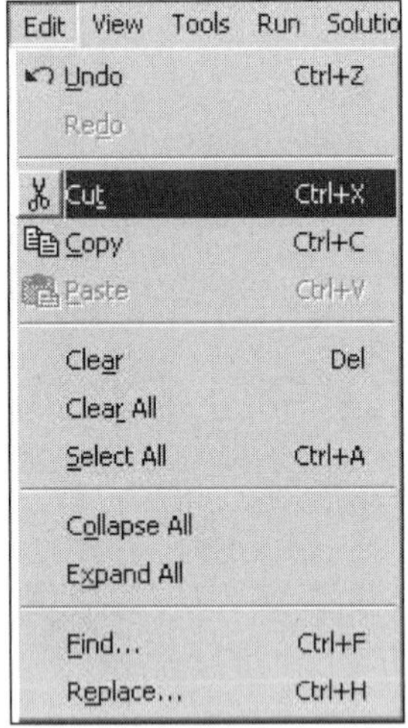

To cut text, first mark it. Then click **Edit → Cut** in the SAS System main menu (or press CTRL-X). The text disappears from the SAS window and is placed on the Clipboard. The Clipboard can hold only one section of text at a time. That is, if you cut one portion of text, then cut a second portion of text, the Clipboard keeps only the second portion of text.

Copying Text

What's New: Copying text no longer clears the mark.

FasTip: Mark the text, then press CTRL-C.

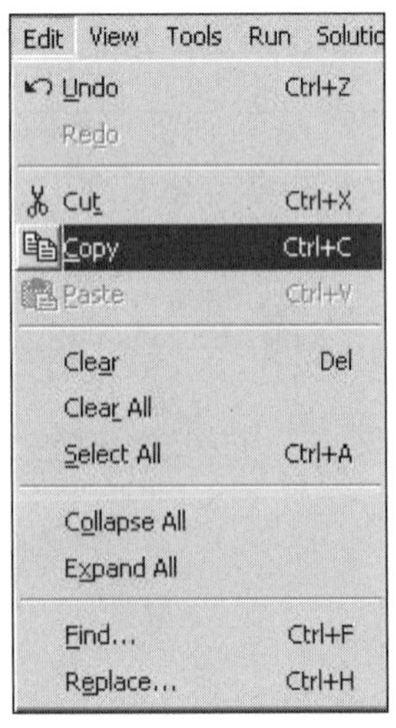

If you want to reuse text but do not want to delete it from its original position, copy it instead of cutting it. First, mark the text. Now click **Edit → Copy** in the SAS System main menu (or press CTRL-C). The text is placed on the Clipboard but remains in its original position as well.

The Clipboard can hold only one section of text at a time. That is, if you copy one portion of text, then copy a second portion of text, the Clipboard keeps only the second portion of text.

Pasting Text

FasTip: Place the cursor at the insertion point and press CTRL-V.

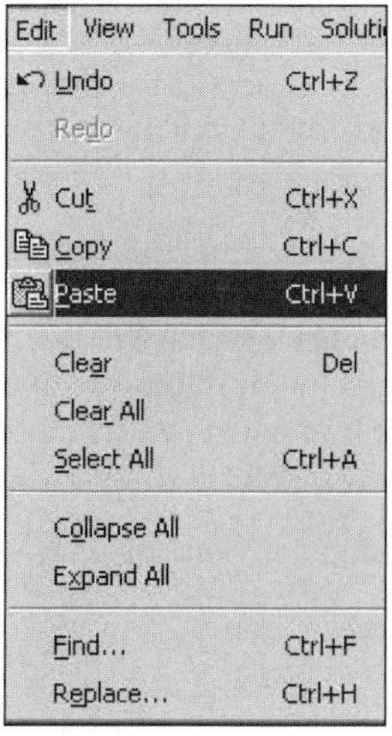

If you have cut or copied text, you can paste it elsewhere in a SAS window or even in another Windows application such as WordPad. To paste text into a SAS window, position your cursor where you want the new text to appear—the text appears after the cursor. Now click **Edit** → **Paste** in the SAS System main menu (or press CTRL-V). The text is pasted into the SAS window. The text is not deleted from the Clipboard, so you can paste it several times in a row if you want.

If you mark text before you paste, the marked text is replaced with the pasted text.

Inserting Text

FasTip: Position the cursor and start typing.

If you want to type new text in a file, position your cursor where you want the new text to appear. If you are in insert mode, the text appears in front of the existing text. If you are in overstrike mode, the text replaces the existing text.

The shape of the cursor indicates whether you are in insert or overstrike mode:

- A block cursor indicates overstrike mode.
- A thin cursor indicates insert mode.

To switch between the two modes, press INSERT.

If you want to replace a chunk of text with new text, mark the text, then start typing. When you type, the marked text is deleted and the new text replaces it.

If you want to append text to a file without opening it, type the new text in the Program Editor window, then use the Save As dialog box to append to the file, as described in "Saving an Existing File" later in this chapter.

Note

> This append technique works only with the Program Editor. It does not work in the Enhanced Editor.

Scrolling

The scroll bars on the right side and bottom of the window can help you scroll. You control how much the window scrolls by how you use the scroll bars.

Scrolling Line by Line: To scroll line by line, click the up or down arrows repeatedly.

Scrolling Character by Character: To scroll character by character horizontally, click the left or right arrows repeatedly.

Scrolling by Larger Increments: To smoothly scroll vertically or horizontally, drag the scroll box inside the scroll bar. Release the mouse button when you have scrolled to where you want to be. To jump vertically through a file, click in the vertical scroll bar. Clicking above the scroll box jumps your cursor toward the top of the window; clicking below the scroll box jumps your cursor toward the bottom of the window. Use the horizontal scroll bar in the same way to move left and right by large increments.

Remember that you can also use the PageDown and PageUp keys alone and in combination with the CTRL key to scroll through your file.

Note

In the Program Editor, you can adjust how much the window scrolls when you press PageDown and PageUp. See "Using the Program Editor instead of the Enhanced Editor" in Chapter 6 for more information. This technique does not work in the Enhanced Editor.

Setting Tab Stops

Tabs are a useful indention tool when typing your code. Both the Program Editor and Enhanced Editor support customized tab stops, but the methods of setting them in each of these windows differ.

Setting Tab Stops in the Enhanced Editor: The Enhanced Editor defaults to tabs every 4 spaces. To change this setting, click **Tools → Options → Enhanced Editor** in the SAS System main menu. This opens the Enhanced Editor Options dialog box. On the **General** tab, use the **Tabs** area to adjust your tab settings. Click **OK** to close the dialog box.

The changes you make via the Enhanced Editor Options dialog box persist from one SAS session to the next. You do not need to issue the WSAVE command.

By default, the tabs in the Enhanced Editor are "real" tabs and are not replaced by spaces (use the Enhanced Editor Options dialog box to change this behavior if you want spaces instead of tabs).

See Chapter 7 for more information on using and customizing the Enhanced Editor.

Setting Tab Stops in the Program Editor: By default, the tab stops in the Program Editor window are set to every 8 spaces. Many times, you may want tab stops at a different place (such as every three spaces). To set new tab stops in the Program Editor window, issue the following command from the command bar:

```
:tan ; :d;
```

Replace *n* in the command with the number of spaces that you want between tab stops. In the Program Editor, tabs are really *n* consecutive spaces.

Note

If you omit the closing semicolon, the tab stop indicator line appears in the Program Editor window (a long line of T's). Issuing the RESET command from the command bar clears this line.

If you want the tab stop settings to be remembered between SAS sessions, issue the WSAVE command from the command bar (make sure the Program Editor window is active when you issue this command).

Dragging and Dropping Text between SAS Windows

FasTip: Use the left-button drag for the default action.

Use the CTRL key plus the left mouse button for copying.

Use the right mouse button to get a move/copy prompt.

After you mark some text, you can drag it to another place in the same window or to another SAS window. As you recall, dragging is when you hold down the mouse button and move the mouse. Dropping is when you release the mouse button when the pointer is at the appropriate position in the destination window.

Why Drag and Drop? Suppose you have some code in the NOTEPAD window that you want to submit. By using drag-and-drop, you can move the text to the Enhanced Editor window without opening any menus.

How to Drag and Drop Text: Here is the basic procedure for dragging and dropping text:

1. Mark the text you want to move and release the mouse button.
2. Place the mouse pointer over the marked text and hold the mouse button down.
3. Drag the pointer to the appropriate position in the destination window and release the mouse button.

You must hold the mouse button down for a second or so before you begin dragging. Otherwise, the mark is changed instead of the text being dragged.

Note

> It is also possible to move text from your SAS session to another Windows application and vice versa. Both the SAS window and the target application must be visible at the same time. To accomplish this, resize the main SAS window as described in "Moving and Resizing Windows" in Chapter 1.

Interpreting the Mouse Pointer: You can drag text from any SAS window to any SAS window that supports text input. For example, you can drag and drop text from the Output window to the Enhanced Editor window but not to the Log window. The mouse pointer indicates which windows accept dropped text:

- If the pointer is over a window that accepts text, the pointer turns into a little box (with or without a + sign next to it).
- If the pointer is over a window that does not accept text, the pointer turns into a "no" icon—a circle with a bar through it.

Whether or not the pointer has a + sign next to it tells you that the text is moved or copied:

-  If the pointer has a + sign next to it, the text is copied from one window to the other.
-  If the pointer has no + sign next to it, the text is moved (that is, deleted) from the original window.

Controlling Whether the Text Is Copied or Moved: To control whether the text is copied or moved, use the CTRL key or either the left or right mouse button, as follows:

- If you hold the CTRL key down while dragging, the text is always copied. Be sure that you release the mouse button before you release the CTRL key. You must first begin to drag, then press and hold the CTRL key. (If you press the CTRL key before beginning to drag, the mark is extended instead of the text being copied.)
- If you use the right mouse button to drag the text, you are asked whether you want to move or copy the text when you release the mouse button at the insertion point.

Use Table 3.1 to help you determine how to control the copying and moving of text.

Table 3.1 Copying and Moving Text with the Mouse

Key and/or Button	Result
Left Mouse Button	moves text from text-editing window to text-editing window copies text from non-text-editing window to text-editing window
CTRL + Left Mouse Button	copies text
Right Mouse Button	prompts you with a popup menu If the destination window is the Enhanced Editor, the menu offers **Move here**, **Copy here**, and **Cancel** choices. If the destination window is the Program Editor, the popup menu choices are **Move**, **Copy**, **Submit**, and **Cancel**.

Searching for Text

What's New: The Find dialog box stays open until you click **Close**.

FasTip: Click **Edit** → **Find**.

Press CTRL-R for repeat find.

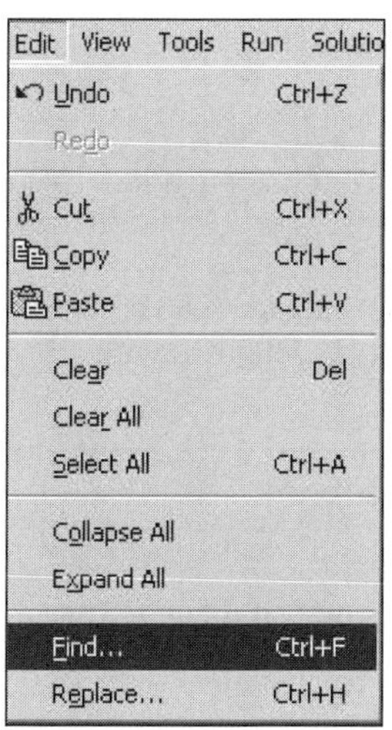

If you have a long program in the Enhanced Editor (or Program Editor, NOTEPAD, or any other text-editing window) and want to find some text, it may be faster to use the Find feature than to scroll through the window. To search for text, click **Edit** → **Find** in the SAS System main menu. A Find dialog box appears, as shown in Figure 3.1.

Figure 3.1 Find Dialog Box

Find Dialog Box for Enhanced Editor | **Find Dialog Box for Other SAS Windows**

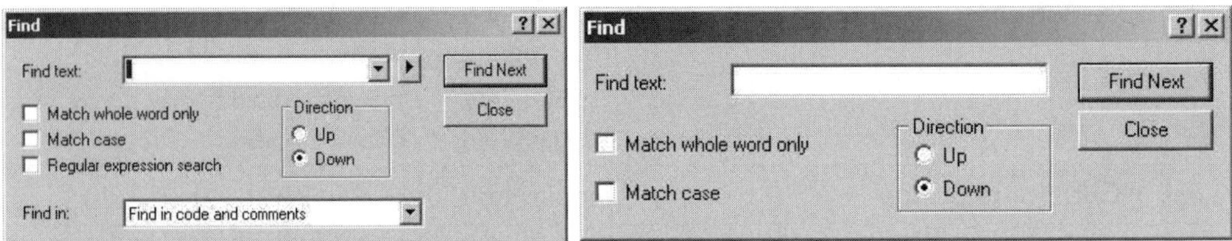

Controlling the Search Parameters: Type the word that you want to find (such as an option name, a table name, or some other keyword) in the **Find text** field. The search is not case sensitive unless you click the **Match case** option.

Note

> The Enhanced Editor version of the Find dialog box remembers the last word searched for from SAS session to SAS session. This is not true of the Find dialog box used for the Program Editor, Log, Output, and other SAS windows. Both versions of the Find dialog box remember the last word searched for during the current SAS session.

If the **Find text** field contains the word "data," by default the search finds both lines containing "DATA A" and "proc datasets." If you want to find only the whole word "data," click the **Match whole word only** option.

For the Enhanced Editor version of the Find dialog box, use the **Regular expression search** option when the text string is a regular expression. A regular expression uses special characters as wildcards to search for a string or substring. For a selection of special characters that you can use in regular expressions, click the arrow that is located to the right of the **Find text** field.

Note

> The search function does not find the occurrence of a word that the cursor is positioned in.

Limiting the Context of the Search: Use the **Find in** field to control where the search occurs. Your choices are in just code, just comments, or both code and comments (the default value).

Note

> The **Find in** field is available only in the Enhanced Editor's Find dialog box.

To search only a specific portion of your text, highlight the text before clicking **Find Next**. The search is limited to only the highlighted text.

Controlling the Search Direction: By default, the search starts at the cursor position and continues forward (down) through the file. If you want to search backward from the cursor position, click the **Up** option. The Find dialog box remembers this direction and retains it for the remainder of your SAS session, unless you change it again.

Performing the Search: When you have the options set to your satisfaction, click **Find Next**. The cursor jumps to the next instance of the word that you wanted to find. In the Program Editor, the Find dialog box closes after the word is found. If no such word is found, a dialog box appears informing you of that fact.

Note

In the Program Editor, Log, and similar windows, a message area at the bottom of the main SAS window displays a message: `WARNING: No occurrences of "word" found.`

Repeating a Search: If you want to search repeatedly for a word, open the Find dialog box again—it remembers the last search you performed. Alternatively, press CTRL-R.

Note

In the Program Editor and similar windows, the search stops at the end of the file. If you want to start searching again at the top, press CTRL-R once more.

In the Enhanced Editor, the search continues until the entire file is searched. For example, if your cursor is in the middle of a file, and you search for "data", the search finds all occurrences of "data" below your cursor, then all the ones above your cursor (assuming the search direction is **Down**) before the "Finished searching" dialog box appears.

Replacing Text

What's New: The Replace dialog box stays open until you click **Close**.

FasTip: Click **Edit** → **Replace**.

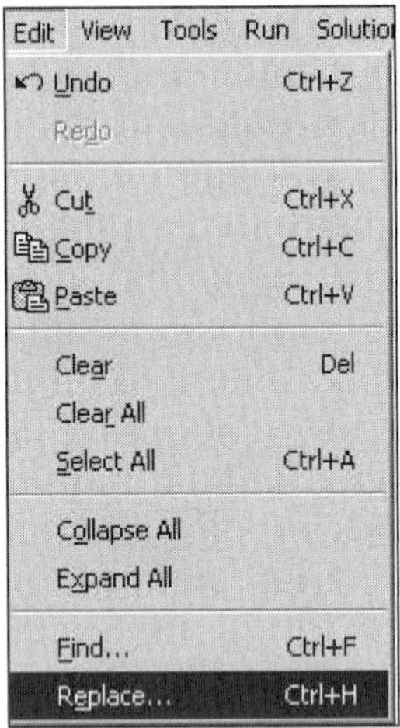

Replacing one string of text with another works similarly to finding text. Click **Edit** → **Replace** in the SAS System main menu. A Replace dialog box appears, as shown in Figure 3.2.

Figure 3.2 Replace Dialog Box

Replace Dialog Box for Enhanced Editor **Replace Dialog Box for Other SAS Windows**

Type the search string in the **Find text** field and the replacement string in the **Replace with** field. Click **Find Next** to find the first occurrence of the text to replace.

Limiting the Context of the Replacement: Use the **Find in** field to control where replacements occur. Your choices are in just code, just comments, or both code and comments (the default value).

Note

The **Find in** field is available only in the Enhanced Editor's Replace dialog box.

To search and replace in only a specific portion of your text, highlight the text before clicking **Find Next**. The search-and-replace operation is limited to only the highlighted text.

Controlling the Search and Replace Parameters: Many of the options in the Replace dialog box are similar to the ones in the Find dialog box. For example, the replacement is not case sensitive unless you click the **Match case** option. The default direction of the search is down; to change this, click the **Up** option. The Replace dialog box remembers this direction and retains it for the remainder of your SAS session, unless you change it again. If you want to ensure that only entire instances of the search string are replaced, click the **Match whole word only** option.

Performing the Replacement: Clicking **Find Next** locates an occurrence of the search string. Click **Replace** to replace the text with the new text string. The text is replaced, and the next occurrence of the search string is highlighted.

Note

> Click **Edit** → **Undo** in the SAS System main menu (or press CTRL-Z) to undo an erroneous replacement.

If you prefer, issue the RCHANGE command from the command bar to repeat replacements. You are not prompted for the replacement.

Replacing All Occurrences of a String: To replace all instances of the search string at once, click **Replace All** in the Replace dialog box instead of **Replace**. Be careful when using **Replace All**—you are not prompted for the replacements, so you might replace a lot of things accidentally if the original string occurs in places that you did not expect. If you find that you've used the **Replace All** feature unadvisedly, click **Edit** → **Undo** in the SAS System main menu to reverse all the changes at once.

To replace all occurrences in a limited section of your text, highlight the text first, then click **Replace in Selection** instead of clicking **Replace All**.

Spell-Checking Your Program

What's New: The spell-checker is not available from the Enhanced Editor. In the Program Editor, the SPELL ALL and SPELL ALL SUGGEST commands are still available, but the **Edit** menu no longer offers the spelling-related menu choices.

The SAS System includes a spell-checker. To access this feature, open your program in the Program Editor window.

Note

> If the Program Editor is not already open, click **View** → **Program Editor** to open it.

Generating a Misspelled Word List: To generate a list of unrecognized words and their corresponding line numbers, issue the following command from the command bar:

```
SPELL ALL
```

The SPELL: Unrecognized Words window opens with the list. Figure 3.3 shows a sample SPELL: Unrecognized Words window.

Figure 3.3 SPELL: Unrecognized Words Window

```
SPELL: Unrecognized Words
 Dictionary: ________

    Unrecognized word        At line

    S                        5
    S                        5
    S                        5
    P                        5
    E                        5
    B                        5
    R                        5
    R                        5
    Y                        5
    DATASHOW                 7
    SAS                      9
    DATMAN                   11
    DATASTEP                 11
    DSOPTION                 11
    PROCS                    14
```

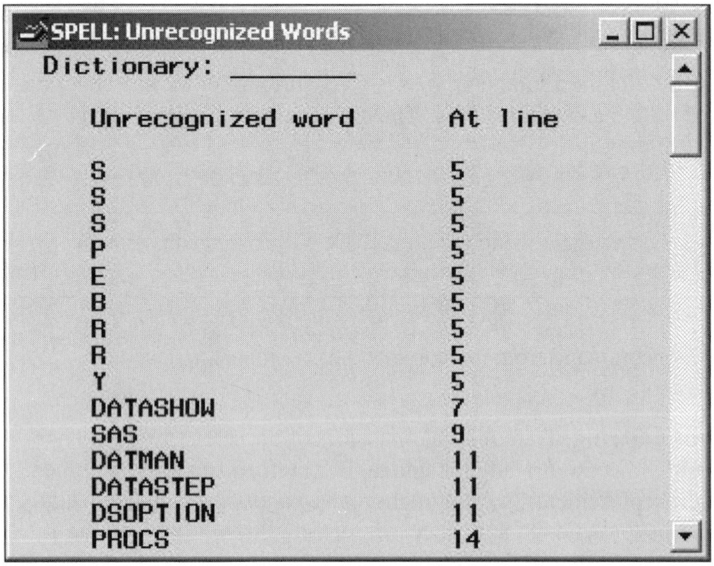

To close the SPELL: Unrecognized Words window, click its Close button.

Letting the SAS System Make Spelling Suggestions: Instead of a mere list of misspelled words, you can choose to let the SAS System make suggestions to replace the questionable spellings. To do so, issue the following command from the command bar:

```
SPELL ALL SUGGEST
```

The SPELL: Suggestions window appears. This window lists the first unrecognized word, the dictionary being used, and the suggestions for the misspelled word. Figure 3.4 shows a sample SPELL: Suggestions window.

Figure 3.4 SPELL: Suggestions Window

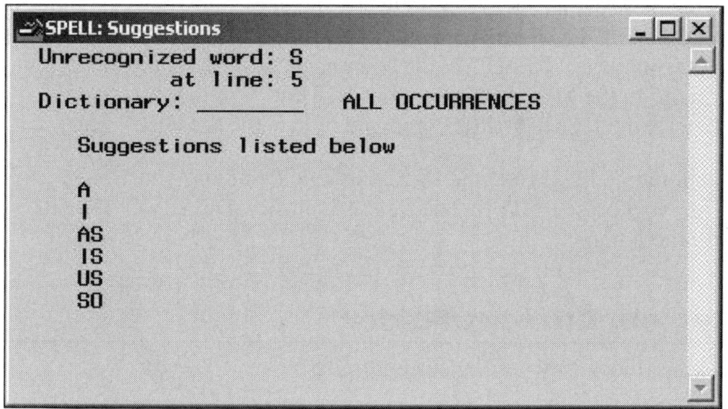

To implement one of the suggestions, click the word with the correct spelling. Then click **Tools** → **Replace** in the SAS System main menu. Alternatively, use the Tab key to move the cursor to the correct spelling, then press ENTER to highlight your choice. Now issue the REPLACE command from the command bar. Only that occurrence is corrected.

If you want all occurrences of that misspelling corrected, highlight the correct spelling, then click **ALL OCCURRENCES** before you do the replace. The message area of the main SAS window tells you how many occurrences were replaced.

Ignoring Suggestions: If you do not want to take action on a word, click the Close button of the SPELL: Suggestions window. It moves to the next word.

Canceling the Suggestion Process: To cancel the whole process of spell-checking and suggesting corrections, issue the CANCEL command from the command bar.

Note

Word replacements that have already been executed are not canceled.

Adding Words to the Dictionary: You can add words to the default dictionary so that they are not flagged as misspelled in future spell-checks. You can also create auxiliary dictionaries. These techniques work in both the SPELL: Unrecognized Words window and the SPELL: Suggestions window.

To add a word to the default dictionary, click the word, or use the Tab key to move the cursor to the word, and press ENTER to highlight it in the SPELL: Unrecognized Words window. This step is not necessary in the SPELL: Suggestions window. Now click **Tools** → **Remember** in the SAS System main menu. Or, issue the REMEMBER command from the command bar. From now on, that word is not flagged as misspelled.

To create an auxiliary dictionary, place your cursor in the **Dictionary** field and type a dictionary name. If one does not exist, create a new name, such as MYDICT. The name must be a valid SAS name. This creates an entry MYDICT.DICTIONARY in your SASUSER.PROFILE catalog. In the SPELL: Unrecognized Words window, all REMEMBER commands now affect the auxiliary dictionary, not the default dictionary. In the SPELL: Suggestions window, you must set the dictionary for each change; otherwise the REMEMBER command affects the default dictionary.

To return to using the default dictionary, click inside the **Dictionary** field and use your Delete and Backspace keys to clear this field. Now press ENTER. The field is blank, and all REMEMBER commands now affect the default dictionary.

Changing the SAS System Current Folder

What's New: Old term = working folder; new term = current folder.

The default current folder in the Windows 2000 environment is now C:\Documents and Settings*Windows-user-name*, if you start the SAS session from the **Start** button menu. For Windows NT users, the current folder defaults to C:\winnt\profiles*Windows-user-name*.

Use the SASINITIALFOLDER system option to set the current folder at SAS System start-up.

FasTip: Double-click the current folder icon in the bottom-right corner of the main SAS window.

The SAS System uses the current folder to look for files and store files, when you do not specify a pathname (such as in the FILENAME or INFILE statement). For SAS 9.1, the default current folder in the Windows 2000 environment is C:\Documents and Settings*Windows-user-name*, if you start the SAS System from the **Start** button menu. If all your files reside in a particular folder, it may be more efficient to change the current folder instead of constantly specifying long pathnames in your SAS statements.

Note

> If you start the SAS session some other way, such as by double-clicking a file with the .SAS extension, the default current folder is different. See "Determining the SAS System Current Folder" in Chapter 11 for more information.

The current folder is displayed in the status bar at the bottom of the main SAS window. For example, in Figure 3.5 the mouse pointer is near the current folder name.

Figure 3.5 Current Folder Displayed in the Main SAS Window

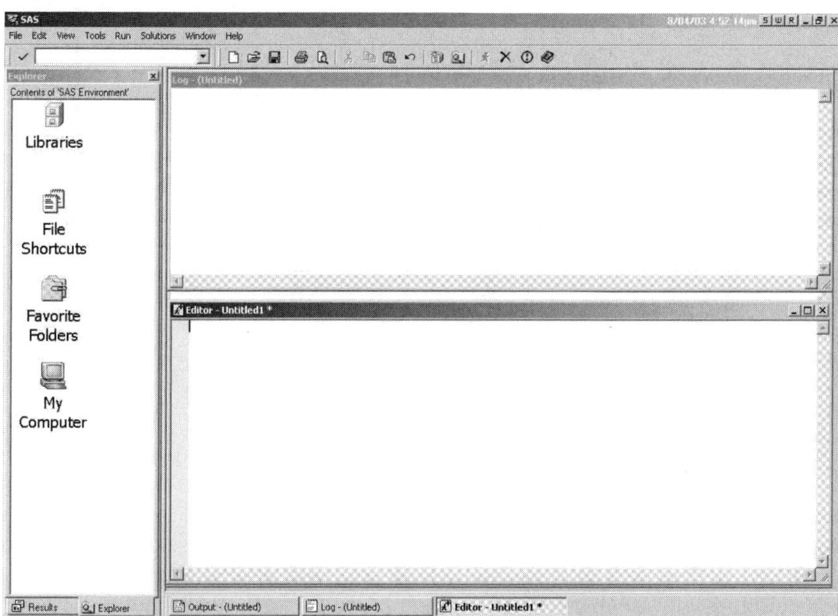

Note

> The Save As and Open dialog boxes do not use the current folder as the default folder at the beginning of a SAS session. Instead, these dialog boxes default to the folder associated with the SASUSER library reference.

Changing the Current Folder during Your SAS Session: To change the current folder, double-click the folder name in the status bar of the main SAS window. The Change Folder dialog box appears, similar to the one in Figure 3.6.

Figure 3.6 Change Folder Dialog Box

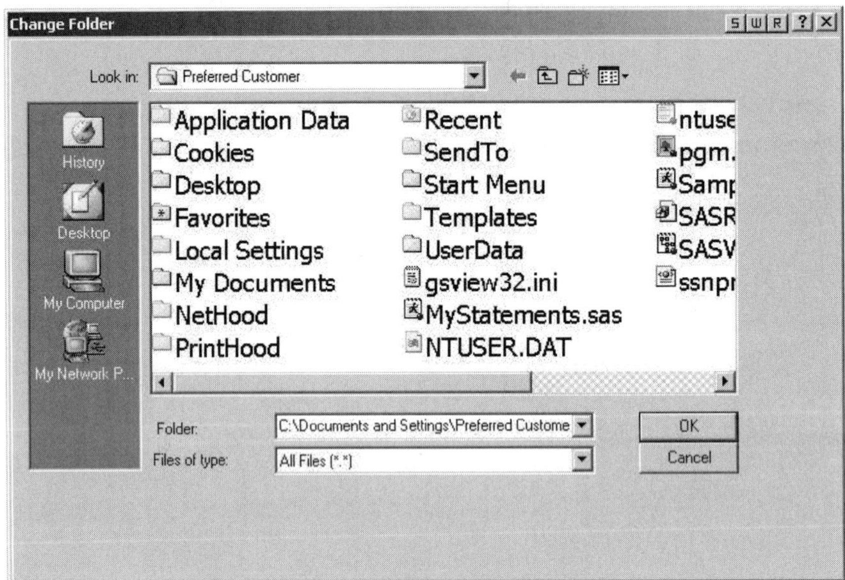

Type the full pathname of the folder in the **Folder** field. Or, you can use the mouse to navigate the list of folders and double-click the folder that you want to use. To move up in the folder hierarchy, click the icon showing a folder with an up arrow, to the right of the **Look in** field.

Once the **Folder** field contains the name of the folder you want, click **OK**. If you change the folder more than once during a single SAS session, the **Folder** field remembers all the folders you have used. To select a previous current folder, click the down arrow next to the **Folder** field and select the correct folder. Then click **OK**.

Note

> Changing the current folder using the Change Folder dialog box is not a permanent change. The next time you invoke the SAS System, the current folder defaults to the last current folder that was permanently set.

An alternative way to open the Change Folder dialog box is to issue the DLGCDIR command from the command bar.

Changing the Current Folder Permanently: To permanently change the current folder, you either change the properties of the program shortcut you use to start the SAS System, or set the current folder using the SASINITIALFOLDER system option.

Changing the Current Folder Using the Program Shortcut Properties: Follow these steps:

1. Navigate to the folder that contains the SAS System shortcut used in the **Start** button menu. For details, see "Altering the Properties of the SAS System Icon in the Windows Start Menu" in Chapter 11.
2. Right-click **SAS 9.1 (English)**, then click **Properties**.
3. When the Properties dialog box appears, click the **Shortcut** tab.
4. Click inside the **Start in** field, and type the name of the folder that you want to use as the SAS current folder. Be sure to include the full pathname of the folder.
5. Click **OK**.

The next time you start the SAS System, the new folder is used as the current folder.

Note

> This change applies only to the shortcut to the SAS System accessed from the **Start** menu. If you have created additional shortcuts to the SAS System (such as on the desktop), you must change each shortcut's properties individually.

Changing the Current Folder Using the SASINITIALFOLDER System Option: The syntax of the SASINITIALFOLDER option is as follows:

```
-SASINITIALFOLDER pathname
```

It is valid only at SAS start-up, so you can put it in your SAS configuration file, or add it to the SAS command. If the pathname contains spaces, remember to enclose the pathname in quotation marks.

Note

> The SASINITIALFOLDER system option changes not only the current folder, but also the default folder used in the Open and Save As dialog boxes.

Opening Files

What's New: Along with the Open dialog box, explore the capabilities of the DLGOPEN, FILEOPEN, and WEDIT commands to open files.

FasTip: Click the Open icon on the SAS tool bar.

This section provides details about opening files into the Enhanced Editor window or other SAS window (such as the Program Editor or NOTEPAD window). There are several methods of opening files, each with its own little twists. Use the one that suits you best.

Note

In most cases, opening a file into the Enhanced Editor opens a new instance of the Enhanced Editor window. By contrast, opening a file into the Program Editor appends the new file to the end of whatever text is already in the Program Editor window.

Before You Begin: It is important to understand one of the main differences between the Program Editor and the Enhanced Editor. With the Program Editor, you can have only one file open at a time. With the Enhanced Editor, you can have multiple files open at once, each in its own instance of the Enhanced Editor window.

Using the Open Dialog Box to Open Files: To open this dialog box, click **File → Open Program** in the SAS System main menu. (If you are using the Program Editor, the menu choice is just **Open**, not **Open Program**.) Figure 3.7 shows a sample Open dialog box.

Figure 3.7 Open Dialog Box

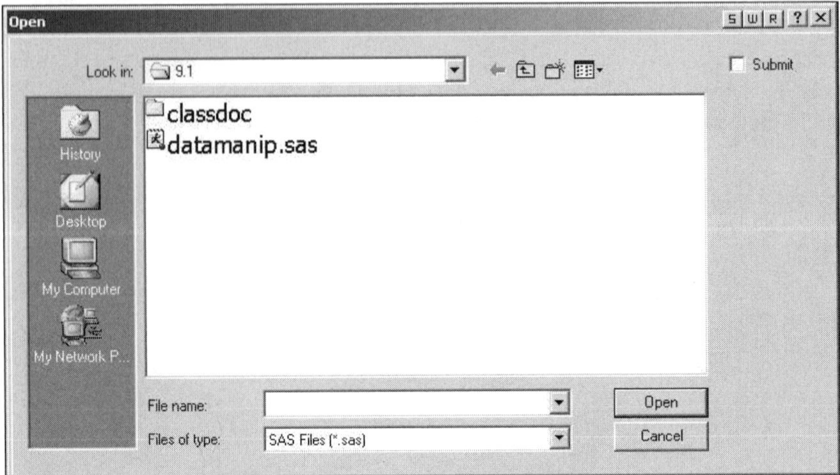

If this is the first time you have opened a file, then by default the Open dialog box shows the contents of the folder associated with the SASUSER library reference. You can type the name of the file that you want to open in the **File name** field. Or, use the **Look in** field and folder list to navigate to the folder where the file is stored. To move up in the folder hierarchy, click the icon showing a folder with an up arrow, to the right of the **Look in** field. To open a subfolder, double-click it in the folder list.

Note

> If the SASINITIALFOLDER system option has been set, the Open dialog box by default shows the contents of the pathname specified by that option, instead of the SASUSER folder.

You may want to "filter" the files listed. If a folder contains many files, you can control which extensions are listed. Click the down arrow next to the **Files of type** field. You can choose to show only files with .SAS, .LOG, .LST, or .DAT extensions, Web files, or all files (*.*). Click your choice to change the value in the field.

Note

> The **Files of type** field does not offer the **Web files** choice for the Program Editor.

When you have found the file you want to open, click its name, then click the **Open** button. The file is copied to the window from which you opened the dialog box (usually the Enhanced Editor). If you click **Submit** in the Open dialog box before you click the **Open** button, the file is immediately submitted. Use this option only with files that contain SAS code.

Using the INCLUDE Command to Open Files: If you prefer, you can issue the INCLUDE command from the command bar to open a file into the Enhanced Editor or Program Editor window. The syntax of the INCLUDE command is as follows:

```
INCLUDE filename
```

If the filename contains spaces, enclose the filename in quotation marks. If the file is not in the current folder, you must type the full pathname of the file.

The INCLUDE command copies a file to the active Enhanced Editor window, but does not submit the code. If there is text already in the window, the included statements are appended to the end of the already existing text.

Using the WEDIT Command to Open Files: You can also issue the WEDIT command from the command bar to open a file into a new instance of the Enhanced Editor window. The syntax of the WEDIT command is as follows:

```
WEDIT "filename"
```

You must always enclose the filename in double quotation marks, even if the filename does not contain spaces.

Using the DLGOPEN Command to Open Files: At its simplest, the DLGOPEN command opens the Open dialog box for the default editor (either the Enhanced Editor or the Program Editor, depending on how your configuration is set). Simply type DLGOPEN in the command bar and press ENTER.

The DLGOPEN command has a complicated syntax, and is actually quite powerful. One of its uses is to filter the files listed in the Open dialog box, as well as to assign an alternate command to use on the file when you click the **Open** button. Here is an example:

```
DLGOPEN FILTER="*.bat" ALTCMD="x"
```

In this case, the Open dialog box opens, and lists only files that have .BAT as their extension. Then, when you select a file and click the **Open** button (or just double-click a file), the X command (see Chapter 13) is used to run the file in a command-prompt window, instead of including it into the default editor window (very handy for Windows batch files). See SAS Help and Documentation for more information on the DLGOPEN command.

Using the FILEOPEN Command to Open Files: Yet another method to open files is using the FILEOPEN command. It is valid only from the Enhanced Editor window.

The syntax for the FILEOPEN command is as follows:

FILEOPEN "*filename*"

You must always enclose the filename in double quotation marks, even if the filename does not contain spaces.

The FILEOPEN and WEDIT commands are similar, but have slight differences. For example, the FILEOPEN command does not always open a new instance of the Enhanced Editor. If the active instance of the Enhanced Editor contains no text and does not have an asterisk (*) in the title bar, the file specified in the FILEOPEN command is included into the active instance, not a new instance. But, if the active instance contains text or has an asterisk in the title bar, the file is included into a new instance of the Enhanced Editor.

Using the Most Recently Used File List: Like many Windows applications, the SAS System remembers the files you have used most recently and lists them in the **File** portion of the SAS System main menu. To see these files, click **File**. To open a listed file, click its name. For example, Figure 3.8 shows the **File** menu with three files listed. Clicking **My SAS Statements.sas** opens that file in the active editor window.

Figure 3.8 File Menu Showing the Three Most Recently Used Files

The exact behavior of clicking a file's name in the most recently used list depends on which editor window you are using and the state of the active editor window:

- If you are using the Enhanced Editor and have already opened a file via the most recently used file list, clicking the same file's name in the list has no effect, except to make that file's already-open Enhanced Editor window active. (No code is included in the window.)
- If you are using the Program Editor, repeatedly clicking a file's name in the most recently used file list appends the file's statements to the end of the Program Editor window, resulting in several copies of the code in one window.
- If you have some text in the Enhanced Editor window but have not saved that text, and then you click a file's name, the file is appended to the end of the already existing text and the title bar changes to the clicked file's name.
- If you have text in the Enhanced Editor window and have saved the text, clicking a file's name in the most recently used file list opens that file in a new instance of the Enhanced Editor.

- If no editor window is open but the Enhanced Editor has not been disabled, clicking a filename in the most recently used file list opens the file into a new instance of the Enhanced Editor.
- If no editor window is open and the Enhanced Editor has been disabled, clicking a filename in the most recently used file list has no effect.

See "Setting Session Preferences" in Chapter 6 for information on customizing the recently used file list.

Creating New Files

Creating a New File from the Enhanced Editor: With the Enhanced Editor, you can create a new, untitled instance of the Enhanced Editor window without affecting any already-open instances of the Enhanced Editor window. To do so, choose one of the following equivalent techniques:

- Click the New icon on the SAS System tool bar.
- Click **File → New Program** in the SAS System main menu.

You can also clear an existing Enhanced Editor window of all content *and* the associated filename by choosing one of the following equivalent techniques:

- Press CTRL-E.
- Right-click in the Enhanced Editor window, and click **Clear All** in the resulting popup menu.
- Issue the CLEAR command from the command bar.

Caution

Be aware that any changes to the original file will be lost if you haven't yet saved them. The Enhanced Editor does NOT prompt you to save changes before the text and filename are cleared.

Creating a New File from the Program Editor: Most of the same techniques work in the Program Editor, with a few twists:

- You can have only one instance of the Program Editor window open at any one time. So, all five of the preceding techniques clear the contents and the associated filename.
- The **Clear All** menu selection is one menu deeper. So, right-click in the Program Editor, click **Edit**, then click **Clear All**.
- The **File** menu choice for a new file is simply **New** (not **New Program**).

- The Program Editor will prompt you if you want to save changes to a file before the text and filename are cleared.

Saving Files

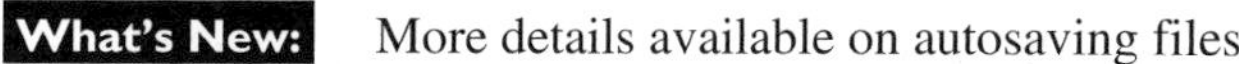

What's New: More details available on autosaving files.

FasTip: Click the Save icon on the SAS tool bar.

In Chapter 2, you learned a little about using the Save As dialog box to save a file. This section provides more details about saving files.

Saving an Existing File: If you have a file open in the Enhanced Editor or other SAS window, the name of the file is listed in the window title bar. For example, in Figure 3.9, the mouse pointer is positioned in the Enhanced Editor title bar, near the filename (My SAS Statements.sas).

Figure 3.9 Program Editor Window Showing the Open Filename

The asterisk at the end of the filename that indicates that the file needs to be saved.

Note

> The asterisk feature is applicable only to the Enhanced Editor; the title bar of the Program Editor does not indicate when the file needs to be saved.

To save the changes under the same filename, click **File** → **Save** in the SAS System main menu. The file is immediately saved.

Note

> The Enhanced Editor assumes you want to replace a file when you click **File** → **Save**. To append, use the FILE command, discussed in "Using the Command Bar to Save a File," later in this chapter.
>
> In the Program Editor, the first time you save an existing file, the File Status dialog box asks if you want to replace or append the data to the existing file. The choice you make in the File Status dialog box becomes the default for your SAS session. If you want to change the replace/append action, use the Save As dialog box to save the existing file. When you double-click the existing filename and then click the **Save** button, the File Status dialog box opens.

Saving a New File: To save a previously unsaved file, click **File** → **Save As** in the SAS System main menu. This opens the Save As dialog box, as shown in Figure 3.10.

Figure 3.10 Save As Dialog Box

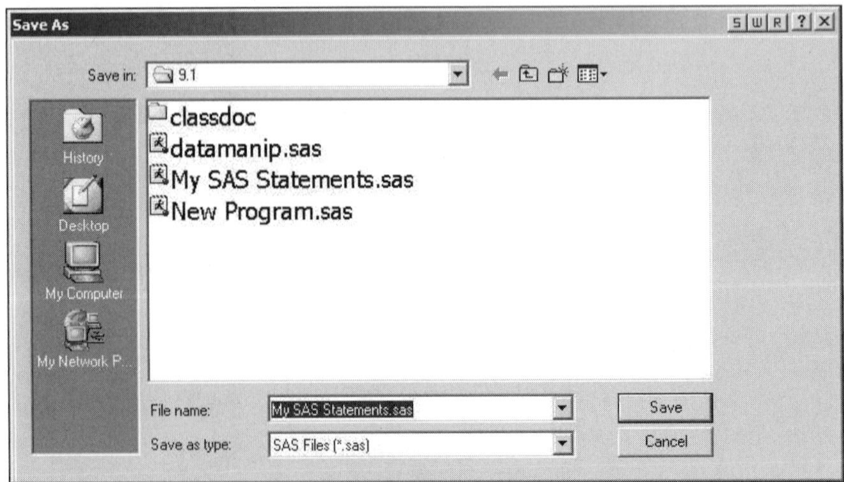

Type the name of the file that you want to save in the **File name** field. Alternatively, use the **Save in** field and folder list to navigate to a different folder, if you want. To open a subfolder, double-click the subfolder's name in the folder list. To move up in the folder hierarchy, click the icon showing a folder with an up arrow, to the right of the **Save in** field.

If you specify a filename that already exists in the folder that you've chosen, you are prompted about replacing the file. If you typed the wrong filename by mistake, click **Cancel** in the prompt dialog box, then type a different filename in the **File name** field.

Use the **Save as type** field to control what file extension is used for the file you are saving. For example, the Enhanced Editor can save files as .sas, .lst, .log, .dat, .htm, .html, and .xml.

Note

> By default, the Save and Save As dialog boxes show the contents of the folder associated with the SASUSER library reference, unless the SASINITIALFOLDER system option has been set.

Using the Command Bar to Save a File: If you prefer, you can issue the FILE command from the command bar. The syntax of the FILE command is as follows:

```
FILE filename
```

For example, the following command saves a file named DATAMANIP.SAS to the current folder:

```
FILE DATAMANIP.SAS
```

If you do not want the file to be saved to the current folder, you must type the full pathname of the file. If the filename and/or pathname contain spaces, enclose the entire pathname in quotation marks.

The FILE command copies the contents of the active SAS window to the file but does not clear the text from the window.

Replacing or Appending New Data in a File: If you want to append the data in a SAS window to an existing file, or specify explicitly that you want to replace an existing file, using the FILE command with the APPEND or REPLACE options is a simple method that works for all SAS windows.

To replace a file, issue the following command from the command bar:

```
FILE filename REPLACE
```

To append to a file, issue the following command from the command bar:

```
FILE filename APPEND
```

Automatically Saving a File: If you'd like the SAS System to save your file automatically at regular intervals while you work on it, follow these steps:

1. Open the Preferences dialog box by clicking **Tools → Options → Preferences** in the SAS System main menu.
2. Click the **Edit** tab, then select the **Autosave every** option.
3. If necessary, adjust the autosave period (the default is every 10 minutes).
4. Click **OK** to save your changes.

Alternatively, issue the following command from the command bar:

```
WAUTOSAVE INTERVAL=minutes
```

Minutes is an integer, specifying the number of minutes between autosaves.

The autosave setting applies to both the Enhanced Editor and the Program Editor. However, the location of the autosave file is different for these two windows:

- The Program Editor autosave file is saved by default to a file named PGM.ASV in the SAS current folder. (See "Changing the SAS Current Folder" earlier in this chapter.) You can change the location of the PGM.ASV file with the AUTOSAVELOC system option.
- The Enhanced Editor autosave file is saved by default to a file named 'autosave of *filename*.$AS', in the following folder: C:\Documents and Settings*Windows-user-ID*\Application Data\SAS\EnhancedEditor. The location is slightly different for Windows NT users.

The AUTOSAVELOC system option does not affect the autosave location for the Enhanced Editor.

Using a Different Text Editor

What's New: Text copied from the Enhanced Editor to another application retains all its formatting, including text color.

Although the SAS System provides the Enhanced Editor, Program Editor, and NOTEPAD windows, you do not have to use them to develop your SAS code if you prefer another text editor. This is one of the major advantages of using the SAS System under Windows—the ability to share information (including text) between applications.

Earlier in this chapter, you learned to cut, copy, and paste text in the SAS System. Most other Windows applications, including text editors and word processing applications, also support cutting, copying, and pasting text. So, you can type your SAS code in the text editor you prefer to use. Then, copy the code to the Clipboard, and paste it into any SAS Text Editor window (such as the Enhanced Editor, Program Editor, NOTEPAD, or SOURCE window). Examples of applications that you may prefer to use instead of the SAS Text Editor include WordPad (which is shipped with Windows), Microsoft Word, and WordPerfect.

Transferring Formatted Text: Formatting, such as bold, underlining, or different font sizes, is not preserved when you paste text into a SAS window. The pasted text in the SAS window is plain unformatted text.

However, text copied from the SAS System to another application does not lose its formatting. As long as the target application supports the Rich Text Format (RTF), text copied from the Enhanced Editor retains all its formatting, including color. Text copied from other SAS windows (such as the Program Editor) does not retain its color formatting when pasted into another application.

Submitting Code from Another Editor: You do not even have to paste code into the SAS System—you can submit it directly from the Clipboard. See "Submitting Code Stored on the Clipboard" and "Using Drag-and-Drop" in Chapter 4.

4 Submitting SAS Code

Introduction

Now that you have learned how to open a file and edit it, your next logical step is to submit the code. You learned one way in Chapter 2, using the **Submit** item in the **Run** menu. But there are many other ways to submit code. Which method you choose depends on the following:

- where your code is (it does not have to be in the Enhanced Editor window, or even in the SAS System)
- your preferences for using menus, function keys, tool bars, and the command bar/command line.

This chapter also presents information on the following topics:

- stopping a SAS job
- managing your SAS log and output files.

Note

This chapter and the ones preceding it focus on using the interactive features of the SAS System. The SAS System also supports batch processing, where you do not interact at all with it and no SAS session windows appear on your screen. See Chapter 12 for information on submitting batch SAS programs.

Submitting Code from the Enhanced Editor Window

 **FasTip:** Click the Run icon on the SAS System tool bar.

In Chapter 2, you submitted your code using the menus. This is one of the ways to submit code. Two shortcut methods are to use the tool bar and function keys:

-  To submit code via the tool bar, click the Run icon.
- To submit code via the function keys, press F3.

Note

> Before you use any of these methods, be sure the Enhanced Editor or Program Editor window is the active window.

Submitting a Certain Number of Lines

What's New: The Enhanced Editor now supports the SUBTOP command.

FasTip Click **Run** → **Submit Top Line**.

Click Run → **Submit N Lines**.

Highlight text, then press F3.

Instead of submitting a whole block of code, you can submit a certain number of lines by choosing one of three methods:

- using the **Submit Top Line** menu item
- using the Submit N Lines dialog box
- highlighting text.

Submitting a portion of your code is useful if you want to test the first few lines of a program (such as a group of FILENAME or LIBNAME statements) without running the entire program. Or perhaps the code you want to run is the top portion of an existing file. Use one of these techniques to submit only the portion of code you need. Highlighting only the code you want to submit is a handy method of submitting a section of code from the middle of a file.

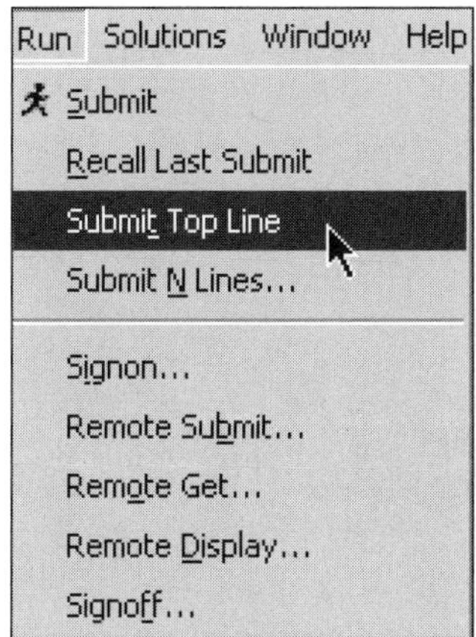

Submitting Only the Top Line: If you want to submit only the top line of code, click **Run → Submit Top Line** in the SAS System main menu.

Alternatively, issue the SUBTOP command from the command bar.

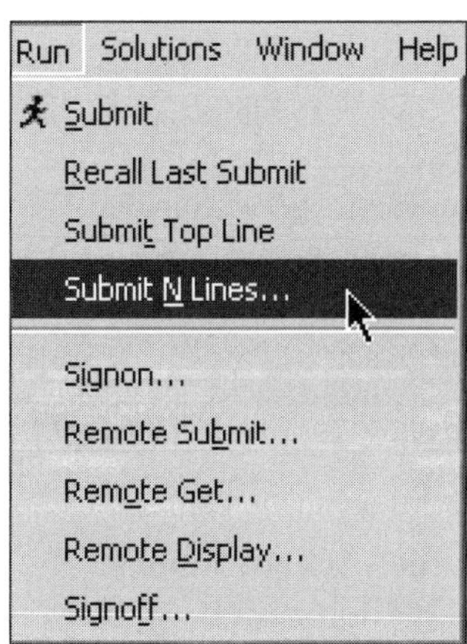

Submitting Several Lines: If you want to submit more than just the top line of code, but all the code that you want to submit is at the top of your program, you can use the Submit N Lines dialog box. Click **Run → Submit N Lines** in the SAS System main menu.

The Submit N Lines dialog box appears, as shown in Figure 4.1.

Figure 4.1 Submit N Lines Dialog Box

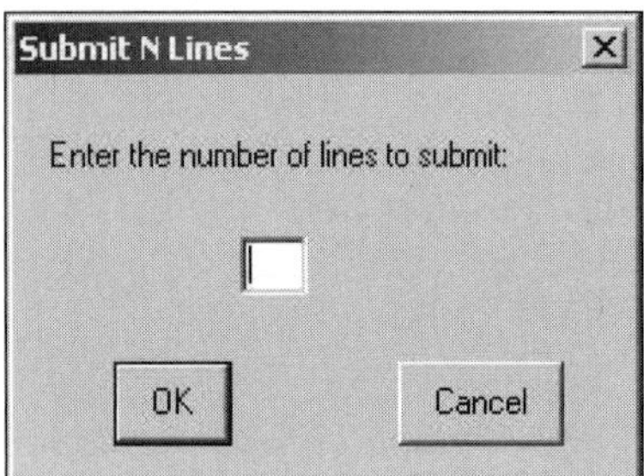

In the text entry field, enter the number of lines you want to submit, then click **OK**.

Alternatively, issue the SUBTOP command from the command bar, indicating how many lines you want to submit:

```
SUBTOP n
```

Submitting Highlighted Text: To submit a section of code in the middle of your program, you cannot use the Submit N Lines dialog box. However, you can highlight the code, then submit the highlighted text (press F3, click **Run** → **Submit** in the menu, click the Run icon, or issue the SUBMIT command).

Submitting Code from the Open Dialog Box

FasTip: Click **File** → **Open**, then choose the filename, click the **Submit** option, and click **OK**.

If you know you want to submit a file (not edit it), when you open the file, click the **Submit** option in the Open dialog box before you click **OK**. When you do click **OK**, the file is immediately submitted.

Submitting Code Stored on the Clipboard

What's New: This option is available only from the Program Editor. The Enhanced Editor does not support this feature.

FasTip: Click **Run** → **Submit Clipboard**.

In a mainframe environment such as z/OS, the SAS System's Program Editor window was your only choice for submitting code. That is, the code you wanted to submit had to be in the Program Editor window before you could run it. Not so for Windows SAS users.

Under Windows, you can develop your code using some tool other than the SAS System and submit the code without ever using the Program Editor window. For example, you might prefer editing text in Word or some other word processing application, as discussed in "Using a Different Text Editor" in Chapter 3.

To use this technique, copy your SAS program to the Clipboard while in the other application. Now switch to your SAS session and click **Run → Submit Clipboard** in the SAS System main menu. The text stored on the Clipboard is submitted to the SAS System. The messages associated with your program appear in the SAS Log window, but the Program Editor window remains empty.

Using Drag-and-Drop

In Chapter 3, you learned how to drag and drop text. You can use this technique to submit code. You can also drag and drop file icons to submit code.

Dragging and Dropping Text: By default, when you highlight a section of text, drag it, and drop it into the Enhanced Editor or Program Editor window, the text is included—but not submitted. You cannot drop text over a non-text-editing SAS window, such as the Log window.

Note

In the Program Editor (but not the Enhanced Editor), you can use the right mouse button instead of the left mouse button to drag and drop the text. In this case, a popup menu lets you click **Submit** (as well as **Move** and **Copy**). This technique works only for text dragged from one SAS window to another and from applications that support dragging with the right mouse button.

Dragging and Dropping File Icons: When you look at the contents of a folder in the SAS Explorer, each file is represented by an icon. To submit a file that contains SAS code, open the SAS Explorer and display the folder that contains the file you want to submit. Also, make sure the other SAS window (such as the Enhanced Editor, Program Editor, Log, or Output window) is visible.

Whether the text of the file is only copied to the SAS window or submitted immediately depends on where you drop the file icon:

- To submit the file immediately, drop the icon into the Log or Output window.
- To copy the text of the file to the SAS System without submitting the code, drop the icon into the Enhanced Editor or Program Editor window. In the case of the Enhanced Editor, a new instance of the Enhanced Editor is created.

Including and Submitting Several Files at Once: You can select two or more files in the SAS Explorer:

- When you drop two or more files into the Program Editor window, the files are included sequentially. However, you cannot predict the order in which the programs are included.
- If you use the right mouse button to drag the files to the Program Editor window and click **Submit**, the files are submitted sequentially. However, you cannot predict the order in which the programs are submitted.
- Dropping several files into the Enhanced Editor window opens a separate instance of the editor for each file selected.

You select several files by using the Shift and CTRL keys when you click on the files, as explained here:

- To select a contiguous block of files in the SAS Explorer, click on the first file. Now hold the Shift key down and click on the last file.
- To select several non-contiguous files in the SAS Explorer, click on the first file. Now hold the CTRL key down and click on the other files.

Note

> You can also drag and drop files from the Windows Explorer. See Appendix 3 for more information on the Windows Explorer.

Right-Clicking on File Icons: By right-clicking on a SAS program file icon in the My Favorite Folders window, you can choose to submit the code in several different ways. Open the My Favorite Folders window (see "Using the Favorite Folders Feature" in Chapter 2), and display the folder that contains the SAS program file that you want to submit. Right-clicking the filename displays a popup menu.

In this menu:

- Clicking **Open** copies the program to a new instance of the Enhanced Editor window, but does not submit the code. This is useful if you want to edit the program before submitting it.
- Clicking **Submit** copies the code to a new instance of the Enhanced Editor window and submits the code.
- Clicking **Remote Submit** submits the code to a remote SAS session using SAS/CONNECT software; see Chapter 15 for more information on using SAS/CONNECT software.

Note

> You can also right-click on SAS file icons in the Windows Explorer, with much the same results. An additional feature of submitting a program from the Windows Explorer is that you can also choose to submit the file in batch mode. See Appendix 3 for more information on the Windows Explorer; see Chapter 12 for information on submitting batch SAS programs.

Double-Clicking File Icons: You can double-click on files with .SAS and .SS2 extensions in the SAS Explorer. This technique includes the file into a new instance of the Enhanced Editor window; the code is not submitted.

Note

> You can also double-click SAS file icons in the Windows Explorer, which activates the file using the default "action." Right-clicking on a file icon shows all the valid actions; the default action changes to bold in the list. You can change the default action, such as changing it to **Batch Submit with SAS 9**, which submits the program in batch mode. See Chapter 12 for more information on using the Windows Explorer to submit batch SAS programs.

Dropping File Icons on the SAS.EXE Icon: You can drag and drop SAS program file icons on the SAS.EXE file icon, which submits the program in batch mode. Therefore, this technique is not suitable for programs that require interaction (such as SAS/GRAPH procedures, PROC REPORT windows, or other interactive SAS System components). Unlike other techniques discussed in this chapter, this technique can be used only from the Windows Explorer.

To use this technique, follow these steps:

1. Start the Windows Explorer by right-clicking the **Start** button, then clicking **Explore**.
2. Navigate to the folder that contains the file you want to submit. Now click the file you want to submit, to highlight it.
3. If necessary, open another Windows Explorer window, and display the SAS System folder, where the SAS.EXE file is stored. Under Windows 2000, the default location of the SAS.EXE file is C:\Program Files\SAS\SAS 9.1. To open a second Windows Explorer window, right-click the **Start** button again, and click **Explore**. Use the mouse to resize and move the new window as needed.

Note

> This step is not necessary if the file you want to submit is stored in the same folder as the SAS.EXE file.

4. Drag the program file icon over to the SAS.EXE file icon and release it. As you drag the file icon, an image of the file icon follows your mouse pointer. When the mouse pointer is over the SAS.EXE file icon, the SAS.EXE icon becomes highlighted. When this occurs, release the mouse pointer to submit the program in batch mode. Figure 4.2 shows how your display might look just before you release the mouse pointer.

Figure 4.2 Dropping a File on the SAS.EXE Icon

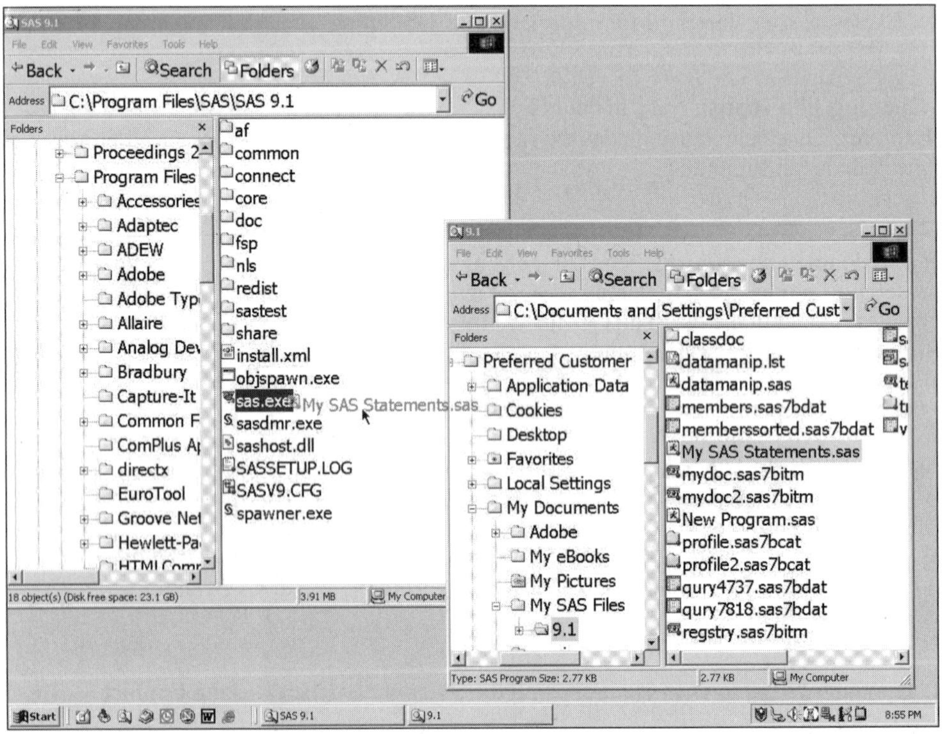

5. The SAS System starts in batch mode and runs the file you selected. Log and list files are created as for any batch program. (See "Understanding Where Batch Logs and Output Go" in Chapter 12.)

Refer to Chapter 12 for additional methods of submitting batch SAS jobs.

Note

> If the SAS System is running when you drop a file icon on the SAS.EXE icon, a second SAS session is started.

Recalling Submitted Code

FasTip: Click **Run → Recall Last Submit**.

By default, the Enhanced Editor does not delete submitted code from the window, so there is no need to recall it. However, you can set your preferences so that the Enhanced Editor is cleared after you submit code (see Chapter 7).

In contrast, the Program Editor window is cleared after you submit code.

To recall submitted code to a window, click **Run → Recall Last Submit** in the SAS System main menu (or press F4). If you have submitted three blocks of code, clicking on **Recall Last Submit** three times recalls the text in the opposite order in which it was submitted, inserting the recalled text before whatever text is already in the window.

Note

> Even if you have submitted text via the Clipboard, the **Submit** option in the Open dialog box, or drag and drop, the **Recall Last Submit** menu choice still recalls your programs.

Interrupting a Submit

FasTip: Click the Attention icon on the SAS tool bar.

If you submit a long program or a program that contains an infinite loop, you may want to abort the program. You can stop a program in two ways:

- stop only the program
- cancel the entire SAS session.

Stopping a Program: To stop a SAS program, click the Attention icon on the tool bar.

Alternatively, press CTRL-BREAK. (The Break key may say "Pause" on it. This key is usually located on the top-right side of your keyboard.)

When you click the Attention icon or press CTRL-BREAK, the Tasking Manager appears. Depending on what the SAS System is busy doing, various tasks are listed in the Tasking Manager dialog box. A sample dialog box is shown in Figure 4.3.

Figure 4.3 Sample Tasking Manager Dialog Box

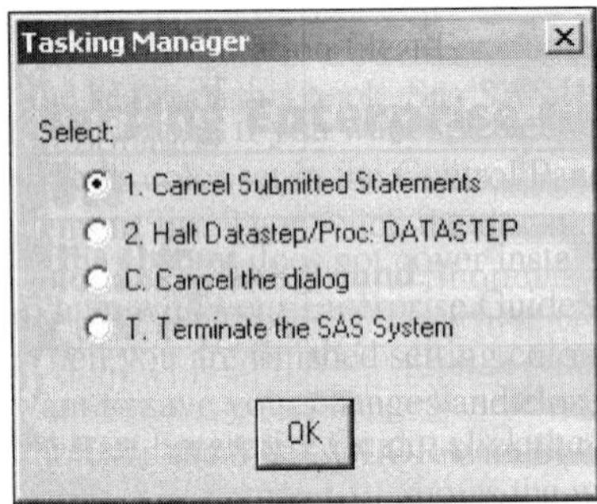

To cancel a procedure or DATA step, click the appropriate radio button in the Tasking Manager dialog box, then click **OK**. This opens the BREAK dialog box. (Figure 4.4 shows the BREAK dialog box.) If you want to end your entire SAS session, click **Terminate the SAS System** in the Tasking Manager dialog box.

If you opened the Tasking Manager by mistake, click **Cancel the dialog**, then click **OK**. This closes the dialog box and enables your program to continue running normally.

Figure 4.4 Sample BREAK Dialog Box

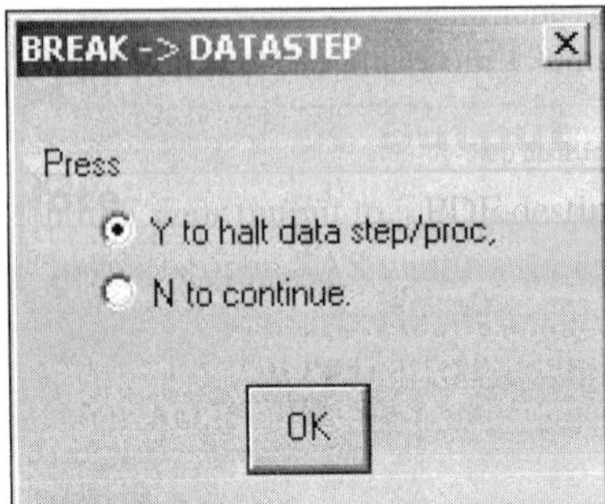

If the BREAK dialog box appears, click **Y to halt data step/proc** to complete the program termination. If you have accessed the BREAK dialog box unintentionally, click **N to continue**. Your program will proceed normally.

Note

It may take several seconds for the Tasking Manager or BREAK dialog box to appear—do not click on the Attention icon or press CTRL-BREAK more than once.

Canceling the Entire SAS Session: If your program has created problems and you think the best thing to do is to start over, cancel the entire SAS session by clicking the SAS System Close button.

Caution

Any unsaved work is lost when you do this, so use it only as an emergency measure, or save your work first.

When All Else Fails... If things are really bad—your display is locked up, and the mouse does not work—try pressing CTRL-ALT-DELETE. This displays a dialog box. Click the **Task Manager** button, then click the **Applications** tab. End any task that is listed as not responding. If this has no effect, press CTRL-ALT-DELETE a second time to reboot your computer.

If CTRL-ALT-DELETE has no effect, you may have to turn your system off—but this is a last-ditch choice and may cause you to lose a lot of work if you have several applications open and have not saved recently. Also, Windows might request to run ScanDisk the next time you boot up.

Managing Your Log and Output Files

When you submit code, the Log window tracks table creation, option setting, procedure statements, and other items. The Output window or the SAS Results Viewer contains the results of your program. To save the log or output of a program, click in the appropriate window to make it the active window. Then, use the Save As dialog box or the FILE command to save the file, as described in "Saving Files" in Chapter 3. Usually, log files are saved with an extension of .LOG and output files have an extension of .LST.

Alternatively, use the Results window to save selected portions of your output. See "Looking at Output" in Chapter 2 for more details on the Results window.

You can also use various system options and the PRINTTO procedure to reroute the log and output to a file or a printer. See Chapter 12 for more information.

If you have selected HTML output instead of listing output, the output appears in the Results Viewer window or in your preferred browser, not in the Output window. In this case, the PRINTTO procedure, LOG, OUTPUT, ALTLOG, and ALTOUTPUT system options do not affect the output destination. For information on controlling HTML output, refer to Chapter 8.

5 Printing

Introduction

What's New: SAS print forms are no longer documented in this book, as this technology is outdated. New features in the SAS printing system, including the Output Delivery System and new system options, make the old-style SAS print form unnecessary and inefficient.

If you are familiar with a mainframe environment like z/OS, you are used to printing by setting system options such as PAGESIZE and LINESIZE and issuing the PRINT command. While the system options and the command still work under Windows, you can also use dialog boxes to set the page and line size. Not only that, but the dialog boxes also enable you to choose fonts, type sizes, and other features. You can even print files such as SAS programs, SAS tables, and SAS output without starting the SAS System, by using the SAS System Viewer (see Appendix 2).

SAS System print jobs are managed by Windows. The dialog boxes you see when printing from SAS are standard dialog boxes for selecting printer options. This chapter explains a bit about how printing works in Windows in general, then addresses printing issues specific to the SAS System.

Although the discussion in this chapter uses the Output window (because often you want to print the output from your code), the principles are the same for any SAS window (such as the Log and SOURCE windows).

This chapter deals primarily with printing from a windowing session. You can also control many aspects of printing with SAS system options. These are discussed in "Printing in Batch Mode" in Chapter 12. Also, except for the first two sections in this chapter, the information here applies only to printing listing-formatted SAS output, not SAS output created with the Output Delivery System in formats such as RTF, HTML, and PDF. For details about printing ODS output, see Chapter 8.

Note

> The dialog boxes and procedures in this chapter are for Windows 2000. If you use a different version of Windows, your dialog boxes might look somewhat different from the ones shown here.

Discovering What Printers Are Available

FasTip: Click the **Start** button, then click **Settings** → **Printers**.

Your computer may be connected to several printers—perhaps a PostScript printer, a plotter, and a network printer. To see which printers are available to your Windows applications, click the **Start** button, then click **Settings**, then click **Printers**. The Printers window appears, similar to the one shown in Figure 5.1. (The Printers window displayed on your screen will be somewhat different from the figure because you will have different printers installed on your system.)

Figure 5.1 Using the Printers Window to See Which Printers Are Available

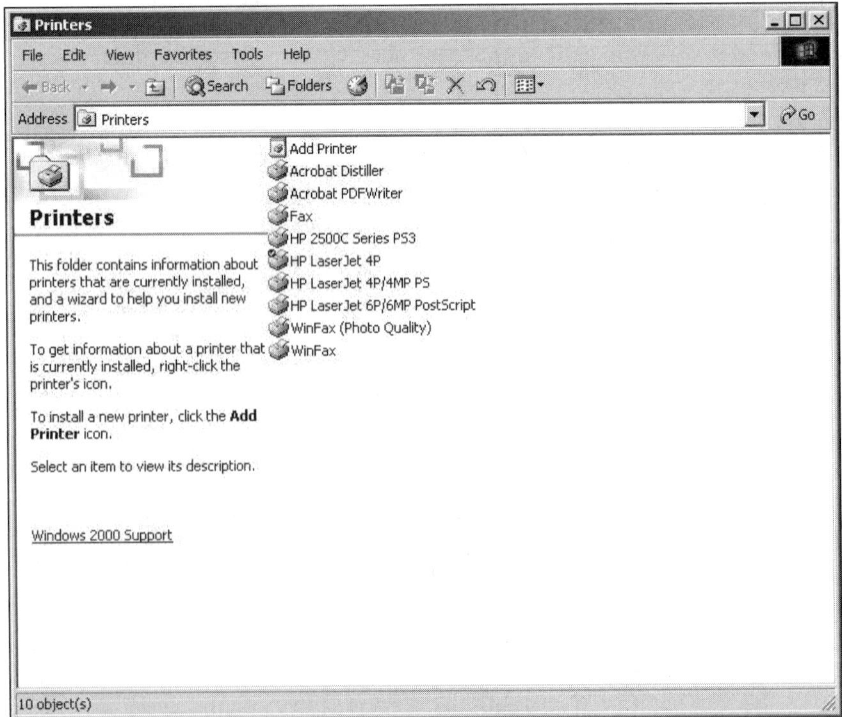

Even though you may have several printers, only one is the default printer—the printer used for a print job if you do not explicitly specify the printer.

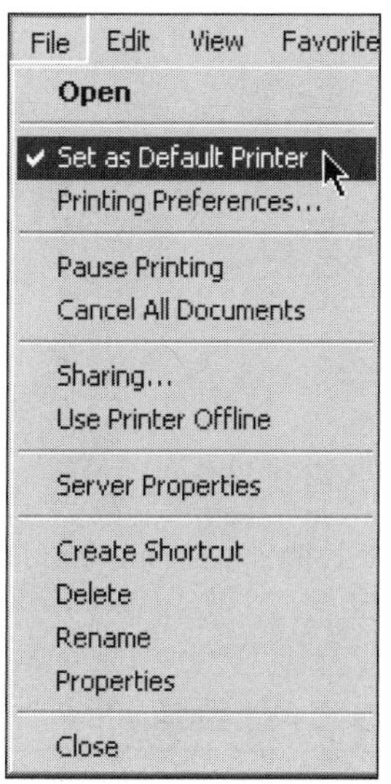

Determining the Default Printer: The check mark on the icon for the "HP LaserJet 4P" printer in Figure 5.1 indicates that this printer is the default printer. You can also determine which printer is the default printer by clicking a printer's icon, then clicking **File** in the Printers window menu. If there is a check mark next to **Set as Default Printer**, that printer is the default printer.

Changing the Default Printer: To change the default printer, first click the icon in the Printers window for the printer you want to use as the default. Then click **File** in the Printers window menu, then click **Set as Default Printer**.

Understanding How Windows Manages Print Jobs

By default, Windows manages all print jobs submitted from Windows applications, including those submitted from the SAS System. Windows routes the jobs to the appropriate printers, monitors the status of the printers, and controls when each job prints. In mainframe terms, this process is similar to a printer spool, except that in the PC environment, you typically have more control over the print jobs. As print jobs accumulate, Windows creates a print queue. Use this print queue to change the order and priority of print jobs, temporarily stop printing a job (pause), resume printing a job, or delete a print job.

Listing Your Print Jobs: To list your print jobs, click the **Start** button, click **Settings**, then click **Printers**. When the Printers window appears, double-click the icon for the printer you want to access. A window similar to the one in Figure 5.2 appears.

Figure 5.2 Listing the Jobs for a Printer

HP LaserJet 4P - Paused

Printer Document View Help

Document Name	Status	Owner	Pages	Size	Subm
Microsoft Word - Printing_old5_.doc		Preferred C...	19	1.74 MB	12:1
Microsoft Word - NewBody.htm		Preferred C...	2	465 KB	12:1
SAS:TemplateExample.sas		Preferred C...	3	58.5 KB	12:1

3 document(s) in queue

When you send a print job from the SAS System or another Windows application, the job is listed in the appropriate printer window. From this window you can pause or rearrange the print jobs; see "Delaying Printing," "Resuming Printing," and "Changing the Order of Print Jobs" later in this chapter.

Configuring Your Printer for Use with the SAS System

FasTip: Click **File → Print Setup** or click **File → Page Setup**.

You may want to configure your printer before you use it with the SAS System. For example, you may decide that you want to print a particular piece of output in landscape mode instead of the default portrait mode.

In general, you'll use the Print Setup dialog box to configure your printer, although you can also use the Print dialog box.

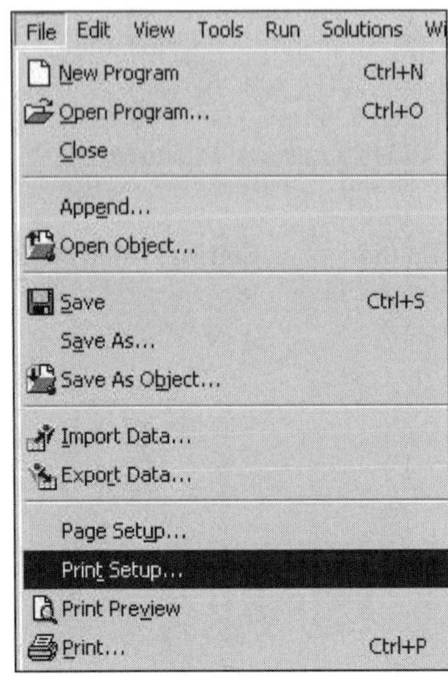

Selecting a Printer for SAS to Use: Click **File → Print Setup** in the SAS System main menu. The Print Setup dialog box appears, similar to the one in Figure 5.3.

Figure 5.3 Print Setup Dialog Box

Note

> The printer configuration options you choose in the Print Setup dialog box persist from one SAS session to the next, with the exception of the printer name. The printer name always defaults to the default printer on your system. See "Discovering What Printers Are Available" earlier in this chapter for more information on determining and changing the default printer.

In this dialog box, use the **Printer** area to specify which printer to use (click the down arrow to display the list of available printers). Click **OK** to close the Print Setup dialog box.

Changing the Page Orientation: To change the page orientation, click **File** → **Page Setup** in the SAS System main menu. The Page Setup dialog box appears, as shown in Figure 5.4.

Figure 5.4 Page Setup Dialog Box

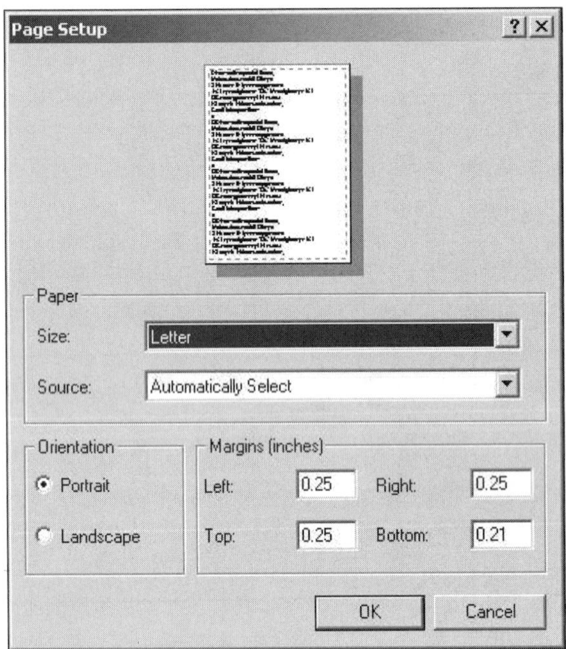

Note

> You can also access the Page Setup dialog box by clicking **Page Setup** in the Print Setup dialog box.

In the Page Setup dialog box, you can adjust the margins and the page orientation. To use landscape mode, select **Landscape**. To change the various margins, either click the up and down arrows beside each value or double-click the margin's text box and type the new value. The SAS System automatically adjusts the page size and line size to fit the new margins. If you want to adjust the paper size or paper source, use the **Size** and **Source** fields to do so.

When you are finished adjusting the page setup, click **OK** to close the Page Setup dialog box.

Changing Other Aspects of Your Output: If you want to change other aspects of the printer setup, explore available options for your printer by opening the Print Setup dialog box, then clicking **Properties** in the Print Setup dialog box. When you click this button, a printer-specific setup dialog box appears. For example, Figure 5.5 shows the printer options dialog box for the HP LaserJet 4P.

Figure 5.5 Example Printer Properties Dialog Box

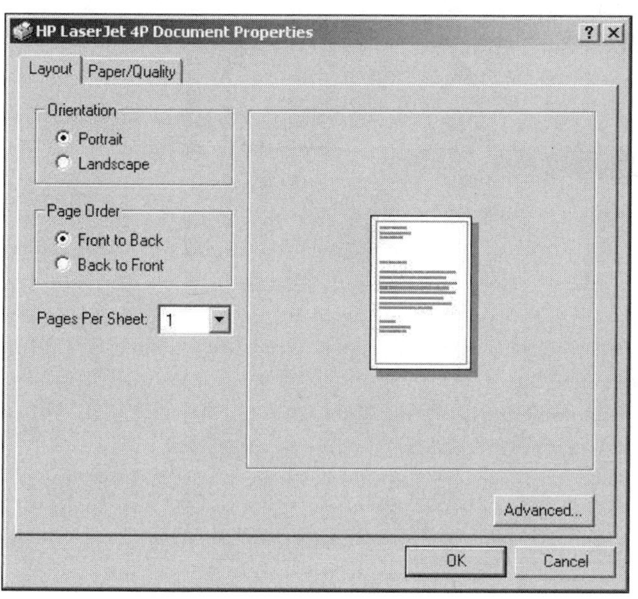

Edit the options, such as page orientation and page order, as appropriate.

Clicking **Advanced** opens yet another printer options dialog box. Your printer manual can help you decipher the available choices.

Note

> The printer properties dialog box shown in Figure 5.5 is also accessible from the Print dialog box, by clicking the **Properties** button.

If the Print Setup and the printer's Properties dialog boxes contain the same parameter (such as landscape versus portrait mode), setting the parameter in one dialog box updates that parameter in the other dialog box.

Clicking **OK** in the various printer properties dialog boxes returns you to the Print Setup dialog box.

Choosing a Printer Font: Clicking **Font** in the Print Setup dialog box opens the Font dialog box, where you can choose the font and type size you want to use for a particular print job. Figure 5.6 shows the Font dialog box.

Figure 5.6 Dialog Box for Setting the Printer Font

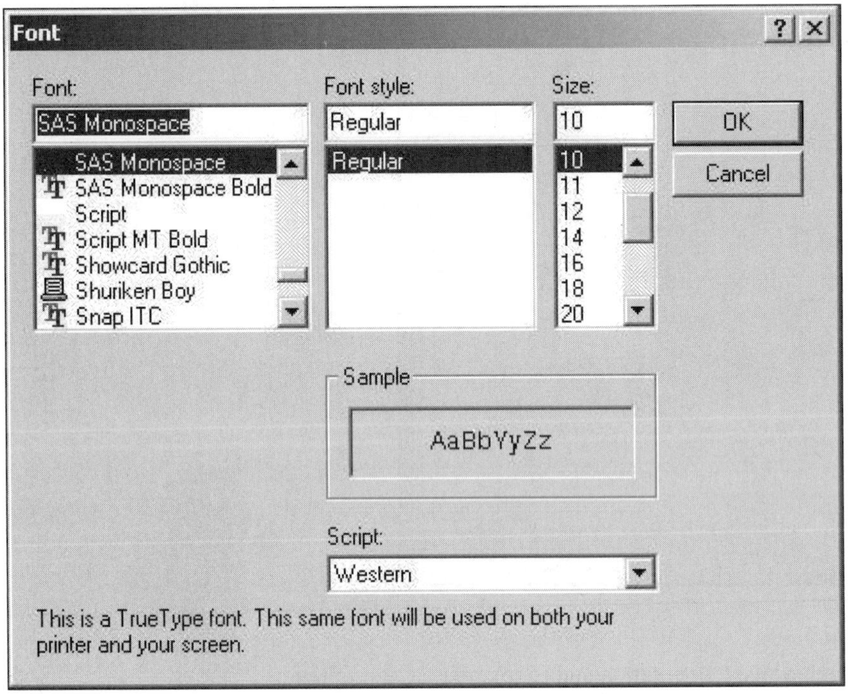

Font

Font: SAS Monospace
SAS Monospace
SAS Monospace Bold
Script
Script MT Bold
Showcard Gothic
Shuriken Boy
Snap ITC

Font style: Regular
Regular

Size: 10
10
11
12
14
16
18
20

OK
Cancel

Sample
AaBbYyZz

Script:
Western

This is a TrueType font. This same font will be used on both your printer and your screen.

By default, the SAS System uses the 10-point SAS Monospace font for your output. To change the font, use the **Font**, **Font style**, and **Size** fields to choose a font you like (scroll if necessary). Monospace fonts (such as Courier and SAS Monospace) work best with SAS output. Proportional fonts (such as Times Roman and Helvetica) do not produce satisfactory results. This is because with monospace fonts each character uses the same amount of space, so columns of data align exactly. Proportional fonts use different amounts of space for different characters, so columns of data may not align correctly.

Note

The fonts the SAS System uses for output and the fonts used in SAS windows are not the same. The font you choose using the **Font** button in the Print Setup dialog box controls the font used for SAS output but not the font used in SAS System windows. See Chapter 6 and Appendix 4 for more information on window fonts.

Resetting Printer Options to the Default: If you have explored the various printer setup dialog boxes and made some changes that produce results you did not expect, return all printer options to their default settings by clicking **Default** in the Print Setup dialog box.

Understanding How the Changes You Make Affect Your Windows Environment: With the exception of the printer name (which always defaults to the default printer on your system), the changes you make via the SAS System Print Setup and Page Setup dialog boxes are permanent. That is, they last, even if you exit the SAS System, until you change them again. However, the changes you make via the SAS System's Print Setup and Page Setup dialog boxes do not affect the printer settings of other Windows applications' (such as Microsoft Word).

Printing the Contents of a SAS Window as Text

What's New: You can now choose to print page numbers and/or line numbers from the Print dialog box. If both your printer and the SAS window you are printing support color printing, you can also choose whether to print in color or not.

FasTip: Click the Print icon on the SAS tool bar. (This bypasses the Print dialog box.)

Suppose you have submitted a SAS program that did not run as you expected. You decide to print the Log window so you can study the error messages. To print a window, first make that window active by clicking in it. Now click **File** → **Print** in the SAS System main menu (or press CTRL-P). The Print dialog box appears, as shown in Figure 5.7.

Figure 5.7 Print Dialog Box

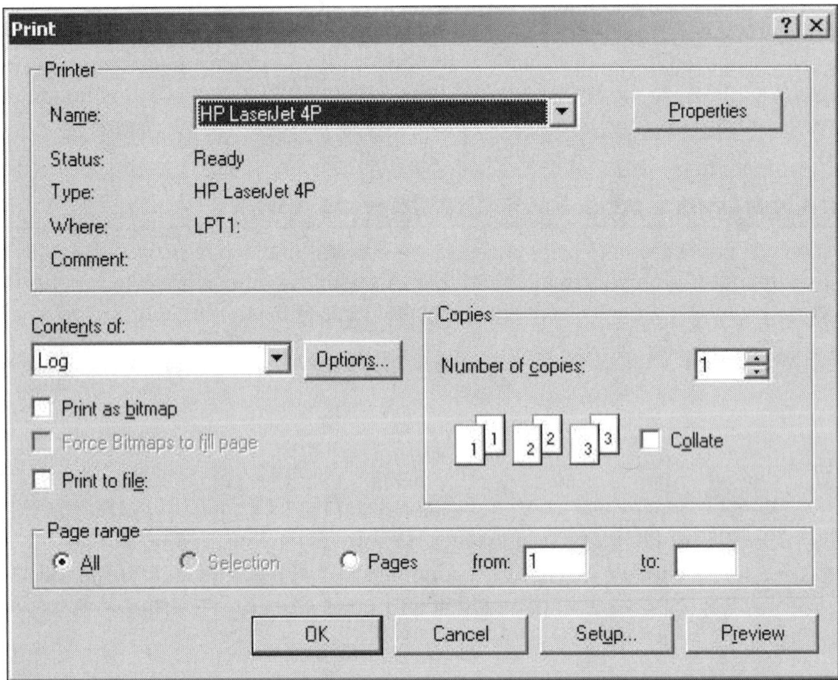

The **Contents of** field displays the title of the active window (in this case the Log window). Adjust the other options in the Print dialog box, as discussed in the following subsections. To submit the print job to the Windows print queue, click **OK**.

Note

Printing from the Results Viewer window differs from printing from most other SAS windows. See "Printing ODS Output" in Chapter 8 for an explanation of printing from the Results Viewer window.

Controlling How Much Information Is Printed: You can specify a page range for your print job. Either select the **All** option in the **Page range** area, or select the **Pages** option and specify the beginning and ending page numbers.

To print only a certain portion of the information displayed in a window, first highlight the portion you want to print. Then, open the print dialog box—the **Selection** option in the **Page range** area is selected. When you click **OK**, only the highlighted portion of the window is printed.

Note

> The Enhanced Editor does not support printing only a selection, and the **Selection** option is grayed out when you print the contents of the Enhanced Editor window. For a workaround, see "Printing the Contents of the Clipboard" later in this chapter.

If you want more than one copy of your output, specify the number of copies in the **Copies** area.

Unless your printer supports collating, the **Collate** option is grayed out.

Configuring the Printer at the Last Minute: If you've forgotten to configure the printer for a job, click **Setup** in the Print dialog box, which opens the Print Setup dialog box. Configure the printer, as described earlier in this chapter. Clicking **OK** in the Print Setup dialog box returns you to the Print dialog box.

Printing Page Numbers: While the default behavior is for listing output from the Output window to have page numbers, the printed SAS log would not by default have page numbers. However, you can add page numbers to your print job by clicking the **Options** button to the right of the **Contents of** field. Figure 5.8 shows the resulting dialog box.

Figure 5.8 Additional Print Options Dialog box

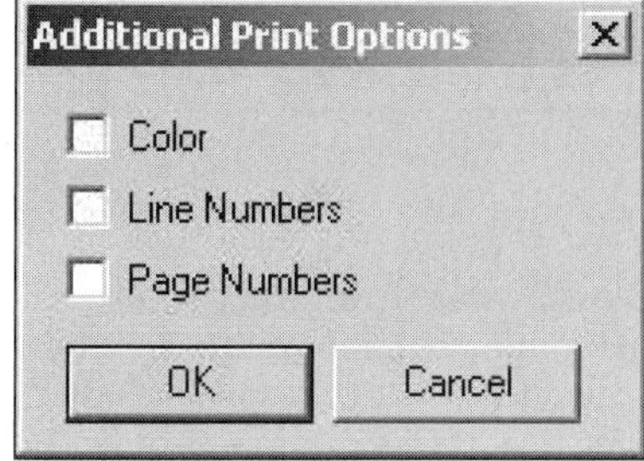

Select the check box for **Page Numbers**, then click **OK**.

Printing Line Numbers: To add line numbers to your print job, click the **Options** button to the right of the **Contents of** field, and select the check box for **Line Numbers**. Now click **OK** to close the Additional Print Options dialog box.

Adding Color to Your Print Job: Assuming you have a color printer, you may want to print in color. To do so, click the **Options** button to the right of the **Contents of** field, and select the check box for **Color**. Now click **OK** to close the Additional Print Options dialog box.

Note

> If you have a color printer and have selected the **Color** option in the Print dialog box, but still get black-and-white output, check the value of the COLORPRINTING system option. If this option is set to NOCOLORPRINTING, you will not get color output.

Not all SAS windows support printing in color. If a SAS window does not support color printing, the **Color** check box does not appear in the Additional Print Options dialog box.

Note

> In particular, the Enhanced Editor does not support color printing.

Bypassing the Print Dialog Box: If you have your print options set the way you want, you might prefer not to see the Print dialog box when you print. Clicking the Print icon on the SAS System tool bar is a quick way to print without opening the Print dialog box.

Note

> Printing from the Results window bypasses the Print dialog box. Before printing from the Results window, be sure your printer is configured properly. See "Looking at Output" in Chapter 2 for more information on the Results window.

Printing the Contents of a SAS Window as a Bitmap

FasTip: Click **File → Print → Print as Bitmap**.

In the previous section, you printed the contents of the Log window as plain text. You can also print the whole window—including the scroll bars, maximize and minimize buttons, title bars, and so on. That is, you create a bitmap of the window.

Bitmap files are useful when you want a picture. For example, the screen shots in this book, such as Figure 5.8, are bitmaps. If you are developing a full-screen application, you may want to print some SAS windows as bitmaps to accompany your documentation. Or, if you are teaching a class, you might want to show your students what a window looks like.

To print a window as a bitmap, click **File → Print** in the SAS System main menu. Now select **Print as Bitmap**. As Figure 5.9 shows, the **Contents of** field indicates that you are going to print the Log window as a bitmap.

Figure 5.9 Print Dialog Box Ready to Print the Output Window as a Bitmap

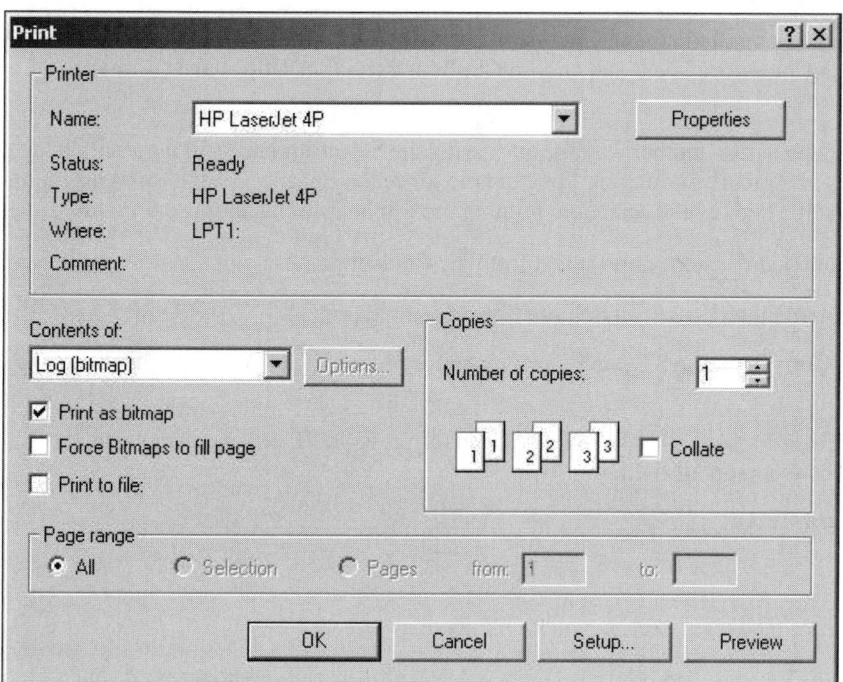

When you have the bitmap option checked, you can choose to print one of several bitmaps. Click the down arrow next to the **Contents of** field. The choices include the following:

- ***active-window* (bitmap)** — prints the active window as a bitmap
- **AWS window (bitmap)** — prints the whole main SAS window as a bitmap
- **Entire screen (bitmap)** — prints the entire screen (including all other visible Windows applications and icons) as a bitmap
- **Clipboard (bitmap)** — prints whatever is stored on the Clipboard as a bitmap.

The last choice, the Clipboard, is discussed in the next section, "Printing the Contents of the Clipboard."

When you click the bitmap option, another option appears: **Force Bitmaps to fill page**. If you select this option, the SAS System scales the output so that it takes up the entire page.

Printing the Contents of the Clipboard

FasTip: Copy the text or graphic to the Clipboard, click **File → Print,** then click the down arrow beside the **Contents of** field and choose **Clipboard (text)** or **Clipboard (bitmap)**.

Printing from the Clipboard is another way (besides using the **Selection** option in the Print dialog box) to print only a portion of your output. For example, since the Enhanced Editor does not support printing just the highlighted selection, printing the Clipboard is a handy workaround.

Printing Text: Follow these steps to print text from the Clipboard:

1. Use your mouse to highlight the section of text you want to print.
2. Click **Edit → Copy** in the SAS System main menu (or press CTRL-C) to copy the text to the Clipboard.
3. Click **File → Print** in the SAS System main menu (or press CTRL-P), and click the down arrow beside the **Contents of** field.
4. Click **Clipboard (text)**.
5. Click **OK**.

The only text that is printed is the section you highlighted.

Printing a Bitmap: You can also print the Clipboard as a bitmap, to print portions of your screen that are valid bitmaps. You must be able to select and copy these bitmaps from the screen. For example, if you select and copy to the Clipboard an icon that appears in the SAS Graphics Editor window, then you can use the **Clipboard (bitmap)** option to print this icon.

To print the Clipboard as a bitmap, follow these steps:

1. Copy the appropriate image to the Clipboard.
2. Click **File → Print** in the SAS System main menu (or press CTRL-P), and click the **Print as Bitmap** option.
3. Click the down arrow beside the **Contents of** field.
4. Click **Clipboard (bitmap)**.
5. Click **OK**.

A message that your printer is now printing the bitmap appears.

Previewing a Print Job

FasTip: Click the Preview icon on the SAS tool bar.

If you have changed a lot of printer configuration options, it may be useful to preview your print job before actually sending it to the printer.

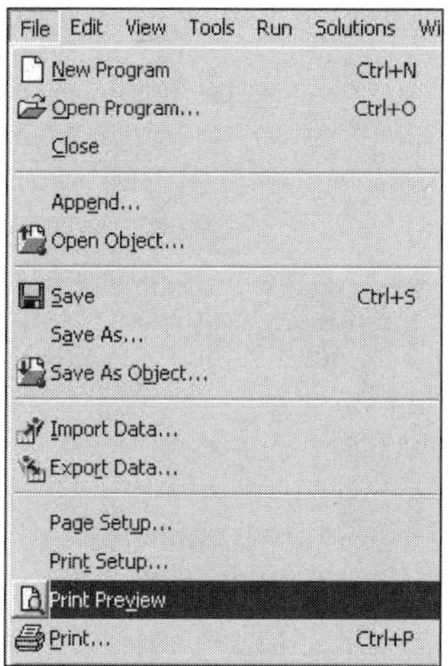

To preview a print job, click in the window you want to print to make the window active. Then, click **File → Print Preview** in the SAS System main menu. For example, Figure 5.10 shows the Print Preview window for the SAS log in landscape mode.

Figure 5.10 Using the Print Preview Window

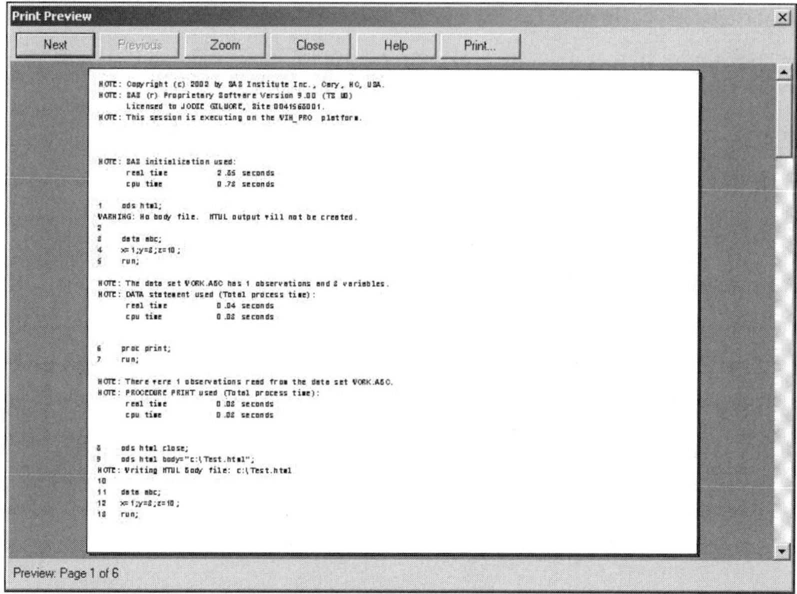

Use the PageUp and PageDown keys to scroll through multiple pages. To see the output in detail, click **Zoom**.

If you are satisfied with how the output looks, click **Print** in the Print Preview window (which opens the Print dialog box), then click **OK** to send the job to the printer.

If you decide you do not want to print, click **Close** in the Print Preview window.

If the output does not appear correctly, click **Print** in the Print Preview window (which opens the Print dialog box), then click **Setup** to configure the printer options. Return to the Print dialog box by clicking **OK** in the printer options dialog box(es), then click **OK** in the Print dialog box to send the output to the printer.

Delaying Printing

You may want to postpone printing a specific job until you check that the printer has the right sort of paper loaded. Or, you may want to pause all your SAS jobs and print them all at once at a more convenient time. Use the Windows Printers window to delay your print jobs.

Note

> The following are general instructions. The menus and exact behavior differ from printer to printer, so you may see menus that look a little different, or experience behavior different from what is documented here.

Delaying a Specific Print Job: To delay the printing of a specific print job, follow these steps:

1. Click **Start → Settings → Printers**.
2. When the Printers window appears, double-click the name of the printer that handles your SAS print jobs, to open that printer's queue.
3. Select a print job by clicking the job name in the queue.
4. Now click **Document → Pause** in the printer's queue window menu.

Delaying an Entire Print Queue: To pause an entire print queue, follow these steps:

1. Click **Start → Settings → Printers**.
2. When the Printers window appears, click the name of the printer that handles your SAS print jobs. This highlights the printer name.
3. Now click **File → Pause Printing** in the Printers window menu.

All print jobs you submit to a paused printer (from the SAS System or any other Windows application) queue up in the printer's queue, but they do not print until you "resume" the printer. Resuming a print job or printer is discussed in the next section.

Resuming Printing

Note

> The following are general instructions. The menus and exact behavior differ from printer to printer, so you may see menus that look a little different, or experience behavior different from what is documented here.

Resuming a Specific Print Job: To release a specific print job, follow these steps:

1. Click **Start** → **Settings** → **Printers**.
2. When the Printers window appears, double-click the name of the printer that handles your SAS print jobs, to open that printer's queue.
3. Now click **Document** → **Resume** in the printer's queue window menu.

Resuming an Entire Print Queue: To release the print jobs for a paused printer, follow these steps:

1. Click **Start** → **Settings** → **Printers**.
2. When the Printers window appears, click the printer name you want to resume.
3. Now click **Printer** → **Pause Printing** in the Printers window menu (this toggles off the check mark beside **Pause Printing**).

Changing the Order of Print Jobs

Note

> The following are general instructions. The menus and exact behavior differ from printer to printer, so you may see menus that look a little different, or experience behavior different from what is documented here.

If you want to print your print jobs in a different order, use the Windows print queue to change the job order by following these steps:

1. Click **Start** → **Settings** → **Printers**.
2. Double-click the icon for the printer you want to affect.
3. Click the job you want to move.
4. Use the mouse to drag the job icon up or down in the list, and drop it in the appropriate spot.

Note

> You must pause the printer before rearranging print jobs.

Canceling Print Jobs

Note

The following are general instructions. The menus and exact behavior differ from printer to printer, so you may see menus that look a little different, or experience behavior different from what is documented here.

Use the Windows print queue to cancel print jobs you no longer want to print. You can cancel a single print job, or you can cancel all print jobs from a printer.

Canceling a Specific Print Job: To cancel a particular print job, follow these steps:

1. Click **Start** → **Settings** → **Printers**.
2. Double-click the icon for the printer you want to affect.
3. When the specific printer window appears, click the job you want to cancel.
4. Click **Document** → **Cancel** in the Printers window menu.

Canceling All Print Jobs: To cancel all print jobs in the Windows print queue for a particular printer, follow these steps:

1. Click **Start** → **Settings** → **Printers**.
2. When the Printers window appears, click the icon for the printer from which you want to cancel print jobs. This highlights the printer name.
3. Now click **File** → **Cancel All Documents** in the Printers window menu.

Adjusting Your Windows Environment

Introduction

When you install the SAS System, it uses default settings that define how your windowing environment looks. For example, these settings affect the menu bar across the top of the main SAS window, the message area at the bottom of the main SAS window, the scroll bars, colors, and so on. However, you can adjust your SAS windowing environment—for example, you can define new tools for the tool bar, replace the menus with command lines, or change the default colors of windows.

You make these changes in several ways. Some changes you make using the Preferences dialog box. To define new tools, you use the Customize Tools dialog box. To customize the SAS Explorer, you use the Explorer Options dialog box. Some options are set using the menus; others are set via commands issued from the command bar.

Besides the changes discussed in this chapter, you can also make many other changes. Because this is a beginner's guide, not all possible options are discussed. For example, if you are developing a SAS/AF application, you can use SAS system options to control how the main SAS window looks and works. Refer to your SAS reference documentation for more information.

Also refer to Appendix 4, "Accessibility and the SAS System," for more suggestions on how you can modify your windowing environment to use the SAS System more productively.

Setting Session Preferences

FasTip: Click **Tools → Options → Preferences**.

The Preferences dialog box controls many aspects of your windowing environment. To open this dialog box, click **Tools → Options → Preferences** in the SAS System main menu. Figure 6.1 shows the first tab of the Preferences dialog box with its default settings.

Figure 6.1 General Tab of Preferences Dialog Box

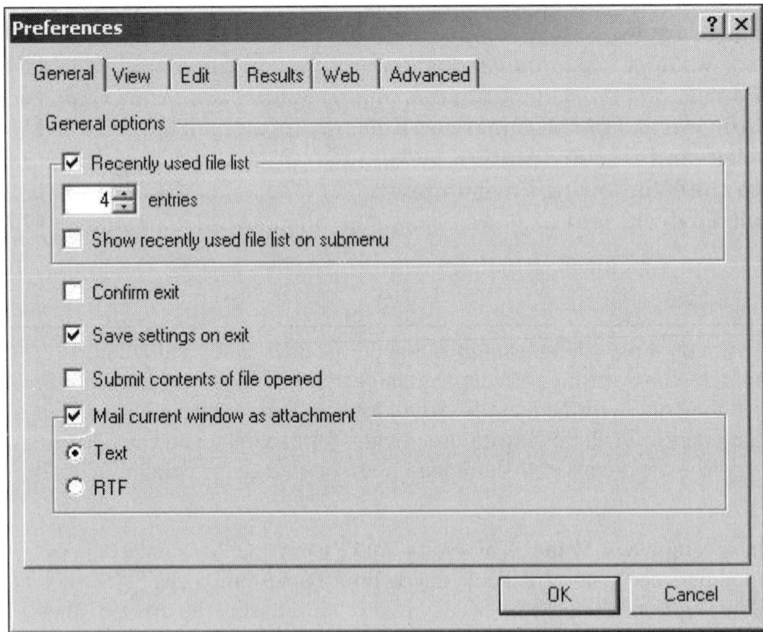

The Preferences dialog box is organized into six tabs:

General	options relating to the general use of the SAS System
View	options relating to the SAS System windowing environment
Edit	options relating to editing
Results	options relating to SAS output
Web	options relating to the Web browser used by the SAS System
Advanced	options relating to less commonly used features of the SAS System.

This chapter mainly discusses the **General** and **View** tabs.

To move to a particular tab, click the tab name. To change a setting, click the option you want to change. For example, by default, on the **General** tab, the **Confirm exit** field is checked. If you do not want the SAS System to ask you if you really want to end your SAS session, click this option to deselect it.
Remember that options with round (radio) buttons next to them are mutually exclusive—you can select only one; you can select one or more options that have square (check) boxes next to them.

When you are finished making changes in the Preferences dialog box, click **OK**. Your changes are saved to your SASUSER profile catalog. These changes remain in effect during your SAS session until you change your preferences again.

Using the General Tab: The following paragraphs explain some of the choices on the Preferences dialog box's **General** tab (shown in Figure 6.1).

- **Recently used file list** — Adjust the number up or down to display more or fewer recently used files in the SAS System's File menu. You can choose to display 0 to 9 files.
- **Confirm exit** — If this option is selected, a dialog box prompts you to confirm whether you really want to end your SAS session. Deselect this option if you want the SAS System to terminate without prompting for confirmation.
- **Save settings on exit** — Select this option to save the placement and attributes of all open SAS windows. Selecting this option is similar to issuing a WSAVE ALL command from the command bar. If this option is not checked, font and color changes are not by default saved from one SAS session to the next.
- **Submit contents of file opened** — Select this option if you always want to submit a file when you open it with the Open dialog box. This option has no effect on files opened by other means (such as from the recently used file list or the INCLUDE command). Selecting this option is equivalent to selecting the **Submit** option in the Open dialog box.

Using the View Tab: The following paragraphs explain several of the choices on the Preferences dialog box's **View** tab, shown in Figure 6.2.

Figure 6.2 View Tab of Preferences Dialog Box

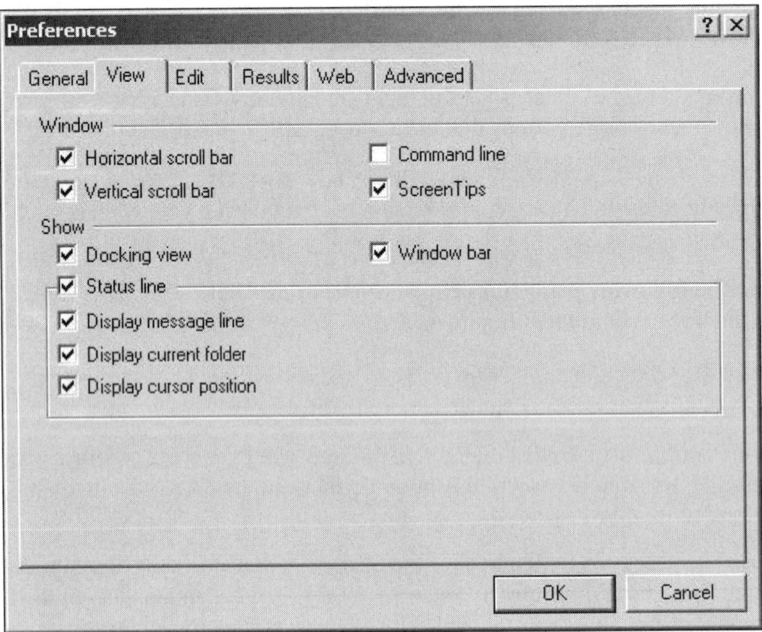

- **Window** — Use this section to turn on or off the vertical and horizontal scroll bars, the command line, and screen tips (helpful hints that appear when you place your mouse pointer over an area in the main SAS window). The **ScreenTips** option in this area does not affect the tool tips that appear when you place your mouse pointer over tools on the SAS System tool bar.
- **Show** — Use this section to control how the status line (at the bottom of the main SAS window) appears. Turn the whole thing off, or turn off portions, such as the message area, the window bar, or the current folder icon.

Note

> You can also disable one or more features of the status line by right-clicking the status line and clicking one of the features (such as **Cursor Position** or **Window Bar**) in the resulting popup menu. Additionally, you can toggle the window bar off and on by issuing the WWINDOWBAR command from the command bar.

To affect how the SAS Explorer and Results windows appear, select or deselect **Docking view**:

- If **Docking view** is not selected, these windows appear anywhere inside the main SAS window, and the menu selections dealing with docking in the **Window** menu are not available.
- If **Docking view** is selected, these windows are "locked" at the left side of the main SAS window. See "Adjusting the Docking View" later in this chapter for more information.

Customizing the Tool Bar and Command Bar

FasTip: Click **Tools → Customize** to change aspects of the command bar and SAS tool bar.

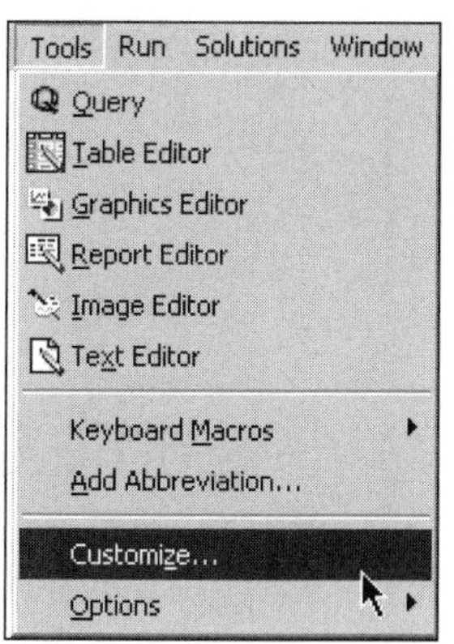

You can customize how the command bar and SAS tool bar look by using the Customize Tools dialog box. Access this dialog box by clicking **Tools → Customize** in the SAS System main menu. Figure 6.3 shows the **Toolbars** tab of the Customize Tools dialog box.

Figure 6.3 Toolbars Tab of the Customize Tools Dialog Box

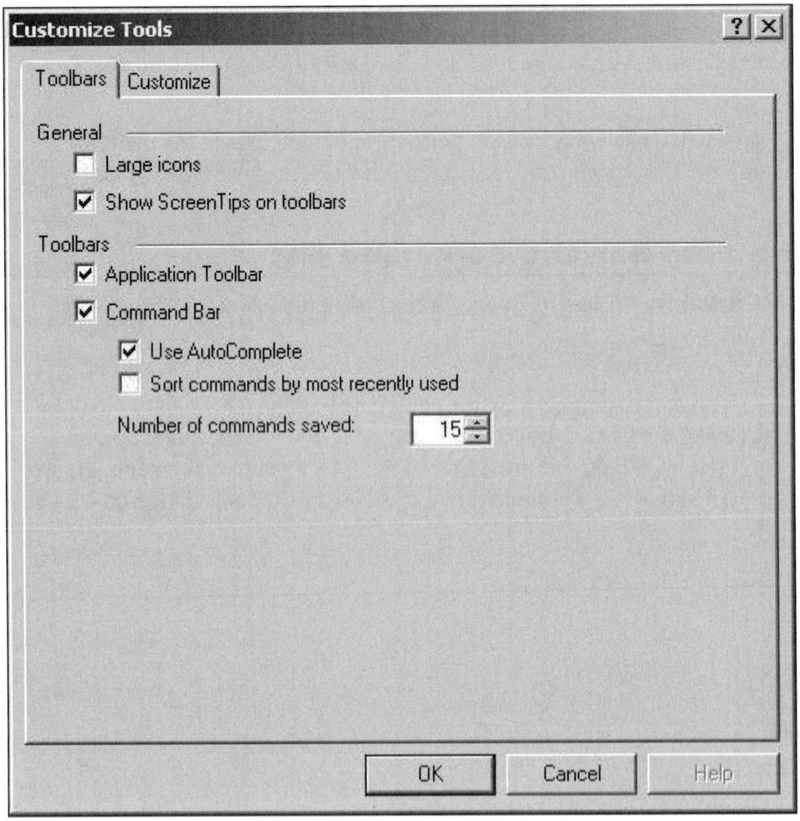

A quick way to access the Customize Tools dialog box is to right-click on the SAS System tool bar, then click **Customize**.

- **Large icons** — Select this option to increase the size of the tool icons in the tool bar (this option does not affect the toolbox). Large tools are most helpful with high-resolution displays because on these displays, the tool bitmaps are small. If you have trouble distinguishing the tools, see if using the larger tools helps. If, when you choose this option, all the tools are no longer visible but extend off the right side of the screen, you do not have a high-resolution display, and you should not use the large tools.
- **Show ScreenTips on toolbars** — Select this option to control whether helpful hints appear when you position the mouse pointer over a tool. For example, if you place your mouse pointer over the Run icon on the SAS System tool bar, the tool tip for that tool says **Submit**, as shown in Figure 6.4. (This option is independent of the **ScreenTips** option on the

View tab of the Preferences dialog box, which affects screen tips for areas of the main SAS window other than the tool bar.)

Figure 6.4 Tool Tips Explain What Tools Do

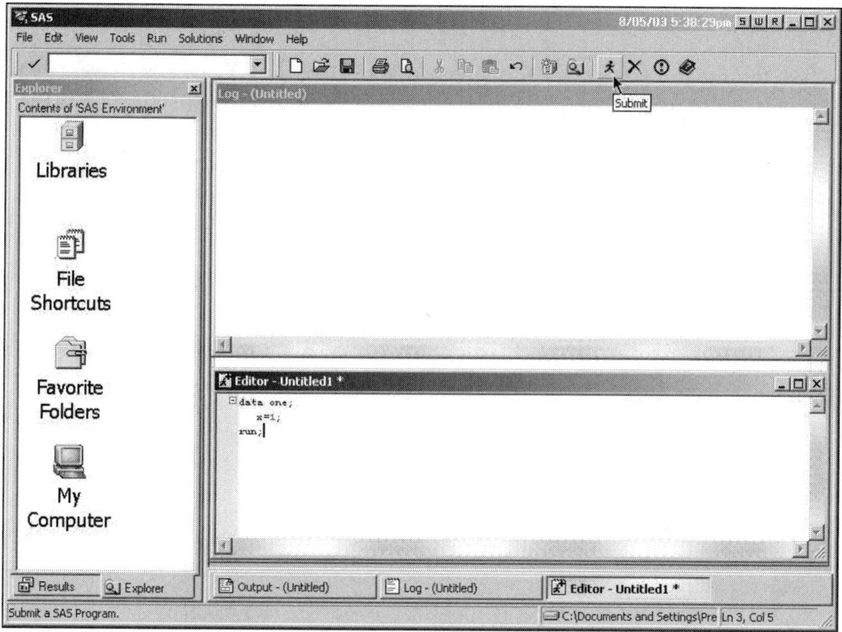

- **Application Toolbar** — This selection controls whether the SAS tool bar appears in the main SAS window.
- **Command Bar** — This selection controls whether a command bar appears in the main SAS window.
- **Use AutoComplete** — This selection activates the autocomplete feature of the command bar. If this feature is on, the SAS System uses the first few characters of a command that you type to guess the command you want, based on commands previously issued in the SAS session.
- **Sort commands by most recently used** — This selection changes the ordering of the list of commands remembered by the command bar. By default, when you click the down arrow to the right of the command bar, the commands are listed in most commonly used order. That is, commands you use most often are toward the top of the list, while less common commands are at the bottom of the list. Selecting this option changes the ordering algorithm used by the command bar, although the list does not immediately reorder itself; the list is gradually reordered as you continue to issue commands.

- **Number of commands saved** — This selection controls the number of commands listed by clicking the down arrow in the command bar. The default number is 15; you can adjust this number up or down to suit your needs.

The **Customize** tab of the Customize Tools dialog box is discussed in "Adding and Editing Tools on the Tool Bar" later in this chapter.

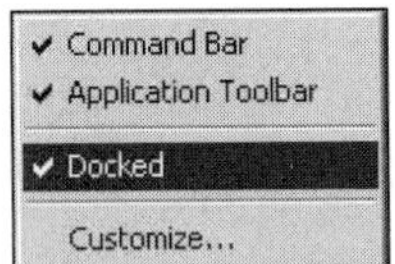

Switching between the Command Bar/Box and Tool Bar/Box: If you prefer to use a command box or SAS toolbox (windows), which can be moved outside the main SAS window, right-click on the check mark to the left of the command bar or on the SAS tool bar. In the resulting popup menu, click **Docked**. Depending on where you right-clicked, the command bar or tool bar now becomes a separate window. Figure 6.5 shows how the main SAS window might look if you undocked the command bar.

Figure 6.5 SAS Session with a Command Box instead of a Command Bar

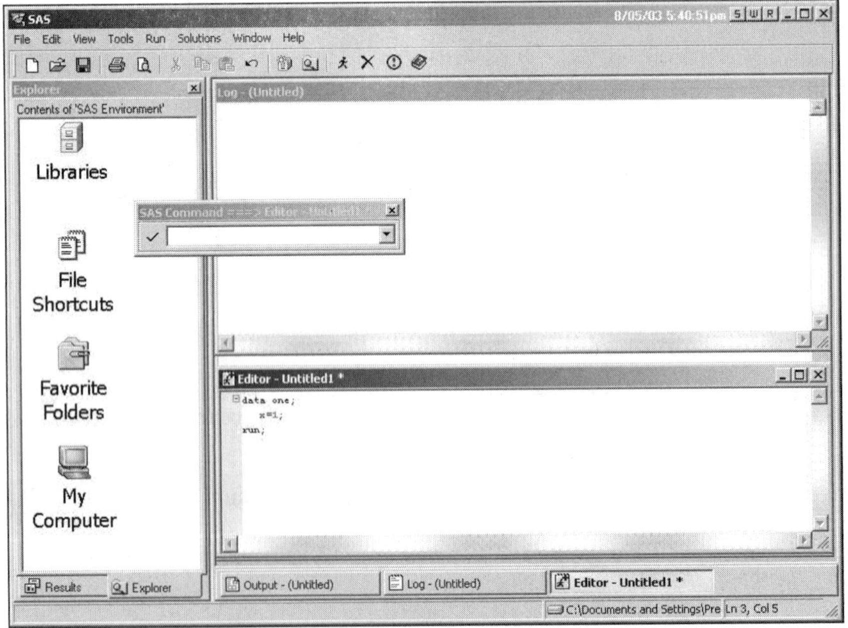

Note

The title bar of the command box shows the active SAS window, to which commands will apply.

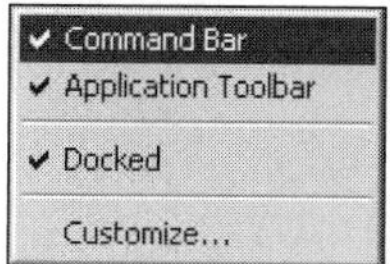

Turning Off the Command Bar or Tool Bar: If you do not want the main SAS window to show the command bar or the SAS tool bar, right-click on the SAS System tool bar and click either **Command Bar** or **Application Toolbar**. Depending on which you clicked on, the command bar or the SAS tool bar disappears.

To display the command bar or SAS tool bar again, simply right-click on the SAS System tool bar again and reselect the appropriate item (**Command Bar** or **Application Toolbar**).

Adding and Editing Tools on the Tool Bar

FasTip: Right-click on the SAS System tool bar, then click **Customize**, then click the **Customize** tab.

Use the TOOLLOAD command to load alternative tool bars.

The tool bar across the top of the main SAS window is a handy way to execute commands. While the default tools may be sufficient for many users, you may want to add a tool, change the icon for a tool, or otherwise edit the look and feel of the tool bar.

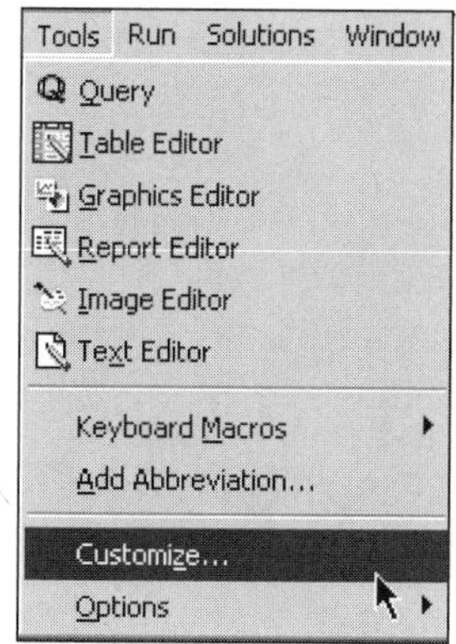

To begin editing the tool bar, click **Tools** → **Customize** in the SAS System main menu. The Customize Tools dialog box opens. Click the **Customize** tab, which is shown in Figure 6.6.

Figure 6.6 Customize Tab of the Customize Tools Dialog Box

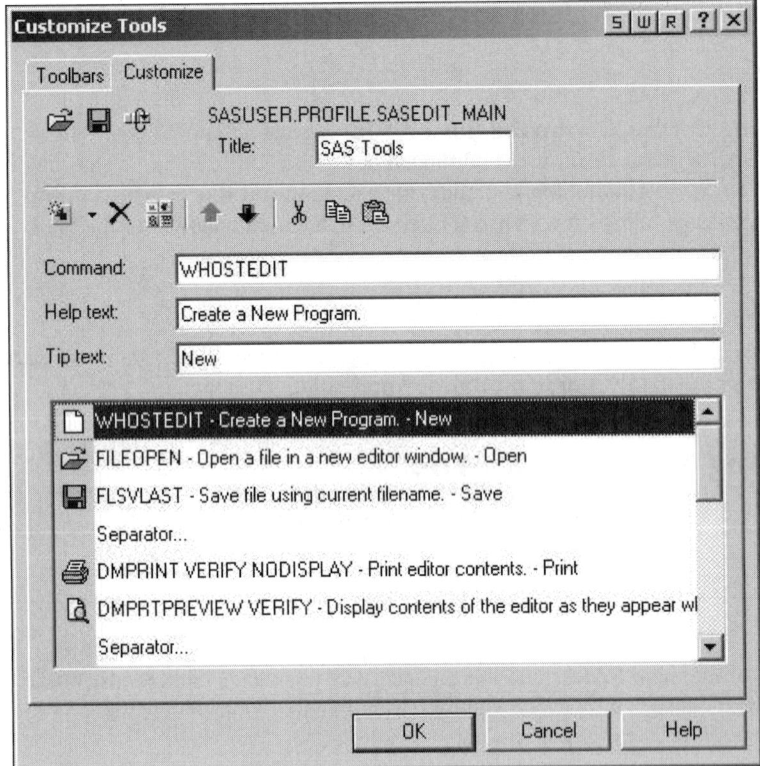

This section shows you how to

- add a tool to the tool bar
- edit an existing tool
- create an alternate tool bar
- associate a tool bar with a specific SAS window.

For information on other tasks, such as changing the order of tools, deleting tools, and so on, click the **Help** button on the **Customize** tab of the Customize Tools dialog box.

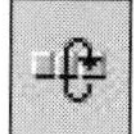

Returning to the Default Tools: Before you begin to make changes, remember that you can always return to the default tools by clicking the **Restore Defaults** icon on the **Customize** tab. When you do so, you are asked if you really want to return the definitions to their default values. Click **Yes**, then click **OK** to close the Customize Tools dialog box. When prompted to save your changes, click **Yes**.

Adding a Tool: The following example illustrates adding a new tool to the default SAS tool bar. Open the Customize Tools dialog box and follow along:

1. Make the Enhanced Editor window active by clicking in it.
2. Open the Customize Tools dialog box by clicking **Tools** → **Customize** in the SAS System main menu. Now click the **Customize** tab of this dialog box.
3. Click the down arrow next to the **Add Tool** icon, and click **Blank Tool**. Tools are added before the tool that is highlighted in the list of tools.

   A blank line and blank icon appear in the list of tools.
4. Click in the **Command** field once to move your cursor, and type the SAS windowing command you want the tool to execute. If you want the tool to execute a string of commands, separate the commands with semicolons.

   For example, type the following to create a tool for submitting code stored on the Clipboard:

   ```
   GSUBMIT
   ```
5. Click in the **Help Text** field, and type the help string that appears in the main SAS window message area when you hold your mouse pointer over the tool. For example, type

   ```
   Submit code from the Clipboard
   ```
6. Click in the **Tip Text** field, and type the help string that appears in the tool tip (the short description that appears under the tool when you place your mouse pointer over a tool). For example, type

   ```
   Submit Clipboard
   ```

   As you type in the **Command**, **Help Text**, and **Tip Text** fields, your characters are copied to the tool definition in the list of tools.

   Figure 6.7 shows how the **Customize** tab looks after you have typed all this text in.

Figure 6.7 Adding a Tool

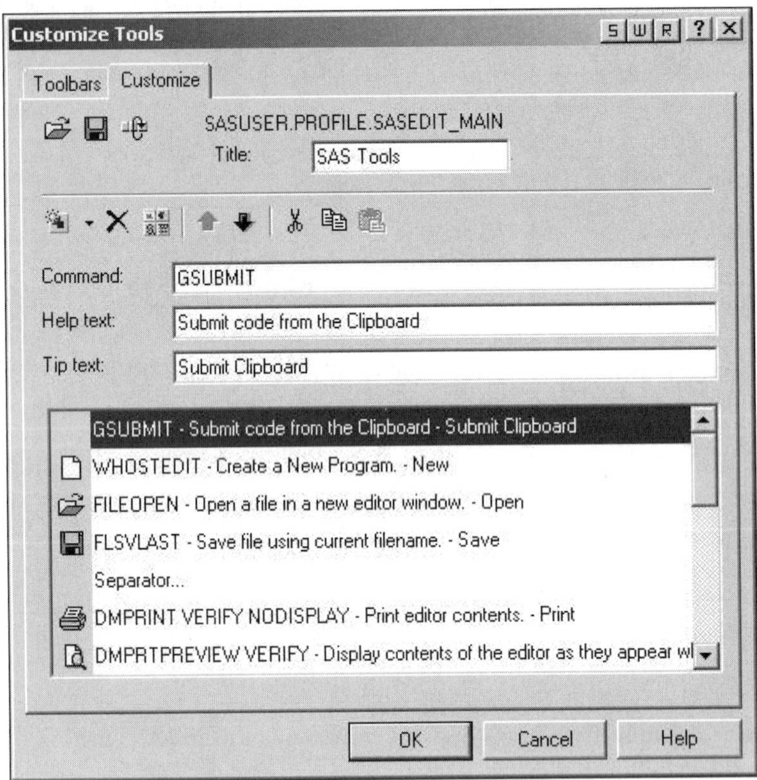

7. To pick an icon for the new tool, click the **Change Icon** icon. The Bitmap Browser dialog box opens, as shown in Figure 6.8.

Figure 6.8 Bitmap Browser Dialog Box

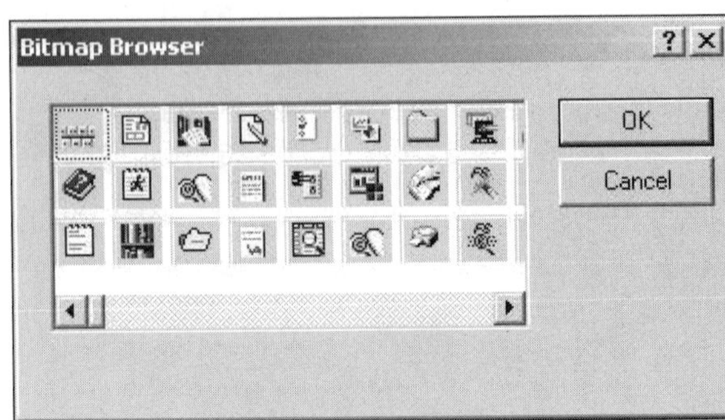

8. Click the icon you want, then click **OK**. The icon appears by the new tool.

   For example, because you already have a submit tool that uses the jogger icon, you may want to choose a different icon for the new tool. Click the jogger-on-a-page icon (second icon from the left in the middle row).

9. To save your changes, click **OK** in the Customize Tools dialog box. When asked if you want to save your changes, click **Yes**. Your new tool appears on the tool bar. Figure 6.9 shows the SAS tool bar with the mouse pointer pointing to the new tool.

Figure 6.9 Tool Bar with the New Tool Added

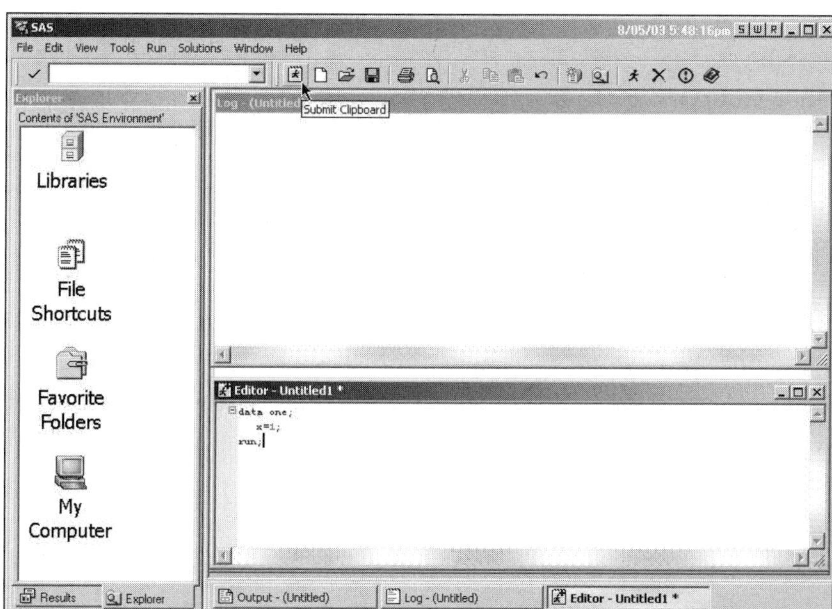

Increasing the Number of Visible Tools: Only a certain number of tools will fit on the SAS System tool bar at one time. The exact number of visible tools depends on your screen resolution. If you find that you have defined a lot of tools and some of them disappear off the right edge of the tool bar, you can try a couple of tricks.

One way to maximize the space usage on the tool bar is to use the **Customize** tab of the Customize Tools dialog box to delete the separators between tools.

To increase the space available for tools, you can resize the command bar by placing the mouse pointer over the vertical double bar that appears to the right of the command bar (the pointer turns into a double-headed arrow). Drag this bar to the left, making the command bar smaller.

You can also choose to make the command bar into a command box (see "Switching between the Command Bar/Box and Tool Bar/Box" earlier in this chapter), which leaves more room for tools on the tool bar.

Editing an Existing Tool: You do not have to accept how the tool icons look—you can choose a different icon for a tool. For example, you may not think that the icon for the tool that opens the New Library dialog box is intuitive:

Change the icon for a tool by following steps similar to those in this example:

1. Open the Customize Tools dialog box by clicking **Tools** → **Customize** in the SAS System main menu. Now click the **Customize** tab.
2. Use the scroll bar in the list of tools to scroll down until the tool you want to change is visible. In this example, we're going to change the tool with the open file drawers and the command LIBASSIGN.
3. Click that line in the list of tools. It is highlighted, as shown in Figure 6.10.

Figure 6.10 Customize Tools Dialog Box with New Library Tool Highlighted

4.  Click the **Change Icon** icon to display the Bitmap Browser dialog box.

   Be sure you are scrolled all the way to the left in the dialog box. Click the second icon from the left in the bottom row—it looks like this:

5. Click **OK** in the Bitmap Browser dialog box. The icon changes in the tool list. Click **OK** in the Customize Tools dialog box to save your changes; click **Yes** when prompted.

   Similarly, edit other parts of a tool by clicking its line in the tool list, then clicking in the **Command**, **Help Text**, or **Tip Text** fields and editing the contents of these fields.

Creating an Alternative Tool Bar: One of the most powerful aspects of the SAS System's tool bar is that you can create several tool bars and load whichever set of tools you need for a specific SAS session. For example, you can create a tool bar for each SAS/AF application you write.

This section walks you through creating a small tool bar. One tool prints and clears the Output window; the other tool saves the text of the window in RTF format. The following two sections show you how to load a specific tool bar and how to return to the original tool bar.

To create a new tool bar, follow steps similar to those in this example:

1. Click **Tools** → **Customize** in the SAS System main menu. The Customize Tools dialog box opens; click the **Customize** tab.

   Each tool bar you create is stored as a catalog entry. The title bar of the **Customize** tab shows the catalog entry name for the tool bar you are editing (the entry type, TOOLBOX, does not appear in the title bar). The SASUSER.PROFILE.SASEDIT_MAIN entry is the default tool bar for the Enhanced Editor.

2. In the **Title** field, give your new tool bar a title. This title serves as a descriptive label for the tool bar.

   Highlight the contents of the **Title** field by marking it with the mouse. Now type your new title. For example, type

   ```
   My Personal Tool Bar
   ```

3. 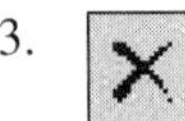 To delete tools you do not want, click the tool in the tool list, then click the **Remove Tool** icon.

   Remove all the tools and separators.

4.  Now add your own tools. In this example, we add two tools. Click the down arrow next to the **Add Tool** icon, then click **Blank Tool**.

   In the **Command** field, type

   ```
   Output; DLGPRT; CLEAR
   ```

   In the **Help Text** field, type

   ```
   Print the Output window and clear it
   ```

   In the **Tip Text** field, type

   ```
   Print/clear Output
   ```

5.  Click the **Change Icon** icon to open the Bitmap Browser dialog box and choose an appropriate icon.

   For example, choose the printer icon that is approximately in the middle of the collection of icons (use the scroll bar to move to the right), in the bottom row:

   .

6. For the second tool, click the down arrow next to the **Add Tool** icon, then click **Blank Tool**. The **Command**, **Help Text**, and **Tip Text** fields should look like this:

   ```
   WRTFSAVE "C:\Myfile.rtf"
   Save the active window text as an RTF file
   Save as RTF
   ```

7. Click the **Change Icon** icon again and choose another icon. For example, choose the first icon in the bottom row:

   .

8. Now you are ready to save your new catalog entry. Click the **Save the Toolbar** icon.

The Save Tools dialog box appears. You can save the entry in any catalog. For this example, we'll store it in the SASUSER.PROFILE catalog and give it a name of PERSONAL. Double-click in the **Entry** field to highlight the entry name and type `PERSONAL`. Figure 6.11 shows how the dialog box should look when you have done this.

Figure 6.11 Save Tools Dialog Box

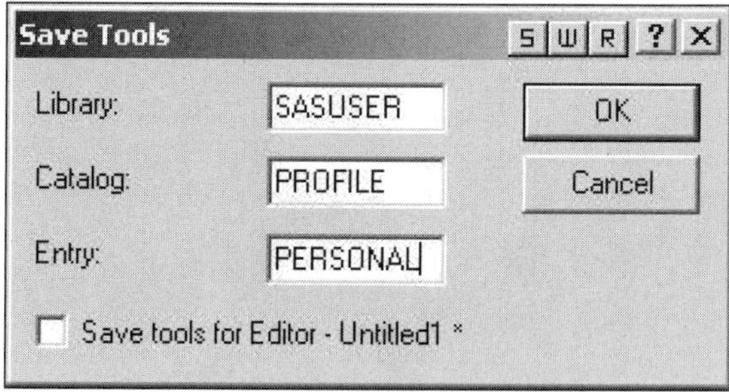

9. Now click OK. This writes the new catalog entry to the SASUSER.PROFILE catalog.
10. Notice that the title bar of the Customize Tools dialog box now says SASUSER.PROFILE.PERSONAL. Click **OK** to close the Customize Tools dialog box.

Loading a Specific Tool Bar: To load your new tools, use the TOOLLOAD command. The basic syntax is as follows:

```
TOOLLOAD tool-set
```

For example, to load the tools you created in the previous section, issue the following command from the command bar:

```
TOOLLOAD SASUSER.PROFILE.PERSONAL
```

Figure 6.12 shows the main SAS window with the new tools loaded.

Figure 6.12 Using the New Tool Bar

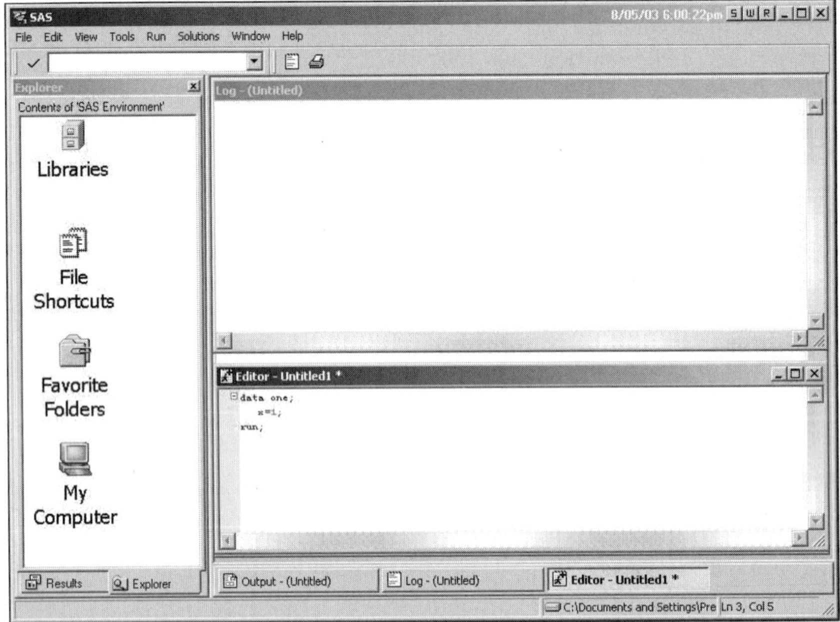

Note

> The Enhanced Editor requires a more complete syntax of the TOOLLOAD command. When issuing this command from an Enhanced Editor window, use the following form:
>
> ```
> TOOLLOAD WINDOW BAR tool-set
> ```

Instead of loading a tool bar manually with the TOOLLOAD command, you can associate a tool bar with a particular window and have that tool bar load automatically every time you open the window. See "Associating a Tool Bar with a Specific SAS Window" on the next page for more information.

You can also create a tool that invokes another tool bar—simply create a tool with the appropriate TOOLLOAD command in the **Command** field of the **Customize** tab of the Customize Tools dialog box.

Loading the Default Tool Bar: To return to the default tool bar, issue the following command from the command bar:

```
TOOLLOAD SASUSER.PROFILE.TOOLBOX
```

Note

For the Enhanced Editor, the command to load the default tool bar is

```
TOOLLOAD WINDOW BAR SASUSER.PROFILE.SASEDIT_MAIN
```

Associating a Tool Bar with a Specific SAS Window: Because you perform different tasks from different windows, it may be helpful to have a tool bar for each window. Follow these steps to set the window for a tool bar:

1. Click in the window with which you want the tool bar associated (this makes the window active).
2. Open the Customize Tools dialog box by clicking **Tools** → **Customize** in the SAS System main menu; now click the **Customize** tab.
3. Create a new tool bar, as described earlier in this chapter.
4. Click the **Save the Toolbar** icon in the Customize Tools dialog box. When the Save Tools dialog box appears, enter the catalog entry information, and also click in the check box next to the line that reads **Save tools for *active-window***.

The new tool bar is saved, and when you switch to the tool bar's window, the tool bar is automatically loaded.

Customizing the SAS Explorer

FastTip: Click **Tools** → **Options** → **Explorer**.

In Chapter 2 you learned how to use the SAS Explorer to manage SAS files. You can customize the SAS Explorer so that it better meets your file-management needs. To customize the SAS Explorer, open the Explorer Options dialog box by clicking **Tools** → **Options** → **Explorer** in the SAS System main menu. (Make sure that the SAS Explorer window is active before accessing the SAS menu.) Figure 6.13 shows the Explorer Options dialog box.

Figure 6.13 Explorer Options Dialog Box

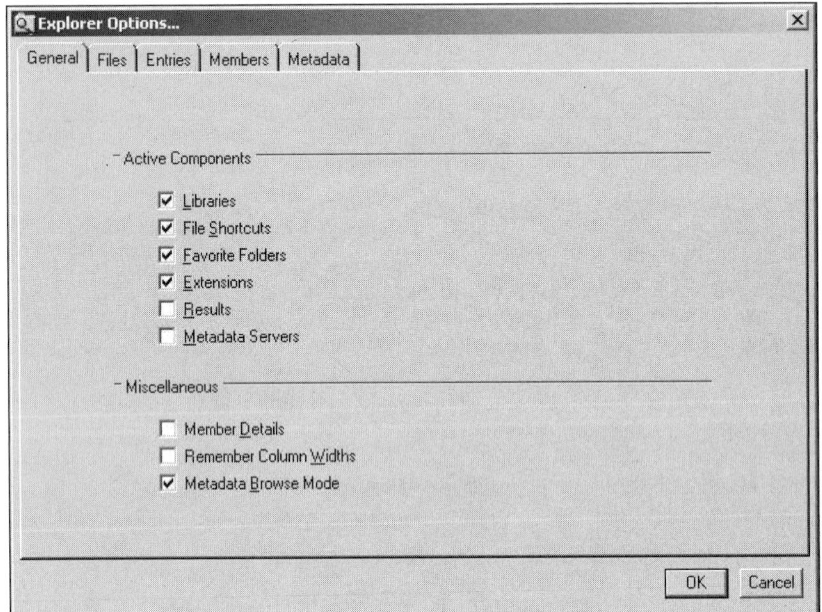

Caution

> The changes you make in the Explorer Options dialog box affect the SAS Registry. The SAS Registry keeps track of file types and actions (such as Open or Print) associated with those file types. For more details on the SAS Registry, including the REGEDIT command, refer to Appendix 5 and SAS Help and Documentation.

The following paragraphs get you started by explaining how to use several features of the Explorer Options dialog box.

To close the Explorer Options dialog box, click **OK**.

Changing the Default SAS Explorer Contents: By default, the SAS Explorer window shows four icons: **Libraries**, **File Shortcuts**, **Favorite Folders**, and **My Computer**. Two other icons, **Results** and **Metadata Servers**, are not shown by default. You can customize which icons are shown in the SAS Explorer by using the Explorer Options dialog box.

Begin by clicking the **General** tab in the Explorer Options dialog box. Folders that are listed by the SAS Explorer have a check mark next to them.

Note

> The My Computer icon is associated with the **Extensions** list item.

Use the check boxes next to each folder's name to include or remove that folder from the SAS Explorer display. If a SAS Explorer window is currently open, it is automatically refreshed when you close the Explorer Options dialog box.

Adjusting SAS Data Library Member Types: When you double-click a SAS data library in the SAS Explorer window, the window shows you the contents of the SAS data library; the **Members** tab of the Explorer Options dialog box controls what types of library members are listed and what actions are associated with those member types. Table 6.1 lists some of the more commonly known member types.

Table 6.1 Some of the SAS Data Library Members Listed in the SAS Explorer Window

Type	Description
ACCESS	Access descriptor
CATALOG	Catalog of entries
FDB	Financial database
MDDB	Multi-dimensional database
TABLE	Data tables (previously called data sets)
PROGRAM	Compiled DATA step code
VIEW	SQL, DATA step, or database interface views

The icon shown in the **Type** column is the icon shown in the SAS Explorer window, representing that member type.

You can change and add actions associated with any of the member types by clicking the member type in the **Type** column, then clicking the **Edit** button. See SAS Help and Documentation for further information.

Caution

> You can use the **Hide** button to remove a default member type from the list. But doing so will impair your ability to use this type of SAS file from the SAS Explorer. For hidden member types, you can add them back to the SAS Explorer display by clicking **Unhide** on the **Member** tab of the Explorer Options dialog box.

Adjusting Catalog Entry Types: When you double-click a SAS catalog in the SAS Explorer window, the window shows you the contents of the catalog, listing all the catalog entries; the **Entries** tab of the Explorer Options dialog box controls what types of catalog entries are listed and what actions are associated with those entry types.

This tab works like the **Members** tab, except that now the **Type** column shows all the catalog entry types that are currently listed by the SAS Explorer window, along with a description of each entry type.

The icon shown in the **Type** column is the icon shown in the SAS Explorer window, representing that entry type.

You can change and add actions associated with any of the entry types by clicking the entry type in the **Type** column, then clicking the **Edit** button. See SAS Help and Documentation for further information.

Caution

You can use the **Hide** button to remove a default catalog member type from the list. But doing so will impair your ability to use this type of SAS file from the SAS Explorer. For hidden catalog member types, you can add them back to the SAS Explorer display by clicking **Unhide** on the **Entries** tab of the Explorer Options dialog box.

Adjusting External File Types: The **Favorite Folders** and **My Computer** icons in the SAS Explorer show the contents of your computer system (such as floppy drives and your hard drive). You can customize the actions associated with various file types.

Begin by clicking the **Files** tab in the Explorer Options dialog box. Now the **Type** column shows all the external file types that are currently listed by the SAS Explorer window, along with a description of each file type.

The icon shown in the **Type** column is the icon shown in the SAS Explorer window, representing that file type.

You can change and add actions associated with any of the file types by clicking the file type in the **Type** column, then clicking the **Edit** button. See SAS Help and Documentation for further information.

Caution

> You can use the **Hide** button to remove a default file type from the list. But doing so will impair your ability to use this type of file from the SAS Explorer. For hidden file types, you can add them back to the SAS Explorer display by clicking **Unhide** on the **Files** tab of the Explorer Options dialog box.

Adjusting the Docking View

By default, when the SAS System starts up, the SAS Explorer and Results windows open and are locked at the left side of the main SAS window. This is called the "docking view."

Undocking a Specific Window: You can "undock" a specific window by following these steps:

1. Make the window active by clicking in it.
2. Click **Window** → **Docked** in the SAS System main menu. The check mark next to **Docked** disappears.

The window is now like other SAS windows and can be moved around inside the main SAS window.

Disabling the Docking View: To undock all windows, open the Preferences dialog box by clicking **Tools** → **Options** → **Preferences** in the SAS System main menu. Click the **View** tab, and deselect **Docking view**. Now all windows are undocked and the **Window** menu choices dealing with docking are disabled.

Redocking Windows: To redock a particular window, make it active, then click **Window** → **Docked** in the SAS System main menu.

Adjusting the Size of Docked Windows: To change the size of a docked window, place your mouse pointer over the docked window border (the pointer turns into a double-headed arrow). Now drag the border where you want. Clicking **Window** → **Size Docking View** (or issuing the WDOCKVIEWRESIZE command from the command bar) automatically places your mouse pointer over the window border. Just drag the border, then click when it is where you want it.

To exit from resize mode without resizing the docking view, press ESC.

Minimizing and Maximizing Docked Windows: Although docked windows do not show the Minimize and Maximize buttons like other windows, they can be minimized. To do so, right-click in the title bar of a docked window, then click **Minimize** in the resulting popup menu. The entire docking area (including both the SAS Explorer and Results windows) is minimized, showing only its name (**Docking view**) in the window bar across the bottom of the main SAS window.

To maximize the docking area, click **Docking view** in the window bar.

Undocking the Command Bar and Tool Bar: To undock the command bar (which changes it to a command box) or the tool bar (which changes it to a toolbox), right-click one of the following:

- the check mark to the left of the command bar
- anywhere on the tool bar.

In the resulting popup menu, click **Docked**. This changes the bar to a floating box, and erases the check mark next to **Docked** in the popup menu. Repeat this process to redock the command bar or tool bar.

Changing Colors

FasTip: Use the SASCOLOR window (affects all SAS windows).

Issue the COLOR command (affects individual SAS windows).

Click the **Start** button, then click **Settings** → **Control Panel**, then double-click the **Display** icon. Now click the **Appearance** tab (affects all Windows applications).

You can customize your SAS session by changing the color of windows and window elements. For example, you may not like the default stark white background of the Enhanced Editor, Log, and Output windows. Also, you may want titles in the Output window to appear in a certain color (default is blue) but footnotes in a different color. And you may want to adjust the color of title bars, scroll bars, and other window "decorations." Decide what you want to change, and whether you want to change the attribute

- for all windows in your SAS session
- for only a particular SAS window
- for all windows in all applications.

Deciding Which Method to Use: The three methods of changing colors and their effects in the SAS System are

- SASCOLOR window—affects all SAS windows
- COLOR command (issued from any SAS window)—affects only the SAS window from which the command is issued
- Display Properties window, from the Windows Control Panel—affects all windows in all Windows applications, including the SAS System.

Each method lets you change the colors of a variety of window attributes; sometimes there is overlap, where an attribute can be changed by more than one method. In this case, one method has precedence over another.

Note

The SASCOLOR window and the COLOR command do not affect HTML output displayed in the Results Viewer window. To change the colors used to display HTML output, you must select a style on the **Results** tab of the Preferences dialog box or use the TEMPLATE procedure to define a new style. See Chapter 8 for more information.

Understanding the Precedence of Color Specifications: The Windows Control Panel overrides all other methods of color specification. For example, even though the COLOR command supports the SCROLLBAR option, it has no effect, because scroll bars are controlled by the Control Panel. Any specifications you make with the COLOR command override options set by the SASCOLOR window.

Using the SASCOLOR Window: Use the SASCOLOR window to set colors for all SAS windows. Table 6.2 shows the window elements supported by the SASCOLOR window.

Table 6.2 Elements Supported by the SASCOLOR Window

Background	Secondary Background
Border	Secondary Border
Banner	Command
Message	Error
Warning	Note
Foreground	Label
Row Label	Informational Text
Column Label	Help Main Topic
Help Link	Help Subtopic and Syntax
Selected Area	Source
Data	Footnote
Header	Title
Byline	

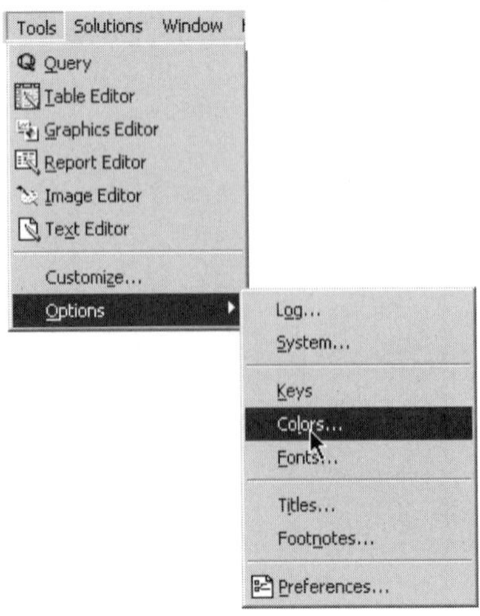

Open the SASCOLOR window by clicking **Tools** → **Options** → **Colors** in the SAS System main menu.

Note

This menu choice is not available if the Enhanced Editor window is active.

Figure 6.14 shows the SASCOLOR window.

Figure 6.14 SASCOLOR Window

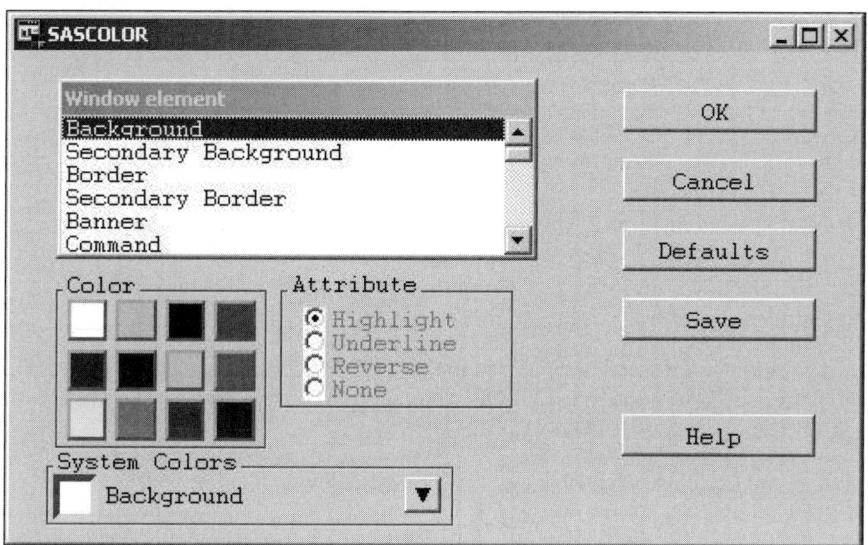

Note

> You can also issue the SASCOLOR command from the command bar to open the SASCOLOR window.

First, choose a window element by selecting one from the **Window element** list. Use the scroll bar to view the whole list. Select the element by clicking it.

If the window element you have chosen supports attributes such as highlighting, reversing, or underlining, these attributes are listed in the **Attribute** area. Unavailable attributes are grayed out and not selectable. Click any attribute you want the window element to have. Now choose a color from the **Color** area. To change more window elements, choose a different element, then set its attributes and color.

The **System Colors** area of the SASCOLOR window allows you to link the color of SAS window elements to colors set by the Windows Control Panel. The three choices for system colors are **Foreground**, **Background**, and **Secondary Background**. Table 6.3 shows how these choices correspond to the choices in the Display Properties window of the Control Panel (on the **Appearance** tab).

Table 6.3 How SASCOLOR Window System Colors Relate to the Control Panel Window Elements

Choice in SASCOLOR Window	Control Panel Window Element	Control Panel Window Element Attribute
Foreground	Window	Font Color
Background	Window	Item Color
Secondary Background	3D Objects	Item Color

For example, if you want selected text in SAS windows always to be the same color as the 3D Objects color set in the Control Panel, select **Selected Area** in the SASCOLOR window **Window element** list. Then, click the down arrow to the right of the **System Colors** area and click **Secondary Background**.

When you are finished setting colors and attributes in the SASCOLOR window, click **OK** if you want to save your changes and close the SASCOLOR window. If you want to save your changes but leave the SASCOLOR window open, click **Save**.

When you click **OK** or **Save**, a catalog entry named SAS.CPARMS is created in your SASUSER.PROFILE catalog.

If you change several window elements but decide you do not like your changes, return to the default configuration by clicking **Defaults** in the SASCOLOR window.

To get information on what the various window elements are, click the **Help** button in the SASCOLOR window. This opens the Using This Window help topic for the SASCOLOR window.

Note

Although the SASCOLOR window affects all SAS windows, if you have changed a window element's color with the COLOR command and then issued a WSAVE command to save your changes, that window's element is not affected by the changes you make via the SASCOLOR window. (See "Saving Your Changes" on the next page for more information on WSAVE.)

Note

Currently open SAS windows do not reflect the new colors you have chosen from the SASCOLOR window until you close the windows and reopen them.

Using the COLOR Command: Use the COLOR command to set colors for a specific SAS window. You can issue the COLOR command from almost any SAS window. The basic syntax is

COLOR *window-element color*

where *window-element* is the name of a part of a window (like banner, note, or message) and *color* is an abbreviation for a supported color. Table 6.4 shows the window elements supported by the COLOR command, and Table 6.5 shows the supported colors and their abbreviations.

Table 6.4 Window Elements Supported by the COLOR Command

Background	Border	Banner
Command	Message	Scroll Bar
Byline	Data	Error
Footnote	Header	Mtext
Note	Numbers	Source
Text	Title	Warning

Table 6.5 Color Abbreviations Used by the COLOR Command

B	blue	R	red	G	green
C	cyan	P	pink	Y	yellow
W	white	K	black	M	magenta
A	gray	N	brown	O	orange

Note

Not all window elements listed in Table 6.4 are valid for all SAS windows. For example, the Header element is not valid in the Log window.

Saving Your Changes: If you issue the COLOR command and then end your SAS session, the default colors return the next time you invoke the SAS System. To make the changes permanent for a window, perform one of the following actions:

- To save the colors set in just one window, issue the WSAVE command from the command bar after the COLOR command. This saves the window's attributes to an entry in your SASUSER.PROFILE catalog, with the name *active-window*.WSAVE.

- To save the colors set in all windows (as well as all other window attributes), select **Save settings on exit** on the **General** tab of the Preferences dialog box. This is similar to issuing a WSAVE ALL command from the command bar, and creates .WSAVE entries for all open SAS windows.

If you've saved changes but then decide to return to the default configuration, delete the appropriate entries from your SASUSER.PROFILE catalog. These entries include all entries that have the WSAVE icon. To decide which .WSAVE entries to delete, display the contents of your PROFILE catalog in the SAS Explorer window, then click **View → Details** in the SAS System main menu. The **Description** column explains what each entry is. (You may have to scroll or resize the right pane of the SAS Explorer window to see the **Description** column.)

Caution

Deleting entries that begin with a window name can also delete attributes other than color, such as customized key definitions.

Using the Control Panel's Display Properties Window: Use the Control Panel's Display Properties window to set colors for all windows in all Windows applications. Table 6.6 shows the window elements supported by the Display Properties window.

Note

The instructions for this section are for Windows 2000. If you are using another version of Windows, the dialog boxes may differ from those shown here.

Table 6.6 Window Elements Supported by the Display Properties Window

3D Objects	Active Title Bar
Active Window Border	Application Background
Desktop	Inactive Title Bar
Inactive Window Border	Menu
Message Box	Selected Items
Tooltip	Window

To open the Control Panel's Display Properties window, click the **Start** button, then click **Settings → Control Panel**. Now double-click the **Display** icon. The Display Properties window opens. Click the **Appearance** tab. The window now looks like the one shown in Figure 6.15.

Figure 6.15 Appearance Tab of the Windows Display Properties Window

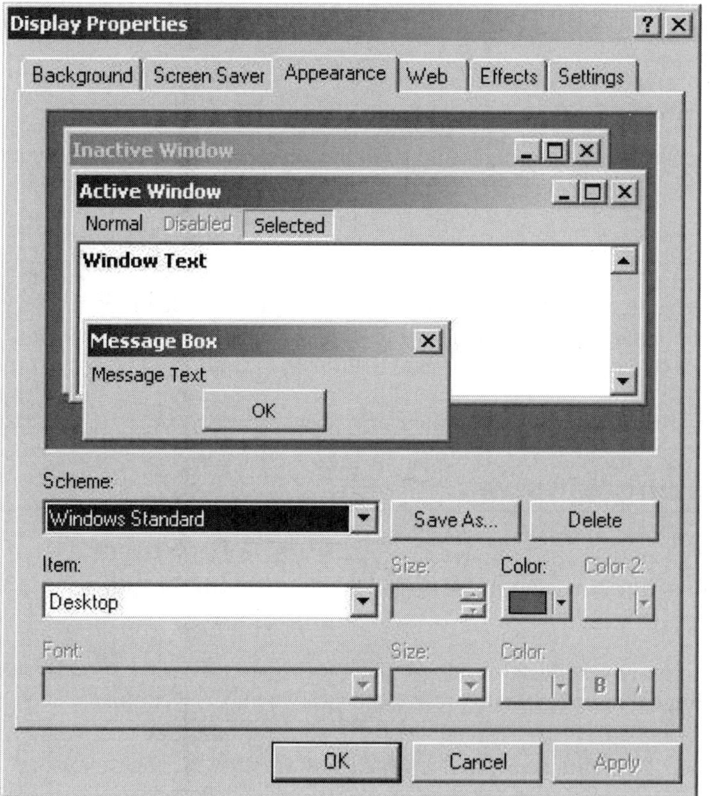

The window attributes you set on the **Appearance** tab of the Display Properties window affect all applications installed on your system. For example, if you set active title bars to be orange, the SAS System title bar is orange, and so is the title bar for Microsoft Word, and even the Control Panel.

To set the color of a particular window attribute, follow these steps:

1. Click the down arrow next to the **Item** field, and use the scroll bar to scroll to the element you want to set. For example, about halfway down the list you see **Menu**.
2. To select an element, click it. The name of the element appears in the **Item** field.
3. Click the **Color** button to the right of the **Item** field, then click the colored square that represents the color you want for the window element. For window elements that also contain text, you can click the **Color** button to the right of the **Font** field to change the text color.

For example, tool tips are normally light yellow with black text. If you prefer light green with magenta text, click the light green rectangle displayed by the **Color** button next to the **Item** field. Then click the **Color** button next to the **Font** field, and click the magenta rectangle.

When you click a color, the sample window on the left side of the **Appearance** tab reflects your changes, showing the effect.

4. If you want to change other window elements, use the **Item** list to select another element, then select its color. When you are finished, click **OK** to close the Display Properties window and save your changes.

Warning

> Be careful when you are selecting elements and colors. For example, it is possible to set both the window text and the window background to white, and if you do, you won't be able to see anything. While you can fix this by going back to the Display Properties window, it is disconcerting to say the least.

Resizing and Organizing Windows

What's New: Tiling is now available in both horizontal and vertical patterns.

FasTip: Click **Window → Tile Horizontally**, **Tile Vertically**, **Cascade**, or **Resize**.

In Chapter 1, you learned how to move and resize windows using the mouse. You can also affect how windows are arranged within the main SAS window by using the menus and commands.

Minimizing Windows: To minimize a window (that is, reduce it to an icon), click the minimize button.

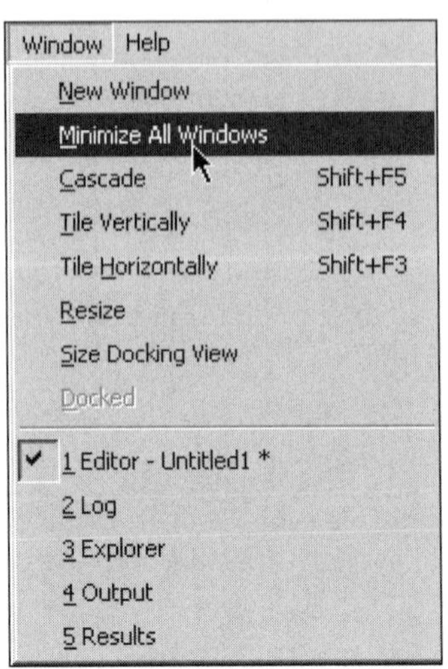

If you want all your SAS windows minimized, click **Window → Minimize All Windows** in the SAS System main menu.

Tiling Windows: A quick way to make all open windows visible at once is to tile them. This arranges them in a mosaic pattern within the main SAS window. You can choose between vertical tiling and horizontal tiling.

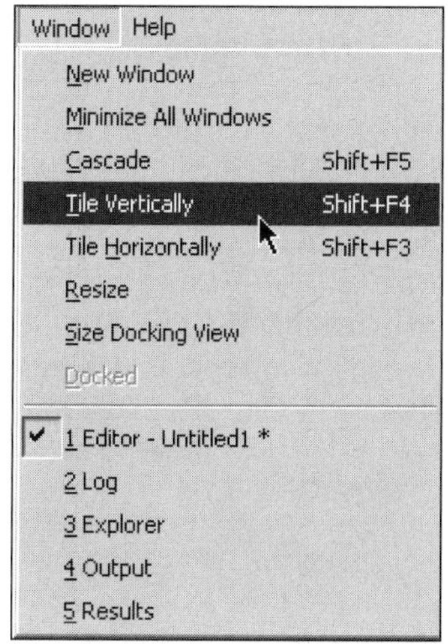

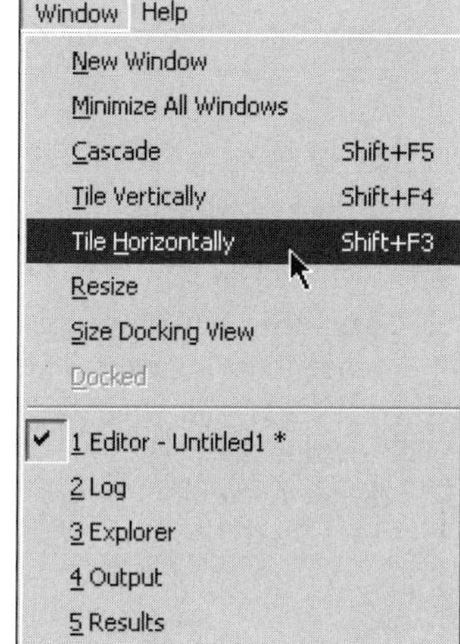

To tile your windows, click **Window → Tile Vertically** or **Window → Tile Horizontally** in the SAS System main menu. Figure 6.16 shows a SAS session with three vertically tiled windows.

Figure 6.16 SAS Session with Vertically Tiled Windows

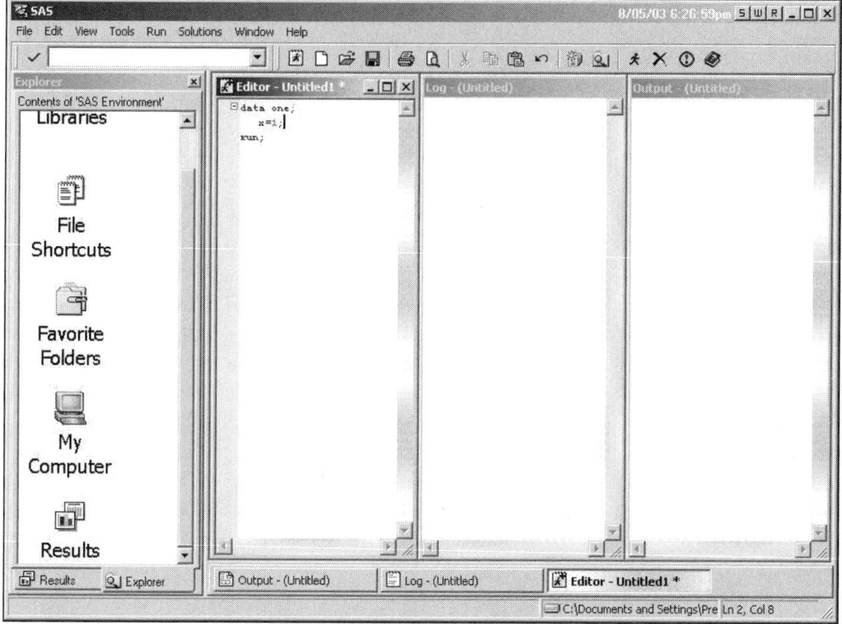

If you prefer to use commands, issue the TILE command from the command bar.

Note

The TILE command and pressing SHIFT-F4 are equivalent to clicking **Window → Tile Vertically**. Pressing SHIFT-F3 is equivalent to clicking **Window → Tile Horizontally**.

Note

The tiling menu choices do not tile docked windows.

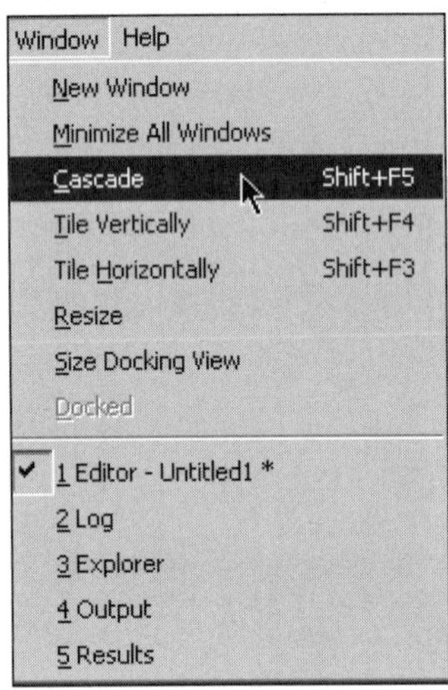

Cascading Windows: An alternative to tiling windows is to arrange them in layers, so that each window's title bar is visible. To cascade your windows, click **Window → Cascade** in the SAS System main menu. Figure 6.17 shows a SAS session with three cascaded windows.

Figure 6.17 SAS Session with Cascaded SAS Windows

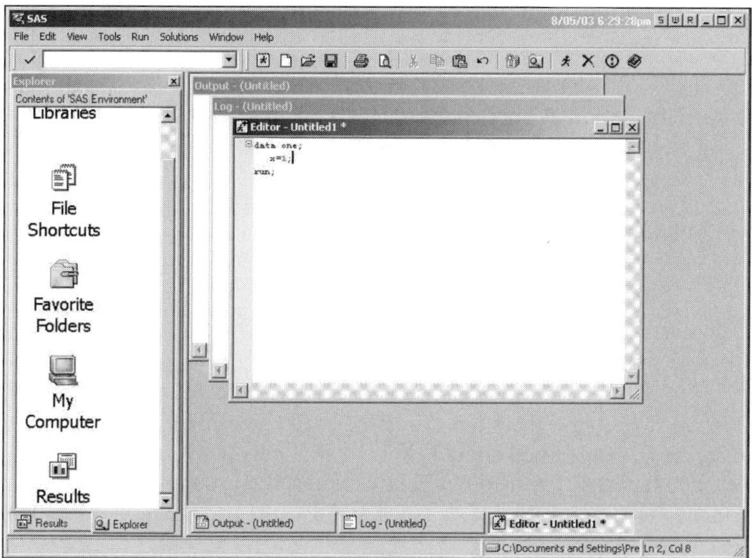

If you prefer, issue the CASCADE command from the command bar or press SHIFT-F5.

If you want a different window on top but still want the windows cascaded, first switch to the window you want, then reissue the CASCADE command. The windows are cascaded with the active window on top.

Note

> The **Cascade** menu choice does not cascade docked windows.

Undoing Your Changes: If you decide you do not want your windows tiled or cascaded, return to the default arrangement by clicking **Window** → **Resize** in the SAS System main menu. If you prefer to use commands, issue the RESIZE command from the command bar.

Note

> The **Resize** menu choice also resets other window attributes, such as size and position. It does not affect docked windows.

Defining Function Keys

FasTip: Click **Tools → Options → Keys**, then redefine the key definitions.

While the point-and-click features of Windows applications are a boon to many users, you may not like this approach to issuing commands. You can issue commands to the SAS System in other ways, bypassing the menus.

Three common alternatives to using the menus are

- function keys
- keyboard shortcuts
- command-line commands.

Earlier in this chapter, you learned how to use the **View** tab in the Preferences dialog box to turn on command lines. And in Chapter 1, you learned about keyboard shortcuts (such as CTRL-C for Copy) and hotkeys (the underlined letters in the menus). This section shows you how to define function keys (such as F1 or SHIFT-F10) and other keys (such as CTRL-H and the mouse buttons) for use with the SAS System.

Many function keys come defined with the SAS System, and you can add and change the default definitions. To see what keys have been defined, open the KEYS window by clicking **Tools → Options → Keys** in the SAS System main menu. Figure 6.18 shows the default KEYS window.

Figure 6.18 KEYS Window

KEYS <DMKEYS>
Key Definition
F1 help
F2 reshow
F3 end; /*gsubmit buffer=def
F4 recall
F5 wpgm
F6 log
F7 output
F8 zoom off;submit
F9 keys
F11 command focus
F12
SHF F1 subtop
SHF F2
SHF F6
SHF F7 left
SHF F8 right
SHF F9
SHF F10 wpopup
SHF F11
SHF F12
CTL F1
CTL F2
CTL F3
CTL F11
CTL F12
ALT F1
ALT F2
ALT F3
ALT F11
ALT F12
CTL B libname
CTL D dir
CTL E clear
CTL G
CTL H help
CTL I options
CTL J
CTL K cut
CTL L log
CTL M mark
CTL Q filename
CTL R rfind

Use the scroll bars or PageUp and PageDown keys to see what keys are defined. Use Table 6.7 to understand the key name abbreviations.

Table 6.7 Abbreviations Used in the KEYS Window

Abbreviation	Key
SHF	Shift key
CTL	Control key
ALT	Alt key
RMB	right mouse button
MMB[*]	middle mouse button

[*] If you have a two-button mouse, MMB is not listed in the KEYS window.

To define a key, type the command that you want associated with that key in the **Definition** column. To assign a string of commands to a single key, separate the commands with a semicolon.

Note

> You can also define function keys specific to the Enhanced Editor. See Chapter 7 for more information.

Returning to the Default Key Definitions: When you close the KEYS window, the changes you've made are saved to your SASUSER.PROFILE catalog in an entry named DMKEYS. If you ever want to go back to the default key definitions, delete the DMKEYS entry from your SASUSER.PROFILE catalog and close your SAS session. The next time you invoke the SAS System, the KEYS window lists the default function key definitions.

An alternative to deleting the DMKEYS entry is to rename it. (This prevents the SAS System from loading the definitions stored in the file.) Because the SAS System cannot find the DMKEYS entry, it uses the default key definitions. When you want to use your customized definitions again, rename the entry back to DMKEYS.

Note

> Windows also defines some useful keys. Refer to Table 1.1 in Chapter 1 for a list of keys you may find helpful while working with the SAS System.

Changing the Display Font

FasTip: Click **Tools → Options → Fonts**.

You may not like the default font (Sasfont) used in SAS System windows. Or, you may want to change the font size (the default is 8 points for low-resolution screens and 10 points for high-resolution screens). To change the SAS System display font, click **Tools → Options → Fonts** in the SAS System main menu. This opens the Font dialog box.

Note

> The **Fonts** menu choice is not available if the Enhanced Editor is the active window. For information about changing the font used in the Enhanced Editor, see Chapter 7.

Now choose the font and type size you want to use. Figure 6.19 shows the Font dialog box.

Figure 6.19 Font Dialog Box for Changing the Display Font

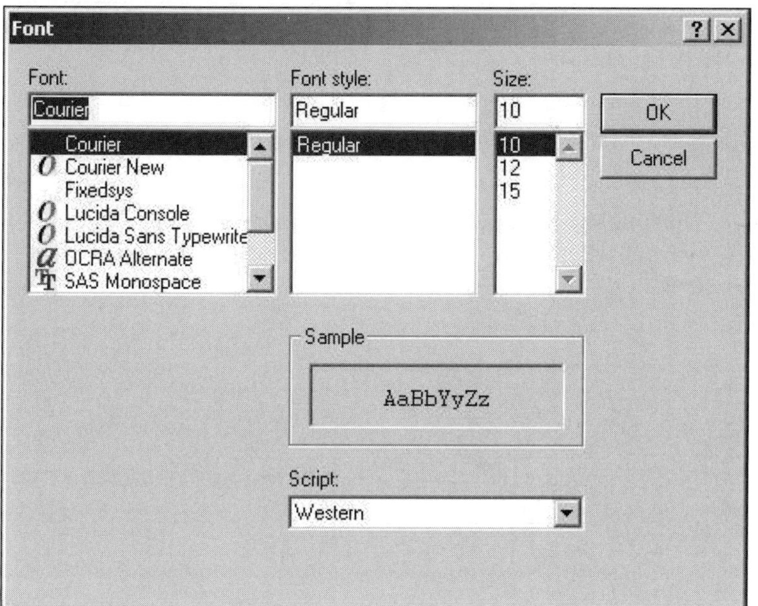

Only monospace fonts work well with the SAS System—proportional fonts do not produce satisfactory results. By default, the SAS System uses the Sasfont font in windows. Other monospace fonts that are common include Courier and IBMPCDOS.

Whether or not the font setting is retained from one SAS session to the next depends on whether you have **Save settings on exit** checked in the Preferences dialog box (see "Setting Session Preferences" earlier in this chapter for more information).

Note

> The font you choose in the Font dialog box accessed through the **Tools → Options** menu affects only the font used in SAS windows. To affect the font used for printer output, use the **Font** button in the Print Setup dialog box. See Chapter 5 for more information.

Appendix 4 contains more information on adjusting the font size used by the SAS System.

Using the Program Editor instead of the Enhanced Editor

What's New: The Program Editor Options dialog box has been redesigned; the Program Editor is no longer the default editor.

Although the Enhanced Editor is the default editor, the Program Editor is only a few mouse clicks away, if you prefer this familiar environment.

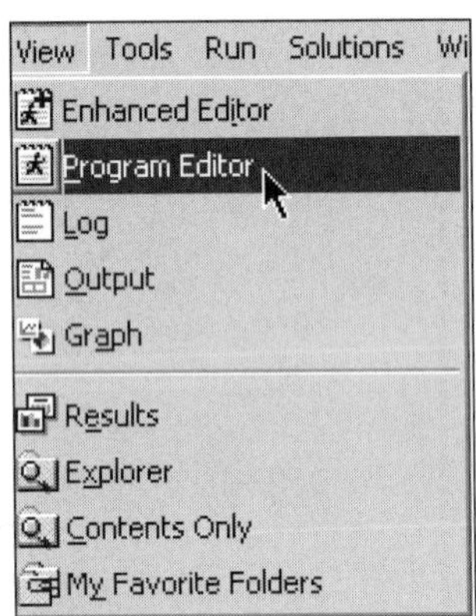

Opening the Program Editor: To open the Program Editor window, click **View → Program Editor** in the SAS System main menu.

If the Program Editor has previously been open and then closed in a SAS session but was not cleared of text, the next time you open the Program Editor, any text that was in the window when it was closed is still there (even if you did not save it).

Note

An alternative method of opening the Program Editor is to issue the WPGM command from the command bar. This works only if the **Use Enhanced Editor** option is deselected on the **Edit** tab in the Preferences dialog box.

Adjusting Program Editor Options: You can adjust many aspects of the Program Editor using the Program Editor Options dialog box. To open this dialog box, make the Program Editor the active window. Now click **Tools → Options → Program Editor** in the SAS System main menu (or issue the EDOP command from the command bar).

Figure 6.20 shows the resulting dialog box.

Figure 6.20 Editor Options Dialog Box for the Program Editor Window

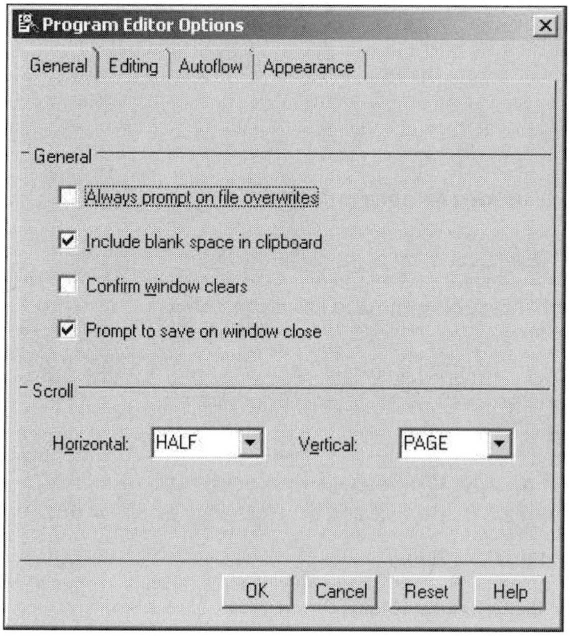

Note

There is a similar Options dialog box for the Log, Output, and NOTEPAD windows, as well.

When you are finished modifying option values on the various tabs, click **OK** to close the Program Editor Options dialog box.

Making the Program Editor the Default Editor: You can change the default editor from the Enhanced Editor to the Program Editor by using the Preferences dialog box. Follow these steps:

1. Click **Tools** → **Options** → **Preferences**.
2. Click the **Edit** tab.
3. Deselect the **Use Enhanced Editor** check box.

An alternative to using the Preferences dialog box is to set the NOENHANCEDEDITOR system option at SAS start-up, such as in the SAS configuration file or in the SAS command.

Although you can still open Enhanced Editor windows through the **View** menu, the next time you start a SAS session, an Enhanced Editor window will not be opened by default. Instead, the Program Editor is used.

Making the Program Editor Window Look Familiar: You may have liked how the Program Editor and other windows looked in older versions of the SAS System in mainframe environments, with line numbers, a command line, no tools, status areas, or scroll bars. You can adjust the settings of various options in the SAS System to emulate the "old" look. Use Table 6.8 to accomplish the tasks that interest you.

Table 6.8 Adjusting the Look and Feel of the Program Editor

To Do This...	Follow These Steps
Activate line numbers	Issue the NUMS ON command from the command bar. **Note:** You can also turn line numbers on in other SAS Text Editor windows, such as NOTEPAD and Source.
Turn on command lines	1. Click **Tools** → **Options** → **Preferences** in the SAS System main menu to open the Preferences dialog box. 2. Click the **View** tab. 3. Select **Command line**. 4. Close the Preferences dialog box.
Turn off the scroll bars and status area	1. Click **Tools** → **Options** → **Preferences** in the SAS System main menu to open the Preferences dialog box. 2. Click the **View** tab. 3. Deselect **Vertical scroll bar**, **Horizontal scroll bar**, and **Status line**. 4. Close the Preferences dialog box.
Turn off the command bar and tool bar	1. Click **Tools** → **Customize** in the SAS System main menu. 2. Deselect **Command Bar** and **Application Toolbar**. 3. Close the Customize Tools dialog box.

Customizing the SAS Help and Documentation System

While SAS Help and Documentation is extensive, you may find it useful to add your own help files to the system. For example, your company may have customized applications, or coding rules, or other information you'd like to make available to SAS users.

The key to adding files to SAS Help and Documentation is the HELPREGISTER system option. This option is valid in the SAS configuration file or the SAS command. It has the following basic syntax:

```
-HELPREGISTER "menu-string" file-location "status-line-message"
```

For example, the following system option specification adds the C:\CodingGuidelines.htm file to the SAS **Help** menu (the code must be on a single line in the SAS configuration file):

```
-HELPREGISTER "Coding Guidelines" C:\CodingGuidelines.htm
"Guidelines for SAS programmers at Our Company"
```

Figure 6.21 shows the new file in the **Help** menu and shows the explanatory text in the status line of the main SAS window.

Figure 6.21 Adding Custom Help Files to the Help Menu

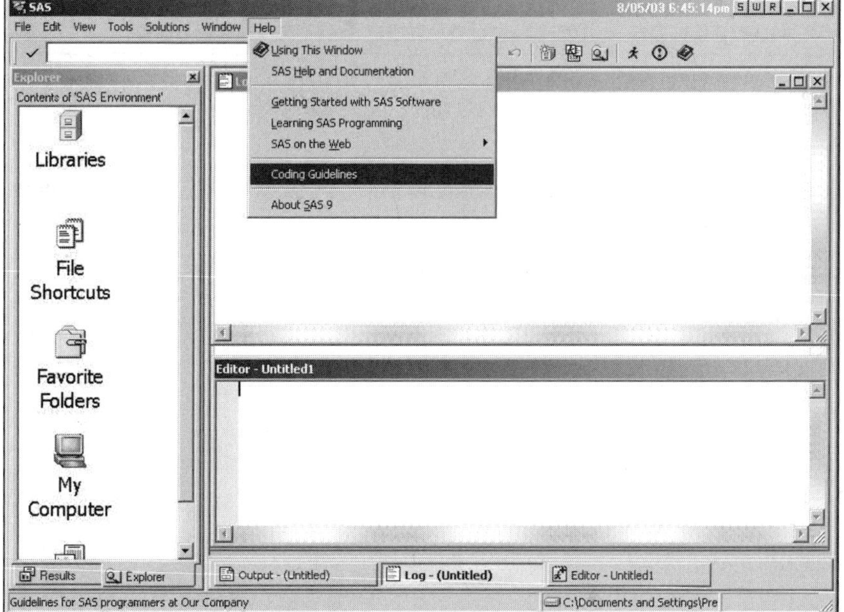

There are a few more parameters you can use with the HELPREGISTER system option, to control exactly what topic displays, and to specify the file type exactly. More details and examples of the HELPREGISTER system option are available from the SAS System online help.

Note

> Any parameter value that contains spaces must be enclosed in double quotation marks. You can also use the HELPLOC system option to specify the folder or subfolder that contains help files, then just specify the filename in the *file-location* parameter.

Use multiple HELPREGISTER system option specifications to add multiple files to the **Help** menu. You can add up to 20 files to the **Help** menu.

Note

> Only WinHelp (.hlp), HTML (.htm), and Microsoft HTML Help (.chm) files will work with the HELPREGISTER system option.

Customizing the Table of Contents and Index: It is possible to provide a customized table of contents and index that are displayed when you click **SAS Help and Documentation** in the **Help** menu, using the HELPTOC and HELPINDEX system options. A full discussion of this topic is beyond the scope of this book; see SAS Help and Documentation for more information.

Saving Your Changes to the Windowing Environment

After you've made changes to your SAS windowing interface, you may not want to make these changes again. You can tell the SAS System to save all the changes you've made. Or, you can save the changes only to a particular window.

Saving All Your Changes: To save all the windowing interface changes you have made, follow these steps:

1. Click **Tools** → **Options** → **Preferences** in the SAS System main menu.
2. In the Preferences dialog box, click the **General** tab.
3. Select the **Save settings on exit** option.
4. Click **OK**.

Following these steps is equivalent to issuing a WSAVE ALL command from the command bar, and creates an Awswsave.WSAVE entry and several other WSAVE entries in your SASUSER.PROFILE catalog.

Saving Changes to a Particular Window: To save the changes you've made in a particular window but not to other windows, follow these steps:

1. Make the window you want to save active.
2. Issue a WSAVE command from the command bar.

This creates a *window-name*.WSAVE entry in your SASUSER.PROFILE catalog.

Returning to the Default Environment

If you want to undo only one change from among many, you may want to redo the command that implemented the change. For example, if you have used the COLOR command to change many aspects of several windows and want to save the majority of the changes, your best approach is to reissue the COLOR command for the few window aspects you want to change. Or, if you are happy with most of the settings in the Preferences dialog box but want to change one of them, open the dialog box, make your change, and click **OK**.

If, however, you want to completely undo a set of changes, such as all color settings or all tool bar changes, use the techniques in Table 6.9 on page 174. Where several actions are listed, try each of them in order—you may have to take several steps to completely return to the default settings.

Note

To see the entry types for catalog entries in the SAS Explorer window, click **View → Details** in the SAS System main menu. You may have to scroll or resize the SAS Explorer window to see the **Type** column. You can also use the **Description** field in the SAS Explorer window to help find specific entries.

Table 6.9 Returning to the Default Windowing Environment

Window Element	To Return to Default Settings
Keys	Delete or rename the Dmkeys entry in your SASUSER.PROFILE catalog.
Tools	Open the Customize Tools dialog box, click the **Customize** tab, and click the Restore Defaults icon: . Delete all .TOOLBOX entries in your SASUSER.PROFILE catalog.
Colors	Open the SASCOLOR window and click **Defaults**. Delete all .WSAVE entries in your SASUSER.PROFILE catalog. Delete the SAS.CPARMS entry in your SASUSER.PROFILE catalog.
Preferences	Delete the *xyz*wsave entries from your SASUSER.PROFILE catalog, where *xyz* represents the various tabs in the Preferences dialog box.
Window size and position	Click **Window** → **Resize** in the SAS System main menu. Delete .WSAVE entries with a window name from your SASUSER.PROFILE catalog. Delete or rename the DMSDEF entry in your SASUSER.PROFILE catalog. Restart your SAS session.

7 Using Advanced Features of the Enhanced Editor

Introduction

Chapter 3 showed you how to perform the basic editing tasks while using the Enhanced Editor. But this powerful editor goes far beyond just typing in and saving programs. Browse through this chapter, and see how the Enhanced Editor can make your programming more efficient.

Note

> The screen captures in this book are in grayscale. To see color versions of the screens in this chapter, visit this book's Companion Web Site. The URL of this Web site is listed in the "Welcome to SAS 9.1 for Windows" section at the beginning of this book.

Overview of Enhanced Editor Features

The Enhanced Editor offers several features found in other code editors (such as HTML editors) that enable you to program and debug more easily. Some of these features are as follows:

- context-sensitive help for the SAS language and procedures
- color schemes for keywords, data, and other programming elements, with the ability to create your own color schemes
- keyboard macros that play back a series of editing commands
- text abbreviation shortcuts that save time when you have to enter long, repetitive strings of text
- bookmarks associated with lines of code so you can easily navigate long programs

- support for user-defined keywords
- hierarchical structure for SAS code, with the ability to expand and collapse blocks of code
- support for multiple views of the same file
- support for file types other than .sas.

These features are discussed in detail in the rest of this chapter. The majority of the chapter illustrates these features via a tutorial.

Getting Help

What's New: With SAS 9.1, the context-sensitive help is expanded to include all SAS language element names.

FastTip: Press F1 to receive help on the keyword or procedure name in which the cursor is positioned.

Even if you have been a SAS programmer for decades, sometimes it is helpful to be reminded of a statement's syntax. With the Enhanced Editor, such help is only one keystroke away. Simply place the cursor somewhere in a SAS keyword in your code, then press F1.

When you do so, the Enhanced Editor accesses SAS Help and Documentation and displays the relevant help topic. For example, if you place your cursor in the keyword DATA, the DATA statement help topic appears. If there is more than one relevant help topic, a topic list box appears from which you can select the appropriate topic.

Preparing for the Tutorial

The best way to learn how to use something is to just DO IT. Therefore, the rest of this chapter presents a tutorial that teaches you how to use the Enhanced Editor. Before beginning the tutorial, follow these steps:

1. Close your SAS session (if you have one open already), and restart SAS. This will give you a clean slate to work with.
2. Clear the Log window (**Edit** → **Clear all**).
3. Maximize the Enhanced Editor window.

This chapter assumes you have read at least Chapters 1–4 of this book, and know how to open and save files, use the menus and dialog boxes, and perform basic navigation in the Enhanced Editor window.

Modifying the Appearance of Code

The Enhanced Editor chooses a default color scheme with which to display your code. To see this default color scheme, open the DATAMANIP.SAS program we worked with in Chapter 2. Figure 7.1 shows how the screen should look.

Figure 7.1 Code with the Default Color Scheme in the Enhanced Editor Window

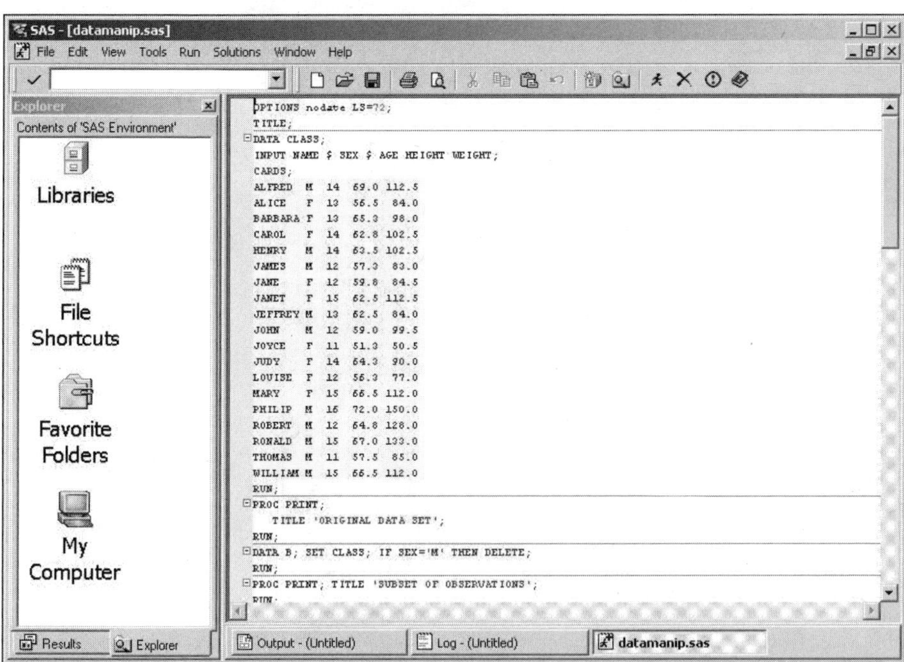

As you can see from viewing the program on screen, keywords are in different shades of blue, CARDS data are highlighted in yellow, and quoted strings are purple, while numeric strings (such as the value of the LS option in the first line of code) are green.

To choose a different color scheme, or to define your own, use the Enhanced Editor Options dialog box. Open this dialog box by clicking **Tools → Options → Enhanced Editor** in the main SAS System menu. Figure 7.2 shows this dialog box.

Figure 7.2 Enhanced Editor Options Dialog Box

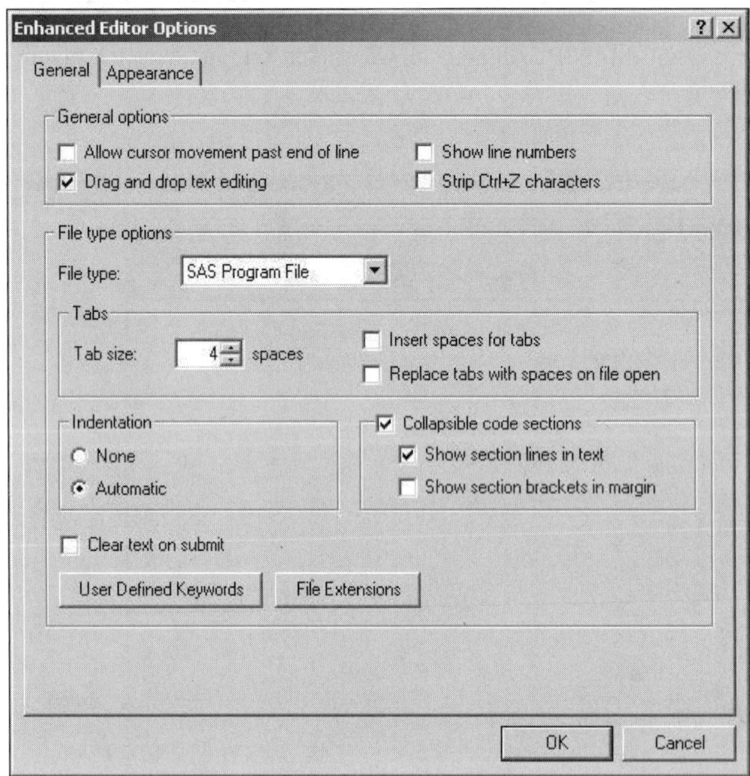

Click the **Appearance** tab, which is shown in Figure 7.3.

Figure 7.3 Appearance Tab of the Enhanced Editor Options Dialog Box

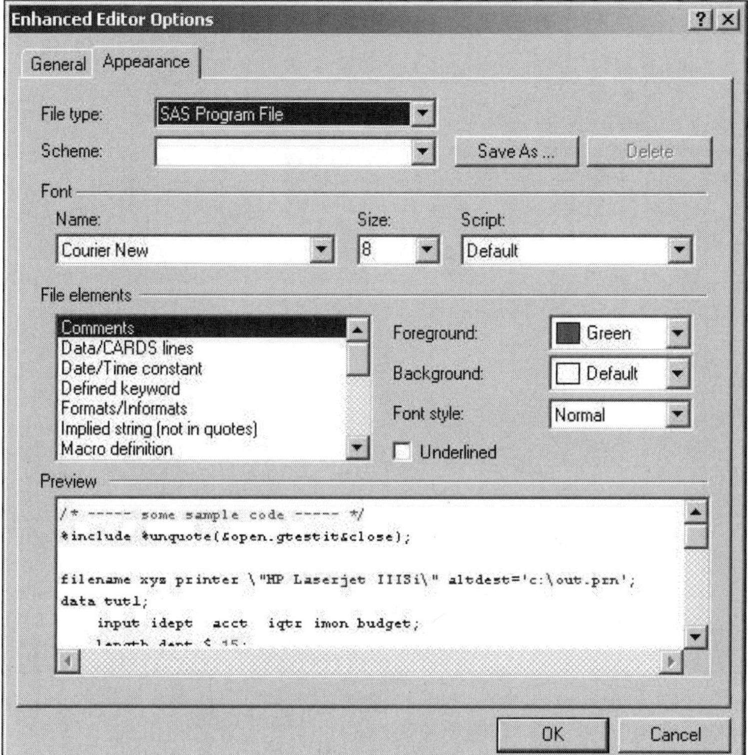

Choosing a Predefined Color Scheme: To choose a different predefined color scheme, click the down arrow next to the **Scheme** field, and choose a scheme other than **Default**. For example, choose **Retro**. The **Preview** field at the bottom of the dialog box shows what the color scheme will look like. In the Retro scheme, procedure names are purple, and CARDS data has no highlighting. Figure 7.4 shows the DATAMANIP.SAS program displayed with the Retro scheme.

Figure 7.4 Retro Color Scheme

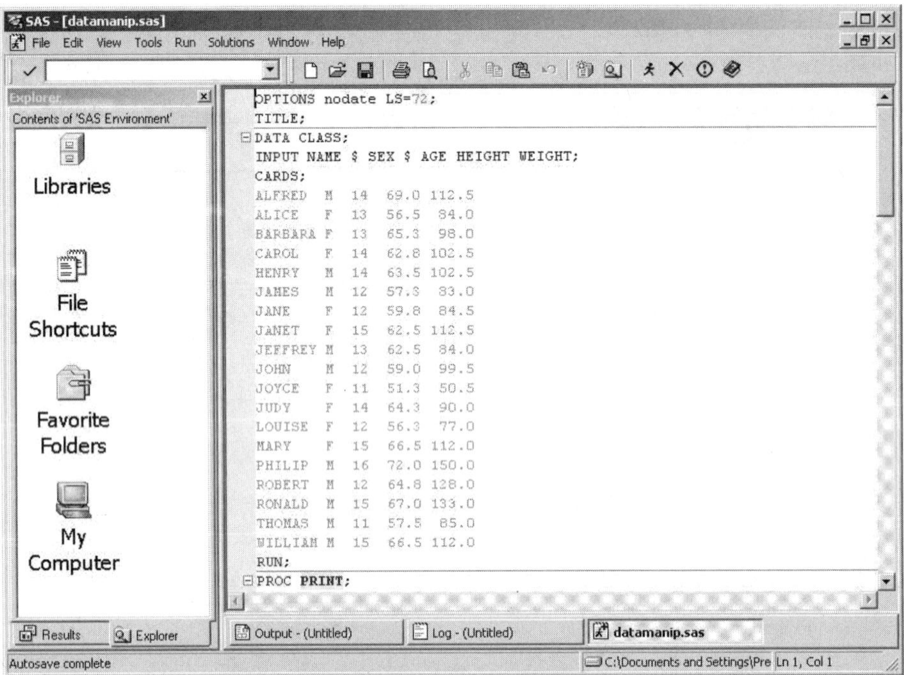

Defining Your Own Color Scheme: If none of the defined color schemes suit your taste, you can define and save your own color schemes. To work through this section of the tutorial, follow these steps:

1. Open the Enhanced Editor Options dialog box (click **Tools** → **Options** → **Enhanced Editor**) and click the **Appearance** tab.
2. In the **File elements** field, select **Comments**.
3. In the **Foreground** field, click the down arrow, scroll the list up, and click **Maroon**.
4. In the **Background** field, click the down arrow, scroll the list up, and click **Yellow**.
5. In the **File elements** field, select **Data/CARDS lines**.
6. In the **Foreground** field, click the down arrow, scroll the list up, and click **Black**.
7. In the **Background** field, click the down arrow, scroll the list up, and click **Teal**.
8. In the **File elements** field, scroll the list down and select **String constant**.
9. In the **Foreground** field, click **Custom**, which displays the Color dialog box, shown in Figure 7.5.

Figure 7.5 Color Dialog Box Used to Define Custom Colors

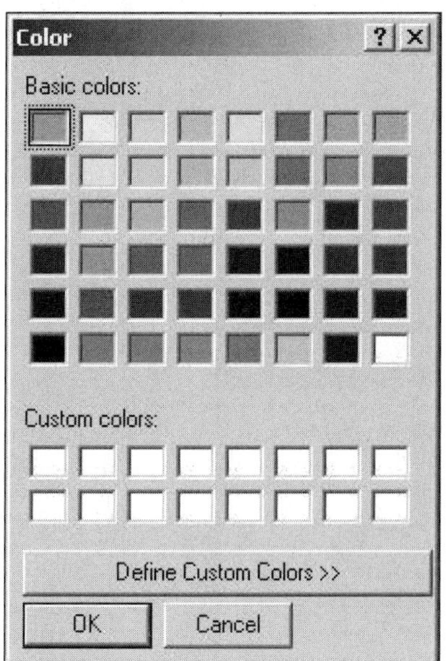

10. In the Color dialog box, choose a color that appeals to you, such as the fourth color selection down on the right side (a sort of electric blue-violet). If none of the colors listed appeal to you, you can click the **Define Custom Colors** button to display a continuous color gradient, and choose a new color from that.
11. Click **OK** to close the Color dialog box.
12. Click the **Save As** button in the Enhanced Editor Options dialog box to save your new color scheme. This displays the Save Scheme dialog box, as shown in Figure 7.6.

Figure 7.6 Save Scheme Dialog Box

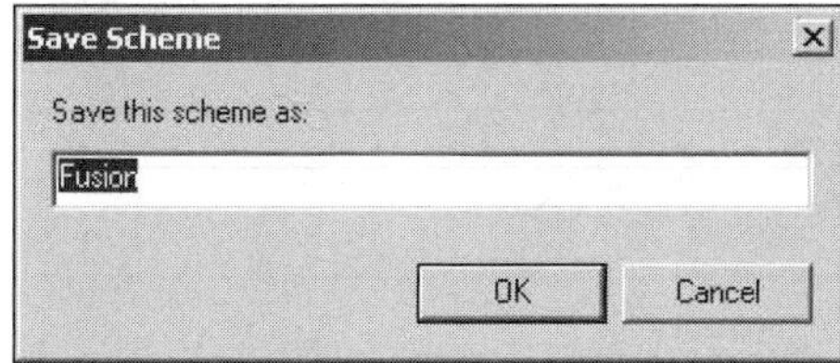

13. Type a new name in the **Save this scheme as** field. For our example, type `MyWildScheme`.
14. Click **OK** to complete the save operation.
15. Click **OK** to close the Enhanced Editor Options dialog box.

Figure 7.7 shows the DATAMANIP.SAS program with the new color scheme.

Figure 7.7 The New Color Scheme in Action

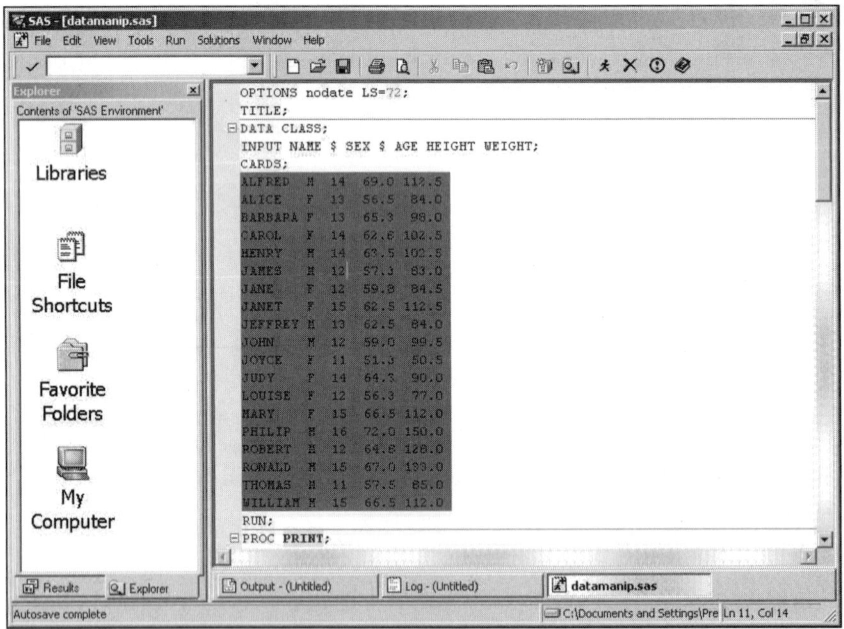

Note

> In this example, we reset the colors for only a few file elements; you can change them all if you want.

Defining and Using Macros

FastTip: Press ALT-SHIFT-R to start and stop recording a macro.

Much of programming lies not in designing elegant solutions, but in the day-to-day drudgery of typing in code. The Enhanced Editor enables you to define macros (much like Microsoft Word macros) that can make your work more efficient. By recording a series of keystrokes and mouse clicks, then assigning that recorded series to a single key, you can shorten the time it takes to accomplish repetitive tasks.

Note

Keystrokes outside of your SAS session (such as in other applications) are not recorded.

Defining a New Macro: The DATAMANIP.SAS program has a lot of code, but not many comments throughout it. For our tutorial, we're going to define a macro that adds a comment block after every RUN statement. (In the next section, we'll use these comment sections to illustrate text abbreviations.) To work through this part of the tutorial, follow these steps:

1. Place your cursor at the beginning of the DATAMANIP.SAS program (CTRL-HOME).
2. To begin recording the macro, click **Tools → Keyboard Macros → Record New Macro**. This puts your SAS session into record mode, and each of your keystrokes or mouse clicks is added to the macro. To remind you that you are in record mode, the cursor changes to a picture of a cassette tape.
3. Now we'll define our "insert comments" macro. First, we need to find a RUN statement. So, click **Edit → Find**, type `RUN;` in the **Find text** field, then click **Find Next**.
4. Click **Close** to close the Find dialog box.
5. Move the cursor to the end of the RUN statement line (press END).
6. Press ENTER twice.
7. Type the following code: `/* Put comment block here */`
8. Press ENTER again. This finishes the keystrokes we want to record.
9. To stop recording, click **Tools → Keyboard Macros → Stop Recording**. This displays the Save Keyboard Macro dialog box, shown in Figure 7.8, where you can give the macro a name and assign the macro to a particular keystroke.

Figure 7.8 Save Keyboard Macro Dialog Box

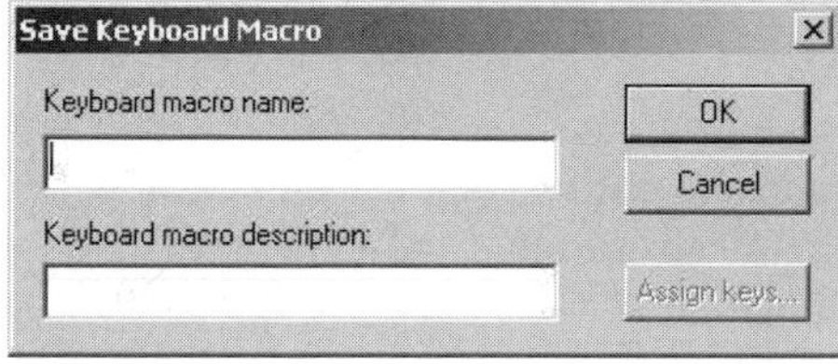

10. For our macro, type `Insert Comment` in the **Keyboard macro name** field.

11. In the **Keyboard macro description** field, type the following: `Inserts a comment block after every RUN; statement.`
12. To assign a keystroke to the macro, click **Assign keys**. This displays the Assign Keys dialog box, as shown in Figure 7.9.

Figure 7.9 Assign Keys Dialog Box

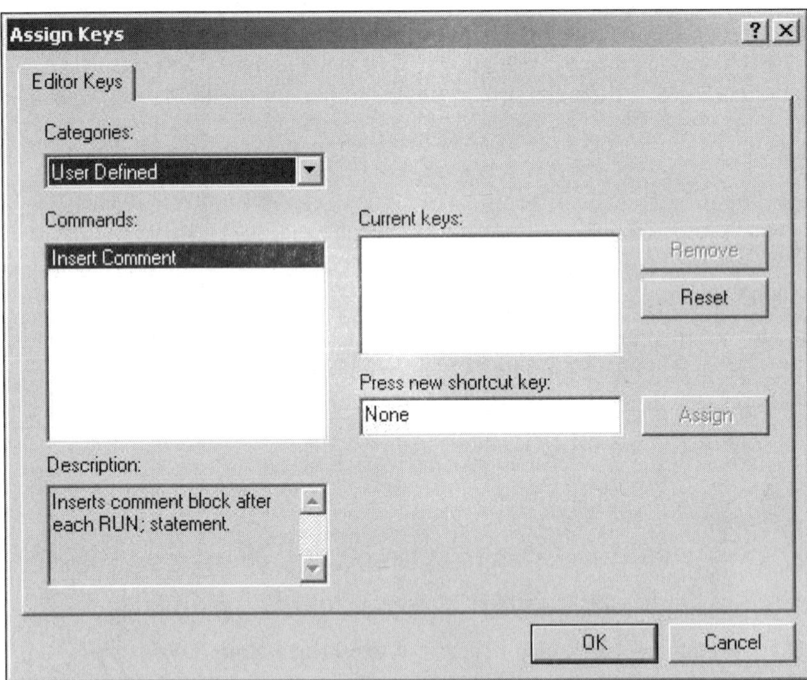

13. Highlight the word **None** in the **Press new shortcut key** field, then press the keystroke you want to assign to the macro. In this case, let's use ALT-I. When you press the keystroke, the field is updated to reflect the key you pressed.

Note

If the keystroke you choose is already assigned to a macro, the text below the **Press new shortcut key** field will indicate what action the keystroke is assigned to. If you want to overwrite the assignment with the new macro, continue. Otherwise, highlight the keystroke name again and try a new keystroke.

14. When the **Press new shortcut key** field contains the keystroke you want to assign to the macro, click **Assign**. The new keystroke is now listed in the **Current keys** field.

Note

> If you want, a macro can have several different keystrokes assigned to it.

15. Click **OK** to close the Assign Keys dialog box.

Your macro is now recorded and ready to use. Macros are not file-specific. Once saved, they can be used in any file you have open in the Enhanced Editor.

Executing a Macro: Now that you have defined the Insert Comment macro, executing it is as simple as pressing the shortcut keystroke you assigned to the macro in the Assign Keys dialog box. When you press ALT-I, the macro is executed, and a comment block appears after the second RUN statement in the DATAMANIP.SAS program. Press ALT-I 24 more times to complete the task of adding a comment block after each RUN statement in the rest of the DATAMANIP.SAS program.

Caution

> Editing changes accomplished with a macro cannot be undone with the UNDO command or its keyboard shortcut, CTRL-Z.

Editing a Macro: Editing a macro works similarly to editing a text abbreviation definition, which is described in the next section.

Defining and Using Text Abbreviations

FasTip: Press CTRL-SHIFT-A to create a new text abbreviation.

Press ENTER to expand a text abbreviation to its full text when the word tip is displayed.

Press ALT-F1 to display the word tip for a text abbreviation name.

Another labor-saving feature of the Enhanced Editor is the ability to associate a short text string with a longer text string, and to expand the short string to the long string with a simple keystroke. (You may have used a similar feature in Microsoft Word, where it is called AutoText.) Text abbreviations are really just a special case of macros, where the macro deletes the text abbreviation name and replaces it with a defined text string.

Defining Text Abbreviations: For our tutorial, we'll define two text strings, to be used in the newly created comment blocks. One string will be for comments for procedure blocks; the other string will be for comments for DATA step blocks. To work through this section of the tutorial, follow these steps:

1. Move the cursor to the beginning of the DATAMANIP.SAS program (press CTRL-HOME).
2. Click **Tools → Add Abbreviation** in the main SAS System menu. This displays the Add Abbreviation dialog box, as shown in Figure 7.10.

Figure 7.10 Add Abbreviation Dialog Box

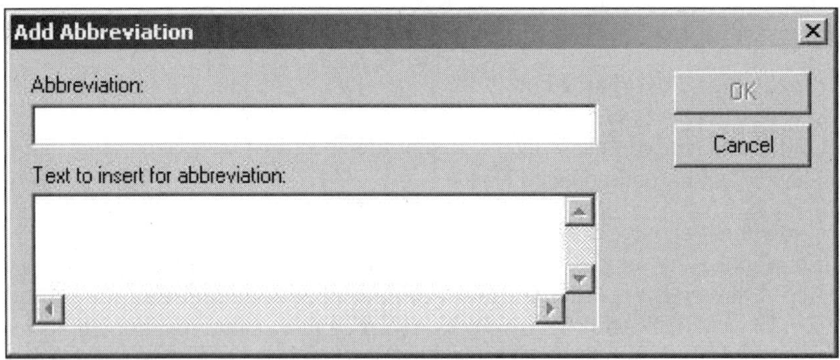

3. Type the short string in the **Abbreviation** field. For our first string, we'll use the abbreviation ProcComm.

4. In the **Text to insert for abbreviation** field, type the full text you want the abbreviation to stand for. For the ProcComm abbreviation, type the following text (with carriage returns, just as it looks here):

```
Purpose of Procedure:
Date Procedure Added:
Name of Programmer:
Data Sets Accessed by Procedure:
Other Notes:
```

5. When you have finished typing the text, click **OK** to close the Add Abbreviation dialog box.

6. Repeat steps 2–5, except use DataComm for the abbreviation name, and use the following text for the full text string:

```
Physical Location for Data Set(s):
Date DATA Step Added:
Name of Programmer:
Other Notes:
```

Using Text Abbreviations: Using defined text abbreviations works as follows:

1. Type the abbreviation.
2. Press ENTER to expand the abbreviation.

To illustrate this, we'll add a procedure comment and a DATA step comment to the DATAMANIP.SAS program, using the ProcComm and DataComm abbreviations. To work through this part of the tutorial, follow these steps:

1. Highlight the words `Put comment block here` in the first comment block.

2. Type `ProcComm`. When you have finished typing the word, a word tip appears that shows the first part of the full text string.
3. Press ENTER. The text is expanded.
4. Now scroll down to the comment block that precedes the next DATA step.
5. Highlight the words `Put comment block here` in the comment block.
6. Type `DataComm`.
7. Press ENTER. The text is expanded.

Note

Pressing TAB will also expand the word tip.

Some things to remember about using text abbreviations:

- The text abbreviation name is case-sensitive. For example, typing `datacomm` or `dataComm` will not cause the word tip to appear in our example.
- If you move your cursor after typing the text abbreviation name, then place the cursor at the end of the text abbreviation name again, you must press ALT-F1 to cause the word tip to appear.

Editing a Text Abbreviation Definition: It is quite probable that after you define a text abbreviation, you will want to edit it at some point. The Enhanced Editor allows you to do so through the macro-editing features. (You can use this same technique to edit any macro you have defined in the Enhanced Editor.)

To illustrate how to edit macros, we will edit the ProcComm text abbreviation we created in the previous section. To work through this part of the tutorial, follow these steps:

1. Click **Tools** → **Keyboard Macros** → **Macros**. This opens the Keyboard Macros dialog box, shown in Figure 7.11.

Figure 7.11 Keyboard Macros Dialog Box

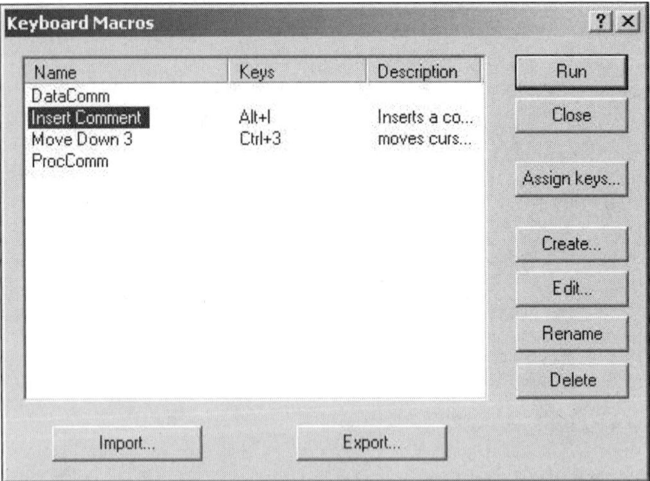

2. Click the macro name, ProcComm, in the **Name** list.
3. Click **Edit**. This displays the Edit Keyboard Macro dialog box, shown in Figure 7.12.

Figure 7.12 Edit Keyboard Macro Dialog Box

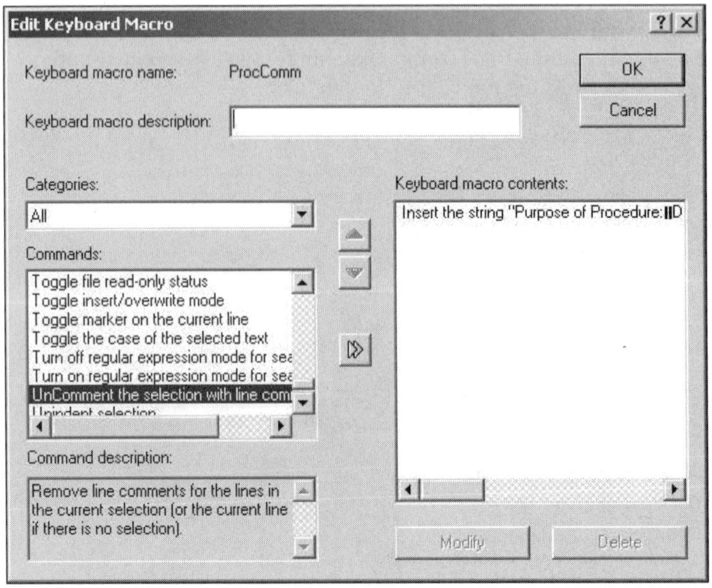

4. The **Keyboard macro contents** box shows the command that inserts the full text string.
5. Double-click on this command, which displays the Insert String dialog box, shown in Figure 7.13.

Figure 7.13 Insert String Dialog Box

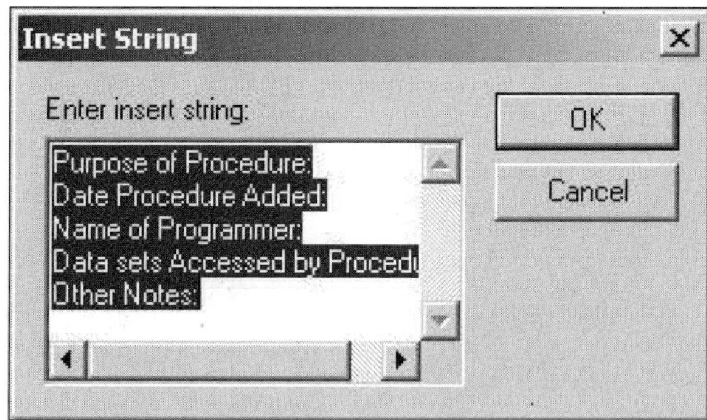

6. Change “Data sets” to “Data Sets” in the next-to-last line.
7. Click **OK** to close the Insert String dialog box.
8. Click **OK** to close the Edit Keyboard Macro dialog box.
9. Click **Close** to close the Keyboard Macros dialog box.

The change you made is now in effect, and will be reflected the next time you use the text abbreviation.

Creating Bookmarks

When working with long segments of code, you may find it useful to bookmark particular lines. For example, if you are walking through a program and get interrupted, bookmarking the line will remind you where you left off when you return to working with the program.

To set a bookmark, place the cursor in the line you want to mark, then press CTRL-F2.

Figure 7.14 shows the DATAMANIP.SAS program with a bookmark next to the comment block for the second DATA step in the program.

Figure 7.14 Example of a Code Bookmark

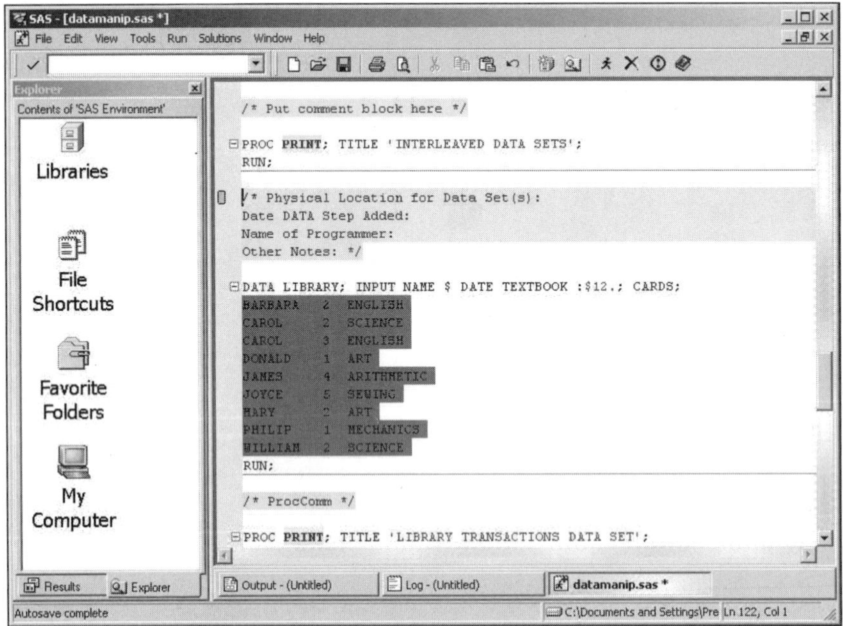

To remove a bookmark, place the cursor in the marked line, and press CTRL-F2 again (it acts as a toggle).

Currently, you cannot move to a specific bookmark. However, you can move to the next bookmark by pressing F2, and to the previous bookmark by pressing SHIFT-F2.

Caution

Currently, bookmarks are not saved with a file. When you close the file, all bookmark information is lost.

Working with Blocks of Code

The Enhanced Editor recognizes the hierarchical structure of the SAS language, and groups code into blocks based on keywords such as PROC and DATA. These blocks are by default expanded, so you can see all your code. To indicate expanded blocks of code, the left margin of the Enhanced Editor displays a minus sign, similar to the icon used in the SAS Explorer and Windows Explorer to indicate expanded directory structures. Figure 7.15 shows the DATAMANIP.SAS program, with the mouse pointer indicating the first code block icon.

Figure 7.15 Mouse Pointer Indicating the Expanded Code Block Icon

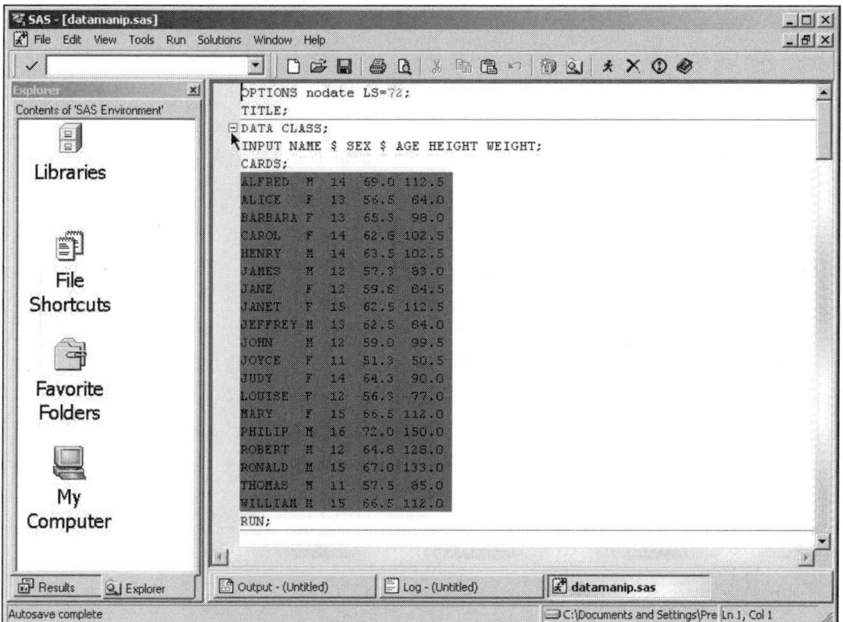

You may find that collapsing some code blocks makes it easier to scroll through your code and find what you are looking for. To collapse a block of code, click the minus sign. The icon changes to a plus sign, and only the first line of the code block is displayed. Figure 7.16 shows the first code block of the DATAMANIP.SAS program in collapsed mode.

Figure 7.16 Mouse Pointer Indicating the Collapsed Code Block Icon

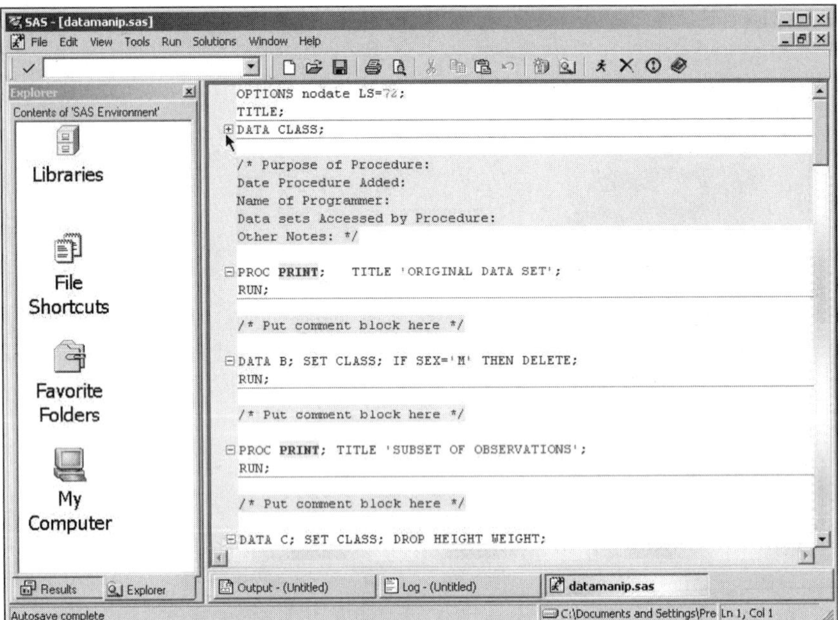

The online help for the Enhanced Editor contains more information about selecting text, pasting text, finding text, and replacing text within collapsed code blocks. To access this help, follow this path: **Help → SAS Help and Documentation → Using SAS Software in Your Operating Environment → Using SAS in Windows → Running SAS under Windows → Using the SAS Editors under Windows → Using the Enhanced Editor**. In the topic window click **Using the Enhanced Editor Window → Using Collapsible Code Sections**.

Working with Multiple Views of the Same File

You may want to look at two parts of your code at the same time. For example, sometimes it can be helpful to see the DATA step that creates a SAS data set, but at the same time be looking at another section of the code that references that data set. (This can help prevent the mental stress of thinking, "Now WHAT did I call that variable…??")

To open a copy of an already-open program displayed in the Enhanced Editor window, first make sure the Enhanced Editor window is active. Now click **Window → New Window** in the SAS System main menu. The SAS Taskbar shows a second Enhanced Editor window is now open. You can resize each of the Enhanced Editor windows to suit your needs. Figure 7.17 shows two copies of the DATAMANIP.SAS program open, with the top copy scrolled to the second DATA step, while the bottom copy displays the first DATA step.

Figure 7.17 Looking at Two Copies of the Same File at the Same Time

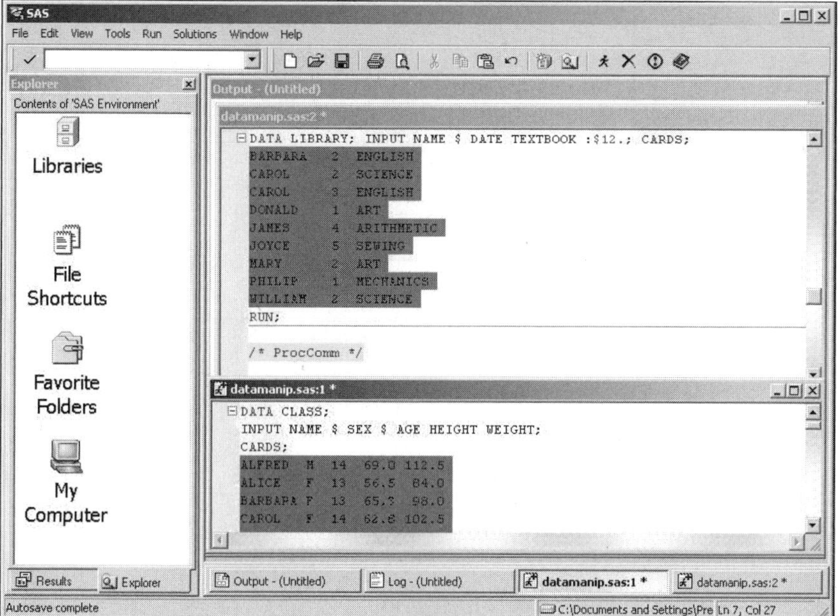

The copies are identified in the Enhanced Editor window title bars by a colon and the copy number (in this case, datamanip.sas:1 and datamanip.sas:2). Any changes you make in one copy are immediately reflected in the other copy. Saving one copy is sufficient to make your changes permanent; you do not need to save both copies.

Creating User-Defined Keywords

As described in "Modifying the Appearance of Code" earlier in this chapter, the Enhanced Editor uses keywords to decide how to display your code, displaying recognized keywords in a different color from the color used for words it does not recognize. You may find it advantageous to add to the default list of keywords. The following section of the tutorial adds the keyword **SASUSER** to the list of keywords recognized by the Enhanced Editor:

1. Click **Tools → Options → Enhanced Editor** in the SAS System main menu.
2. Click the **General** tab.
3. Click the **User Defined Keywords** button (it is located near the bottom-left corner of the Enhanced Editor Options dialog box). This displays the User Defined Keywords dialog box, as shown in Figure 7.18.

Figure 7.18 User Defined Keywords Dialog Box

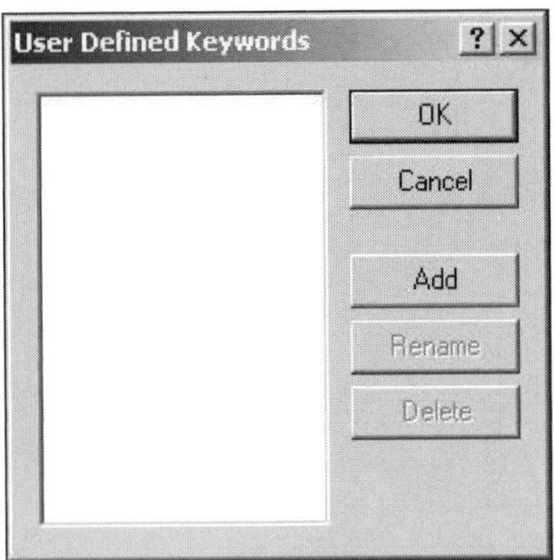

4. Click **Add**.
5. In the resulting highlighted text that says **NewKeyword**, type your user-defined keyword (in our case, SASUSER), then press ENTER. The new keyword is added to the list.
6. Click **OK** to close the User Defined Keywords dialog box.
7. Click **OK** to close the Enhanced Editor Options dialog box.

Now when you type SASUSER in the Enhanced Editor window, that word is displayed in the color chosen for keywords in the Enhanced Editor color scheme.

Keywords are not case-sensitive. Whether you type SASUSER, sasuser, or SasUser, it is still recognized as a keyword.

Using Other File Types

The Enhanced Editor recognizes several other file types besides SAS files, and displays them intelligently. Supported file types include HTML files (.htm and .html), XML files (.xml), and text files (.txt).

You can adjust the color coding used to display these types of files just as you can for .sas files, using the Enhanced Editor Options dialog box as described earlier in this chapter in "Modifying the Appearance of Code." Simply select **HTML Document** (for HTML or XML files) or **Text Document** (for text files) from the drop-down list in the **File type** field, then edit the appearance settings appropriately.

Keyboard Shortcuts

To make your SAS coding even more efficient, the Enhanced Editor supports a number of keyboard shortcuts, and you can define your own keyboard shortcuts as well.

Table 7.1 lists some of the default keyboard shortcuts; you can see the complete list by clicking **Tools → Options → Enhanced Editor Keys**.

Alternatively, follow this path: **Help → SAS Help and Documentation → Using SAS Software in Your Operating Environment → Using SAS in Windows → Appendices → Default Key Settings for Interactive SAS Sessions under Windows → Keyboard Shortcuts within the Enhanced Editor**.

Table 7.1 Partial List of Default Enhanced Editor Keyboard Shortcuts

Press This Key...	To Perform This Action
F1	Get help for the keyword or SAS procedure in which the cursor is located.
CTRL-F1	Execute the last recorded macro.
ALT-SHIFT-R	Start and stop macro recording.
CTRL-G	Go to a specified line.
CTRL-[or CTRL-]	Move the cursor to the matching brace or parenthesis.
ALT-[or ALT-]	Move the cursor to the matching DO/END keyword.
CTRL-SHIFT-W	Clean up white space.
CTRL-/	Add line comment characters to the selection.
CTRL-SHIFT-/	Remove line comment characters from the selection.
CTRL-SHIFT-A	Open the Add Abbreviation dialog box.
ALT-F1	Display the word tip for text abbreviation name when the cursor is at the end of the text abbreviation name.
CTRL-F2	Bookmark an unmarked line, or remove the bookmark from a marked line.
F2	Move the cursor to the next bookmark.
SHIFT-F2	Move the cursor to the previous bookmark.

Defining Your Own Keyboard Shortcuts: Defining your own keyboard shortcuts is equivalent to defining a macro. See "Defining and Using Macros" earlier in this chapter.

8 Using the SAS Output Delivery System

Introduction

What's New: The SAS Output Delivery System (ODS) supports a wide variety of output types beyond HTML, including PDF, RTF, XML, personalized tag sets, statistical graph output objects, and ODS documents.

The TEMPLATE procedure features many enhancements.

The DOCUMENT procedure enables you to generate many types of output and rearrange the output while running code only once.

In addition to the listing of SAS output displayed in the Output window (referred to as the LISTING destination), you can use the SAS Output Delivery System, first introduced in Version 7, to generate many different types of output, including HTML, PDF, FTF, XML, and personalized tag sets. ODS is available to both interactive and batch SAS sessions.

This chapter gives an overview of some of the features of ODS, including a few examples of new SAS 9.1 features. However, there is much more to ODS than you see here. For the full description of ODS capabilities, refer to other ODS-specific SAS documentation (visit support.sas.com to view the *Publications Catalog*).

Note

The screen captures in this book are in grayscale. To see color versions of the screens in this chapter, visit this book's Companion Web Site. The URL of this Web site is listed in the "Welcome to SAS 9.1 for Windows" section at the beginning of this book.

Understanding ODS Terminology

Before you can learn to use ODS, you need to understand some terms commonly used when talking about managing your output with ODS. Table 8.1 provides some definitions to keep in mind as you read the rest of this chapter.

Table 8.1 Basic ODS Terminology

data component	an entity that contains the results (characters and numbers) of a DATA step or PROC step that supports ODS
template	a framework that includes definitions of such things as style, tag set, columns, headers, and footers
style	a presentation design for your output that includes font, color, spacing, justification, and other specifications
output object	a data component paired with a format (template and style)
output object name	the name used for the output object
output destination	the file format in which you want your output stored (such as HTML or PDF)

Creating HTML Output

Using Dialog Boxes to Tell SAS You Want HTML Output: By default, the SAS System creates regular listing output. If you'd prefer output that looks more "Web-ready," you may want to produce HTML output instead. You can then use the .htm files created by SAS in Word documents or on your Web site without further modification.

To tell the SAS System you want to automatically generate HTML output, follow these steps:

1. Open the Preferences dialog box by clicking **Tools → Options → Preferences** in the SAS System main menu.

2. Click the **Results** tab. This tab is shown in Figure 8.1.

Figure 8.1 Results Tab of the Preferences Dialog Box

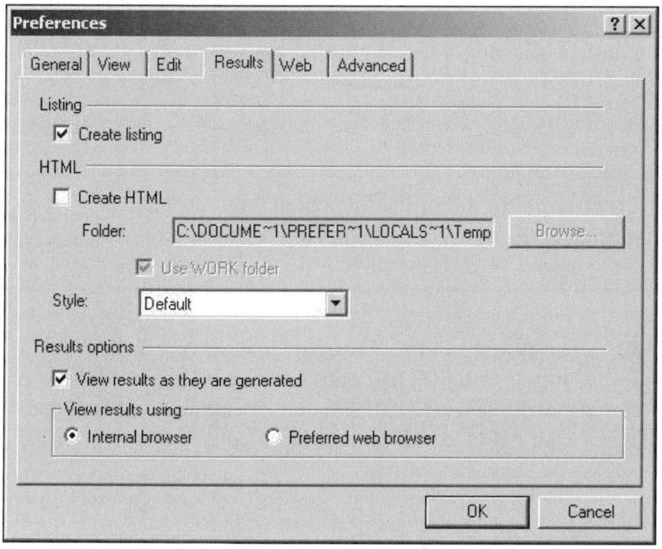

3. Select the **Create HTML** option and deselect the **Create listing** option.

   Note

   > If you want both HTML and listing output, select both the **Create listing** and **Create HTML** options; in this case, the listing output goes to the Output window and the HTML output goes to the .htm file and is displayed in the Results Viewer window.

4. To select a style, click the down arrow next to the **Style** field, and click the style you want.

   Caution

   > The style you choose affects all subsequent SAS output, until you change the style again.

5. By default, the HTML output is written to a temporary .htm file in your WORK data library.

   The default filename is sashtm#.htm. The # starts at 0 (and the 0 is omitted from the filename) and increases by one each time output is generated. (So, for example, if your code contains two PROC PRINT steps, two .htm files are created: sashtm.htm and sashtm1.htm.)

   To specify a permanent file for your HTML output, follow these steps:

   a. Deselect the **Use WORK folder** choice.

   b. Click in the **Folder** field and specify the folder where you want the output stored.

The filenames created in this folder are the same as the names of the temporary files: sashtm#.htm.

6. Decide whether you want to view the HTML output in the internal SAS browser (the default) or your preferred Web browser (such as Microsoft Internet Explorer or Netscape), and select the appropriate option.

   Note

   > If you do not have Microsoft Internet Explorer 4.0 or later installed, you must select **Preferred web browser**. The internal SAS browser (Results Viewer window) is not available without IE.

Using SAS Statements to Tell SAS You Want HTML Output: Instead of using the Preferences dialog box to tell the SAS System you want HTML output, you can also use SAS statements to control the Output Delivery System. Several ODS statements enable you to set the output destination and attributes and to select or exclude individual output objects from your results.

Note

> The following sections assume that you are familiar with HTML. If you are not, you should obtain an HTML user's guide before continuing.

The following steps guide you through the general process of creating HTML output.

1. **Open the HTML Output Destination.**

   To select HTML as your output destination, use the following ODS statements:

   ```
   ODS HTML FILE = 'filename.html';
   ODS LISTING CLOSE;
   ```

   The first ODS statement opens the HTML output destination and specifies a file where the HTML output is stored. The second ODS statement closes the LISTING output destination. If you omit this statement, output is written to both the HTML and LISTING destinations.

   Note

   > Although output is written to the HTML file when you submit code, you cannot view the output until you close the HTML output destination, as described in the section on the next page.

2. **Run Code That Generates Output.**

```
data test;
   x=1;
   y=2;
run;

proc print;
run;
```

3. **Close the HTML Output Destination.**

   Unless you specify otherwise, after you use the ODS statement to open the HTML output destination, all subsequent output is written to that destination. You cannot view the output until the HTML destination is closed.

   To close the HTML output destination, use the following ODS statement:

```
ODS HTML CLOSE;
```

   If you closed the LISTING destination in step 1, and now want to use the LISTING destination again, submit the following statement to reopen the LISTING destination:

```
ODS LISTING;
```

Depending on the options you select on the **Results** tab in the Preferences dialog box, HTML output is displayed using the internal SAS HTML browser in the Results Viewer window, or in an external browser window. To access the Preferences dialog box, click **Tools** → **Options** → **Preferences** in the SAS System main menu.

Figure 8.1 shows the output of the sample PROC PRINT code in the Results Viewer window.

Figure 8.1 Simple HTML Output Using the Internal SAS Browser

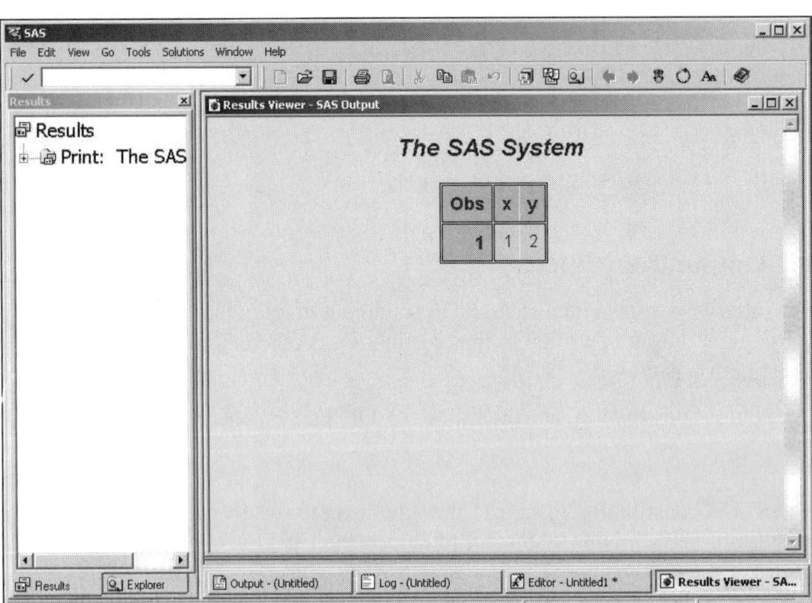

Creating an HTML Table of Contents: If your code generates a lot of output, you may find a table of contents useful. Use the following ODS statement to generate a table of contents and display that table of contents in a frame:

```
ODS HTML PATH = "HTML-folder" (URL=NONE)
        FRAME = "frame-file.htm"
         BODY = "filename.htm"
     CONTENTS = "contents-file.htm";
```

In this ODS statement, the PATH option defines the folder in which the FRAME=, BODY=, and CONTENTS= files are created. When you display the resulting frame file, the table of contents is linked to the body of the output. Clicking on an entry in the table of contents displays the corresponding output object in the body of the output.

Note

> The syntax given for creating a table of contents is actually one of several methods; this particular method is guaranteed to work with all Web browsers.

The following program creates an HTML table of contents. The CONTENTS= option in each of the PROC PRINT statements creates a meaningful label for the output in the HTML table of contents.

```
ods listing close;
ods html path = "C:\"(url=none)
         frame = "frame.htm"
         body = "body.htm"
         contents = "toc.htm";

data test;
   x=1;
   y=2;
run;

proc print contents="Data for Test";
run;

data test2;
   w=5;
   z=7;
run;

proc print contents="Data for Test2";
run;

ods html close;
ods listing;
```

The Results Viewer window shows only the actual output (but not the table of contents); to see the table of contents, open the file referenced in the FRAME= option of the ODS HTML statement with your preferred browser. For example, Figure 8.2 shows the table of contents and body files viewed in Internet Explorer.

Figure 8.2 Sample HTML Output with a Table of Contents

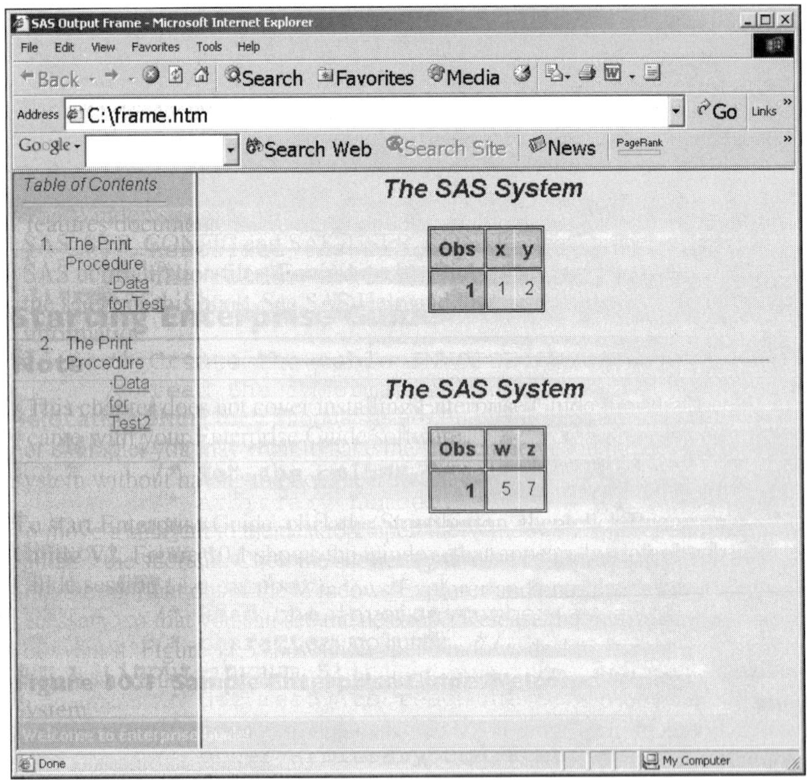

Note

> By default, SAS 9.1 generates standardized HTML tags. To generate HTML 3.2 tags, use the keyword HTML3 instead of HTML in the ODS statement.

Creating PDF Output

Sending your output to a PDF destination is similar to sending output to an HTML destination.

Note

> Unlike generating HTML output, you cannot use the Preferences dialog box to generate PDF output. You must use SAS statements to generate PDF output.

To generate PDF output, use the ODS PDF statement. For example, the following program sends the output of the two PRINT procedures to the default PDF destination file, SASPRT.PDF:

```
ods listing close; /* optional */
ods html close; /* optional */
ods pdf;

data test;
   x=1;
   y=2;
run;

proc print;
run;

data test2;
   w=5;
   z=7;
run;

proc print;
run;

ods pdf close; /* necessary to see the output */
ods listing;
```

Warning

If you close an ODS destination, then open and write to it again, the contents of the file that the destination points to are replaced by default. Furthermore, any previous output objects listed in the Results window that were once written to that file remain—and now display the wrong data (that is, they no longer display the data they once contained, but rather the latest data written to the file). Therefore, to avoid confusion, you may want to clear the Results window before submitting output again to the same ODS destination. It is possible to append output to an ODS destination; see the online SAS ODS documentation for details.

To send the PDF output to a specified file, add the FILE= option to the ODS PDF statement. For example, the following statement indicates that output should be written to a file named C:\SALESDATA.PDF:

```
ODS PDF FILE="c:\salesdata.pdf";
```

The PDF output is displayed within the Results Viewer window if you have selected the internal SAS System browser as your default results viewer. If you selected "Preferred Browser" in the Preferences dialog box, the PDF file opens in your preferred browser. Figure 8.3 shows some PDF output in the Results Viewer window.

Figure 8.3 Sample PDF Output in the Results Viewer Window

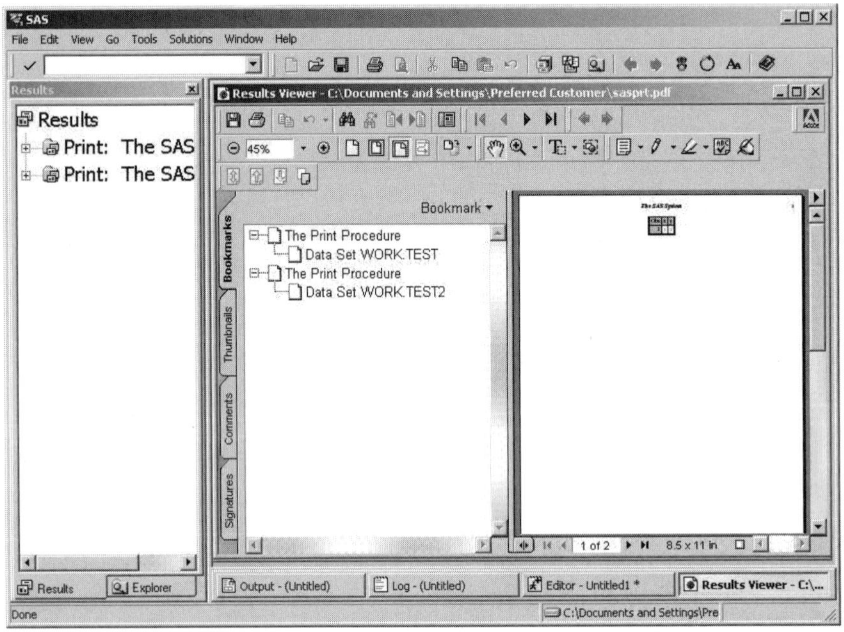

Note

To view PDF output, you must have Acrobat Reader 4.0 or later installed on your machine. For more advanced ODS PDF features, you'll need the full installation of Adobe Acrobat.

Viewing ODS Output

If you've told the SAS System that you want to view ODS output (such as HTML or PDF output) using the internal browser (see "Creating HTML Output" earlier in this chapter), click **Results Viewer** in the window bar to see your output. By default, the Results Viewer window displays the current (latest) ODS output.

Figure 8.4 shows a sample Results Viewer window with some output.

Figure 8.4 Looking at HTML Output in the Results Viewer Window

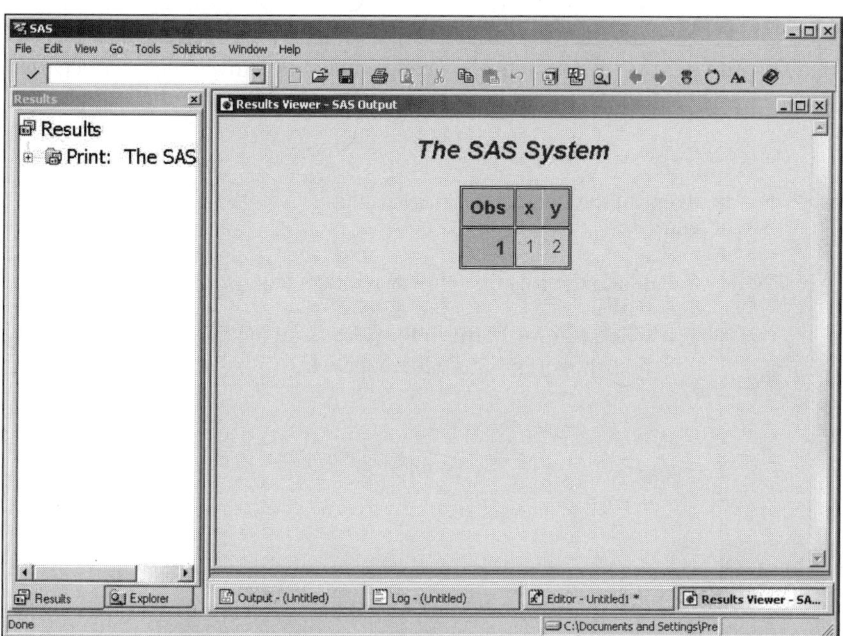

To navigate in the Results Viewer window, right-click in the window to display the popup menu. Click **Forward** and **Back** to move to different pages of your output. Within each page of output, use the scroll bar and the PageUp and PageDown keys to change the view. Use the Results window to display a different output object. See "Looking at Output" in Chapter 2 for an explanation of using the Results window.

You can use your preferred Web browser to view HTML output, instead of the internal SAS System browser. If you have selected this option in the Preferences dialog box, your output automatically appears in your Web browser after you submit the code.

Viewing a Particular File: If you close the Results Viewer window, you can open it again by double-clicking the appropriate output object in the Results window.

If the output object is no longer displayed in the Results window, but the physical file still exists, issue the WBROWSE command from the command bar to display the output, using your preferred Web browser or application (for example, PDF files are opened in Acrobat Reader or Acrobat). The syntax for using the WBROWSE command to display a particular file is as follows:

WBROWSE "*filename*"

Using the SAS System Viewer to View Output: A final method of viewing your SAS output is to use the SAS System Viewer. See Appendix 2 for more information on using the SAS System Viewer.

Printing ODS Output

The printing interface for printing from the Results Viewer window differs from the interface you see when printing from the rest of the SAS System (such as printing the Log or Output window).

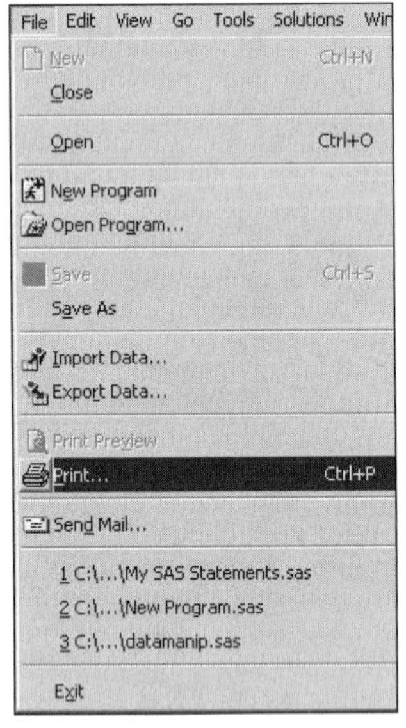

To print the contents of the Results Viewer window, follow these steps:

1. Make the Results Viewer window active.
2. Click **File → Print** in the SAS System main menu. The dialog box shown in Figure 8.5 appears.

Figure 8.5 Print Dialog Box Used by the Results Viewer Window

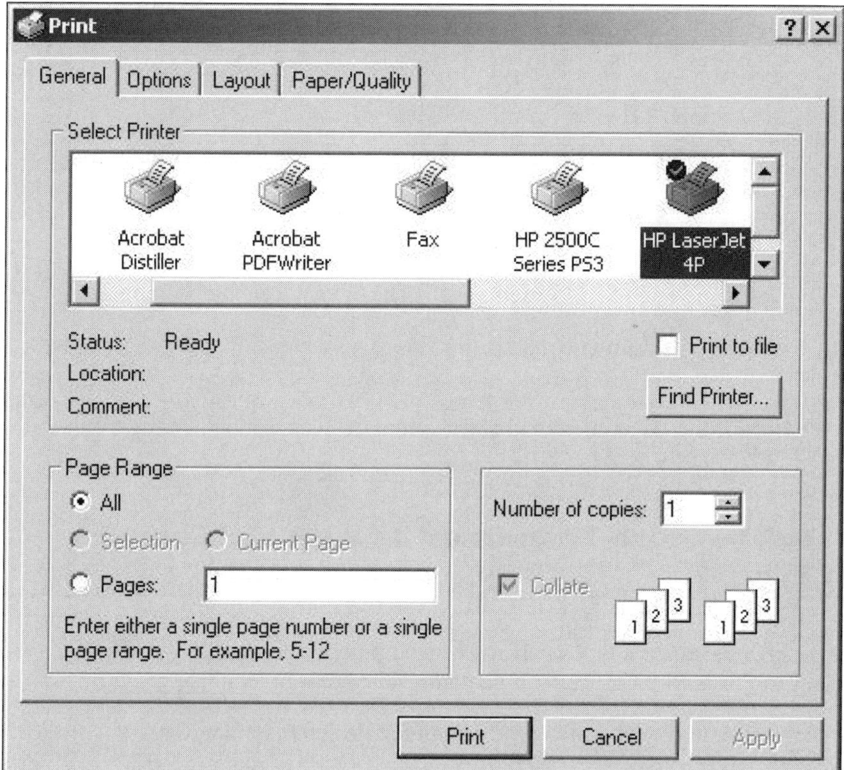

3. Choose the correct destination printer in the **Select Printer** area by clicking on the printer's icon.

4. Then, select the correct page range and number of copies in the **Page Range** and **Number of copies** areas.

5. Click **Print** to send the contents of the Results Viewer window to the selected printer.

Note

> No matter how many output objects are listed in the Results window, only the currently selected output object displayed in the Results Viewer window is printed.

Printing from Your Preferred Browser or Application: For information about printing from your preferred browser or application (such as Acrobat Reader), see that product's own documentation.

Editing and Saving the HTML Source Code

You may want to edit the HTML source code for your output. For example, you could change the <TITLE> tag, then save the code to a new file. To do this, follow these steps.

1. In the Results window, click the HTML file you want to edit.
2. Right-click and select **Edit Source** in the resulting popup menu. The HTML source code is displayed in a new window.
3. Edit the source code as necessary.
4. Click **File** → **Save As** in the main SAS System menu. The Save As dialog box appears.
5. Type the new name in the **File name** field and click **OK**. This saves the output to a file with a file type of .HTM.
6. If you want to see the effect of your changes, click the Refresh Content icon on the Results Viewer window tool bar.

Sending Output to More Than One File with the Same Destination Type

Whether you create PDF, HTML, RTF, or other forms of output, you may want to have several instances of the same ODS destination type open at the same time. For example, you may want to create a "plain" file as well as a file that uses a more complicated design template.

The following program uses the ID= option to send output to two separate PDF files:

```
ods pdf (id=plain) file="c:\PlainOutput.pdf";
ods pdf (id=fancy) style=FancyPrinter
    file="c:\FancyOutput.pdf";

data fruit;
   length name $15 color $15;
   input name $ color $;
   datalines;
Orange orange
Apple  red
Banana yellow
Pear   green
;
run;

data veggies;
   length name $15 color $15;
   input name $ color $;
   datalines;
```

```
Cauliflower white
Broccoli    green
Beet        red
Carrot      orange
Eggplant    purple
;
run;

proc print data=fruit;
run;
proc print data=veggies;
run;

ods pdf (id=plain) close;
ods pdf (id=fancy) close;
```

When this program runs, the Results window shows two PROC PRINT entries, which in turn show two versions of each data set's data, as shown in Figure 8.6.

Figure 8.6 Results Window Showing Two PDF Versions of Output for Each Data Set

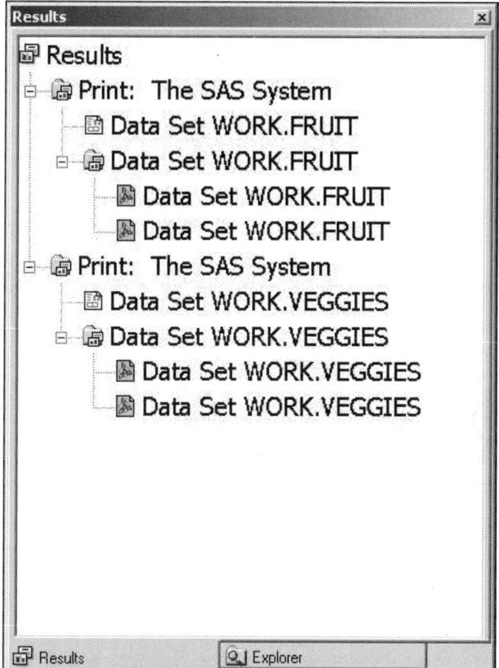

Note

In Figure 8.6, the two PDF files have the same name (Data Set WORK.*name*), although the Results Viewer window title bar specifies the filename (C:\PLAINOUTPUT.PDF or C:\FANCYOUTPUT.PDF). Currently, you cannot separately label the different destinations within each output node.

Figure 8.7 shows the two versions of the output side-by-side (with the Acrobat Navigation window hidden; the two Results Viewer windows are also resized). As you can see, the FancyPrinter style referenced in the second ODS PDF statement in the program (displayed in the left-hand Results Viewer window) uses an italic font for the column and row labels, while the default output created by the first ODS PDF statement uses no italics.

Figure 8.7 Comparison of the Two PDF Files

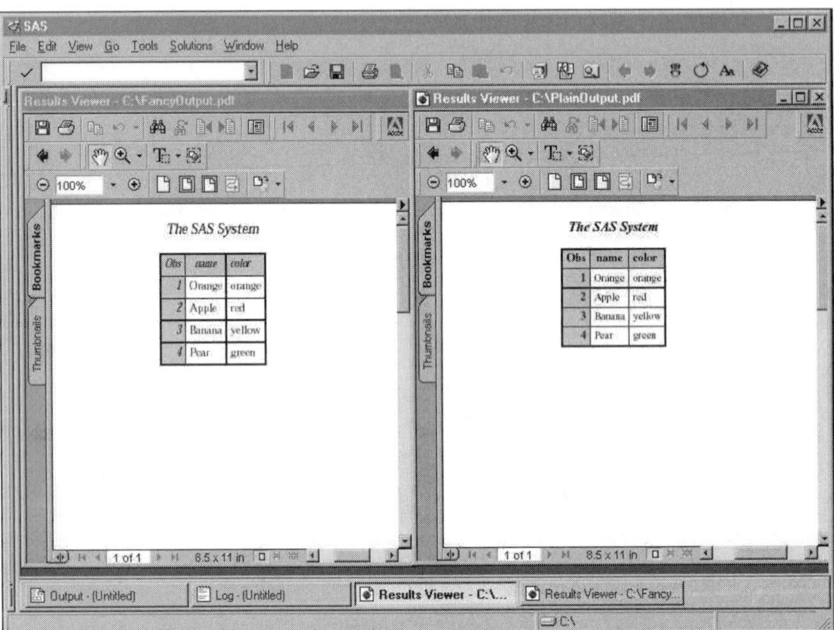

Controlling Which Output Objects Are Included in Your Output

If your SAS program generates more output than you need, the Output Delivery System lets you select individual output objects from your output. To select the output objects, follow these steps:

1. **Turn ODS Tracing On.**
   The first step is to discover the names of the various output objects generated by your program. Use the ODS TRACE statement with the ON and LABEL options to display all the output object names. (This statement writes these names to the SAS log.) The LABEL option records a brief description of the contents of the output object. (This label is identical to the label that identifies the output object in the Results window.)

   Here is how this statement looks:

   ```
   ODS TRACE ON / LABEL;
   ```

   For example, if you submit the following code, the SAS log contains the results shown in Figure 8.8.

   Note

In Figure 8.8, the SAS log is displayed using the Windows Notepad editor.

   ```
   ods trace on/label;

   data test;
      do i = 1 to 150;
         group = (i > 50);
         x = normal(123);
         y1 = uniform(123);
         y2 = uniform(567);
         output;
      end;
   run;

   proc means;
      by group;
      title 'Means Step';
   run;
   ```

Figure 8.8 SAS Log Displaying the Results of the ODS TRACE Statement

```
Untitled - Notepad                                    8/06/03 5:22:21pm
File  Edit  Format  Help
    ods trace on/label;

    data test;
       do i = 1 to 150;
          group = (i > 50);
          x = normal(123);
          y1 = uniform(123);
          y2 = uniform(567);
          output;
       end;
    run;

NOTE: The data set WORK.TEST has 150 observations and 5 variables.
NOTE: DATA statement used (Total process time):
      real time           0.32 seconds
      cpu time            0.06 seconds


    proc means;
       by group;
       title 'Means Step';
    run;

Output Added:
-------------
Name:       Summary
Label:      Summary statistics
Template:   base.summary
Path:       Means.ByGroup1.Summary
Label Path: 'The Means Procedure'.'group=0'.'Summary statistics'
-------------
NOTE: The above message was for the following by-group:
      group=0

Output Added:
-------------
Name:       Summary
Label:      Summary statistics
Template:   base.summary
Path:       Means.ByGroup2.Summary
Label Path: 'The Means Procedure'.'group=1'.'Summary statistics'
-------------
NOTE: The above message was for the following by-group:
      group=1
NOTE: There were 150 observations read from the data set WORK.TEST.
NOTE: PROCEDURE MEANS used (Total process time):
      real time           0.59 seconds
      cpu time            0.09 seconds
```

In Figure 8.8, two output objects are recorded, because there are two sections that begin "Output Added:". As you can see, both output objects have the same name (Summary). However, adding the LABEL option to the ODS TRACE statement lets you see that the output objects have unique label paths (the lines beginning with "Label Path:").

2. **Select or Exclude Output Objects.**
   Having used the ODS TRACE statement to determine the output object names and label paths, you can select and exclude individual output objects by specifying their names in the appropriate ODS statement.

   To select an output object (that is, include the output object in the output), use the ODS SELECT statement:

   ODS SELECT *name-1 name-2 ... name-n*;

To exclude output objects, use the ODS EXCLUDE statement:

ODS EXCLUDE *name-1 name-2 ... name-n*;

If the output object names are not unique, you can substitute the output object's label path for the name:

ODS SELECT *label-path-1 label-path-2 … label-path-n*;

ODS EXCLUDE *label-path-1 label-path-2 … label-path-n*;

3. **Turn ODS Tracing Off.**
   Turn off the tracing feature by submitting the following statement:

   ODS TRACE OFF;

Example—Selecting an Output Object: The following program selects only the Group 1 statistics output object from the PROC MEANS step, using the ODS SELECT statement just before the PROC MEANS step. Also, ODS HTML statements have been added to open the HTML destination and to tell the SAS System where to store the HTML output.

(You can use the same technique with other destinations, such as RTF and PDF.)

```
ods html body='c:\body2.htm';

data test;
   do i = 1 to 150;
      group = (i > 50);
      x = normal(123);
      y1 = uniform(123);
      y2 = uniform(567);
      output;
   end;
run;

   /* Select a single output object. Note the use of */
   /* quotation marks in the label path. */
ods select "The MEANS Procedure"."group=1"."Summary
           statistics";

proc means;
   by group;
   title 'Means Step';
run;

ods html close;
ods listing;
```

Figure 8.9 shows the output from this program.

Figure 8.9 Selecting Only One Output Object from a PROC MEANS Step

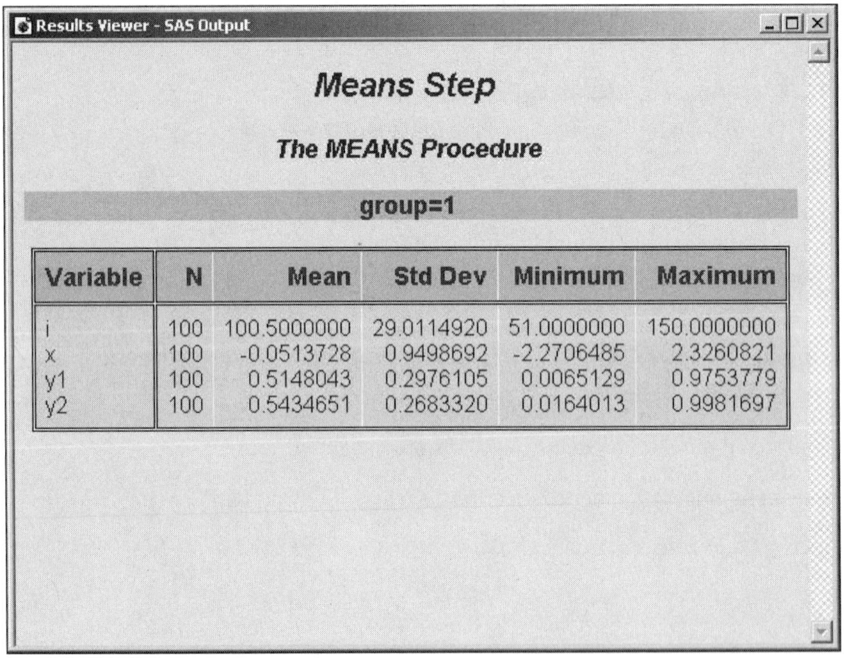

Results Viewer - SAS Output

Means Step

The MEANS Procedure

group=1

Variable	N	Mean	Std Dev	Minimum	Maximum
i	100	100.5000000	29.0114920	51.0000000	150.0000000
x	100	-0.0513728	0.9498692	-2.2706485	2.3260821
y1	100	0.5148043	0.2976105	0.0065129	0.9753779
y2	100	0.5434651	0.2683320	0.0164013	0.9981697

Modifying and Creating Styles: The TEMPLATE Procedure

The Preferences dialog box (see Chapter 6) offers several distinct style definitions. However, at some point you may need to define your own style definitions. The TEMPLATE procedure allows you to do this. While a detailed discussion of the TEMPLATE procedure is beyond the scope of this book, the examples shown in this section should get you started on the road toward customizing and perfecting the look and feel of your SAS output.

Definitions and Concepts: First, let's review some terminology and concepts. When you view SAS output, much of it is organized in tabular form. The appearance of the cells (centered or left-justified, size of font, background color, and so on); the color of titles, BY-group labels, footers, and headers; the background color; and many other attributes can be controlled through the TEMPLATE procedure.

The relevant terms and definitions from the *ODS User's Guide* are repeated in Table 8.2 for your convenience.

Table 8.2 ODS Template Terminology

style definition	controls the overall appearance (color, font face, font size, and so on) of your output. Each style definition is composed of style elements.
style attribute	specifies a value for one aspect of the data presentation. For instance, the BACKGROUND= attribute controls the color for the background of an HTML table, and the FONT_STYLE= attribute specifies whether to use a roman, a slant, or an italic font.
style element	is a collection of style attributes that apply to the presentation of a particular aspect of the output, such as column headers or cell data. Examples of style elements may also specify default colors and fonts for output that uses the style definition.
table element	is a collection of attributes that apply to a particular column, header, or footer. Typically, these attributes specify something about the data rather than about their presentation. For instance FORMAT= specifies the SAS format to use in a column. However, some attributes describe presentation aspects of the data.
table definition	describes how to render the output for a tabular output object. A table definition determines the order of table headers and footers, the order of columns, and the overall appearance of the output object that uses it. Each table definition contains or references table elements.
template store	is a SAS file that stores the definitions (style, table, and so on) that SAS provides and the definitions that you create using the TEMPLATE procedure. Definitions that SAS provides are in the template store SASHELP.TMPLMST. You can store your definitions in any template store where you have write access. **Note:** Template stores are not visible using the SAS Explorer or Windows Explorer.

Note

Style definitions specified with the TEMPLATE procedure do not affect the LISTING destination. However, attributes that control the structure of a table or the presentation of data values *do* affect the LISTING destination.

Style definitions are object-oriented in nature. In particular, they use "inheritance" to pass along various style and table attributes. The default style definition is the "parent of all parents," from which other style definitions can inherit attributes. As an example, the fancyPrinter style definition is based on the Printer style definition. Attributes that aren't changed in the new definition remain the same as in the parent style definition.

Getting Started with PROC TEMPLATE: The TEMPLATE procedure offers both a strictly programmatic interface and a graphical interface. We'll begin by using the graphical interface, and work our way to the necessary statements.

Perhaps the easiest way to begin to use PROC TEMPLATE is to see how the SAS System itself uses PROC TEMPLATE to build the fancyPrinter style from the default printer style. Then, we'll build our own style.

Begin your exploration of the TEMPLATE procedure by following these steps:

1. To begin, make the Results window active by clicking in it. (If the Results window is not already open, open it by clicking **View → Results**.)
2. Right-click the uppermost Results node.
3. In the resulting popup menu, click **Templates**.
4. Click **Sashelp.Tmplmst** in the left-hand panel.
5. Double-click **Styles** in the right-hand panel.

Note

As an alternative to steps 2 and 3, make the Results window active, then click the Templates icon on the SAS System tool bar. Or, issue the ODSTEMPLATES command from the command bar.

Figure 8.10 shows the resulting Templates window.

Figure 8.10 Templates Window

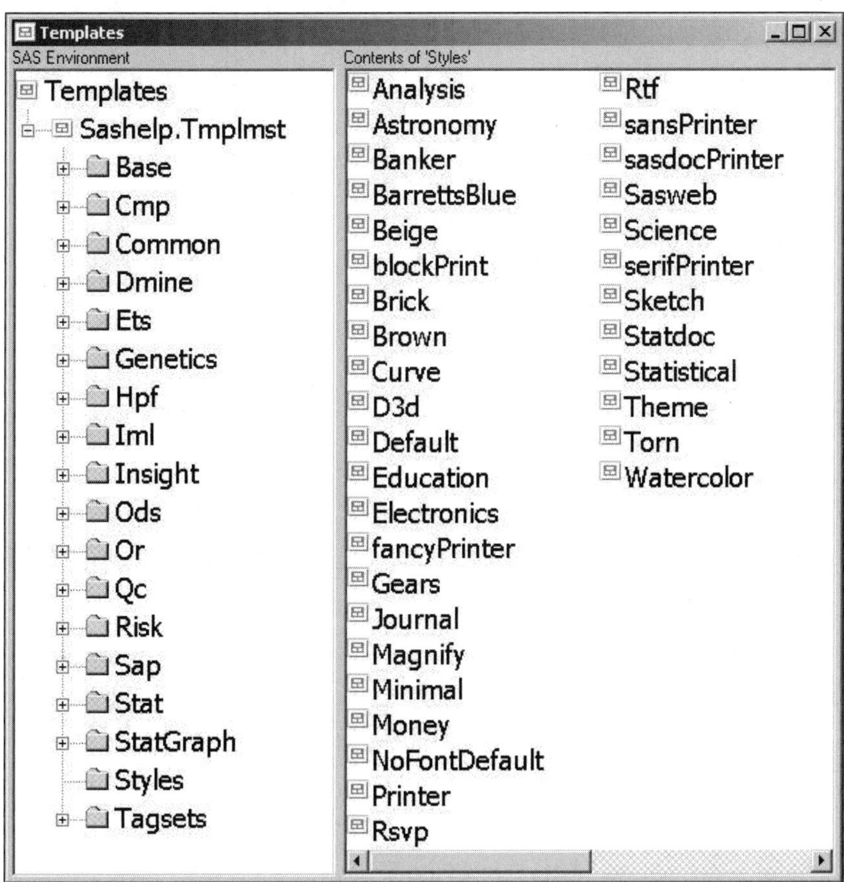

6. Double-click the **fancyPrinter** style definition. This displays the TEMPLATE procedure statements the SAS System uses to create the fancyPrinter style definition, as shown in Figure 8.11.

Figure 8.11 Template Browser Window

```
Template Browser
proc template;
   define style Styles.fancyPrinter;   ❶
      parent = styles.Printer;   ❷
      replace fonts /   ❸
         'TitleFont2' = ("Palatino, Arial, Times Roman",13pt,Bold Italic)
         'TitleFont' = ("Palatino, Arial, Times Roman",13pt,Bold Italic)
         'StrongFont' = ("Palatino, Book Antiqua, Times Roman",10pt,Bold)
         'EmphasisFont' = ("Palatino, Book Antiqua, Times Roman",10pt,Bold
         Italic)
         'FixedEmphasisFont' = ("Courier",10pt,Italic)
         'FixedStrongFont' = ("Courier",10pt,Bold)
         'FixedHeadingFont' = ("Courier",10pt,Bold)
         'BatchFixedFont' = ("SAS Monospace, Courier",8pt)
         'FixedFont' = ("Courier",10pt)
         'headingEmphasisFont' = ("ITC Zaph Chancery, Palatino, Times Roman",
         13pt,Bold Italic)
         'headingFont' = ("ITC Zaph Chancery, Palatino, Times Roman",12pt,
         Italic)
         'docFont' = ("Palatino, Times Roman",10pt);
      replace GraphFonts /
         'GraphDataFont' = ("Times Roman",8pt)
         'GraphValueFont' = ("Times Roman",10pt)
         'GraphLabelFont' = ("Times Roman",12pt,Bold)
         'GraphFootnoteFont' = ("Times Roman",12pt,Bold)
         'GraphTitleFont' = ("Times Roman",14pt,Bold);
      style Table from Output /   ❹
         rules = ALL
         cellpadding = 4pt
         cellspacing = 0.25pt
         borderwidth = 0.75pt;
      style Graph from Graph
         "Graph attributes" /
         cellspacing = 0.25pt
         borderwidth = 0.75pt;
   end;
run;
*** END OF TEXT ***
```

In Figure 8.11, the circled numbers have been added to explain the code:

❶ Give the new style definition a name (in this case, fancyPrinter).

❷ Specify which style definition you are going to use as a base (also known as a parent)—in this example, Printer.

❸ Use the REPLACE statement to replace style elements in the parent style definition. Here, we replace the font elements and the graph font elements.

❹ Use the STYLE statement to modify elements in the parent style definitions. Here, we modify the rules, cell padding, cell spacing, and border width.

See "The REPLACE Statement versus the STYLE Statement" later in this chapter for a full explanation of these two techniques.

Note

> To get a good feel for what style and table attributes are available, it is instructive to study the source code for the default style definition, as well as for a few more of the predefined style definitions such as Printer, fancyPrinter, and Brown.

Creating Your Own Style Definition: Now that you see how PROC TEMPLATE works, you can use the same technique to modify various style and table elements and attributes to suit your needs. Here we present a simple example that starts with the Default style, then changes several attributes, creating a new style called MyWebStyle.

For purposes of comparison, Figure 8.12 shows the results of the following two PROC PRINT steps, using the default style. (The data sets referenced in the PROC PRINT steps were created earlier in this chapter.)

```
options nodate;
ods listing close;

ods html path = "C:\"(url=none)
         frame = "NewFrame.htm"
         body = "NewBody.htm"
         contents = "NewToc.htm";

footnote "~ Report prepared by Farmer Bob ~";

proc print data=fruit contents="Fruit Data";
   title "Fruit Data from My Farm";
run;

proc print data=veggies contents="Veggie Data";
   title "Veggie Data from My Farm";
run;

ods html close;
ods listing;
```

Figure 8.12 Results Using the Default Style Definition

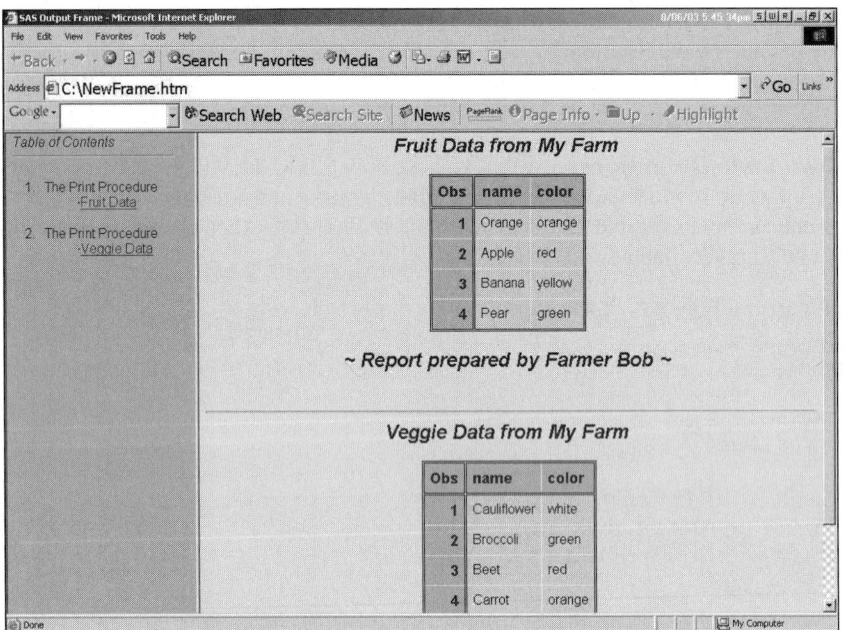

Now we'll use PROC TEMPLATE to define a new style definition that modifies a number of the attributes of the data presentation and table of contents. At the end of the following code, we print out the same data, using the new style. The code is fairly long, but the comments explain what each step does.

```
proc template;
   /* Give the new style definition a name (MyWebStyle). */
   /* It is stored in the default location, which is the */
   /* SASUSER.TEMPLAT template store, accessed through the */
   /* Templates window. This is a permanent file, not a */
   /* temporary file, and persists from one SAS session to */
   /* the next. */
define style MyWebStyle;
   /* Specify the parent style definition as a starting
      point. */
parent = styles.default;

   /* Replace the old color list with a new color list. */
replace color_list /
      'fgB2' = cx0066AA
      'fgB1' = cx004488
      'fgA4' = cxAAFFAA
      'bgA4' = cx880000
```

```
      'bgA3' = cxD3D3D3
      'fgA2' = cx0000FF
      'bgA2' = cxFFFF99 /* a darker yellow */
      'fgA1' = cx000000
      'bgA1' = cxCCFFFF /* a light blue */
      'fgA' = cx000000 /* black */
      'bgA' = cxFFFFCC; /* a light buff yellow */

    /* Replace the foreground and background colors for
       the title and footnote areas. */
replace titlesandfooters /
      foreground = colors("systitlefg")
      background = colors("systitlebg");

    /* Modify the font used for footnotes. */
style SystemFooter from SystemFooter /
   font = Fonts('TitleFont') font_size=1
   font_weight = demi_light;

    /* Modify the font used for column headers. */
style header from header /
      font_style = italic;

    /* Replace the commonly used text phrases. */
replace text /
      "prefix1" = "PROC "
      "suffix1" = "--"
         /* title for table of contents */
      "Content Title" = "Content Map"
      "Pages Title" = "Pages"
      "Note Banner" = "Note"
      "Warn Banner" = "Warning:"
      "Error Banner" = "Error:"
      "Fatal Banner" = "Fatal:";

    /* Replace the commonly used HTML snippets. */
replace html from html /
    /* Cause the table of contents title to be
       centered. */
   'expandAll' = "<center><SPAN
onClick=""if(msie4==1)expandAll()"">"
    /* End the centering. */
   'posthtml flyover line' = "</center></SPAN><HR size=""3"">"
   'prehtml flyover line' = "<SPAN><HR size=""3"">"
   'posthtml flyover' = "</SPAN>"
   'prehtml flyover' = "<SPAN>"
   'break' = "<br>"
   'Line' = "<HR size=""3"">"
```

```
   'PageBreakLine' = %nrstr("<p style=""page-break-after:
always;""> </p><HR size=""3"">");

    /* Modify how tables are presented. */
style table from table /
      rules = rows /* rules only between rows */
      cellspacing = 3 /* increase cell spacing */
      bordercolorlight = colors("databg")
      bordercolordark = colors("link1")
      borderwidth = 3;

    /* Increase the size of the table of contents
       area. */
style frame from frame /
     contentsize = 30%;

    /* Modify some of the colors used in the table
       of contents. */
style contents from contents /
      visitedlinkcolor = colors("systitlefg")
      foreground = colors('systitlefg');

    /* Modify the font used in the table of contents
       heading. */
style ContentTitle from ContentTitle /
     font = fonts('headingEmphasisFont');

    /* Modify the behavior of the leaf nodes in the table
       of contents. Notably, remove the ugly "middle dot"
       type bullets. */
replace IndexItem from IndexItem /
   leftmargin = 6pt
   listentryanchor = on
   background = colors('contentbg')
   foreground = colors('conentryfg');

    /* Modify more table of contents features, such as
       adding more space between output items and using a
       more attractive bullet. */
style ContentItem from ContentItem /
   posthtml = '<br>'
   bullet = "disc";
end;
run;

ods listing close;
options nodate;
```

```
     /* Add the STYLE= option to the ODS statement so the new
        style definition is used. */
   ods html path = "C:\"(url=none)
            frame = "NewFrame.htm"
            body = "NewBody.htm"
            contents = "NewToc.htm"
            style=MyWebStyle;

   footnote "~ Report prepared by Farmer Bob ~";

   proc print data=fruit contents="Fruit Data";
      title "Fruit Data from My Farm";
   run;

   proc print data=veggies contents="Veggie Data";
      title "Veggie Data from My Farm";
   run;

   ods html close;
   ods listing;
```

Figure 8.13 shows the results of this program, using the new style definition.

Figure 8.13 HTML Output Using the New Style Definition

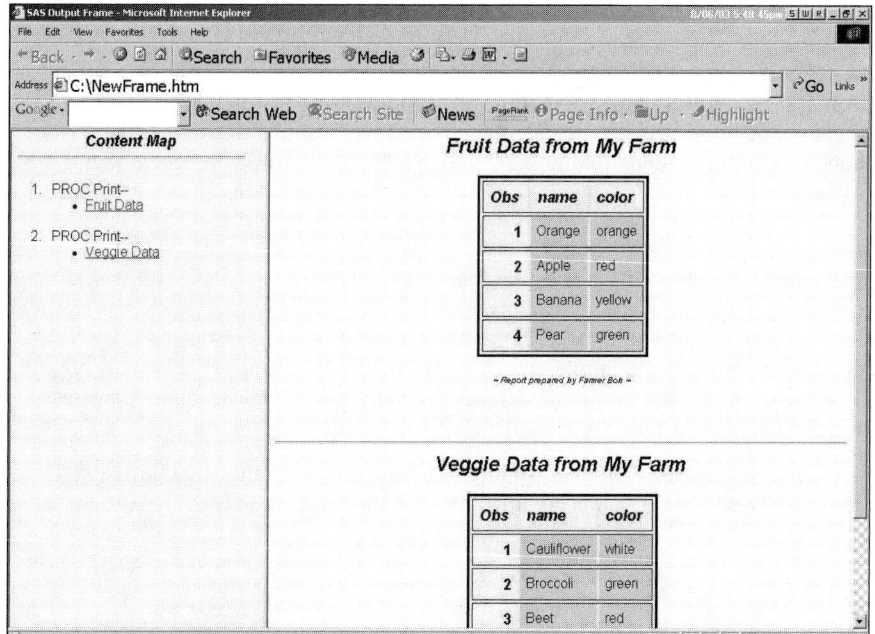

In Figure 8.13, you can see many changes from the default output appearance that was shown in Figure 8.12, including the following:

- Background colors are a more visually interesting light and dark buff color.
- Footnote text is smaller.
- Column and row headers stand out from the actual data because they appear in a bright, contrasting color.
- Table borders use light and dark colors to emulate a 3-D effect.
- The Table of Contents frame has a more attractive, informative title, and the bullets in the output object list are nicely formatted.

The REPLACE Statement versus the STYLE Statement: You'll notice in the example program that some parts of the new style definition are created using the REPLACE statement, while others use the STYLE statement. Neither statement actually affects the parent style definition, but the statements do differ significantly in how they affect the new definition's contents and attribute inheritance.

- Use the REPLACE statement to cause both the specified style element and all its child style elements to inherit the new attribute settings. Any attribute settings that are in the parent style element but aren't listed in the new style element are not included in the new style definition. Using the REPLACE statement enables you to eliminate unwanted parent style attributes from new style definition.

  Caution

  > The REPLACE statement can have unforeseen effects if used unwisely. Removing style attributes from a style definition means that these attributes aren't available to any of the parent style element's child style elements either. Therefore, it is important to know which style elements are children of a particular parent style element, before you decide to use the REPLACE statement.

- Use the STYLE statement to modify one or more attributes in the parent style element, or to add new attributes to a style element. Attributes you don't list in the new style element remain unchanged. However, changes you make to a parent style element are not inherited by child style elements. For example, the example program uses the STYLE statement to modify the POSTHTML and BULLET attributes in the ContentItem style element. But these changes would not be reflected by any child style elements of ContentItem.

It may be helpful when planning your template strategy to draw an inheritance tree for the style elements you want to change to see if you need attribute inheritance or not.

Note

> The MyWebStyle style definition used in the preceding example works fine for simple PROC PRINT steps and other uncomplicated procedures such as PROC CONTENTS. However, it may need further customization to be fully functional for other procedures that produce more complex output.

Creating a Cascading Style Sheet (CSS): The style created by PROC TEMPLATE is stored in a SAS template store and cannot be accessed outside the SAS System. If you would like to use the style outside the SAS System (such as in Enterprise Guide), you must create a CSS file that is stored as an external file. To do so, add the STYLESHEET option to your ODS HTML statement, as in the following example:

```
ods listing close;
ods html file="c:\Test.html"
    style=MyWebStyle stylesheet="c:\MyWebStyle.css";

data one;
x=1;
run;

proc print;
run;

ods html close;
ods listing;
```

When you submit this code, the MyWebStyle style definition is used to print the output, and the style is also output to a CSS file named C:\MYWEBSTYLE.CSS.

Learning More about PROC TEMPLATE: The TEMPLATE procedure offers far more than is illustrated by the simple examples in this chapter. SAS offers several good books on the subject; see "Welcome to SAS 9.1 for Windows" at the beginning of this book for some titles you may find useful.

Generating Reusable, Permanent Output: The DOCUMENT Procedure

What's New: The DOCUMENT destination offers great flexibility for output.

The Documents window provides a graphical point-and-click interface to the DOCUMENT procedure.

If you already thought being able to choose among several SAS output file formats was great, and being able to control how you wanted the output to look was even better, wait until you learn about the DOCUMENT destination and PROC DOCUMENT.

In the old world, after you ran a procedure and generated output in a certain format, that was it. If you wanted the data in a different format ("Oops—I really wanted a PDF file…"), you had to run the procedure again. Rerunning procedures just to reformat the data is expensive in terms of CPU and I/O resources. Not only that, but if your data were no longer available, rerunning the procedure may not even be possible. And, some data would simply benefit from a different order of presentation than the standard SAS procedure hierarchy.

The DOCUMENT destination and the DOCUMENT procedure solve these problems by enabling you to generate permanent, reusable, reorganizable output. Once you have the pieces, you can combine them, organize them, and format them in any order or manner you want, as many times as you want, without rerunning any procedures.

Like the TEMPLATE procedure, the DOCUMENT procedure is far more powerful and complex than one or two simple examples can hope to demonstrate. But this section should whet your appetite for learning more about the DOCUMENT destination and procedure—see SAS Help and Documentation for detailed information.

As an alternative to the DOCUMENT procedure, you can use the DOCUMENTS window, which is discussed briefly at the end of this chapter.

Example Using PROC DOCUMENT: Let's set up a sample scenario, and see how the DOCUMENT destination and procedure can enhance the organization of your data. Our example data set SASUSER.MEMBERS contains the name, address, and member status (active or inactive) of each member of a club. You decide to run PROC TABULATE to see how many active and inactive members there are in each distinct zip code area, and PROC FREQ to see the percentage of active and inactive members in each zip code area.

Here is the code for this example:

```
ods html path = "C:\"(url=none)
         frame = "DocFrame.htm"
         body = "DocBody.htm"
         contents = "DocToc.htm";

options nodate;

proc sort data=sasuser.members out=sasuser.MembersSorted;
   by city_state_zip name;
run;

title "Proc TABULATE Step";
proc tabulate data=sasuser.MembersSorted;
   by city_state_zip;
   class city_state_zip status;
   table city_state_zip,status;
run;

title "Proc FREQ Step";
proc freq data=sasuser.MembersSorted;
   by city_state_zip;
   table status;
run;
```

```
ods html close;
ods listing;
```

Figure 8.14 shows some sample output from this code. The table of contents frame shows the standard output hierarchy.

Figure 8.14 Example of Standard Output Hierarchy, Organized by Procedure

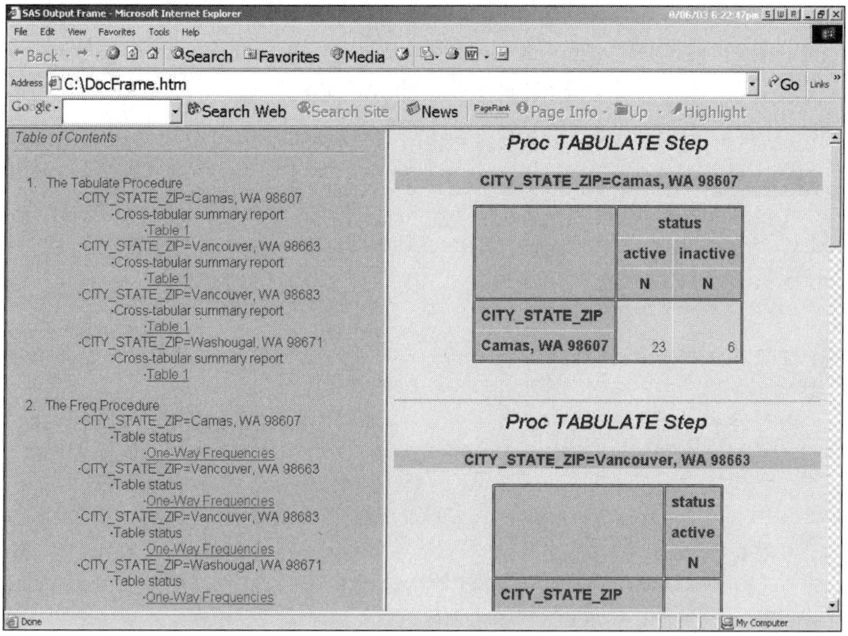

As you can see, all the PROC TABULATE results are shown first, followed by all the PROC FREQ results. But in many cases, it would make more sense to present the results of both procedures for the first BY group, then the results of both procedures for the next BY group, and so on. SAS 9.1 makes this possible by letting you create a permanent but flexible form of your output, which you can then re-render in any way you want.

The basic steps to creating reusable output are as follows:

1. Write the output to the DOCUMENT destination.
2. Determine the names of the output objects so you can reference them.
3. Use the DOCUMENT procedure to reorder the output.
4. Use the DOCUMENT procedure to display the output using the new order.

Here are more details on each step.

1. **Write the Output to the DOCUMENT Destination:** The DOCUMENT destination works like any ODS destination:

   ODS DOCUMENT NAME=*document-name*(WRITE);

   If you specify a one-level name, such as MYDOC, for *document-name*, the output document is stored in the WORK data library and deleted at the end of your SAS session. To create a permanent output document, use a two-level name such as SASUSER.MYDOC.

The following program uses the DOCUMENT destination to create a permanent record of the TABULATE and FREQ procedure output from our club data example:

```
ods document name=sasuser.mydoc(write);

options nodate;

proc sort data=sasuser.members out=sasuser.MembersSorted;
   by city_state_zip name;
run;

title "Proc TABULATE Step";
proc tabulate data=sasuser.MembersSorted;
   by city_state_zip;
   class city_state_zip status;
   table city_state_zip,status;
run;

title "Proc FREQ Step";
proc freq data=sasuser.MembersSorted;
   by city_state_zip;
   table status;
run;

ods document close;
```

When this code finishes executing, the file SASUSER.MYDOC contains all the output created by the TABULATE and FREQ procedures.

2. **Determine the Names of the Output Objects:** Before you can recombine the output objects, you need to know their names. The LIST statement of the DOCUMENT procedure writes the necessary information to the current output destination. For example, the following program lists the output objects associated with our example:

```
ods listing;
title "Names of Output Objects in SASUSER.MYDOC";
proc document name=sasuser.mydoc;
   list/levels=all;
run;
   /* Like other interactive procedures, PROC DOCUMENT */
   /* requires a QUIT statement. */
quit;
ods listing close;
```

Figure 8.15 shows the resulting SAS output in the Output window. As you can see, the output is organized in a hierarchy that resembles directories.

Figure 8.15 Listing the Output Objects with PROC DOCUMENT

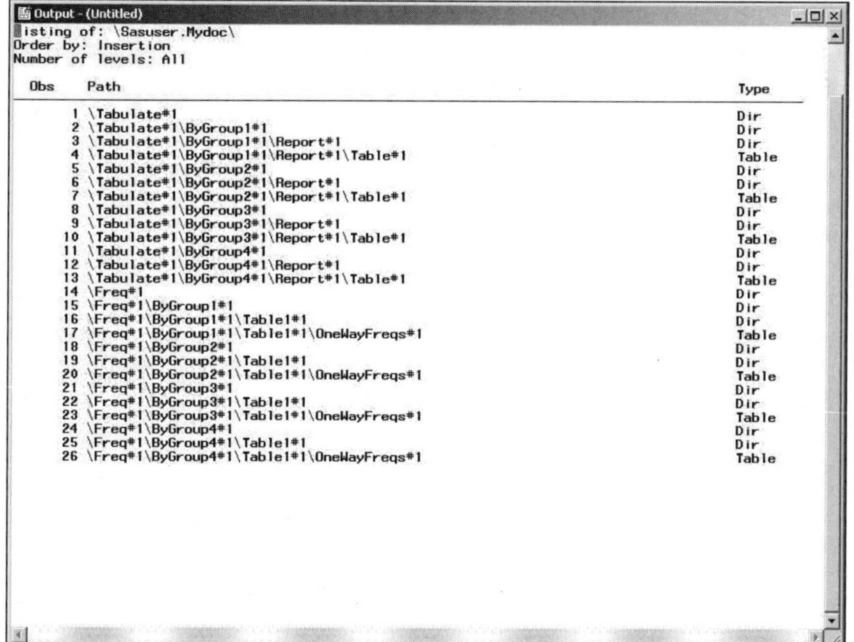

Output - (Untitled)

Listing of: \Sasuser.Mydoc\
Order by: Insertion
Number of levels: All

Obs	Path	Type
1	\Tabulate#1	Dir
2	\Tabulate#1\ByGroup1#1	Dir
3	\Tabulate#1\ByGroup1#1\Report#1	Dir
4	\Tabulate#1\ByGroup1#1\Report#1\Table#1	Table
5	\Tabulate#1\ByGroup2#1	Dir
6	\Tabulate#1\ByGroup2#1\Report#1	Dir
7	\Tabulate#1\ByGroup2#1\Report#1\Table#1	Table
8	\Tabulate#1\ByGroup3#1	Dir
9	\Tabulate#1\ByGroup3#1\Report#1	Dir
10	\Tabulate#1\ByGroup3#1\Report#1\Table#1	Table
11	\Tabulate#1\ByGroup4#1	Dir
12	\Tabulate#1\ByGroup4#1\Report#1	Dir
13	\Tabulate#1\ByGroup4#1\Report#1\Table#1	Table
14	\Freq#1	Dir
15	\Freq#1\ByGroup1#1	Dir
16	\Freq#1\ByGroup1#1\Table1#1	Dir
17	\Freq#1\ByGroup1#1\Table1#1\OneWayFreqs#1	Table
18	\Freq#1\ByGroup2#1	Dir
19	\Freq#1\ByGroup2#1\Table1#1	Dir
20	\Freq#1\ByGroup2#1\Table1#1\OneWayFreqs#1	Table
21	\Freq#1\ByGroup3#1	Dir
22	\Freq#1\ByGroup3#1\Table1#1	Dir
23	\Freq#1\ByGroup3#1\Table1#1\OneWayFreqs#1	Table
24	\Freq#1\ByGroup4#1	Dir
25	\Freq#1\ByGroup4#1\Table1#1	Dir
26	\Freq#1\ByGroup4#1\Table1#1\OneWayFreqs#1	Table

3. **Use the DOCUMENT Procedure to Reorder the Output:** With this information, we can write a program to organize the data exactly how we want it to appear.

```
      /* Specify a new document name in which to store the reorganized
         output. */
proc document name=sasuser.mydoc2;
       /* Create a subdirectory for each of the BY-group values. */
       /* Also create a label for each subdirectory. */
    make Camas;
    setlabel Camas 'City=Camas, WA 98607';
    make Vancouver1;
    setlabel Vancouver1 'City=Vancouver, WA 98663';
    make Vancouver2;
    setlabel Vancouver2 'City=Vancouver, WA 98683';
    make Washougal;
    setlabel Washougal 'City=Washougal, WA 98671';

       /* Make the active directory the Camas directory. */
    dir ^^\Camas;
       /* Copy specific output objects from the original
          document to the new document. The '^' character
          represents the current directory. */
    copy \sasuser.mydoc\Freq#1\ByGroup1#1\Table1#1\OneWayFreqs#1
          to ^;
    copy \sasuser.mydoc\Tabulate#1\ByGroup1#1\Report#1\Table#1 to ^;
       /* Make the active directory the Vancouver1 directory. */
    dir ^^\Vancouver1;
       /* Copy specific output objects from the original
          document to the new document. The '^' character
          represents the current directory. */
    copy \sasuser.mydoc\Freq#1\ByGroup2#1\Table1#1\OneWayFreqs#1
          to ^;
    copy \sasuser.mydoc\Tabulate#1\ByGroup2#1\Report#1\Table#1 to ^;
       /* Make the active directory the Vancouver2 directory. */
    dir ^^\Vancouver2;
       /* Copy specific output objects from the original
          document to the new document. The '^' character
          represents the current directory. */
    copy \sasuser.mydoc\Freq#1\ByGroup3#1\Table1#1\OneWayFreqs#1
          to ^;
    copy \sasuser.mydoc\Tabulate#1\ByGroup3#1\Report#1\Table#1 to ^;
       /* Make the active directory the Washougal directory. */
    dir ^^\Washougal;
       /* Copy specific output objects from the original
          document to the new document. The '^' character
```

```
         represents the current directory. */
   copy \sasuser.mydoc\Freq#1\ByGroup4#1\Table1#1\OneWayFreqs#1
         to ^;
   copy \sasuser.mydoc\Tabulate#1\ByGroup4#1\Report#1\Table#1 to ^;
   run;
quit;
```

4. **Use the DOCUMENT Procedure to Display the Output Using the New Order:** Now that the SASUSER.MYDOC2 document contains the output in the order we want, we can use PROC DOCUMENT to display the output. Note that the following program uses the customized style definition created in the PROC TEMPLATE section of this chapter. Of course, you could use any style you want.

```
ods listing close;
ods html path = "C:\"(url=none)
         frame = "NewDocFrame.htm"
         body = "NewDocBody.htm"
         contents = "NewDocToc.htm"
         style = MyWebStyle;

options nodate;

proc document name=sasuser.mydoc2;
   replay;
   run;
quit;

ods html close;
ods listing;
```

Figure 8.16 shows the result of this program (that is, the contents of the SASUSER.MYDOC2 document). Note that the output is now organized by zip code, with the PROC FREQ and PROC TABULATE results grouped together.

Figure 8.16 Reorganized Output

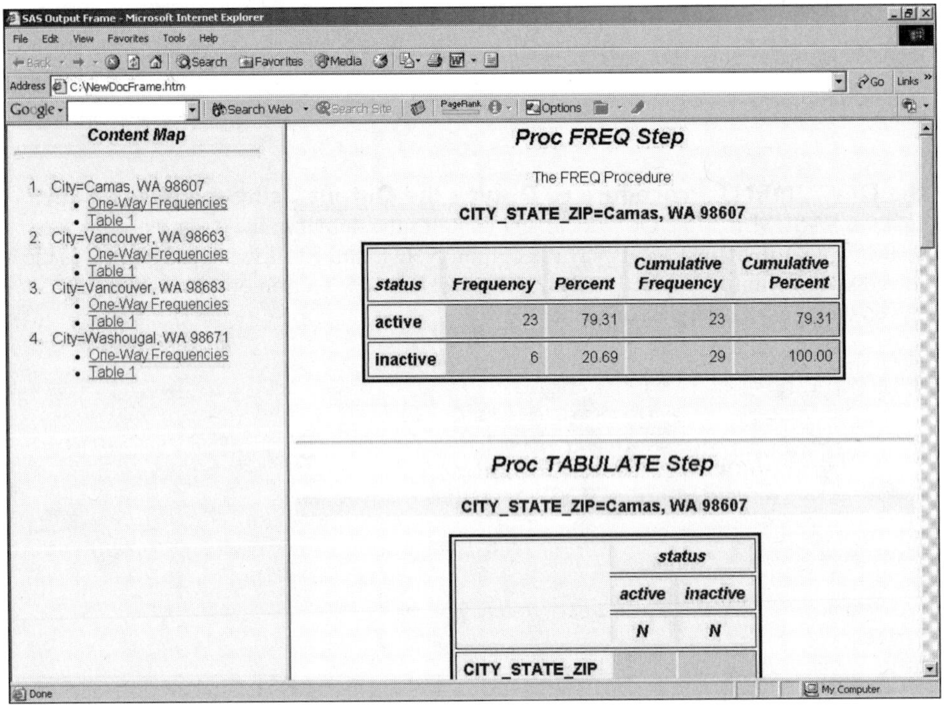

If we decided that we wanted PDF output instead of HTML output, generating the PDF file is as simple as changing the ODS statement and redisplaying the output with PROC DOCUMENT:

```
ods listing close;
ods pdf file="c:\NewOutput.pdf"
    style = MyWebStyle;

options nodate;

proc document name=sasuser.mydoc2;
   replay;
   run;
quit;

ods pdf close;
ods listing;
```

Using the Documents Window: Once you have used PROC DOCUMENT to create the output objects, you can use the Documents window to rearrange your output, instead of using programming statements. To open the Documents window, make the Results window active, then click **View → Documents**. For example, Figure 8.17 shows the Documents window, with the MYDOC and MYDOC2 documents created earlier in this chapter.

Figure 8.17 Sample Documents Window

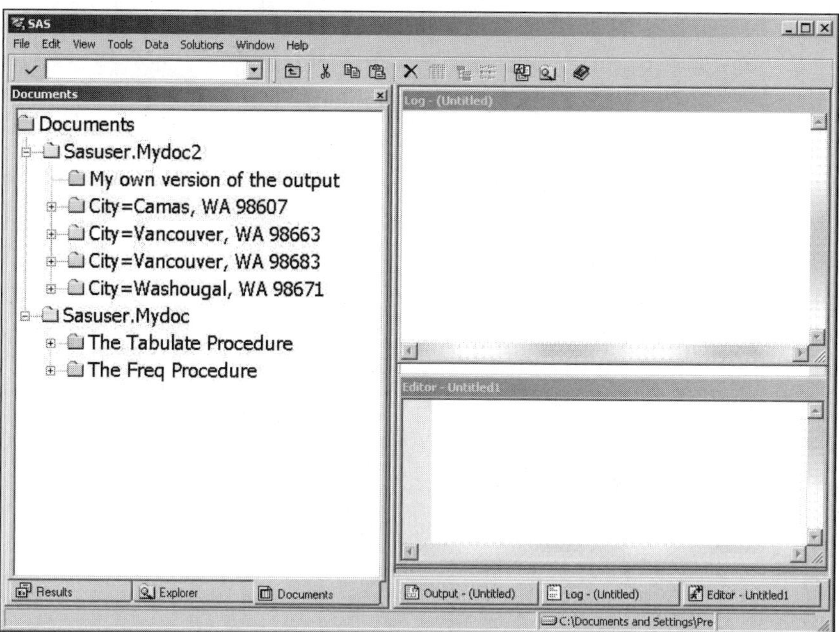

You can highlight a node or subnode, then use the right-click popup menu to cut, copy, and paste output objects into whatever order you want; exclude output objects from the document; and redisplay the document. For more information on the Documents window, see SAS Help and Documentation.

9 Managing SAS Files

Introduction

What's New: The V604 engine is available in SAS 9.1; however, the V606 engine is not a valid engine name in SAS 9.1—use V6 instead.

In 64-bit environments, the V6 engine is read-only.

It is often best to manage SAS files such as SAS tables and catalogs using the SAS System's file management capabilities.

This chapter first discusses some data protection issues you should consider before deciding how to manage your SAS files. Then, it shows you how to perform the following file management tasks:

- renaming and deleting SAS files using the SAS Explorer window
- moving and copying SAS files using the SAS Explorer window
- managing your SAS library references and file shortcuts
- managing your SAS catalogs.

Note

The Windows Explorer, discussed in Appendix 3, is also useful for managing files. For example, depending on the security settings of a folder, you may not be able to rename, move, or copy SAS programs using the SAS Explorer. For folders with restricted security settings, you must perform these tasks using the Windows Explorer.

Understanding Data Protection

What's New: Accessing passwords for SAS tables is done through the Properties window.

The Windows environment and the SAS System both provide data protection services. Which one you choose (or you may choose to use both) depends on how you plan to access and manage your files.

Setting SAS System Passwords: The SAS System lets you assign passwords to SAS tables. These passwords control file access and are assigned using the READ=, WRITE=, and ALTER= data set options.

- READ= allows read-only access to the file.
- WRITE= allows read and write access to the file (including the ability to modify, delete, and add columns).
- ALTER= allows read and write access to the file, plus the ability to delete the file, rename columns, and create indexes.

If you do not specify the correct password with the correct option, you cannot access the file. See SAS Help and Documentation for the syntax of these data set options.

Warning

> If you forget the password, you will not be able to access your protected SAS files. Therefore, you may want to record the password in a safe place.

Warning

> Remember that SAS password protection does not prevent you from deleting files using the Windows Explorer.

You can modify the READ=, WRITE=, and ALTER= values from the SAS Explorer. To do so, right-click the SAS table name, then click **Properties**. In the resulting dialog box, click the **Passwords** tab. You should see a dialog box similar to the one shown in Figure 9.1.

Figure 9.1 Properties Dialog Box

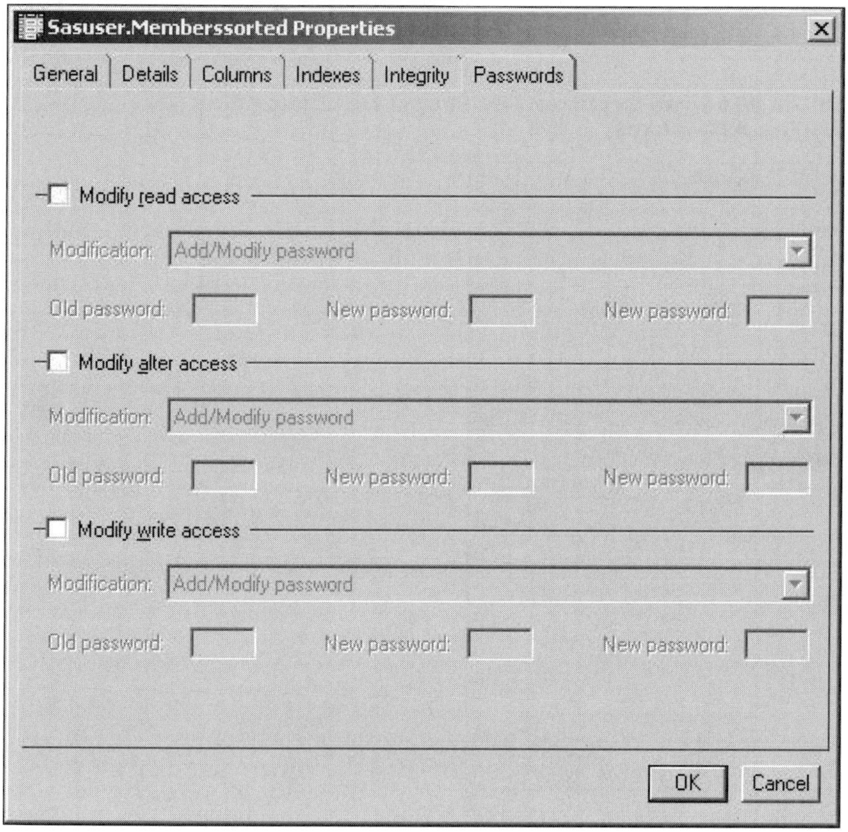

Click the appropriate check box (Read, Alter, or Write). Type the old password (once) and new password (twice) for the appropriate option, then click **OK**.

To clear a password, click the down arrow next to the **Modify** field, and select **Clear password**. Now click **OK**.

Using File Attributes: You can also use the Windows Explorer to set file attributes, which are different from SAS System passwords. Here are the steps to display a file's attributes in the Windows Explorer:

1. Open the Windows Explorer by right-clicking the **Start** button, then clicking **Explore**.
2. Display the folder containing the file for which you want to display attributes.
3. Right-click the file for which you want to see attributes.
4. Click **Properties** in the popup menu. The Properties dialog box for the file appears.

For example, Figure 9.2 shows the Windows Explorer Properties dialog box for a SAS program file named MYSTATEMENTS.SAS.

Figure 9.2 Using the Windows Explorer File Properties Dialog Box to Set File Attributes

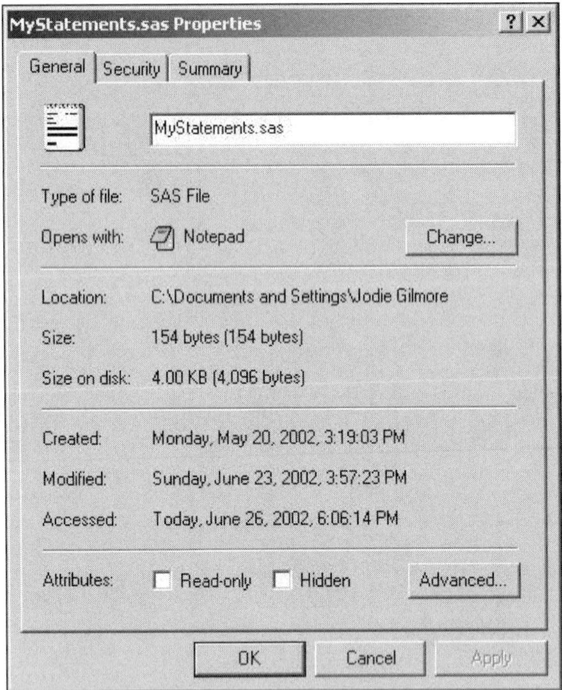

In the Properties dialog box, choose one or more of the following attributes:

- **Read-only** means users cannot write to the file, rename it, or delete it. All they can do is read it.
- **Hidden** means the file is not listed by default in the Windows Explorer's folder listings.

Turn file attributes on and off by clicking their respective check boxes. The **Advanced** button allows you to further tweak file attributes.

Note

Windows also provides other file-protection devices, such as lists of authorized users. Use the following help path to learn more: **Start** → **Help** → **Security**.

Understanding SAS System Data Protection and Windows File Protection: Setting passwords in the SAS System does not affect file access outside the SAS System. For example, if you use the READ= data set option to mark a table read-only, you can still delete it using the Windows Explorer. Therefore, if you depend on SAS System data protection, you should perform all your file management from within the SAS System using the SAS Explorer window, the COPY procedure, and other SAS System file management features.

On the other hand, file attributes set with the Windows Explorer Properties dialog box do affect the SAS System. For example, if you mark the program DATAMANIP.SAS as read-only using the Windows Explorer Properties dialog box and then try to save it from the Enhanced Editor window, you receive an "Insufficient authorization" error in your SAS log.

Similarly, if you have marked a file as hidden, it is not listed in the SAS System dialog boxes (for example, Open and Save As).

Renaming SAS Files

FasTip: Right-click the SAS filename in the SAS Explorer window, then click **Rename** in the popup menu.

You can rename SAS files from the SAS Explorer or from the Active Libraries window.

Warning

Be careful when you rename files; some files, such as the SASUSER.PROFILE catalog, must have a particular name in order to work. In general, it is safe to rename catalogs and other files you have created; do not rename files created automatically by the SAS System.

Using the SAS Explorer to Rename SAS Files: To use the SAS Explorer to rename SAS files, follow these steps:

1. Double-click the SAS data library for which you want to see the contents.
2. Continue to drill down to the SAS file you want to rename (double-clicking a catalog name if necessary).
3. Right-click the file you want to rename, then click **Rename** in the popup menu. A dialog box appears, as shown in Figure 9.3.

Figure 9.3 Rename Dialog Box for Renaming SAS Files from the SAS Explorer

Rename
Rename Veggies
Veggies
OK
Cancel

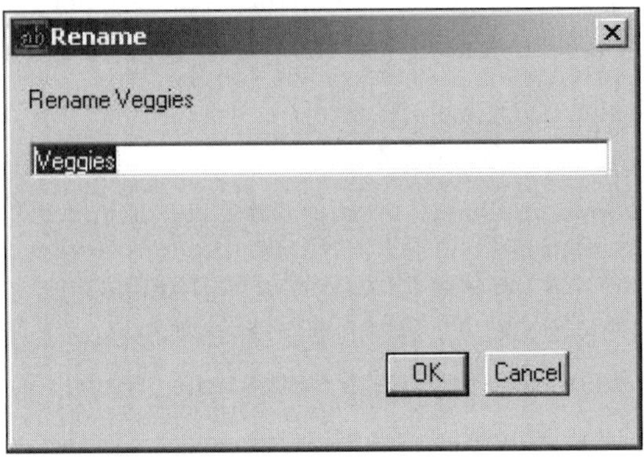

4. Type the new name in the text entry field, then click **OK**.

Note

> Remember that SAS 9.1 supports long names for most types of SAS files—you are no longer limited to eight characters.

Using the Active Libraries Window to Rename SAS Files: You can also rename SAS files from the Active Libraries window. To open this window, issue the LIBNAME command from the command bar. Figure 9.4 shows a sample Active Libraries window.

Figure 9.4 Active Libraries Window

LIBNAME
Active Libraries
Name
Engine
Type
Host Path Name
Sashelp
V9
Library
('C:\Program Files\SAS\SAS System\9.0\nls\en\SASCFG' 'C:\...
Sasuser
V9
Library
C:\Documents and Settings\Jodie Gilmore\My Documents\My...
Work
V9
Library
C:\DOCUME~1\JODIEG~1\LOCALS~1\Temp\SAS Temporary..

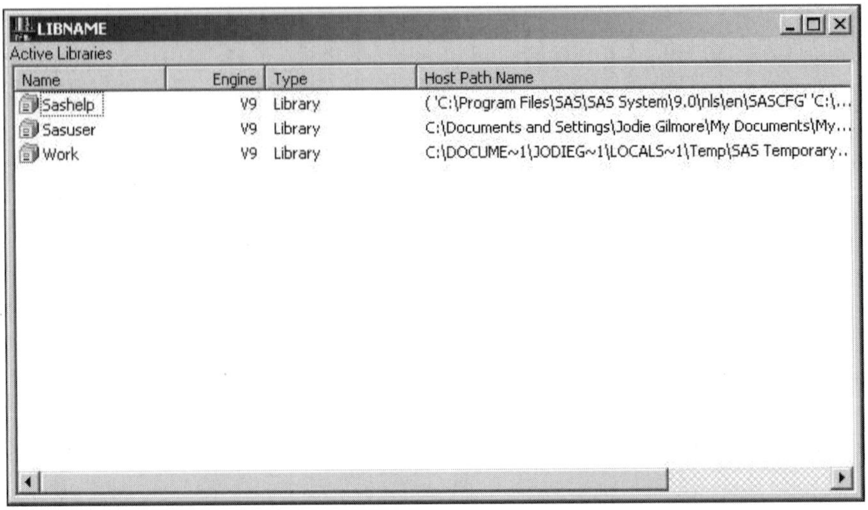

Navigate in this window as you would in the SAS Explorer window (without the tree view) until the file you want to rename is displayed. Now right-click the filename, and click **Rename** in the popup menu. Type the new name in the text entry field, then click **OK**.

Note

> You may need to resize or even close the docked windows in your SAS session to see the entire Active Libraries window. Even then, you will probably have to scroll to see the **Modified** field on the far right side of the window, unless you are using a high-resolution display.

Deleting SAS Files

FasTip: Right-click the SAS filename in the SAS Explorer window, then click **Delete** in the popup menu.

You can delete SAS files from the SAS Explorer or from the Active Libraries window.

Warning

> Be careful when you delete files; some files, such as the SASUSER.PROFILE catalog, are necessary for the SAS System to work properly. In general, it is safe to delete catalogs and other files you have created; do not delete files created automatically by the SAS System.

Note

> If you try to delete a file that is protected by the ALTER= data set option, you are prompted to enter the correct password before the file is deleted.

Using the SAS Explorer to Delete SAS Files: To use the SAS Explorer window to delete SAS files, follow these steps:

1. Double-click the SAS data library for which you want to see the contents.
2. Continue to drill down to the SAS file you want to delete (double-clicking a catalog name if necessary).
3. Right-click the file you want to delete, then click **Delete** in the popup menu.
4. When asked whether you are sure you want to delete the file, click **OK**.

Using the Active Libraries Window to Delete SAS Files: You can also delete SAS files from the Active Libraries window. To open this window, issue the LIBNAME command from the command bar. Figure 9.4 shows a sample Active Libraries window.

Navigate in this window as you would in the SAS Explorer window until the file you want to delete is displayed. Now right-click the filename, and click **Delete** in the popup menu. When asked whether you are sure you want to delete the file, click **OK**.

Warning

Files deleted using the SAS Explorer window or other methods within the SAS System are not sent to the Windows Recycle Bin, and therefore they cannot be easily recovered. To recover such files, you must have a third-party file restoration utility, such as Norton Utilities.

Moving and Copying SAS Files Using the SAS Explorer

The SAS System provides the COPY procedure, and it works the same under Windows as it does under any other operating system. But if you prefer the object-oriented method of moving and copying files, use the SAS Explorer to move and copy files from one folder to another.

Note

Moving files from one folder to another involves deleting a file from the original folder. If you have protected your SAS tables with the ALTER= data set option (which prevents you from deleting the file without providing the password), you must specify the password to move these tables.

Moving Files with Drag-and-Drop: To move a file using the drag-and-drop technique in the SAS Explorer, follow these steps:

1. Navigate until the file you want to move is displayed in the right pane of the SAS Explorer (use tree view).
2. Use the right mouse button to drag the file into the left pane and drop the file on the SAS data library or catalog to which you want to move the file.
3. When the popup menu appears, click **Move**. The file is moved to the new folder.

Copying Files Using Drag-and-Drop: To copy a file using the drag-and-drop technique in the SAS Explorer, follow these steps:

1. Navigate until the file you want to copy is displayed in the right pane of the SAS Explorer (use tree view).
2. Use the right mouse button to drag the file into the left pane and drop the file on the SAS data library or catalog to which you want to copy the file.
3. When the popup menu appears, click **Copy**. The file is copied to the new folder.

Copying Files Using the Popup Menus: To copy a file using the popup menus in the SAS Explorer, follow these steps:

1. Navigate until the file you want to copy is displayed in the right pane of the SAS Explorer (use tree view).
2. Right-click the file you want to copy. Click one of the following popup menu items:

- **Copy**, if you want to copy the file to a different SAS data library. Go to step 3 and then step 4.
- **Duplicate**, if you want to create a copy of the file in the same SAS data library. Go to step 5 and then step 6.

3. If you clicked **Copy**, now navigate in the SAS Explorer until the contents of the target SAS data library or catalog are displayed in the right pane.
4. Right-click in the right pane, and click **Paste**. The SAS file is now copied to the target SAS data library, and you are finished (do not continue with steps 5 and 6).
5. If you clicked **Duplicate**, a dialog box appears, as shown in Figure 9.5.

Figure 9.5 Duplicate Dialog Box for Duplicating SAS Files from the SAS Explorer

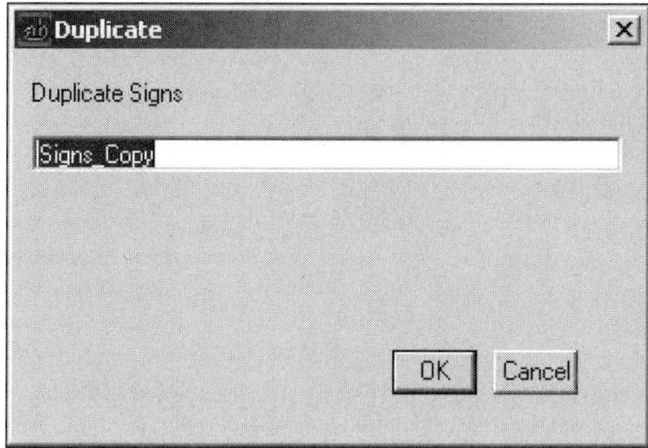

6. Type the new name for the duplicate SAS file in the Duplicate dialog box, then click **OK**. The new SAS file appears in the right pane of the SAS Explorer.

Selecting More Than One File to Move or Copy: You can move or copy more than one file from the original folder to the target folder. To do so, use the Shift and Control keys in combination with your left mouse button to select multiple files, as described here:

- To select several contiguous files, click the first filename, hold the Shift key down, and click the last filename.
- To select several files that are separated by files you do not want to select, click the first filename, hold down the Control key, and click the subsequent filenames.

Note

If you select more than one file and then choose **Duplicate**, a Duplicate dialog box appears for each SAS file you selected. Enter the new name and click **OK** to progress to the next dialog box.

Managing SAS Data Libraries

What's New: SAS Explorer features replace old library-maintenance dialog boxes.

There is no longer a Libraries tool on the SAS System tool bar (although there is still a New Library tool).

In 64-bit environments, the V6 engine is read-only.

FasTip: Use the SAS Explorer to list the active SAS data libraries, or issue the LIBNAME command to see a similar active library references list.

 Click the Add New Library icon on the SAS tool bar to create a new library reference.

SAS data libraries are central to using the SAS System. The SAS System offers several easy ways to manage SAS data libraries.

Listing Active Library References: If you have assigned many library references (also called librefs) during a SAS session, it is often difficult to remember which library reference points to which folder.

You can view active library references in two ways:

- Double-click the Libraries icon in the SAS Explorer window—this displays all currently defined library references.
- Use the Active Libraries window to display a list of currently assigned library references. To open the Active Libraries window, issue the LIBNAME command from the command bar.

To see the members of a particular library, double-click the library reference (in either the SAS Explorer or Active Libraries window).

To see the engine and physical pathname associated with each library reference listed in the SAS Explorer, click **View → Details** in the SAS System main menu.

Figure 9.4 earlier in this chapter shows a sample Active Libraries window. Like the detailed SAS Explorer view, the Active Libraries window shows you which SAS engine is associated with each library and the library's physical pathname.

Note

> You may need to resize or even close the docked windows in your SAS session to see the entire Active Libraries window. Even then, you will probably have to scroll to see the **Modified** field on the far right side of the window, unless you are using a high-resolution display.

Viewing the Contents of a SAS Data Library: To view the contents of a particular data library, double-click its name in the SAS Explorer or Active Libraries window.

Creating a New Library Reference: To create a new library reference, click the Add New Library icon on the SAS tool bar.

Alternatively, you can right-click the Libraries icon in the SAS Explorer, then click **New** in the popup menu. In either case, the New Library dialog box opens, as shown in Figure 9.6.

Figure 9.6 New Library Dialog Box

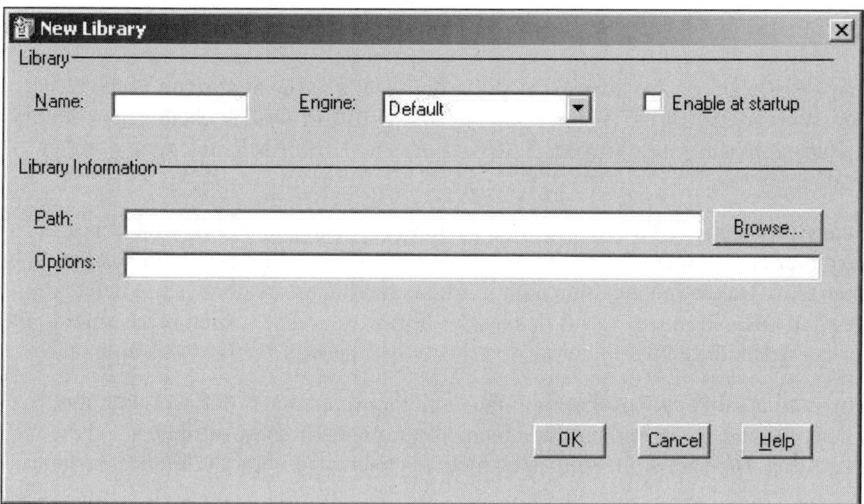

This dialog box works like a point-and-click LIBNAME statement.

Type the new library reference in the **Name** field. Use the **Browse** button to find the folder you want to associate with the library reference. When you have found the folder you want, click **OK**. This copies the folder name to the **Path** field in the New Library dialog box. Alternatively, you can type the folder name directly into the **Path** field. Choose the engine you want to associate with the library reference by clicking the down arrow next to the **Engine** field and clicking the correct engine name. (The default engine is V9.)

Note

SAS 9.1 includes the V604 engine; however, the V606 engine is not a valid engine name in SAS 9.1—use V6 instead.

Type any options you want to associate with the library reference in the **Options** field. The options you can enter depend on which engine you select for the library. For example, to create a read-only SAS 9.1 SAS data library, you can specify the following in the **Options** field:

```
ACCESS=READONLY
```

When you have filled in all the fields, click **OK**. This creates the new library reference.

Creating a Concatenated SAS Data Library: To create a library reference that points to a concatenation of folders, click in the **Path** field in the New Library dialog box and enter a quoted list of folders contained inside parentheses. For example, if you want the library reference to point to both the folders C:\BACKUP and C:\Old Files, enter the following in the **Path** field:

```
('c:\backup' 'c:\old files')
```

Assigning Library References Automatically: If you select **Enable at startup** in the New Library dialog box, a library definition is stored in your SASUSER.PROFILE catalog. The library reference is available as soon as you start your SAS session—no LIBNAME statement or other action is necessary.

Deleting a Library Reference: To delete a library reference, display the library reference in either the SAS Explorer or the Active Libraries window. Right-click the library reference you want to delete, then click **Delete** in the popup menu. When asked if you really want to delete the library reference, click **OK**. (Remember, this deletes the library reference, which is a pointer to the folder, but it does not delete the actual folder.)

Editing Attributes of a Library Reference: Once a library reference is defined, with its name, associated engine, and associated physical path, you cannot edit these attributes "on the fly" during your SAS session. Here are some suggested methods to change library reference attributes:

- Delete the library reference, then define it again with the new attributes.
- Use LIBNAME statements to assign your library references, and store these statements in an AUTOEXEC.SAS file. When you need to modify a library reference definition, edit the AUTOEXEC.SAS file, then restart your SAS session. For more information about using AUTOEXEC.SAS files, see "Creating and Editing the Autoexec File" in Chapter 11.
- Use the New Library dialog box and the **Enable at Startup** check box to define your library references, then export the SAS registry to a text file. You can then edit the library reference definitions in this text file, and then import the edited text file back into the SAS registry. Appendix 5 shows how to use this approach.

Caution

Editing the SAS registry file can seriously affect your SAS session, and is not for beginning SAS users.

Managing File Shortcuts

FasTip: Double-click the File Shortcuts icon in the SAS Explorer window, or issue the FILENAME command.

Chapter 2 showed you how to create a file shortcut (also called a fileref) using the SAS Explorer. However, once you create several file shortcuts, it can be hard to remember which shortcut points to what file.

You can display the active file shortcuts in two ways:

- Double-click the File Shortcuts icon in the SAS Explorer window.
- Open the Active File Shortcuts window by issuing the FILENAME command.

If you want to see details about each file shortcut in the SAS Explorer window, such as the physical pathname associated with each file shortcut, click **View → Details** in the SAS System main menu.

Figure 9.8 shows a sample Active File Shortcuts window.

Figure 9.8 Active File Shortcuts Window

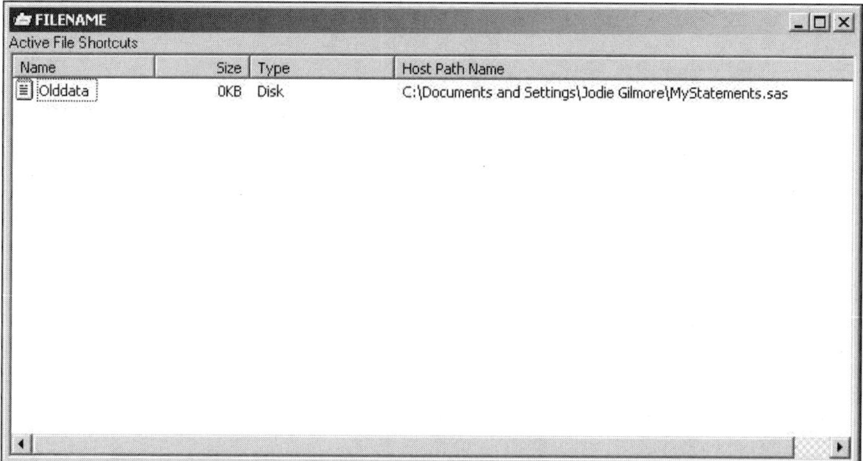

The Active File Shortcuts window lists each file shortcut, the physical file that the file shortcut points to, and other attributes as appropriate (such as file size and file type). You may have to scroll right in the window to see all the information.

Managing SAS Catalogs

While you can manage your catalogs programmatically with the CATALOG procedure, you may find it easier to use the SAS Explorer and Active Libraries windows to rename, move, copy, and delete SAS catalog entries.

If the entry is an executable entry, such as NOTEPAD.SOURCE or a BUILD entry, double-clicking an entry opens that entry. This is the same as pointing at the entry name, right-clicking to activate the popup menu, and clicking **Open**. Other possible actions, depending on the type of entry you are pointing at, include clicking **Rename**, **Delete**, and **Copy**.

Warning

Be careful renaming catalog entries—some entries have required names (such as SAS.CPARMS). In general, it is safe to rename entries you have created but not entries created automatically by the SAS System. Also, exercise care when deleting entries. For example, if you delete the entry GENWSAVE.WSAVE, you lose all the general preferences you have set via the Preferences dialog box.

Using SAS Enterprise Guide: A Primer

Introduction

SAS Enterprise Guide provides the full power of the SAS System in a more Windows-like intuitive interface. Enterprise Guide can serve as a productivity and decision-making tool that enables you to easily

- organize your data
- perform data analysis
- create graphs
- generate reports.

What's more, you can combine all these types of components into *projects*, which enable you to more easily answer vital business questions and distribute important information throughout your organization. And, you are not limited to the data residing on your own machine. It is possible, through Enterprise Guide servers, to access data anywhere in your organization.

Some of the more commonly used features of Enterprise Guide include the following:

- query tools to help you access the data you need
- task wizards that guide you through data analysis and reporting tasks
- a color-coded editor (similar to the Enhanced Editor)
- publishing options that enable you to rapidly disseminate information to coworkers.

Getting More Information: This chapter introduces you to using SAS Enterprise Guide's interface and capabilities. You can obtain more information on Enterprise Guide through its online help, and by visiting www.sas.com/products/guide. Enterprise Guide also provides a tutorial, which you can access from the Enterprise Guide Welcome window or from the Enterprise Guide **Help** menu (click **Help → Getting Started Tutorial**).

Note

The information in this chapter applies to Version 2.0 of SAS Enterprise Guide. Some of the features documented here may not be available or may work differently in other versions.

Starting Enterprise Guide

Note

This chapter does not cover installing Enterprise Guide. For that, see the documentation that came with your Enterprise Guide software.

To start Enterprise Guide, click the **Start** button, then click **Programs → SAS → Enterprise Guide V2**. Figure 10.1 shows the window that appears by default when you begin an Enterprise Guide session.

Figure 10.1 Sample Enterprise Guide Welcome Window

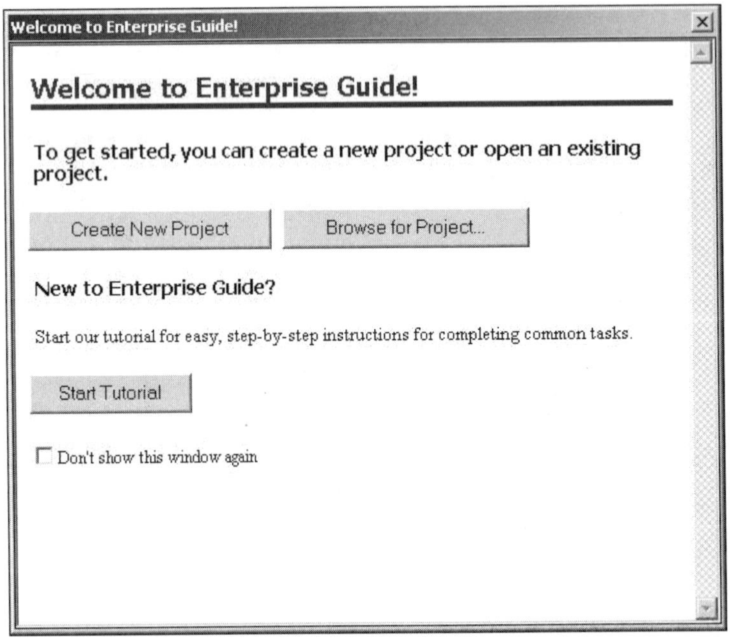

If you have already created projects with Enterprise Guide, these would be listed in an area titled **Recent Projects**. You can use this window to access the Enterprise Guide tutorial, create a new project, or browse through the files on your computer for an existing project.

For now, just close the window to access the Enterprise Guide session, a sample of which is shown in Figure 10.2.

Figure 10.2 Sample Enterprise Guide Session at Start-up

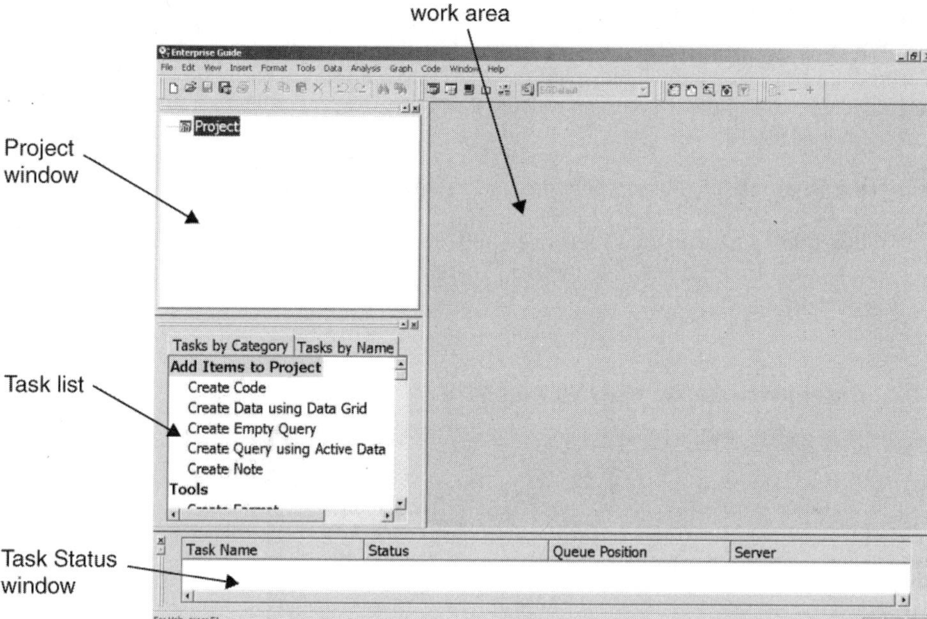

Figure 10.2 also labels the various portions of the Enterprise Guide window, such as the Project window, the Task list, and the work area.

Project window: This portion of the Enterprise Guide session displays the name of the currently open project, and all the project's components (sometimes called nodes). In Figure 10.2, the project does not yet have any components.

Task list: To help you build your projects and perform data analysis and reporting, the Task list displays commonly used tasks. The tasks are organized by category (such as **Add Items to Project** and **Descriptive**) and by name (such as **Append Table** and **Box Chart**) on two separate tabs.

Task Status window: This window displays the status of running tasks.

Work area: The remaining portion of the Enterprise Guide window is the work area, where data and results are displayed.

Creating or Opening a Project

Understanding Projects: It is important to understand that a project is a logical collection of components. For example, a project can "contain" a number of tables. In actuality, the project contains only pointers to those tables, not the tables themselves. Therefore, if you delete one of the tables from a project, you do not delete the actual data, but only the pointer to it. The physical SAS data set continues to reside on your system. Similarly, you can rename a component in a project, such as a SAS program. But in doing so, you do not change the physical filename of the object.

Projects form the basis of Enterprise Guide. Essentially, a project is a collection of related components. For example, a project might consist of a few tables, a couple of SAS programs, some predefined queries against the tables, and some predefined reports based on the data in the tables. The project groups all these components together into a logical collection that can then be easily distributed or accessed.

Creating a New Project: To create a new project, follow these steps:

1.  Click **File** → **New** in the Enterprise Guide main menu. Alternatively, click the New icon on the Enterprise Guide toolbar. This displays the New dialog box, as shown in Figure 10.3.

Figure 10.3 Enterprise Guide New Dialog Box

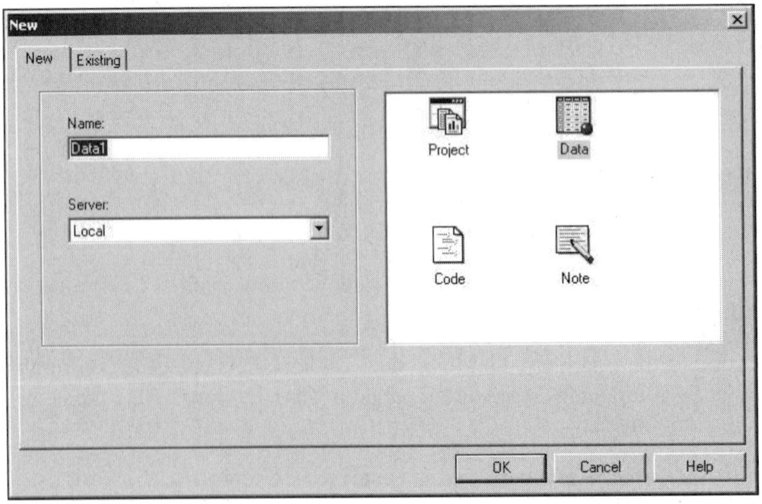

2. Click **Project**, then type a name such as `MyFirstProject` in the **Name** field.
3. Click **OK**.

Now the Project window lists the project you just created.

Opening an Existing Project: You can have only one project open at a time. To open an existing project, follow these steps:

1. Close any already-open project by clicking **File** → **Close *project-name*** in the Enterprise Guide main menu.
2. Click **File** → **Open** in the Enterprise Guide main menu. This displays the Open dialog box.
3. Click the **Existing** tab.
4. Be sure the **Open as** field is set to **Project**.
5. Select the appropriate project file (project files have an extension of .SEG).
6. Click **OK** to open the project.

Saving a Project

FasTip: Click the Save Project icon on the toolbar.

Like most files, a project must be saved before the changes you have made to it become permanent. To save a project, follow these steps:

1. Be sure the project name is highlighted in the Project window.
2. Click **File** → **Save *project-name*** in the Enterprise Guide main menu.
3. If you have previously saved the project, the project is immediately saved.
4. If this is the first time you have saved the project, the Save As dialog box appears, where you can name the project and select the folder in which it is to be saved. Click **Save** in the Save As dialog box to complete the save.

Adding a Data Component to a Project

FasTip: Click the Insert Data icon on the toolbar.

Gone are the days when you needed to know DATA step syntax to enter data. Entering data into Enterprise Guide is as easy as entering data into a table in a word processing application.

Creating a New Table: Here are the steps for creating a table in Enterprise Guide:

1. Be sure the name of the project to which you want to add the table is highlighted in the Project window.
2. Double-click **Create Data Using Data Grid** in the Task list. A data grid, with the table's name in the title bar, appears in the work area, as shown in Figure 10.4.

Figure 10.4 Enterprise Guide Work Area with New Data Grid

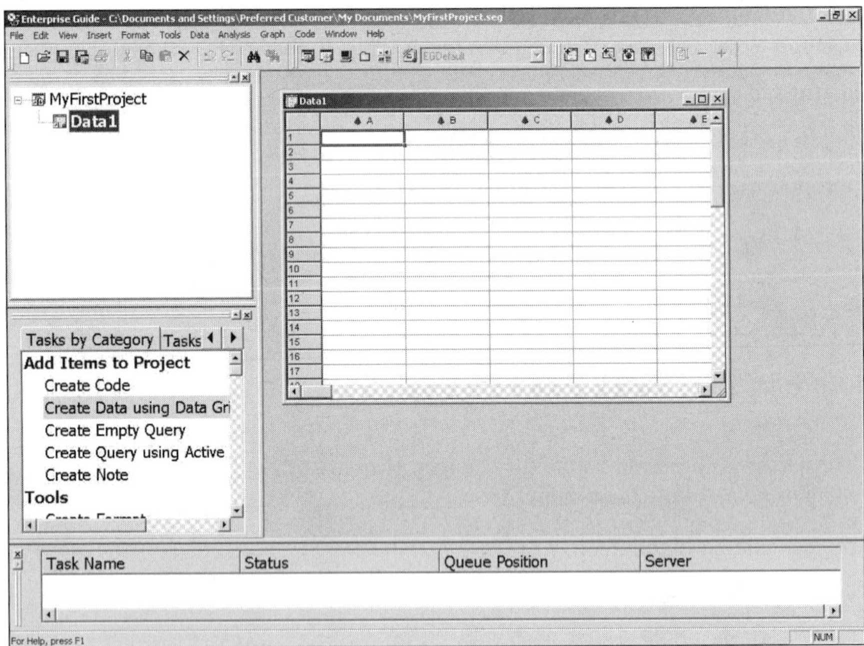

You can move the data grid around in the work area, and maximize or minimize it, as you can with any window. You may find that maximizing both the Enterprise Guide session and the data grid window makes it easier to enter and work with data.

Renaming Data Grid Columns: The columns are by default named A, B, C, and so on. To rename a column, follow these steps:

1. Right-click the column name, and click **Properties** in the resulting list. This displays the Properties dialog box, as shown in Figure 10.5.

Figure 10.5 Enterprise Guide Properties Dialog Box

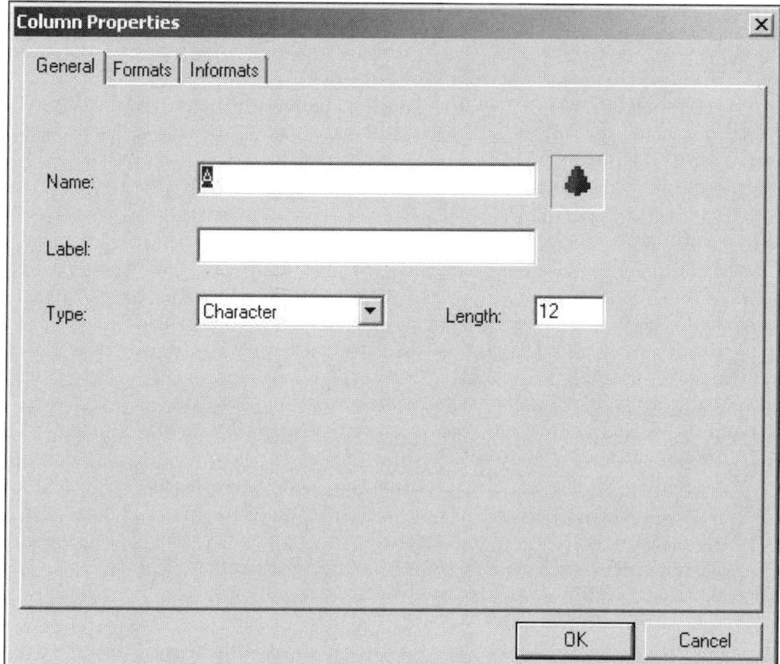

2. Fill in the **Name** and **Label** fields as appropriate, then set the **Type** and **Length** fields.
3. Click **OK** to close the Properties dialog box.
4. Repeat steps 1–3 for each column that you want to rename. For example, Figure 10.6 shows a data grid with the first four columns renamed.

Figure 10.6 Enterprise Guide Data Grid with Renamed Columns

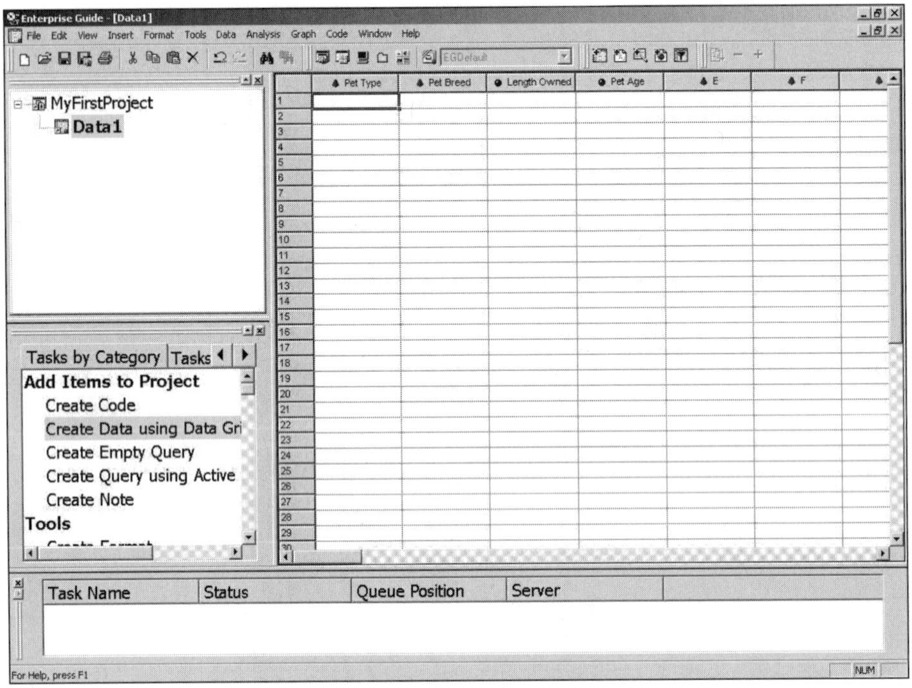

Entering Data into the Data Grid: Now that you have the columns named, you are ready to enter the data. This works just like entering data into a spreadsheet such as Microsoft Excel. For example, pressing TAB moves the cursor to the next cell, and the arrow keys move the cursor up and down the rows. Figure 10.7 shows the data grid after 25 rows of data have been entered.

Figure 10.7 Enterprise Guide Data Grid with Data

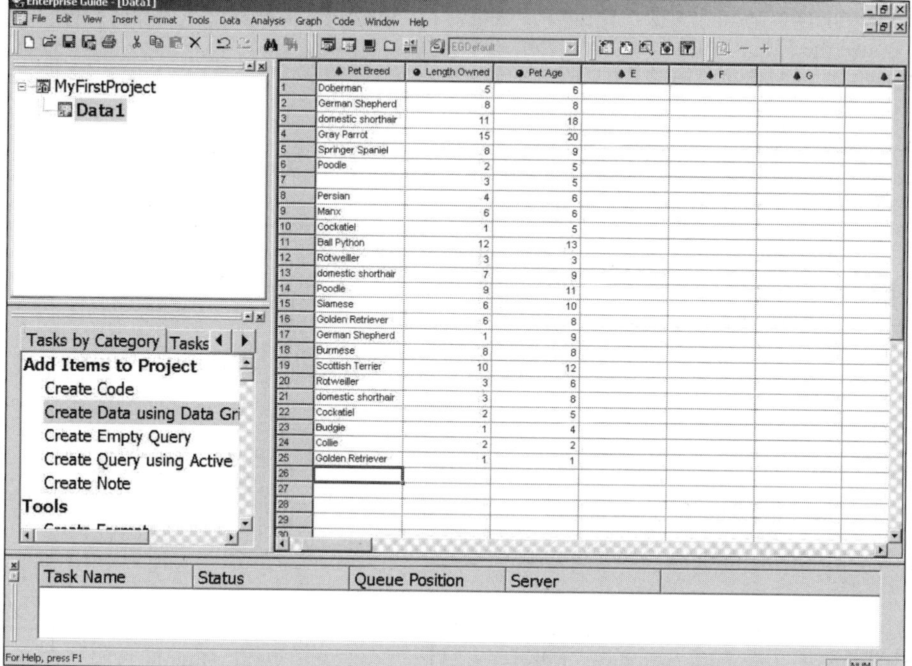

Note

While you are entering data into the data grid, the table is temporary. It is not stored permanently until you save it.

Saving Your Table: To move the data from the temporary WORK SAS data library to a permanent location, you must save the data you just entered. To do so, follow these steps:

1. Right-click on the data component in the Project window, and click **Save *data-name*** in the resulting popup menu. This displays the Save As dialog box.
2. Give the data component the name you want it to have, and navigate to the appropriate folder in which you want the data saved. For example, you might give it the name PetData (the file extension defaults to .SAS7BDAT).
3. Click **Save** to complete the save.

Renaming a Data Component: The default name of "Data1" may not be the most helpful name for your newly created data component. To rename the data component, simply right-click it in the Project window, then click **Rename** in the resulting popup menu. Type the new name (such as "PetData"), and press ENTER.

Note

Renaming a component in the Project window does not rename the physical file. To rename the physical file, use the **File → Save As** menu choice.

Caution

Do NOT rename components of Enterprise Guide projects using the Windows Explorer. If you do so, Enterprise Guide will not be able to open the files.

Adding an Existing Table to a Project: Besides creating data "on the fly" using the data grid, you can also add existing tables to your project. To do so, follow these steps:

1. In the Project window, right-click the name of the project to which you want to add the table.
2. Click **Insert** in the resulting popup menu.
3. When the New Dialog box appears, click the **Existing** tab.
4. Navigate to where the data are stored, and select the data.
5. Click **OK** to complete the insert action.

Note

When you add an existing table to a project, it is added in "Protected" mode (that is, read-only). See the following section, "Switching between Read-Only and Update Mode," for more information.

Switching between Read-Only and Update Mode: Because the data components of a project are merely pointers to physical data files and are often used only for informational purposes, Enterprise Guide provides a way to protect your data from unintended changes. You cannot change the protection mode of a data component unless it is open.

To change a data component from protected to update mode, follow these steps:

1. Double-click the data component in the Project window to open it.
2. Click **Data → Protected** (which has a check mark next to it) in the Enterprise Guide main menu.
3. When the dialog box appears, asking you if you are sure you want to change to update mode, click **Yes**.

The **Protected** menu selection acts as a toggle, so selecting it again will change the data component back to read-only.

Adding a Report to a Project

Collecting data is all well and good—but to be useful, data must be turned into information. Enterprise Guide provides all kinds of tools to transform data into information. In this section, we'll run two simple reports on the PETDATA table:

- One resembles a PROC PRINT with a BY statement.
- One provides some summary statistics, resembling a PROC MEANS with a BY statement, as well as some graphs (if you have SAS/GRAPH licensed).

Using the List Data Task: On the **Tasks by Category** tab of the Task list, the **Descriptive** category contains several types of reports you can generate. The following example shows how to use the **List Data** task to generate a report that shows the pet data organized by pet type (dog, cat, bird, etc.). To work through this example, follow these steps:

1. Select the PETDATA table in the Project window by clicking it.
2. Scroll the Task list to the **Descriptive** category.
3. Double-click the **List Data** task. This displays the List Data dialog box, as shown in Figure 10.8.

Figure 10.8 Enterprise Guide List Data Dialog Box

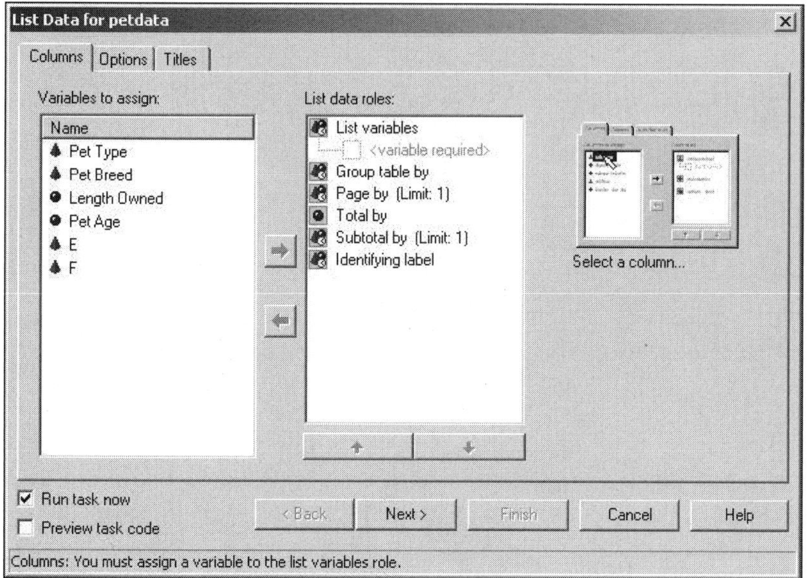

4. The first thing to do is to tell Enterprise Guide what variables you want to list. For our example, we'll include all the variables. You include a variable by dragging its name from the **Variables to assign** list and dropping it on the **List variables** role in the **List data roles** list.

5. Since we want to include several variables, click **Pet Type**, hold the Shift key down, and click **Pet Age**. All four variables are now highlighted.

6. Drag the highlighted variables over to the **List data roles** list and drop them.

7. For our example, we want to group the data by type of pet. To accomplish this, click in the **Variables to assign** list to clear the highlighting.

8. Now drag **Pet Type** from the **Variables to assign** list and drop it on the **Group table by** role. Figure 10.9 shows how the List Data dialog box should look at the end of step 8.

Figure 10.9 Enterprise Guide List Data Dialog Box with Defined Report

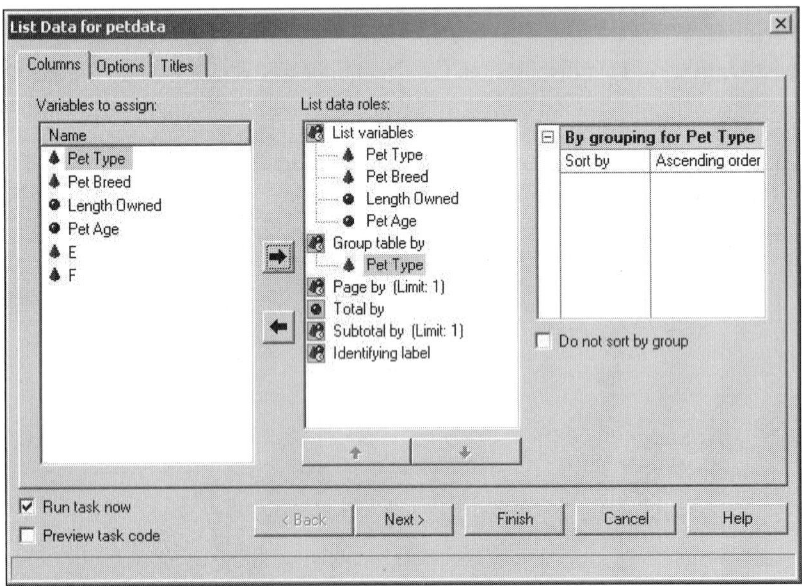

9. Click **Next**. This displays the **Options** tab of the List Data dialog box. For our example, we won't change anything here.

10. Click **Next** again. This displays the **Titles** tab of the List Data dialog box, as shown in Figure 10.10.

Figure 10.10 Titles Tab of Enterprise Guide List Data Dialog Box

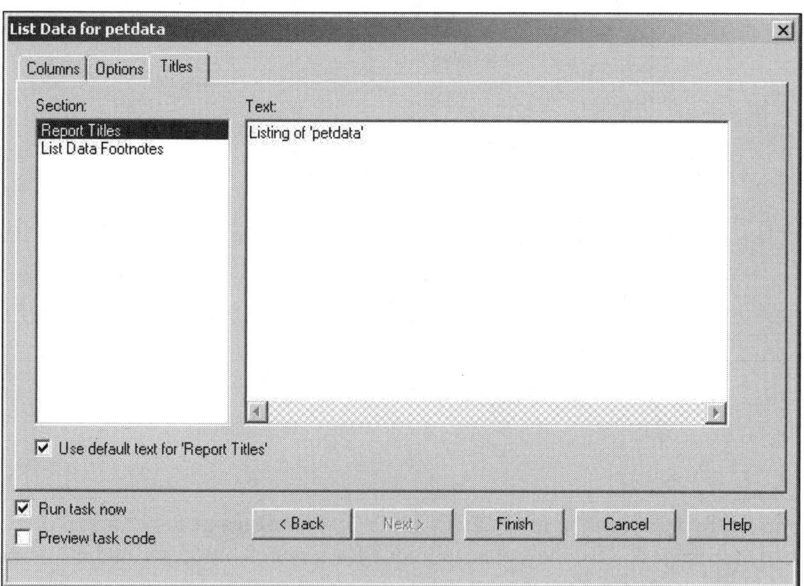

11. Type your preferred title in the **Text** area, such as `Pet Data Report`.

12. Click **Finish**.

The report is displayed in the Enterprise Guide work area, in a window titled HTML for List Data. The report along with its code and log is added to the Project window, as you can see in Figure 10.11. (In Figure 10.11, the report has been maximized so you can see more of the data.)

Figure 10.11 Report Added to the Project

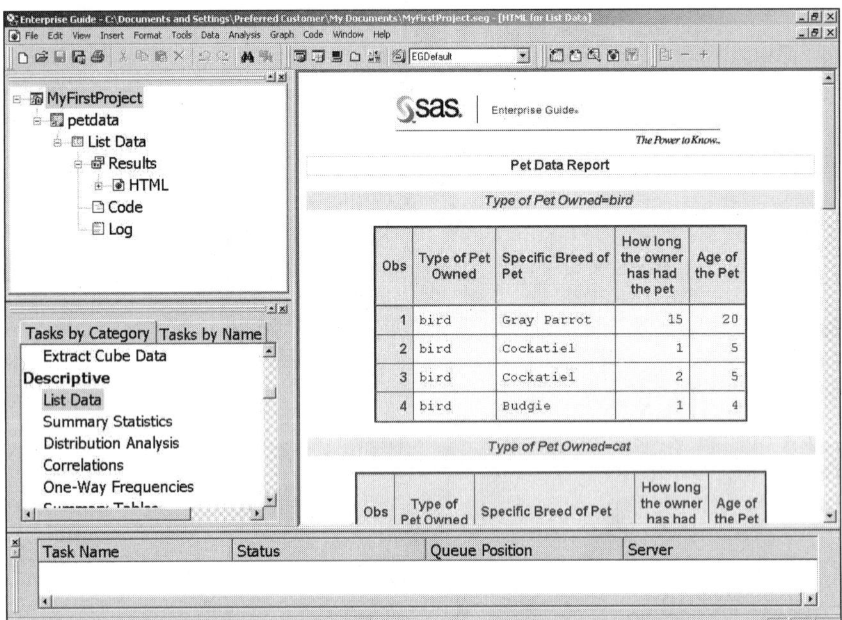

You can change the name of the report in the Project window from **List Data** to something more informative, such as **Pet Data Report**. Use the same technique for renaming as described in "Renaming a Data Component" earlier in this chapter.

Using the Summary Statistics Task: Now we'll add a second report that provides some statistics about the average age of each type of pet and the average time owners have owned each type of pet. To work through this example, follow these steps:

1. Select the PETDATA table in the Project window by clicking it.
2. Scroll the Task list to the **Descriptive** category.
3. Double-click the **Summary Statistics** task. This displays the Summary Statistics dialog box, as shown in Figure 10.12.

Figure 10.12 Summary Statistics Dialog Box

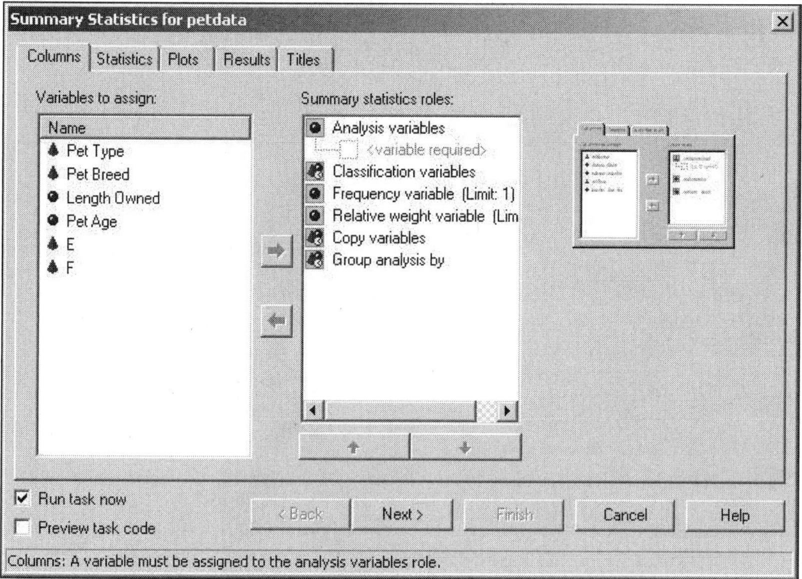

4. We want to analyze the variables Length Owned and Pet Age. So, highlight these two variables in the **Variables to assign** list (use the Shift key), then drag them over to the **Analysis variables** role and drop them.

5. To group the results by type of pet, drag the **Pet Type** variable from the **Variables to assign** list and drop it on the **Group analysis by** role.

6. Click **Next**. This displays the **Statistics** tab of the Summary Statistics dialog box, as shown in Figure 10.13.

Figure 10.13 Statistics Tab of Summary Statistics Dialog Box

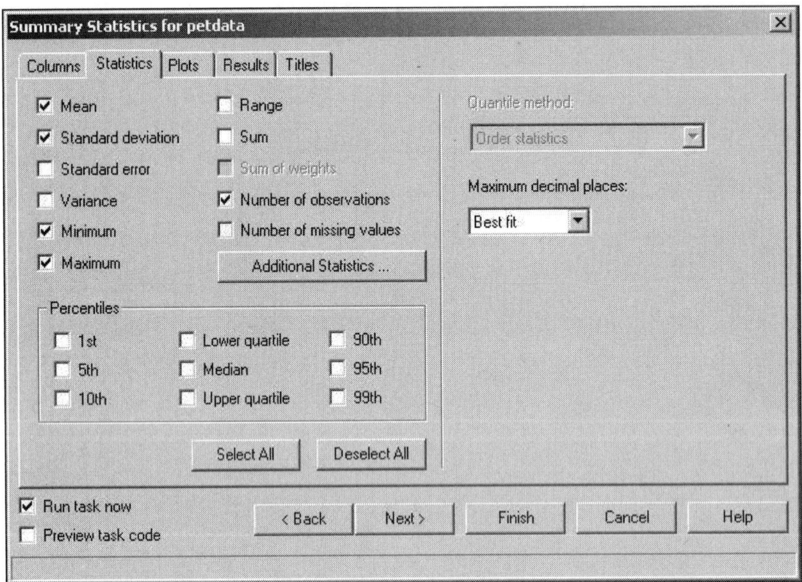

7. Deselect **Standard Deviation**, and change the value of the **Maximum decimal places** field to 0.

8. Click **Next**. This displays the **Plots** tab of the Summary Statistics dialog box, as shown in Figure 10.14.

Figure 10.14 Plots Tab of Summary Statistics Dialog Box

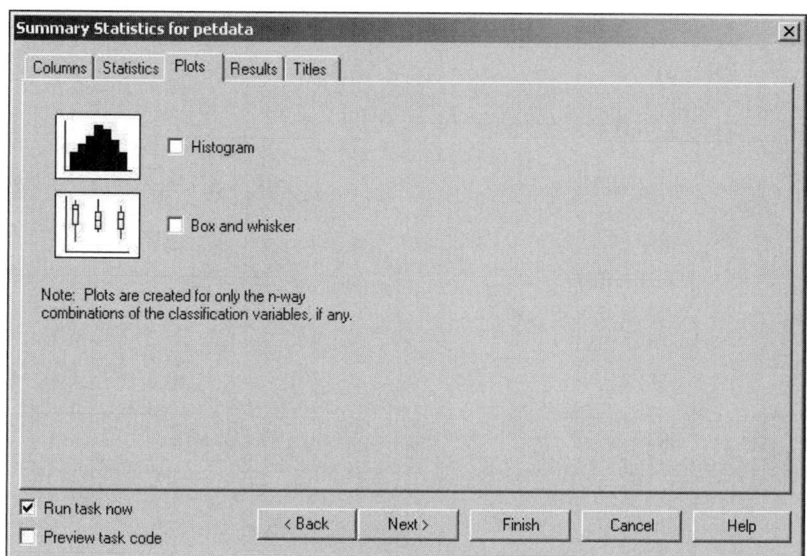

9. Select **Histogram**.
10. Click the **Titles** tab of the Summary Statistics box, which is shown in Figure 10.15.

Figure 10.15 Titles Tab of Summary Statistics Dialog Box

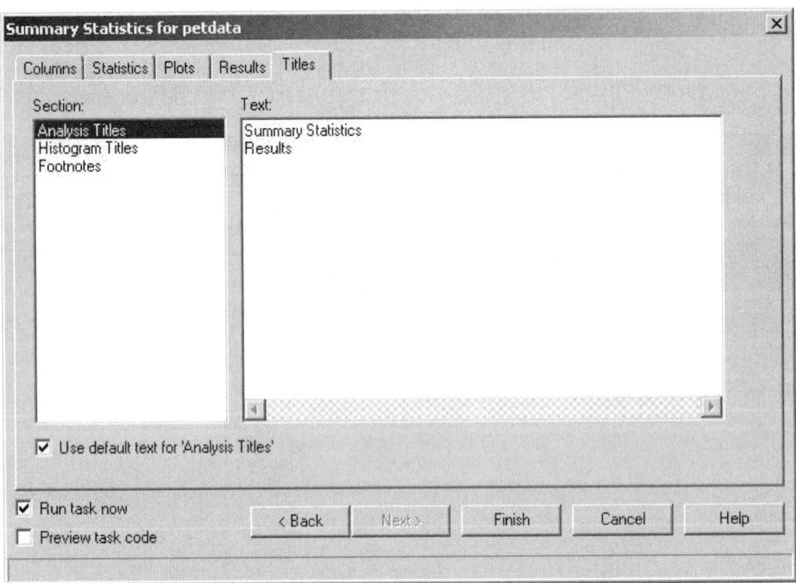

11. Give the analysis report a meaningful title in the **Text** field, such as `Summary Statistics for Pet Data: Analysis`.

12. Click **Histogram Titles** in the **Section** area, and give this a meaningful title too, such as `Summary Statistics for Pet Data: Histograms`.

13. Click **Finish**.

The report is displayed in the Enterprise Guide work area, in a window titled HTML for Summary Statistics. The report along with its code and log is added to the Project window, as you can see in Figure 10.16. (In Figure 10.16, the report has been maximized so you can see more of the data.)

Figure 10.16 Statistics Report Added to the Project

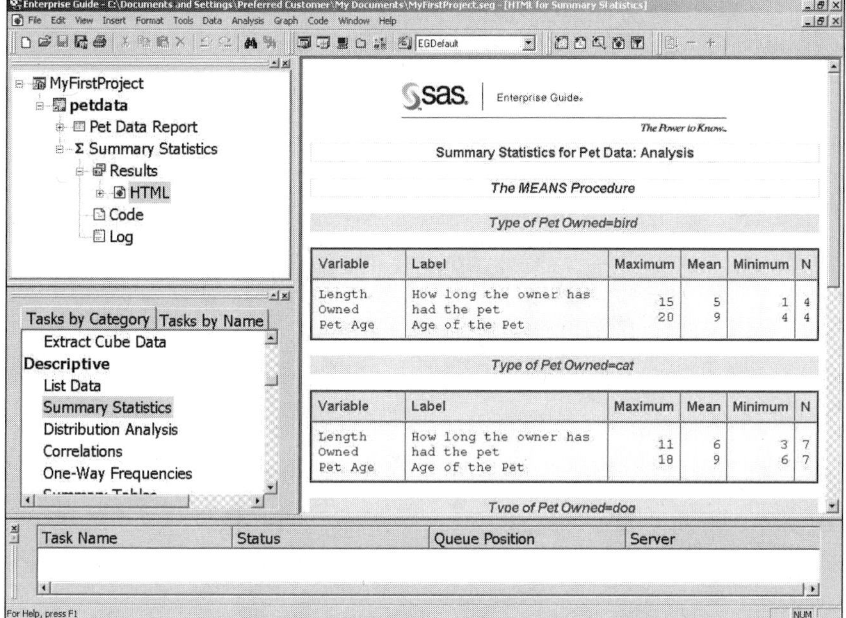

Scroll the HTML for Summary Statistics window, and you can see the histograms.

Note

Creating the histograms requires that you have a license for SAS/GRAPH software.

You can change the name of the report in the Project window from **Summary Statistics** to something more informative, such as **Summary Statistics for Pet Data**. Use the same technique for renaming as described in "Renaming a Data Component" earlier in this chapter.

Adding a Note to a Project

FasTip: Click the Insert Note icon on the toolbar.

You may find it useful to add a note to a project, where you can document the purpose of the project, considerations for the data, instructions for running the SAS code, or other information you think users of the project will find useful. To add a note to a project, follow these steps:

1. Be sure the project name to which you want to add the note is highlighted in the Project window.
2. Double-click **Create Note** in the Task list. A text-entry window appears in the work area, as shown in Figure 10.17.

Figure 10.17 Enterprise Guide Note Window

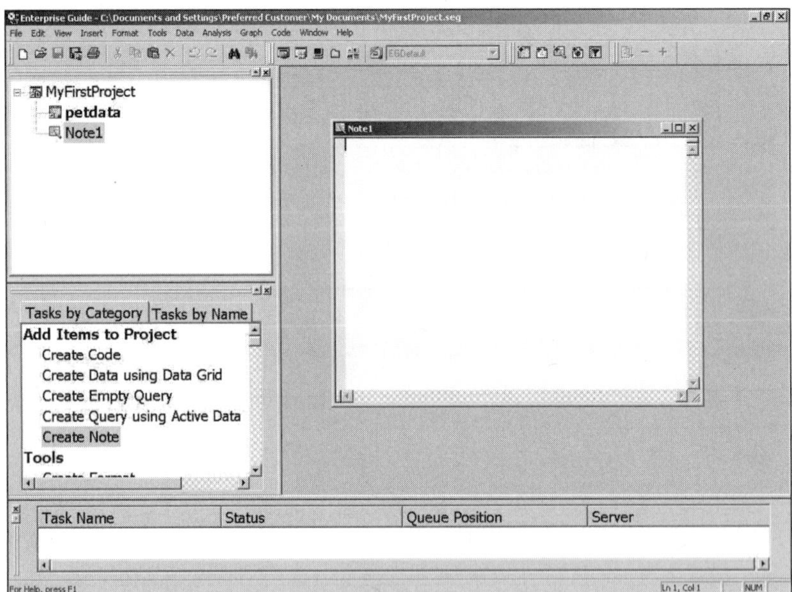

3. Type the information into the text-entry window.

To close the text-entry window, click its Close icon.

Adding a Query to a Project

FasTip: Click the Create Query icon on the toolbar.

Use the Query Builder to add a query to a project. Queries can be as simple or as complex as you want; the following example creates a query against the PETDATA table, selecting only the dogs from the list of pets. To see how the Query Builder works, follow along with this example, which is broken into various sections.

Beginning the Query

1. Open the PETDATA table by double-clicking it in the Project window. The data appear in the work area.
2. Select the project to which you want to add the query by clicking its name in the Project window.
3. In the Task list, double-click **Create Query Using Active Data** in the **Add Items to Project** category (on the **Tasks by Category** tab). This displays the Query Builder, shown in Figure 10.18.

Figure 10.18 Enterprise Guide Query Builder

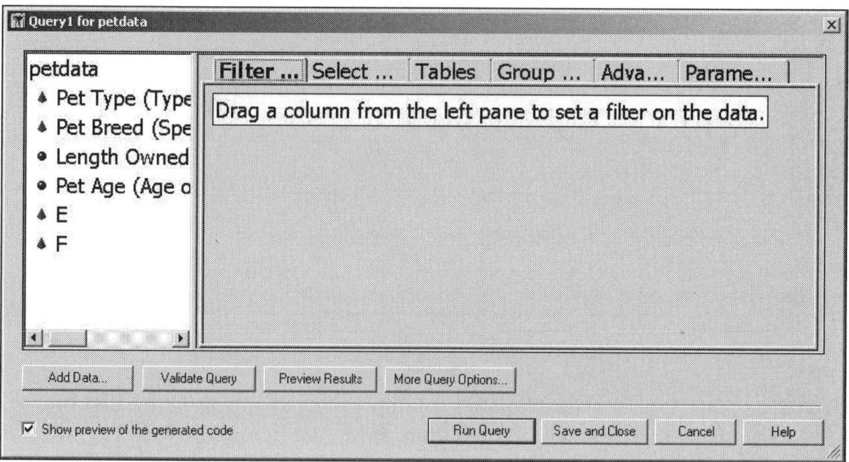

Adding a Filter: Think of a filter as a pictorial WHERE statement. For example, you might want to see the data associated with only one type of pet, or pets over a certain age. The following steps set up a filter so that the results of the query show only dogs from the PETDATA table.

1. Drag the **Pet Type** column name from the list on the left into the filter area on the right, and release it. This opens the Edit Filter Condition dialog box, as shown in Figure 10.19.

Figure 10.19 Enterprise Guide Edit Filter Condition Dialog Box

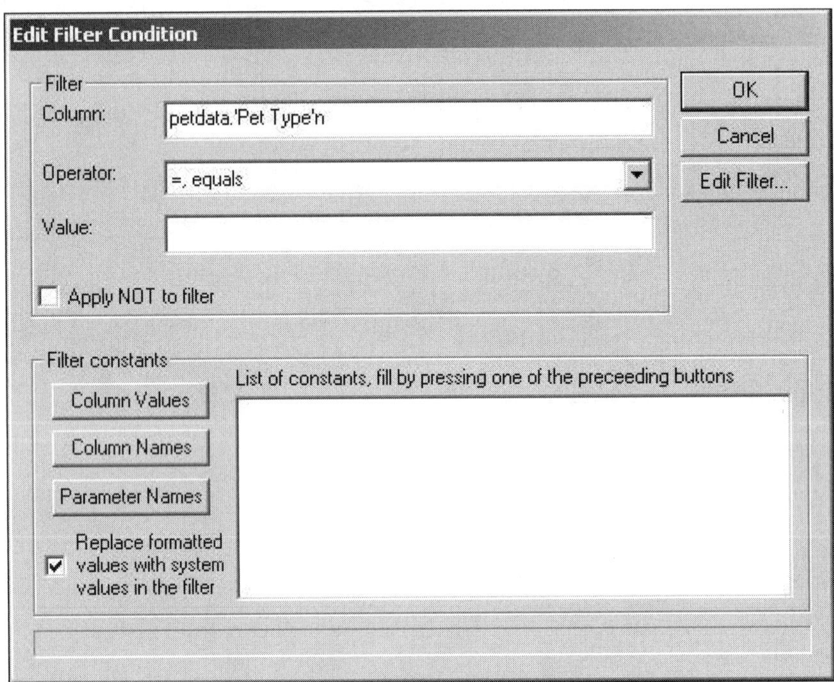

2. Click **Column Values**, which causes the available column values to appear in the **List of Column Value constants** box to the right of the button, as shown in Figure 10.20.

Figure 10.20 Displaying Column Values in the Enterprise Guide Edit Filter Condition Dialog Box

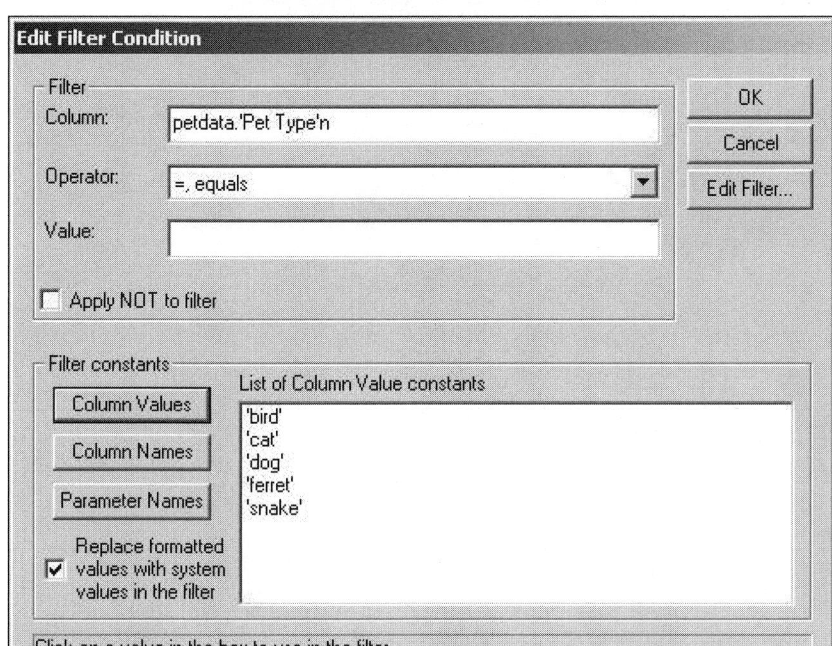

3. Click **'dog'** in the constant list, which copies that value to the **Value** field.
4. Click **OK** to close the Edit Filter Condition dialog box. Now the Query Builder displays the filter, as shown in Figure 10.21.

Figure 10.21 Enterprise Guide Query Builder, Showing Filter

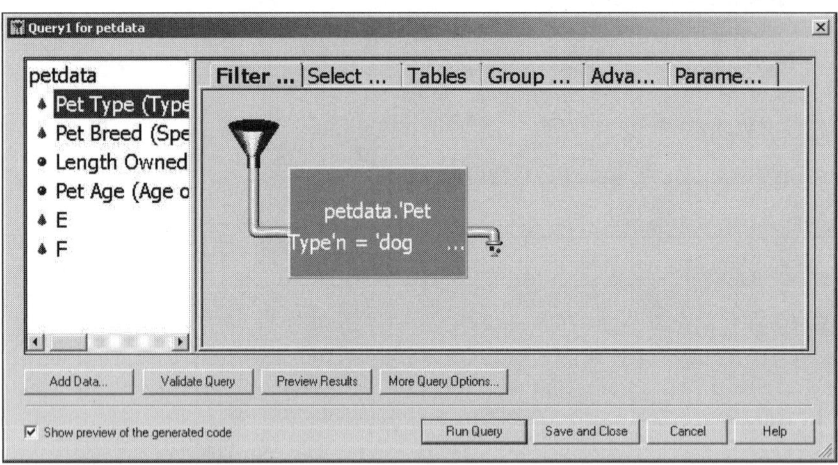

5. Click **Save** and **Close** to complete the query building operation.
6. As a last step, you might want to change the name of the query you just built to something more intuitive than "Query 1 for Petdata." For example, you could rename it "All Data for Dogs." Use the same approach as described in "Renaming a Data Component" earlier in this chapter.

Running a Query: To execute the query, right-click the query in the Project window. In the resulting popup menu, click **Run this Query**. For example, Figure 10.22 shows the results of the "All Data for Dogs" query.

Figure 10.22 Results of an Enterprise Guide Query

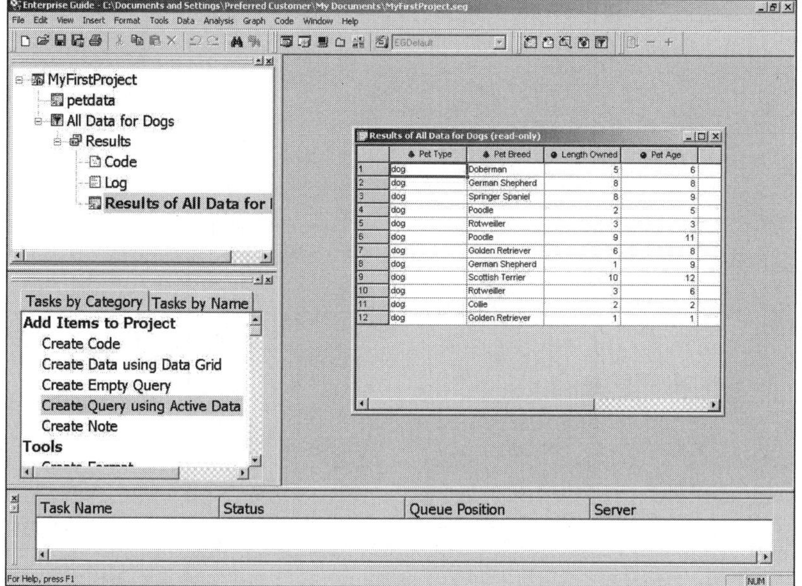

As you can see from the Project window in Figure 10.22, the results of the query include the code generated by the query, the SAS log, and the selected data.

Adding Files from Other Applications to a Project

Any file on your system can be added to an Enterprise Guide project—you are not limited to adding only SAS files. For example, you could add a Word document or an HTML file to a project. Follow these steps to add another type of file to a project:

1. Right-click on the project name in the Project window, and in the resulting popup menu, click **Insert**.
2. Click the **Existing** tab.
3. Make sure the **Open as** field is set to **Auto**.
4. Navigate to the file you want to add, select it, and click **OK**. The file is added to the project and is opened in the work area. For example, Figure 10.23 shows a Microsoft Word file added to the project.

Figure 10.23 Microsoft Word File Added to an Enterprise Guide Project

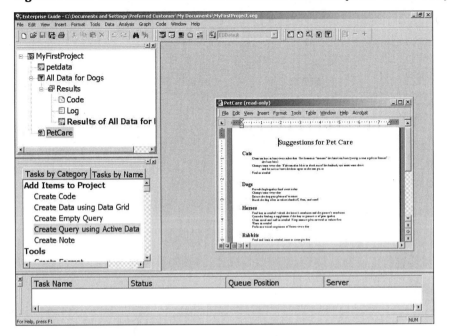

Adding a SAS Program to a Project

FasTip: Click the Insert Code icon on the toolbar.

Note

The Enterprise Guide editor is similar to the Enhanced Editor in the SAS System, and it defaults to the same color scheme as the Enhanced Editor. Changing the color scheme in either Enterprise Guide or the SAS System affects the color scheme in the other application.

Although you can use the Task list to perform many data reporting and analysis tasks, you may find it necessary or useful to include SAS code with your project. Follow these steps to add a SAS program to a project:

1. Select the project to which you want to add the query by clicking its name in the Project window.
2. In the Task list, double-click **Create Code** in the **Add Items to Project** category (on the **Tasks by Category** tab). This opens the code editor in the work area, as shown in Figure 10.24.

Figure 10.24 Adding Code to an Enterprise Guide Project

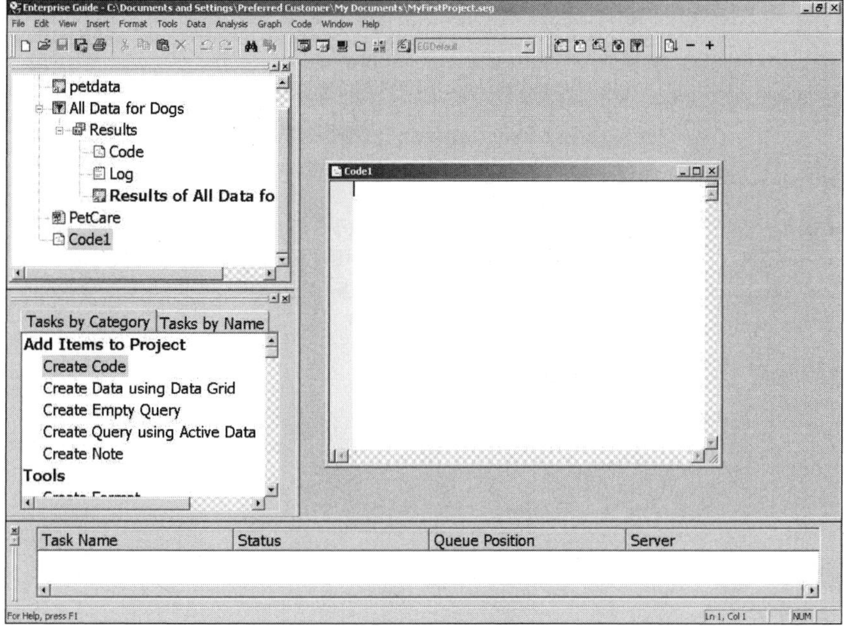

3. Type your SAS program. If you are not familiar with the Enhanced Editor, refer to Chapter 7.
4. When your program is complete, close the Editor window.

Running a Program: You can run your program from Enterprise Guide without starting the SAS System. Press F3 from the Editor window, or click the Run icon on the toolbar.

By default, when you submit code, Enterprise Guide displays any tables created by the code and any output created. These are added to the project. You can suppress the display of the log and output by customizing your session preferences, as described in "Setting Enterprise Guide Preferences" later in this chapter.

Sharing Enterprise Guide Data with Other Programs

Enterprise Guide makes it easy to send your data and other project components to other programs, such as Microsoft Word and Microsoft Excel. For example, suppose you wanted to export the results of the "All Data for Dogs" query, illustrated in "Adding a Query to a Project" earlier in this chapter, to a Microsoft Word document. To do so, follow these steps:

1. Be sure the data you want to send to the other application are open and active.

2. Click **File** → **Send To** → **Microsoft Word** in the Enterprise Guide main menu.

The data are copied into a Microsoft Word table in a new, unsaved document.

Customizing Enterprise Guide

One of the most powerful aspects of Enterprise Guide is the fact that you can customize it to suit your needs. The following sections describe how to perform a few of these customizations.

Displaying and Hiding Toolbars: Enterprise Guide includes several toolbars, such as View, Project, Editor, and MDDB. You can choose to display all, none, or some of these toolbars. To change which toolbars are displayed, click **View** → **Toolbars** in the Enterprise Guide main menu. The resulting submenu is shown in Figure 10.25.

Figure 10.25 Available Enterprise Guide Toolbars

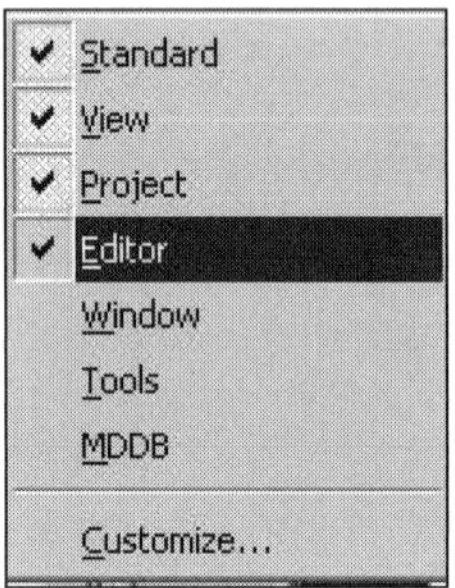

Toolbars with a check mark next to them are displayed. Clicking a toolbar name toggles the display mode of that toolbar (shown or hidden).

Whether a toolbar opens in the docked area at the top of the window or in a separate, movable window depends on how the toolbar was last displayed.

- To move a stand-alone toolbar to the docked toolbar area, double-click in the toolbar title bar.
- To move a docked toolbar to a stand-alone window, double-click in the toolbar itself (but not on a specific tool).

Using the Style Manager: Enterprise Guide uses the Output Delivery System (see Chapter 8 for full details on this topic), often referred to as ODS, to format output generated during your Enterprise Guide session. By default, output is displayed using the EGDefault style.

There are several other predefined styles available, and you can create your own.

To begin working with styles in Enterprise Guide, open the Style Manager by clicking the Style Manager icon on the toolbar.

Figure 10.26 shows the Style Manager.

Figure 10.26 Enterprise Guide Style Manager

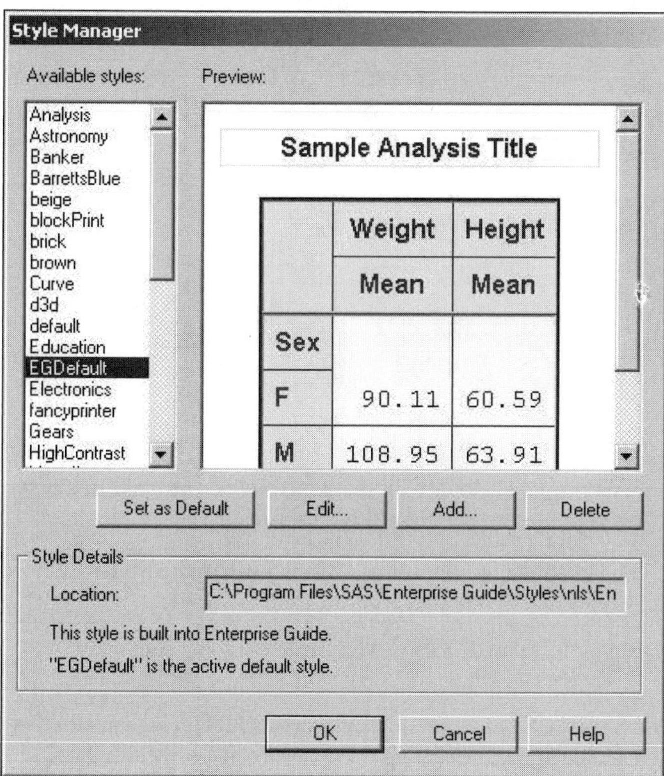

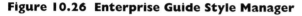

The default style is highlighted when the Style Manager first opens. In Figure 10.26, the default style is EGDefault. To choose another style as the default, select the new style name in the list of available styles, then click **Set as Default**. To help you choose a style, the **Preview** area of the Style Manager shows what the new style would look like.

If none of the styles exactly matches your needs, you can make changes to an existing style, create a new style, or add styles from an external source.

To make changes to an existing style or create a new one, click **Edit** in the Style Manager. This opens the Edit Style dialog box, as shown in Figure 10.27.

Figure 10.27 Edit Style Dialog Box

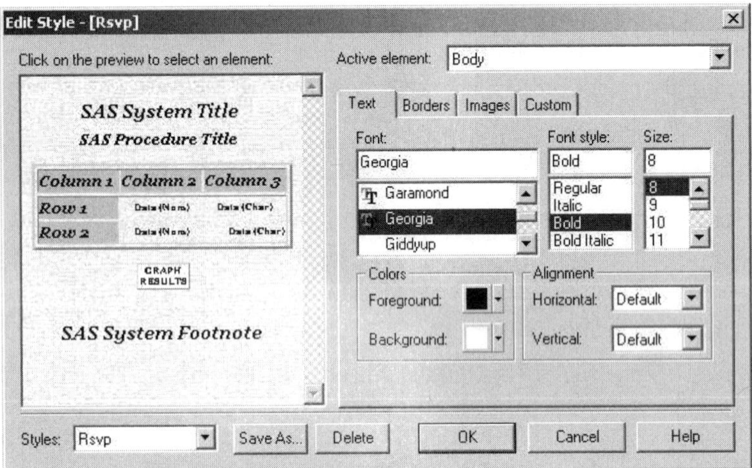

Use the **Text**, **Borders**, **Images**, and **Custom** tabs, along with the **Active element** field, to create the style you want. Then, depending on your intent, do either of the following:

- Click **OK** to apply the changes you have made to the active style, shown in the **Styles** field as well as in the title bar of the Edit Styles dialog box.
- Click **Save As** to save the changes you have made to a new style, leaving the active style unchanged.

If you have created a Cascading Style Sheet (CSS) file outside Enterprise Guide, you can add that style to the list of available Enterprise Guide styles. "Creating a Cascading Style Sheet (CSS)" in Chapter 8 describes one way to create a CSS file.

To add a style from an external source, click **Add** in the Style Manager dialog box. This displays the Add New Style dialog box, as shown in Figure 10.28.

Figure 10.28 Add New Style Dialog Box

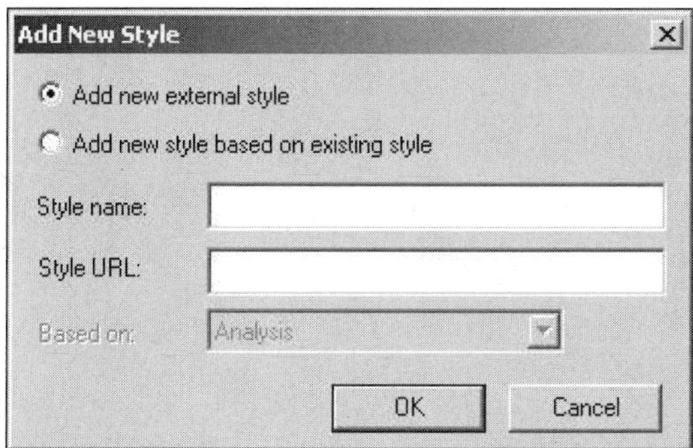

Be sure **Add new external style** is selected, then type the style name in the **Style name** field. For example, if you wanted to use the CSS file created in Chapter 8, you would type `MyWebStyle` in the **Style name** field.

In the **Style URL** field, type the full pathname for the CSS file, including the filename and extension. For example, to use the CSS file created in Chapter 8, you would enter `C:\MYWEBSTYLE.CSS`. The CSS file could reside on your Web server or on your local machine. Click **OK** to add the external file to Enterprise Guide's style list.

Note

> If the style you added does not appear in the list of available styles, try using Windows Explorer to create a Styles subfolder in the following folder: C:\Documents and Settings*Windows-userid*\Application Data\SAS\Enterprise Guide\. Now try adding the style again.

Setting Enterprise Guide Preferences: Similar to the Preferences dialog box in the SAS system, the Options dialog box allows you to affect numerous aspects of your Enterprise Guide session. To access the Options dialog box, click **Tools → Options** in the Enterprise Guide main menu. Figure 10.29 shows this dialog box.

Figure 10.29 Enterprise Guide Options Dialog Box

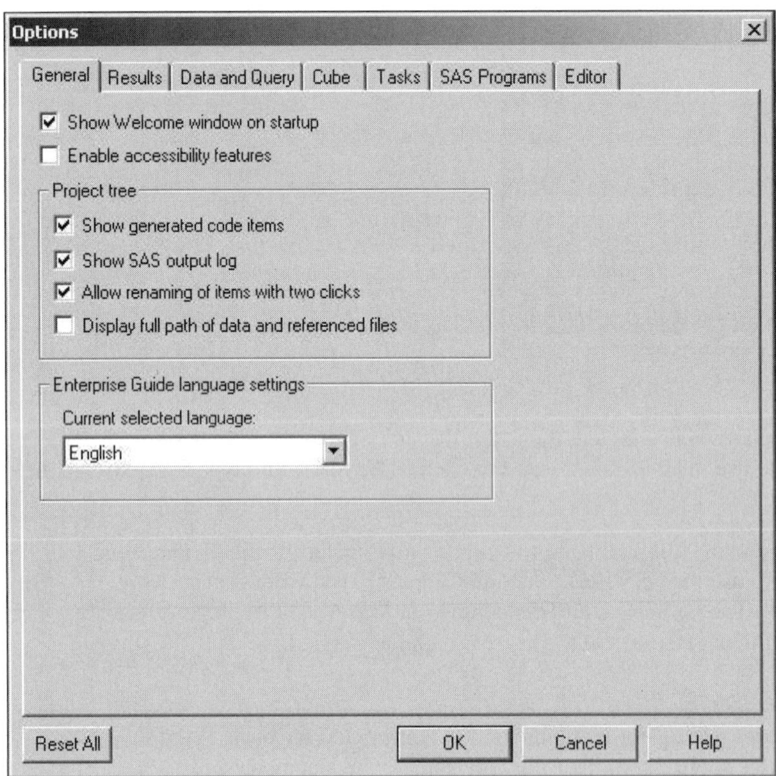

As you can see from Figure 10.29, this dialog box offers seven tabs where you can set preferences and options for just about every aspect of your Enterprise Guide session.

Explore each tab, and experiment with various settings to see if they suit you. If you make changes you don't like, use the **Reset All** button to return to the default settings.

Customizing the Arrangement of Windows: Like most Windows applications, Enterprise Guide supports tiling open windows (both horizontally and vertically) as well as cascading (layering) them. Use the **Window** menu choice to tile or cascade the open windows.

Some windows in Enterprise Guide, such as the Project window and the Task list, are docked by default. You can undock them by right-clicking in the docked window and clicking **Dock** in the resulting popup menu (which clears the check mark and undocks the window). You can also prevent the window from ever being docked by clicking **Allow Docking** in the popup menu.

Undocking a window leaves that window along the left-hand side of the Enterprise Guide session. To have the window displayed in the Enterprise Guide work area, right-click in the window and click **Float In Main Window** in the resulting popup menu.

Note

> Once you have selected **Float In Main Window** for a particular window, the next time you undock that window, it moves to the main window even if the float feature is turned off for that window. That is, undocking returns the window to the last place it was moved to.

More Customizations: Other possible types of customization, which are discussed in the Enterprise Guide online help, include the following:

- customizing the toolbar tool icons
- adding user code to tasks
- creating editor macros (see "Defining and Using Macros" in Chapter 7 for more information)
- adding tools to the toolbar
- adding menu items to the **Tools** menu.

Conclusion

This chapter has gotten you started with Enterprise Guide. But don't stop there. Enterprise Guide is full of useful tools, wizards, and features that can make your job of organizing, analyzing, reporting, and distributing data and information much easier. Check out the tutorial, or simply read through the excellent online Enterprise Guide help to find out how to customize your own tasks and dialog boxes, write background Visual Basic scripts to run reports, or perform some of the other customizations and advanced tasks that Enterprise Guide supports.

11 Customizing Your Start-up Files and SAS System Options

Introduction

Under every operating system, the SAS System uses two start-up files: the configuration file and the autoexec file. This chapter explains how these two files work under Windows and how to modify them. Much of the information is similar to that for other operating systems, so you should become adept quickly at using these files under Windows.

As a reminder, here are the differences between the configuration and autoexec files:

- The configuration file sets SAS system options. These options control various aspects of the SAS System, such as the size of the main SAS window, printer options, and more. When you install the SAS System, a default configuration file named SASV9.CFG is created in the !SASROOT folder (the folder in which you install SAS).

- The autoexec file executes SAS programming statements immediately after the SAS System starts. The default name for the autoexec file is AUTOEXEC.SAS. No autoexec file is created at SAS System installation—if you want one, you must create it yourself.

Under Windows, you can also specify SAS system options in the **Target** field of the Properties dialog box for the SAS System icon, or after the SAS command in the Run dialog box. The system options you specify in this way are used in addition to the system options in the configuration file. Later in this chapter, "Altering the Properties of the SAS System Icon in the Windows Start Menu" provides more information about this technique.

If you want to alter the value of a SAS system option while SAS is running, use the SAS System Options window, as described in "Customizing SAS System Options during Your SAS Session" later in this chapter.

Determining the SAS System Current Folder

An important concept related to SAS configuration and SAS autoexec files is the SAS current folder—the folder that SAS uses to look for files and store files when a specific pathname isn't given. For example, if you do not specify a pathname for a file specified in the FILENAME statement, the SAS System looks for the file in the current folder.

Note

The Save As and Open dialog boxes do not default to the current folder; rather, they default (at the beginning of a SAS session) to the folder associated with the SASUSER library reference.

The simplest case for the current folder is when you start your SAS session using a program shortcut, such as starting SAS from the Windows **Start** menu. In that case, the current folder is the pathname specified in the **Start in** field in the Properties dialog box for the SAS System shortcut that you used. (See "Altering the Properties of the SAS System Icon in the Windows Start Menu" later in this chapter for details on how to find where the **Start** menu SAS System shortcut is stored.)

Note

It is not recommended to leave the **Start in** field blank.

Things start getting more complicated when you use the Windows Run dialog box or a command-prompt window to start the SAS System. In this situation, two scenarios have two different results:

- If you specify a path to SAS.EXE, the current folder is the path that you specify as part of the SAS command. This is true, even if the SAS.EXE file actually is not in that folder. If the SAS.EXE file is not in the folder you specify in the path, Windows searches the paths named in the PATH Windows environment variable for a file named SAS.EXE. But the current folder remains the path you specified in the command.
- If you specify just SAS.EXE as the command (no path to the file), then the current folder is the path from which you issued the command.
  - For the Run dialog box, this translates to C:\.
  - For commands issued from command-prompt windows, it is the pathname that appears before the command prompt. For example, if you change directories to C:\SASBOOK, and then type SAS.EXE at the command prompt and press ENTER, the SAS System starts up, using C:\SASBOOK as the current folder.

Note

> Issuing the SAS command from a command-prompt window or the Run dialog box with no pathname assumes that the folder that contains the SAS.EXE file is listed in the PATH Windows environment variable.

Effect of the SASINITIALFOLDER System Option: If the SASINITIALFOLDER system option is specified at SAS System start-up (such as in the SAS configuration file or in the SAS command), the pathname specified by the option becomes the current folder, overriding any other rules.

Note

> The SASINITIALFOLDER system option also affects the default folder used in the Open and Save As dialog boxes (which normally default to the folder associated with the SASUSER library reference).

Editing Your Start-up Files: An Overview

Warning

> To edit your configuration file or autoexec file, you must use a text editor that saves the file as plain text. (If you use a word processing application, be sure to save the file as a plain ASCII text file without formatting codes.)

Here are two text editors to choose from:

- Windows Notepad editor
- SAS Text Editor window, such as the Enhanced Editor, Program Editor, or NOTEPAD window.

Note

> If you use a SAS window to edit your start-up files, you must restart the SAS System to see the effects of your changes.

This section shows you the basics of using the Windows Notepad editor. If you use the SAS System to edit the SAS start-up files, then see Chapter 3 or Chapter 7 for information on using the SAS Enhanced Editor.

Overview of Using the Windows Notepad Editor: You can open a file with the Windows Notepad editor in several ways.

- To start the Windows Notepad editor without opening a particular file, either click **Start** → **Programs** → **Accessories** → **Notepad**, or submit NOTEPAD as the command in the Windows Run dialog box.

- To start the Windows Notepad editor and open a file at the same time, display the file's folder in the Windows Explorer, then right-click the file's name. In the resulting popup menu, click **Open With → Notepad**.

If you are creating a new file, simply start typing. To edit an existing file, click **File** in the Notepad menu, then click **Open**. Type the name of the file you want to edit in the **File name** field, and click the **Open** button. The file is copied to the Notepad window.

Use your cursor arrow keys and the PageUp and PageDown keys to move to where you want to make your changes. When you have finished editing the file, click **File** in the Notepad menu, then click **Save**. (If the file has not been saved before, give the file a name in the Save As dialog box and then click the **Save** button.)

To close the Notepad editor, click **File → Exit** in the Notepad menu.

Making Changes to the SAS Configuration File

Although the default configuration file that is created when the SAS System is installed may be sufficient for some users, you may need to add or modify option specifications.

There are many required system options in the default configuration file. Unless you are certain of your changes, do not edit the existing option specifications. When you add options, you should not add them in the portion of the file that the SAS System INSTALL utility controls. Figure 11.1 shows the SASV9.CFG file open in the Notepad editor; add your options above the boxed comment.

Figure 11.1 SASV9.CFG File Open in the Windows Notepad Editor

```
SASV9.CFG - Notepad
File  Edit  Format  Help

/* This is the OEM character set                                */
/* -FORMCHAR "³ÄÚÂ¿ÃÅ´ÀÁÙ+=|-/\<>*" */

/* This is the ANSI character set (for SAS Monospace font and ANSI Sasfont) */
-FORMCHAR ",ƒ„…†‡ˆ‰Š‹Œ+=|-/\<>*"

/* This is the ANSI character set                               */
/* -FORMCHAR "|----|+|---+=|-/\<>*" */

/*-------------------------------------------------------------\
| WARNING:  INSTALL Application edits below this line.  User    |
|           options should be added above this box comment.     |
|           INSTALL Application maintains and modifies the      |
|           following options; -SASAUTOS, -SASHELP, -SASMSG,   |
|           -PATH, and -MAPS.  It also maintains and modifies   |
|           the following CONFIG variables with the -SET option;|
|           INSTALL, USAGE, LIBRARY, SAMPSIO, SAMPSRC, SASCBT,  |
|           and SASEXT01-SASEXT50.  It preserves all lines above |
|           the line containing 'DO NOT EDIT BELOW THIS LINE'.  |
\-------------------------------------------------------------*/

/* DO NOT EDIT BELOW THIS LINE - INSTALL Application edits below this line */
/* * * * * * * * * * * * * * * * * * * * * * * * * * * * * * * * * * * * * */
```

After opening the configuration file in the editor of your choice, use the scroll bars or the PageDown key to scroll to the boxed comment shown in Figure 11.1. Click the blank line right above the box and press ENTER twice. Now type your new option specifications. Precede each option with a hyphen (dash).

Note

It is possible to have several SAS configuration files, located in different folders, with the same name. Be sure you are editing the correct SAS configuration file.

Types of SAS System Options: There are two kinds of system options—the on/off kind and the kind that take a value. For example, the SPLASH option is an on/off option. It controls whether the SAS System logo and copyright information appear when the SAS System initializes. To suppress the logo (also called the splash screen), specify NOSPLASH.

The FONT option is an example of a system option that takes a value. It controls the screen font that the SAS System uses. Here is how these two options might look if you add them to your configuration file:

```
-NOSPLASH
-FONT 'Sasfont' 12
```

Some options can take both the on/off and value forms. The PRINT option is an example of this kind of option. Notice that for options that take values, you do not use an equal sign—you use only a space between the option name and its value.

Discovering Which System Options Are Available: One way to find out which system options are available under Windows is to follow this help path: **Help → SAS Help and Documentation → Using SAS Software in Your Operating Environment → Using SAS in Windows → Features of the SAS Language for Windows → System Options under Windows.**

(You might want to put this page in your Help Favorites—see "Customizing SAS Help and Documentation" in Chapter 6 for instructions.)

A list of operating system–specific options is displayed. To see the syntax and description of an option, click its name.

For example, Figure 11.2 shows the help that is available for the AUTOEXEC system option.

Figure 11.2 Example Help Window for SAS System Options

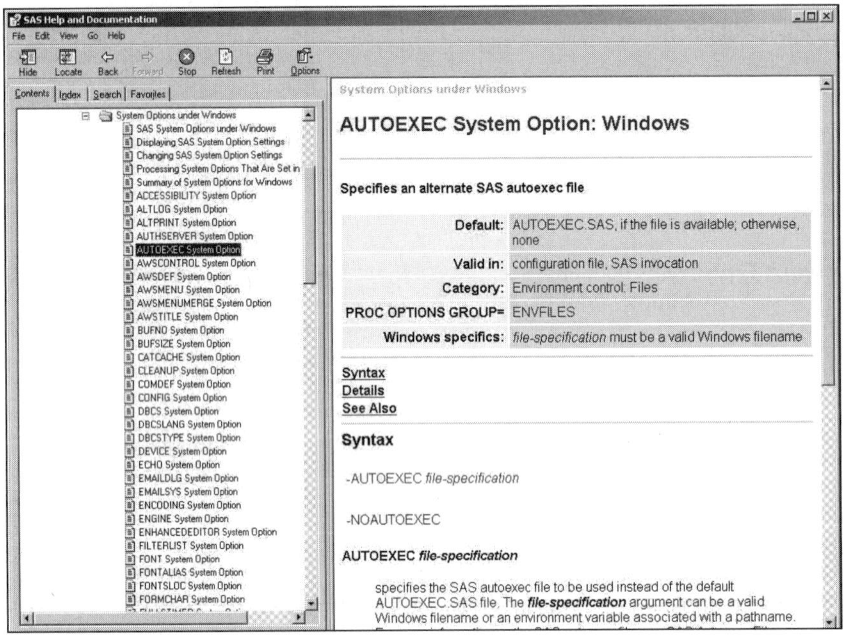

Another way to see all the available options is to submit the following code:

```
proc options;
run;
```

Creating and Editing the Autoexec File

The autoexec file contains SAS programming statements that are executed before your SAS session begins. Use the autoexec file to customize and automate your SAS session. Here are some ways to use your autoexec file:

- set SAS system options with the OPTIONS statement
- issue windowing commands with the DM statement
- define SAS library references and file shortcuts with the LIBNAME and FILENAME statements
- perform data processing with DATA and PROC statements
- invoke SAS/AF applications with the AF statement.

For example, suppose your reports need a special line size, and you find yourself creating the same library reference every time you invoke the SAS System. Suppose you also need to see all your open windows at once. Your AUTOEXEC.SAS file might look like this:

```
options linesize=50;
libname currdata 'c:\saledata\current';
dm 'tile';
```

When your SAS session initializes, the line size is set to 50, the CURRDATA library reference is created, and the Log, Enhanced Editor, and Output windows are tiled (in a vertical manner).

No AUTOEXEC.SAS file is created when the SAS System is installed, so you must create it yourself. If you use the Windows Notepad editor, open the editor and begin typing your SAS statements.

To save the file, click **File → Save As** in the Notepad editor menu. In the **File name** field, type the pathname of where you want the file to be saved. Be sure to include the filename itself (such as "C:\Documents and Settings*Windows-user-name*\AUTOEXEC.SAS") and to enclose the complete pathname in double quotation marks. Now click the **Save** button. To close the editor, click **File → Exit** in the Notepad editor menu.

Caution

If you do not enclose the pathname in double quotation marks, Notepad will append .txt to the filename, which will make the file unusable for your SAS session.

You can also use the SAS Enhanced Editor or Program Editor to create and save your AUTOEXEC.SAS file. If you or someone else has already created an autoexec file, edit it using the same techniques as described for the configuration file.

Note

Remember to end each statement with a semicolon. There is no size limitation on the autoexec file—it can contain as many SAS programming statements as you want.

Some system options are not valid in the OPTIONS statement, and therefore you cannot specify them in the autoexec file. The autoexec file cannot contain system options that affect the SAS System initialization (such as ALTLOG or SPLASH). To see if a system option is valid in the OPTIONS statement, only at SAS System start-up, or both, look up the option in SAS Help and Documentation. In particular, refer to the **Valid in** section in the option's help topic.

Note

It is possible to have several SAS autoexec files, located in different folders, with the same name. Be sure you are editing the correct SAS autoexec file.

Note

> If you are using the SASINITIALFOLDER system option to control the SAS current folder, place your SAS autoexec file in a different folder from the one specified by this option.

Specifying Configuration Files and Autoexec Files in the SAS Command

Once you have created or edited the SAS configuration and autoexec files to your satisfaction, getting the SAS System to use them is simple.

Use the CONFIG system option to specify the SAS configuration file in the SAS command. For example, you can edit the **Target** field in the Properties dialog box for the SAS System shortcut, or you can type the command in the Windows Run dialog box. If the pathname for the configuration file contains spaces, enclose the pathname in quotation marks. Here is an example SAS command that specifies a configuration file and its location:

```
"C:\Program Files\SAS\SAS 9.1\sas.exe" -CONFIG "C:\Production
Projects\sasv9.cfg"
```

Note

> You can specify multiple CONFIG options in a single command. You must repeat the CONFIG option for each file.

Telling the SAS System where the autoexec file is works similarly, except you use the AUTOEXEC system option, as in the following sample command:

```
"C:\Program Files\SAS\SAS 9.1\sas.exe" -AUTOEXEC "C:\Production
Projects\autoexec.sas"
```

Note

> You can specify only one autoexec file. If you place more than one AUTOEXEC system option specification in the SAS command, the one that appears last in the list is the one processed by the SAS System.

Altering the Properties of the SAS System Icon in the Windows Start Menu

When you click the Windows **Start** menu (accessed by clicking the **Start** button) to start an application, Windows uses properties to control how that application behaves. For example, for the SAS System, properties can specify which folder to use as the current folder, which system options to use at invocation, and whether the application begins as a normal-size, maximized, or minimized window.

To begin, you must find the **Start** menu shortcut for the SAS System. Because everyone's PC is configured differently, your shortcut may be located in a different place than documented here. In general, the **Start** menu shortcuts for the SAS System (for Windows 2000) are stored in the following path: C:\Documents and Settings\All Users\Start Menu\Programs\SAS.

Note

> One way to find the SAS shortcut is to use the Windows Explorer's Search feature. Type `9.1` in the search box. Although there will be several files in the search results, you should be able to pinpoint the SAS shortcut fairly easily.

Once you have located the correct folder, you are interested in editing the properties associated with the shortcut named (by default) **SAS 9.1 (English)**. Of course, if you specified a different name for the shortcut or are using a different language, the shortcut will have a different name.

To change the system options used in the SAS command that starts the SAS System, use the Properties dialog box. To access this dialog box, follow these steps:

1. Right-click the **SAS 9.1 (English)** icon, then click **Properties**.
2. Click the **Shortcut** tab.
3. Click in the **Target** field, and use the Backspace and Delete keys to delete any system options you do not want to use; type any new system options after the SAS.EXE. Remember that each system option begins with a hyphen and does not use an "=" between the option name and the option value.
4. When you have finished editing the **Target** field, click **OK**. The next time you use the **Start** menu to open the SAS System, the new system options will be in effect.

Note

> This change applies only to the SAS System shortcut that is accessed from the SAS System program group in the Windows **Start** menu. If you have created additional shortcuts to the SAS System (such as on the desktop), you must change each shortcut's properties individually.

Using the Run Dialog Box to Specify SAS System Options

You can use the Run dialog box to specify SAS System options, instead of editing your SAS configuration file or the properties of the SAS System icon. This technique is useful when you need the options only occasionally.

To open the Run dialog box, click the **Start** button, then click **Run**.

Type the full pathname of the SAS.EXE file in the **Open** field, followed by whichever system options you want to use for that session. For example, if you do not want to see the SAS logo when the SAS System starts up, type the following in the **Open** field:

```
"c:\Program Files\SAS\SAS 9.1\sas.exe" -nosplash
```

The quotation marks are necessary, because the pathname contains spaces. The pathname for your SAS.EXE file may be different from the one shown here. Click **OK** to start the SAS System.

The system options that you add to the **Open** field in the Run dialog box are used in conjunction with the options in the SAS configuration file (that is, they do not replace the configuration file). Because the **Open** field can contain up to 255 characters, you can specify many system options. If you need more space than this, put the options in your configuration file instead.

Note

It is important to know where the SAS System looks for SAS configuration files, so you are sure you are using the configuration file you want. See "Understanding How SAS Searches for Configuration and Autoexec Files" below.

Understanding the Precedence of System Options

System options can appear in several places, so it is important to know which specifications take precedence:

- An OPTIONS statement in the autoexec file has the last word and overrides options that are specified in the SAS command, the SAS configuration file, or the Run dialog box.
- SAS system options that are specified in the SAS invocation command override options in any processed SAS configuration file. For example, if the same option is specified in the SAS configuration file and in the SAS command in the **Open** field of the Run dialog box, the option in the dialog box takes precedence.

In summary, SAS system options that are encountered later in the processing always override those options that are specified earlier.

Understanding How SAS Searches for Configuration and Autoexec Files

With a Config File Here, and a Config File There... The default Windows 2000 installation of SAS 9.1 places three SAS configuration files (SASV9.CFG) on your system:

- One in your C:\Documents and Settings*Windows-user-name* folder
- One in the C:\Program Files\SAS\SAS 9.1 folder
- One in your language-specific SAS folder (such as C:\Program Files\SAS\SAS 9.1\nls\en).

(The pathnames are somewhat different for Windows NT users.)

By default, the second of these config files consists of only a CONFIG system option, pointing to the language-specific folder config file.

Why so many config files?

The SAS System uses a fairly detailed algorithm to find a config file if one is not specified in the SAS command. Since the SAS System cannot start without a config file, having duplicate config files in various strategic places enables the SAS System to find a config file when it needs one.

How SAS Finds the Configuration File: Because there are several ways to specify a SAS configuration file, it can be hard to tell which configuration files are processed, and in what order.

Here are the basic rules that the SAS System uses to find the configuration files for a particular SAS session:

1. If you specify a configuration file in the SAS invocation command (such as from the Windows Run dialog box) using the CONFIG SAS system option, then this is the *only* configuration file used. You can specify multiple CONFIG options in a single command. In this case, the SAS System uses all the files you specify, processing them in the order in which they appear in the SAS command.
2. If you start the SAS System from the Windows **Start** menu or another SAS System shortcut (see "Altering the Properties of the SAS System Icon in the Windows Start Menu" earlier in this chapter), the configuration file specified in that shortcut's **Target** field is used.
3. If the **Target** field or SAS command does not contain a CONFIG option, the SAS System looks for a configuration file with the default name (SASV9.CFG) in the current folder. See "Determining the SAS System Current Folder" earlier in this chapter for details.
4. If the **Target** field or the SAS command does not contain a CONFIG option and there isn't a SASV9.CFG file in the current folder, then the SAS System looks for a SASV9.CFG file in the folder that contains the SAS.EXE file
5. If you double-click a file containing SAS code (such as a .SAS or .SS7 file), the file is opened with the SAS.EXE executable file. For this method of submitting SAS code, you *must* have a SASV9.CFG file in the folder that contains the SAS.EXE file.

Note

If you have Enterprise Guide installed, double-clicking a .SAS file may open Enterprise Guide, not the SAS System. See Chapter 10 for more information on Enterprise Guide.

If the SAS System cannot find a configuration file, it cannot start up, and you will receive some cryptic error messages, similar to the two error dialog boxes shown in Figure 11.3.

Figure 11.3 Sample Error Messages When the SAS System Cannot Find or Read a Configuration File

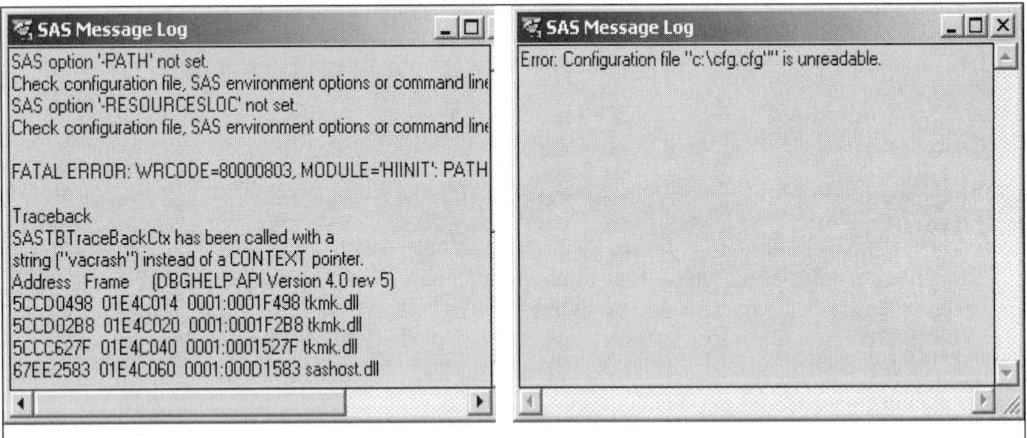

Note

There are other ways to specify SAS configuration files, including several Windows environment variables, that add complexity to these basic rules. See SAS Help and Documentation for more information on these more advanced configuration file specification techniques.

Tracking System Option Settings: A quick way to check the values of system options set in your SAS configuration file is with the VERBOSE system option. Add this option to either the SAS command or the SAS configuration file, using the following syntax:

```
-VERBOSE
```

Then, when you start the SAS System, the system option values are written to the SAS log. This can help you debug your configuration file.

How SAS Finds the Autoexec File: The easiest way to ensure that the SAS System finds and uses the correct autoexec file is to use the AUTOEXEC system option in the SAS command. However, if you not use the AUTOEXEC system option, the SAS System looks in the following places, in this order:

1. The current folder. See "Determining the SAS System Current Folder" earlier in this chapter for details.
2. The paths specified by the Windows PATH environment variable.
3. The root folder of the current drive.
4. The folder that contains the SAS.EXE file.

When the SAS System finds an autoexec file, it processes that one and does not look for others.

The SAS log records the location of the autoexec file that was processed, but does not by default include the statements that were contained in the autoexec file. If you want the SAS log to record the statements from the autoexec file, add the ECHOAUTO system option to the SAS command or SAS configuration file.

Note

> If you know you will not be using an autoexec file, you can streamline SAS System start-up by specifying the NOAUTOEXEC system option in the SAS command. Specifying NOAUTOEXEC keeps the SAS System from searching for an autoexec file.

Accommodating Multiple Users

Sometimes several people use the same PC, and each person may have a different concept of what the SAS session should look like, what it should do, and so on. The same problem arises when people on a network use a single copy of the SAS System.

The answer to this problem lies in setting up configuration and autoexec files for each user. Alternatively, create SAS System shortcuts for each user. The following sections discuss how to use each approach.

Creating Start-up Files for Each User: Suppose three people use the same PC—Nancy, Kurt, and Paulo. Nancy creates sales reports with PROC REPORT, and Kurt uses SAS/GRAPH to produce monthly sales charts. Paulo, a summer intern, does not know much about the SAS System, but he is responsible for using a SAS/AF application to enter weekly sales data into the tables that Nancy and Kurt use. These three users have distinct needs, yet they must share the same software. Separate SAS System start-up files help them use the SAS System efficiently.

Although the default name of the SAS configuration file is SASV9.CFG and the autoexec file is by default named AUTOEXEC.SAS, these files can have any name, as long as you tell the SAS System where to find them. Here are the steps for creating start-up files for each user:

1. Use the Windows Explorer to copy the original SASV9.CFG file to three new files in the same folder.

   The location of the SASV9.CFG file can vary from computer to computer. A quick way to find it is to use the Windows Explorer Search feature (click the **Search** button in the Windows Explorer menu bar). If you need help using the Windows Explorer, refer to Appendix 3.

   a. Once you have located the SASV9.CFG file, click **Edit** → **Copy** in the Windows Explorer menu.

   b. Click **Edit** → **Paste**. A file named **Copy of SASV9.CFG** appears in the folder listing.

   c. Change the name of this file to NANCY.CFG.

   d. Repeat steps b and c twice to create KURT.CFG and PAULO.CFG.

2. Have each user edit his or her personal configuration files and save the changes. In particular, each user may want to change the value of the SASUSER system option to point to a personal profile catalog location.

   Note

   > If the folder specified in the SASUSER system option specification does not exist, the SAS System will create the folder for you.

3. Have each user create a file that contains the SAS programming statements they want to have executed each time the SAS System initializes, and save these files with names like AUTONANCY.SAS, AUTOKURT.SAS, and AUTOPAULO.SAS.

   Continuing with our example, here is what each file might contain:

   AUTONANCY.SAS
   ```
   libname sales 'c:\products\saleinfo\qtr4';
   libname expense 'c:\products\expinfo\qtr4';
   proc report;
   ... report-generating statements
   ```
   AUTOKURT.SAS
   ```
   libname sales 'c:\products\saleinfo\qtr4';
   proc gplot;
   ... chart-generating statements
   ```
   AUTOPAULO.SAS
   ```
   libname apps 'c:\products\sasapps';
   af apps.product.entry.menu;
   ```

Now each user has his or her own version of the SAS configuration and autoexec files. All that remains is to tell the SAS System which files to use. When Nancy, Kurt, or Paulo invokes the SAS System, he or she must open the Run dialog box and type the following in the **Open** field:

```
"pathname\sas.exe" -CONFIG "pathname\xyz.CFG" -AUTOEXEC
"pathname\AUTOxyz.SAS"
```

where *pathname* is the pathname of the sas.exe, *xyz*.CFG, and AUTO*xyz*.SAS files. Substitute the user's name (NANCY, KURT, or PAULO) in place of *xyz*. If the options are already typed, use the cursor arrow keys to position the cursor where the changes need to be made, and type the new name (use the Backspace key, if necessary, to erase extra characters). Click **OK** to start the SAS System. The appropriate start-up files are used.

Creating Copies of the SAS System Icon: Using the Run dialog box to change the options for an application every time you want to use it can be cumbersome. Another approach is to create copies of the SAS System icon, each having its own properties. Each user can double-click the SAS System icon that he or she needs.

A drawback to this approach is that displaying several icons uses system resources. If your Windows desktop is rather cluttered, you may run out of system resources if you add too many more icons.

When you create a copy of a program icon, it is called a shortcut. To create customized SAS System shortcuts, follow these steps:

1. Use the Windows Explorer to find the **Start Menu** shortcut for the SAS System, as described earlier in “Altering the Properties of the SAS System Icon in the Windows Start Menu.”
2. Once you have found the right folder, right-click the **SAS 9.1 (English)** icon.
3. Click **Create Shortcut**. An icon named **SAS 9.1 (English) (2)** appears. Rename this icon to something descriptive, such as **Nancy’s SAS System**.
4. Right-click the new icon, and click **Properties**. The Properties dialog box appears, as shown in Figure 11.4.

Figure 11.4 Properties Dialog Box for the New SAS System Shortcut

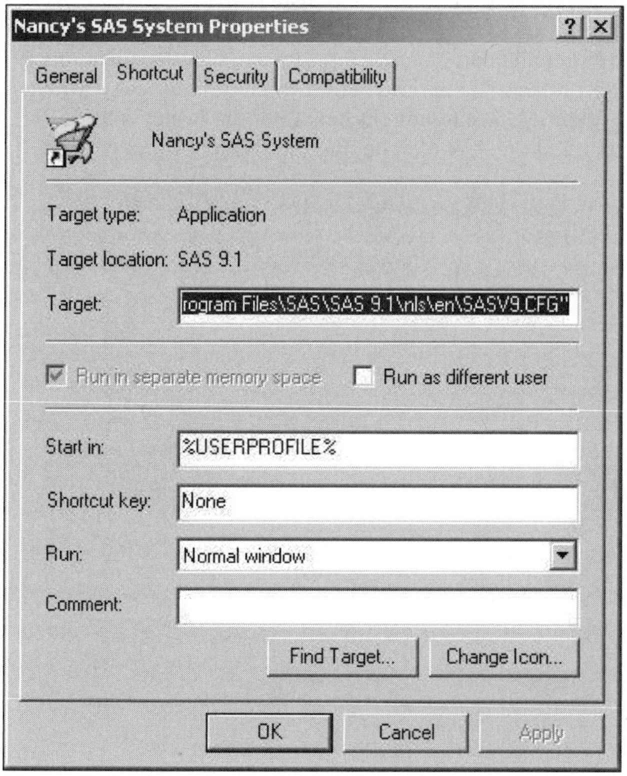

5. Click the **Shortcut** tab, if necessary (it is shown in Figure 11.4).

6. In the **Target** field, edit the SAS system options to suit the individual user, then click **OK**.

Create as many shortcuts as you need.

Note

The Windows operating system also makes available two environment variables, SAS_SYS_CONFIG and SAS_USER_CONFIG, that can be assigned to valid pathnames of SAS configuration files. Environment variables are not a beginner's topic, and are not within the scope of this book. See SAS Help and Documentation and your Windows help for more information.

Relocating Shortcuts: Shortcuts can be moved from their folders to more convenient places. For example, you may want to have the shortcut icons on the desktop so that you can start the SAS System without having to click the **Start** button.

To move a shortcut to the desktop, open the Windows Explorer and display the folder that contains the shortcut. Click the shortcut you want to move, to highlight it. Now use the mouse to drag the shortcut out of the Windows Explorer and onto the desktop. (Resize other applications if necessary, so that you can see the desktop.) Release the mouse button when the shortcut is where you want it. Figure 11.5 shows how the Windows desktop might look after the Nancy's SAS System shortcut has been dragged onto the desktop. Double-clicking the shortcut starts the SAS System.

Figure 11.5 Windows Desktop with the New SAS System Shortcut

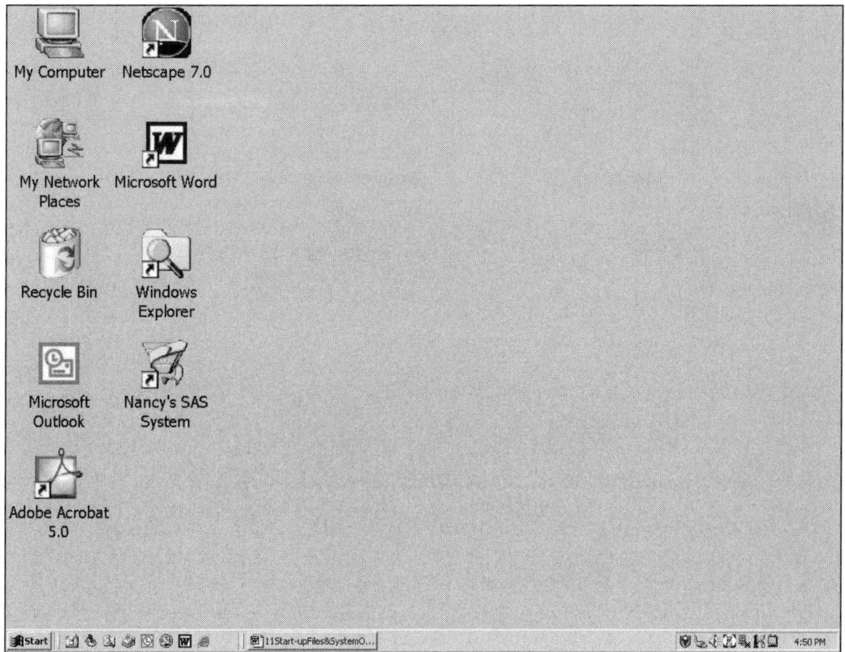

(Your desktop will look somewhat different from that shown here, because you will have different programs installed on your machine.)

Note

If you need help using the Windows Explorer, refer to Appendix 3.

Customizing SAS System Options during Your SAS Session

FasTip: Click **Tools** → **Options** → **System** to open the SAS System Options window.

You can adjust the value of many SAS System options using the SAS System Options window. You can use this window to change any option you can change with the OPTIONS statement. (That is, you cannot edit a system option that is valid only at start-up, such as LOG or SPLASH.)

To open the SAS System Options window, click **Tools** → **Options** → **System** in the SAS System main menu. Figure 11.6 shows the SAS System Options window.

Figure 11.6 SAS System Options Window

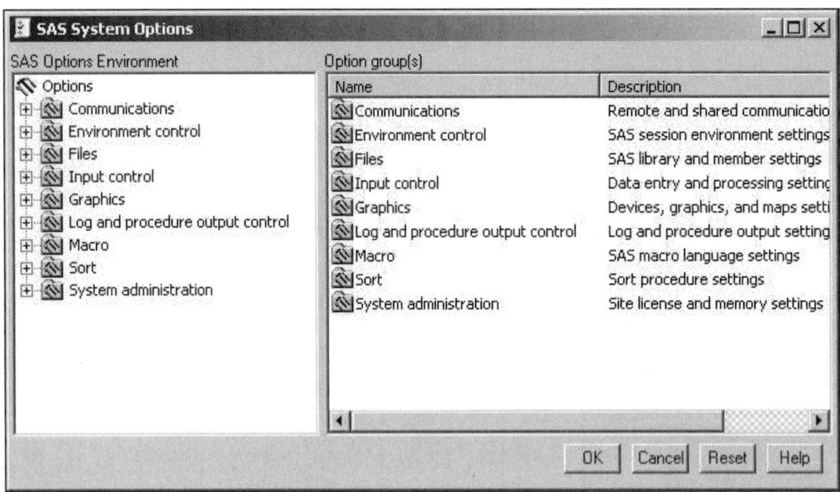

This window works like the SAS Explorer window. Double-click group names in the left pane to expand the group; click a subgroup to see the contents of the subgroup. The option names and their values are shown in the right pane of the window.

To edit the value of an option, double-click the option name in the right pane of the window. This opens the Modify Value dialog box. Figure 11.7 shows a sample Modify Value dialog box (in this case, for the LINESIZE option).

Figure 11.7 Modify Value Dialog Box for Changing SAS System Option Values

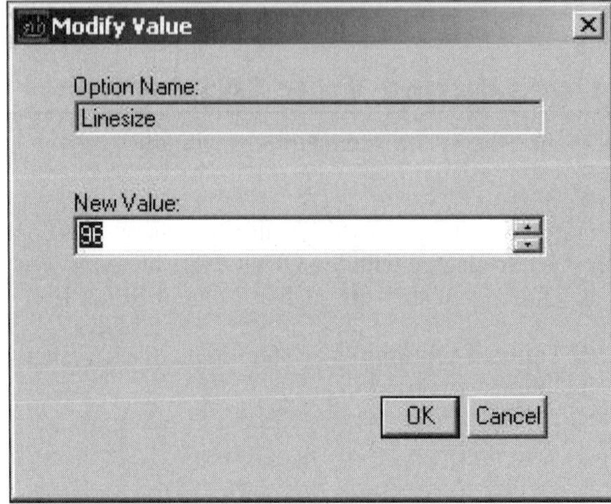

Type the new value in the **New Value** field or select a value from the drop-down list, then click **OK**. The SAS System Options window now shows the updated value.

Note

> Changes that are made in the SAS System Options window affect only the current SAS session; to change the value of a SAS System option permanently, edit your SAS configuration file.

Finding a Particular System Option: Sometimes it is hard to remember which group of options a particular option is stored in. To find an option quickly, right-click in the left pane of the SAS System Options window, then click **Find Option** in the popup menu. This opens the Find Option dialog box, as shown in Figure 11.8.

Figure 11.8 Find Option Dialog Box for Changing SAS System Option Values

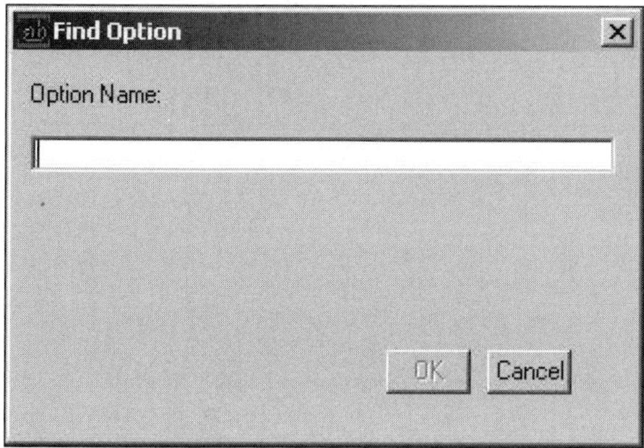

Type the name of the option you want to find, then click **OK**.

Note

> For options that have names such as SPLASH and NOSPLASH, search for the "on" name.

Undoing Your Changes: The SAS System Options window allows you to undo your changes in two ways:

- You can cancel all changes that you have made in the SAS System Options window by clicking the **Reset** button—but you must do this before you close the window. This resets the option values to the values they had when you first opened the SAS System Options window.
- You can reset a particular option to its default value (the value that it had when you installed SAS) by right-clicking the option in the SAS System Options window, then clicking **Set to Default** in the popup menu.

12 Using Batch Mode

Introduction

While Windows is considered a point-and-click operating system, it does support batch execution of the SAS System. If you are more familiar with a mainframe operating system such as z/OS, the Windows definition of batch is not quite the same as the mainframe definition, at least at the technical level. But for practical purposes, think of them as the same: batch execution under Windows means that you do not see any SAS windows, and the SAS programs you submit run without input from you.

The methods for starting a batch job are numerous. Here are some of the more common methods:

- right-clicking a SAS program file icon in the Windows Explorer
- dropping a SAS program file icon onto the SAS.EXE file icon (from the Windows Explorer)
- clicking the **SAS 9.1 (English)** icon in the Windows **Programs** menu
- using the Run dialog box from the **Start** button
- double-clicking a SAS program file icon in the Windows Explorer
- submitting the job from the SAS System Viewer (see Appendix 2)
- starting the SAS job from a command-prompt window.

Which method you use to submit your SAS batch jobs depends on several factors, including how often you submit batch jobs, whether you submit the same program over and over or run lots of different jobs, and, of course, personal preferences.

This chapter first helps you decide when to use batch mode. Then it shows you how to use each of the methods.

Later in the chapter, you learn how to print from a batch job, control where the logs and output are stored, combine using batch and windowing sessions in one job, and submit more than one batch job at a time. Finally, you learn how to interrupt a batch job.

Understanding How Batch Mode Works

When you submit a batch job, you do not interact with the SAS System. When you submit the job, by default you see the SAS System logo appear, followed by the BATCH SAS window, which tells you what program is running and where the log and output files are being stored.

Several system options affect SAS batch processing, including the following:

- NOSPLASH suppresses the SAS logo and copyright screen when the job starts.
- ICON minimizes the BATCH SAS window when the job starts.

You can add these and other system options to your SAS configuration file, as described in Chapter 11.

Deciding When to Use Batch Mode

Batch mode helps save system resources by not using windows, tool icons, scroll bars, and so on. If your programs can run without user input, they may run faster and use fewer system resources in batch mode. Another approach to using batch mode is to split your job in two—run the intensive data creation, analysis, sorting, and so on part in batch mode, then run a windowing session, using the SAS files created by the first job, after all the crunch work is finished. Either way, you use the "expensive" (in terms of system resources) graphical user interface only when needed.

Right-Clicking a File in the Windows Explorer

Perhaps the easiest way to submit a SAS file in batch mode is to use the Windows Explorer. To submit a batch job in this manner, follow these steps:

1. Open the Windows Explorer by right-clicking the **Start** button, then clicking **Explore**.
2. Display the folder that contains the SAS program you want to submit.
3. Right-click this file, then click **Batch Submit** in the resulting popup menu.

Note

> If you need more information on the Windows Explorer, refer to Appendix 3.

Dropping a File on the SAS.EXE Icon in the Windows Explorer

Another easy way to submit batch SAS jobs is to drag and drop SAS program icons onto the SAS.EXE file icon in the Windows Explorer. To use this method, follow these steps:

1. Open the Windows Explorer by right-clicking the **Start** button, then clicking **Explore**.
2. Display the folder that contains the SAS.EXE file icon. (Under Windows 2000, this folder by default is C:\Program Files\SAS\SAS 9.1.)
3. If your SAS program is not stored in the same folder as the SAS.EXE file, open another Windows Explorer window (right-click the **Start** button and click **Explore**). In this second Windows Explorer window, display the folder that contains the SAS program file you want to submit.
4. Use the mouse to drag the file icon you want to submit, and drop it on the SAS.EXE icon. For step-by-step instructions, refer to "Using Drag-and-Drop" in Chapter 4.

By default, the log and output files for the batch job are stored in the following folder in the Windows 2000 environment: C:\Program Files\Common Files\System\Mapi\1033\NT. The location may differ for Windows NT and Windows XP users. Use the Windows Explorer Search function to find the log and output files, if necessary.

Note

> You cannot drop multiple files on the SAS.EXE icon. See "Submitting Multiple Batch SAS Programs" later in this chapter for information on submitting more than one batch file at a time.

Clicking the SAS System Icon in the Start Menu

By default, clicking the **SAS 9.1 (English)** icon in the **SAS** program group begins a SAS windowing session. However, you can add the filename for the SAS program you want to run to the **Target** field of the SAS System's Properties dialog box. Then when you click the **SAS 9.1 (English)** icon, the SAS System runs in batch mode. Because you must edit the Properties dialog box to run a different program, this method is good for SAS users who run the same batch job over and over.

To use this method, follow these steps:

1. Open the Windows Explorer by right-clicking the **Start** button, then clicking **Explore**.
2. Navigate to the folder that contains the **Start Menu** shortcut for the SAS System. (Under Windows 2000, this folder by default is C:\Documents and Settings\All Users\Start Menu\Programs\SAS.)
3. Right-click the **SAS 9.1 (English)** icon, then click **Properties** in the resulting popup menu.
4. When the Properties dialog box appears, click the **Shortcut** tab.

5. Click in the **Target** field, immediately after the closing quotation mark after SAS.EXE. Add a space, then type the name of the SAS program you want to submit. For example, Figure 12.1 shows the Properties dialog box that has a program named C:\SampleProgram.sas added to the **Target** field.

   Be sure that the program name is immediately after the SAS.EXE and before any system options (these start with hyphens).

Figure 12.1 Adding the Program Name to the Target Field

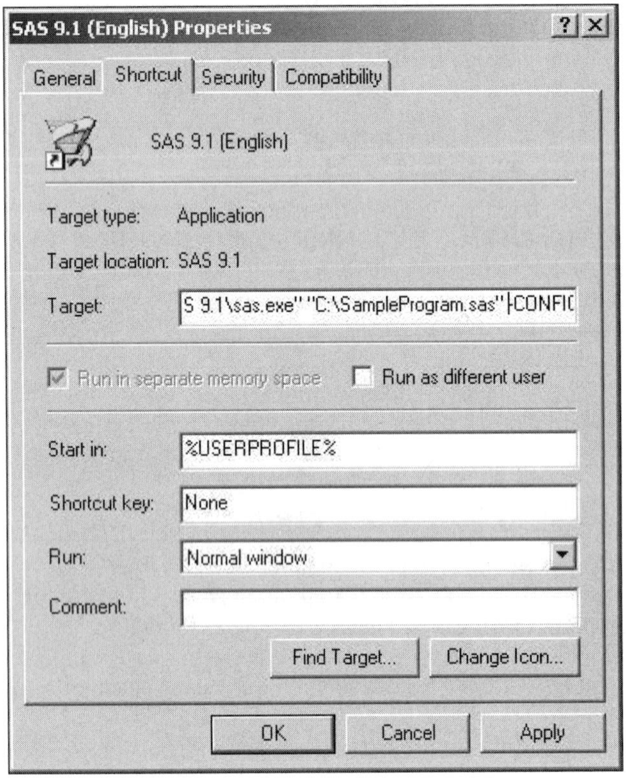

6. Click **OK** to close the Properties dialog box. Now when you click the **SAS 9.1 (English)** icon in the **Start** menu, the SAMPLEPROGRAM.SAS program is submitted in batch mode.

Note

The program name is not a system option, so it does not need a hyphen, as long as it immediately follows the SAS.EXE portion of the **Target** field contents. If you want to place the program name elsewhere, after some system options, use the SYSIN system option to specify the program name.

Note

These changes apply only to the shortcut to the SAS System accessed from the **SAS** program group. If you have created other shortcuts (such as a shortcut to SAS on the desktop), you must change each shortcut's properties individually.

Creating Additional SAS System Shortcuts: Suppose you want to run both windowing and batch jobs. Or, you run three or four different batch jobs, but you still want to start the SAS System in batch mode by clicking the **SAS 9.1 (English)** icon. If this is the case, add additional SAS System shortcuts to the **SAS** program group.

To add another SAS System shortcut to the **SAS** program group, follow these steps:

1. Open the Windows Explorer by right-clicking the **Start** button, then clicking **Explore**.
2. Navigate to the folder that contains the **Start** menu shortcut for the SAS System. (Under Windows 2000, this folder by default is C:\Documents and Settings\All Users\Start Menu\Programs\SAS.)
3. Right-click the **SAS 9.1 (English)** icon, then click **Create Shortcut** in the resulting popup menu. An icon appears named **SAS 9.1 (English) (2)**. Change the name of this icon to something descriptive, such as **Run the SAMPLEPROGRAM File in Batch Mode**. (See Appendix 3 for information on how to rename a file in the Windows Explorer.)
4. Right-click the new icon, then click **Properties** in the resulting popup menu.
5. Click the **Shortcut** tab.
6. In the **Target** field, add the program name after the SAS.EXE portion of the field, as described in the previous section.
7. Click **OK** to close the Properties dialog box.

Repeat these steps to create additional shortcuts, giving each a descriptive name and adding the appropriate filename to the **Target** field.

A drawback of this approach is that each icon takes up system resources. Adding several SAS System shortcuts to your program group can cause system resource problems in the following situations:

- You are running a PC with minimal RAM (Random Access Memory). For best results, your PC should have at least 128M of RAM.

- You run a lot of applications simultaneously.
- You have a lot of icons on your screen.

If you try this method but get error messages about system memory, shut down all other open applications and try again. If the error messages persist, you should probably try a different approach to running your batch jobs.

Starting Your Batch Job from the Run Dialog Box

The Run dialog box enables you to run any program without having to click an icon. Follow these steps to use this method:

1. Click the **Start** button, then click **Run**. The Run dialog box appears, as shown in Figure 12.2.

Figure 12.2 Run Dialog Box

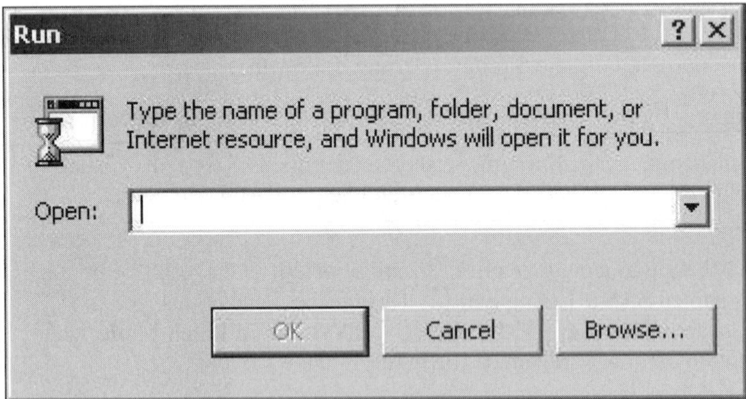

2. Type the following in the **Open** field:

   ```
   C:\SAS-folder\SAS.EXE your-SAS-program
   ```

   For example, if your SAS.EXE file is stored in the C:\Program Files\SAS\SAS 9.1 folder, and the SAS program you want to submit is C:\SampleProgram.SAS, type the following:

   ```
   "C:\Program Files\SAS\SAS 9.1\SAS.EXE"
   "C:\SampleProgram.SAS"
   ```

   Add any necessary system options after the program name.

3. Click **OK**. The program is submitted in batch mode.

Double-Clicking a File Icon in the Windows Explorer

By default, when you double-click a SAS program file with an extension of .SAS, .SAS7BPGM, .SS2, or .SS7 in the Windows Explorer, the SAS System starts in windowing mode. However, you can change the default action so that double-clicking a SAS program file submits the program in batch mode.

To change the default double-click action for the .SAS file extension, follow these steps:

1. Open the Windows Explorer by right-clicking the **Start** button, then clicking **Explore**.
2. Click **Tools** in the Windows Explorer menu, then click **Folder Options**.
3. When the Folder Options dialog box appears, click the **File Types** tab.
4. Scroll through the **Registered file types** list until you see the entry **SAS Program**, as shown in Figure 12.3.

Figure 12.3 Finding the SAS Program Entry in the List of Registered File Types

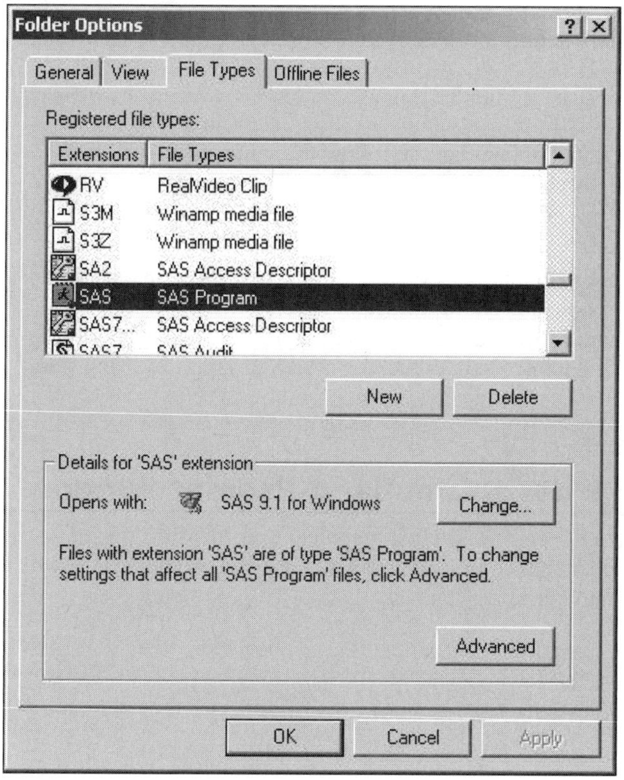

5. Click **SAS Program**, then click **Advanced**.
6. The Edit File Type dialog box appears. In the **Actions** area, click **Batch901**, then click **Set Default**.
7. If you want to add system options to your batch job, click **Edit** in the Edit File Type dialog box. If you do not want to change the system options, skip to step 9.
8. When you click **Edit** in the Edit File Type dialog box, another dialog box opens, titled "Editing action for type: SAS System Program." In the field labeled **Application used to perform action**, click at the end of the text and add the system options you want (for example, LINESIZE, MACRO, and so on). When you've finished adding system options, click **OK**. This returns you to the Edit File Type dialog box.
9. Click **OK** in the Edit File Type dialog box. This returns you to the Folder Options dialog box.
10. Click **Close** in the Options dialog box.

The next time you double-click a SAS program file icon in the Windows Explorer, the program is submitted in batch mode.

Note

> Follow similar steps to change the default action for SAS System stored programs (files with an extension of .SAS7BPGM, .SS7, or .SS2).

Should you ever want to return to the original default action, follow the same steps, except choose the **OpenwithSAS901** action instead of **Batch901** in step 6.

Note

> If you've already started a SAS session by double-clicking a SAS program file icon, and then double-click another, the same SAS session is used for the second file. However, if the first SAS session was started in another manner (for example, by clicking a SAS System shortcut icon or double-clicking the SAS.EXE file icon), double-clicking a SAS program file icon starts a second SAS session.

Starting Your Batch Job from a Command-Prompt Window

Although Windows is generally considered a point-and-click graphical user interface operating system, it does support issuing operating system commands from a command prompt. Therefore, if you want to invoke SAS from a command prompt, you can.

First, open a command-prompt window. One way to do this is to click the **Start** button, then click **Programs → Accessories → Command Prompt**. Now type the following command at the command prompt:

```
"C:\SAS-folder\SAS.EXE" "batch-program.SAS" -CONFIG "C:\SAS-
folder\SASV9.CFG"
```

This command must be all on one line when you type it in. Here is an explanation of the various parts of the command:

- C:*SAS-folder*\SAS.EXE starts the SAS System.
- *batch-program*.SAS is the name of the SAS program you want to submit.
- Specifying the CONFIG system option enables the SAS System to find your SAS configuration file. Add any other system options after the CONFIG option.

Note

If you do not specify the batch program name immediately after the SAS.EXE portion of the command, you must use the SYSIN system option.

The command-prompt window you started the SAS System from is "frozen"; that is, you cannot issue any other commands from this window until you close your SAS session. However, you can start other command-prompt windows.

Printing in Batch Mode

What's New: PRTPERSISTDEFAULT system option.

When you print in batch mode, you do not have access to the Print and Print Setup dialog boxes. However, you can accomplish many of the same things using system options and the PRINTTO procedure. The following list explains some of the most useful techniques for printing in batch mode:

- Use the SYSPRINT and SYSPRINTFONT system options to define the default printer and printer font.
- Use the PRTPERSISTDEFAULT system option to use the same printer from SAS session to SAS session.
- Use various system options to set the number of copies, page orientation, paper size and source, and margins.
- Use the PRINTTO procedure to route the log and procedure output to a printer.
- Use the FILENAME statement and PRINTER keyword to define a file shortcut that points to a printer. Then, use a FILE statement and that file shortcut to send DATA step output to a printer.

Understanding Printer Names: Every printer installed on your system has a unique name. For example, an HP LaserJet 4P printer may have the following name:

HP LaserJet 4P/4MP

To find your printers' names, look in the SAS Print dialog box or in the Control Panel's Printers window. Familiarize yourself with the name of each printer you use, as you need this information when printing in batch mode.

Setting the Default Printer: Use the SYSPRINT system option to set the default printer. The simplest form of the SYSPRINT option is as follows:

SYSPRINT "*printer-name*"

For example, to set the default printer to "HP LaserJet 4P/4MP," specify the following SYSPRINT option in the OPTIONS statement:

```
options sysprint="HP LaserJet 4P/4MP";
```

For more information on the SYSPRINT system option, refer to SAS Help and Documentation.

Using the Same Printer from One SAS Session to the Next: Typically, when you start a SAS session, the printer used is the printer specified by the SYSPRINT system option. If this option is not explicitly set, the printer used is the Windows default printer.

The PRTPERSISTDEFAULT system option allows you to override this behavior. When you start a SAS session using the PRTPERSISTDEFAULT system option, SAS uses the printer used by the last SAS session that was started using PRTPERSISTDEFAULT.

Note

> If you specify both the SYSPRINT system option and PRTPERSISTDEFAULT system option, SAS uses the printer specified by the SYSPRINT system option.

Setting the Default Printer Font: If you do not want to use the default typeface in your batch output, use the SYSPRINTFONT system option.

The simplest form of the SYSPRINTFONT option is as follows:

SYSPRINTFONT '*font-name*' <*point-size*>

For example, if you want to use the Courier New font in 14-point, specify the following OPTIONS statement:

```
options sysprintfont="Courier New" 14;
```

Typeface names are case sensitive; type the font name exactly as it appears in the list of fonts. (Use the SAS Font dialog box to list available fonts.) Remember that only monospace fonts work well with the SAS System—proportional fonts may result in misaligned output.

You can also use the SYSPRINTFONT option to control the weight and style of the font. For example, to specify a 14-point bold italic Courier New font, specify the following:

```
options sysprintfont="Courier New" bold italic 14;
```

Caution

> Once you set the SYSPRINTFONT option, that font and point size are used from then on (in all subsequent batch and interactive SAS sessions), until you set the option again.

To return to the default font and point size, specify the following in your SAS configuration file:

```
-sysprintfont 'SAS Monospace' normal regular 8
```

Alternatively, submit an OPTIONS statement to reset the SYSPRINTFONT option.

Note

> If you are using a high-resolution display, specify a point size of 10 when returning to the default font.

For more information on the SYSPRINTFONT system option, refer to SAS Help and Documentation.

Note

> Not all fonts support italic or bold. For example, the SAS Monospace font does not support italic.

Setting Other Print Job Parameters: Several system options are available that let you set the same print job parameters in batch mode that you can set in the Print Setup and Print dialog boxes. Use Table 12.1 to familiarize yourself with the various printing-related system options.

Table 12.1 System Options for Controlling Print Job Parameters in Batch Mode

Option Name	Quick Summary of Use	Easy Syntax
BOTTOMMARGIN	Sets the bottom margin, in inches	BOTTOMMARGIN=*n*
COLLATE	Turns collation on or off (by default, collation is off)	COLLATE|NOCOLLATE
COPIES	Sets the number of copies printed	COPIES=*n*
DUPLEX	Turns duplexing on or off (see also SAS Help and Documentation for the BINDING option)	DUPLEX|NODUPLEX
LEFTMARGIN	Sets the left margin, in inches	LEFTMARGIN=*n*
ORIENTATION	Sets the page orientation (the default is portrait)	ORIENTATION=PORTRAIT|LANDSCAPE
PAPERDEST	Sets the printer bin to receive output	PAPERDEST=*printer-bin-name*
PAPERSIZE	Sets the paper size (default is LETTER)	PAPERSIZE=*paper-size-name*
PAPERSOURCE	Sets the printer bin that supplies paper to the printer	PAPERSOURCE=*printer-bin-name*
PAPERTYPE	Sets the paper type (such as PLAIN)	PAPERTYPE=*paper-type-name*
RIGHTMARGIN	Sets the right margin, in inches	RIGHTMARGIN=*n*
TOPMARGIN	Sets the top margin, in inches	TOPMARGIN=*n*

Two examples are included in this section, to get you started using these new options.

The following OPTIONS statement sets the top margin to 2 inches (for example, to accommodate a letterhead), the left and right margins to .5 inches, and the number of copies to print to five:

```
options topmargin=2 rightmargin=.5 leftmargin=.5 copies=5;
```

The following OPTIONS statement sets the page orientation to landscape and specifies that the paper is to be legal size and that it comes from the bottom printer paper bin:

```
options orientation=landscape papersize=legal
papersource=bottom;
```

For further information on each option, refer to SAS Help and Documentation.

Note

When you change the value for the TOPMARGIN, BOTTOMMARGIN, LEFTMARGIN, and RIGHTMARGIN system options, the PAGESIZE and LINESIZE system options are automatically recalculated by the SAS System.

Controlling Whether You Use Windows Print Spooling: The HOSTPRINT option controls whether SAS print jobs are sent to the Windows print queue. Specifying NOHOSTPRINT bypasses the Windows print queue.

When you bypass print spooling, you do not always get automatic page feeds. If your output is only one page, you may have to press the Off-line key on your printer, then the FormFeed key, then the Off-line key again to cause the page to eject. You may also have to follow this procedure to get the last page of a multipage print job. Usually, if Windows is spooling your print jobs, page feeds are automatic.

Sending the Log and Procedure Output to the Printer: The PRINTTO procedure enables you to route the SAS log and procedure output to a file shortcut. By setting up a file shortcut that points to the printer, you can direct your log and procedure output to the printer. Follow these steps:

1. Set up a file shortcut that points to the default printer:

```
filename myprint printer;
```

2. Use the PRINTTO procedure to send the procedure output or the SAS log to the MYPRINT file shortcut:

```
    /* Sends the procedure output to the printer. */
proc printto print=myprint;
run;

   /* Sends the SAS log to the printer. */
proc printto log=myprint;
run;
```

3. Submit your code.
4. Submit an empty PROC PRINTTO step, which closes the printer file:

```
proc printto;
run;
```

Note

> You cannot send both the procedure output and the log to the printer at the same time. If you want to print both the log and procedure output, send them to separate files, then print the files.

Sending DATA Step Output to the Printer: If you want to send DATA step output directly to the printer, follow these steps:

1. Set up a file shortcut that points to the default printer:

```
filename myfile printer;
```

2. Submit your DATA step, including a FILE statement that uses the file shortcut you have defined. For example, the following DATA step prints "This is a test":

```
data _null_;

file myfile;
   put 'This is a test';
run;
```

3. Submit your program.

Submitting Multiple Batch SAS Programs

In windowing mode, you submit several programs at once by dragging and dropping the file icons onto the Log window. There is no correspondingly easy way to submit multiple batch files—but it is possible.

The basic approach is to create a "dummy" SAS program that contains %INCLUDE statements for each program you want to submit. Then submit the dummy file as a batch job.

If your dummy program contains only %INCLUDE statements, however, the logs and output from all the files are written to big concatenated log and output files. In addition, the logs do not show the included statements. Therefore, it is usually best to add some other options and statements to control how the logs and output are created and stored. These options and statements can be defined in either the dummy file or the individual SAS programs that you include.

Here is an example dummy file that includes two programs and controls the logs and output. The SOURCE2 system option, specified in the OPTIONS statement, causes the included lines to be listed in the log. The PRINTTO procedure lets you control where the logs and output are stored.

```
      /* Lists the included program */
      /* code in the log. */
   options source2;
      /* Sends log to */
      /* PROG1.LOG. */
   proc printto log='prog1.log' new;
      /* Includes the PROG1.SAS */
      /* program. */
   %include 'prog1.sas';
      /* Resets the page number */
      /* for the output file. */
   options pageno=1;
      /* Sends output */
      /* to PROG2.LST. */
   proc printto print='prog2.lst' new;
      /* Includes the PROG2.SAS */
      /* program. */
   %include 'prog2.sas';
```

The BATCH SAS window does not reflect the PROC PRINTTO information. For example, if your dummy file is named MYBATCH.SAS, the BATCH SAS window indicates that the log and output files are being written to MYBATCH.LOG and MYBATCH.LST. However, the MYBATCH.LST file is never created, and the MYBATCH.LOG file contains only an abbreviated log. The real information is in the PROG1.LOG and PROG2.LST files, as specified in your program.

Understanding Where Batch Logs and Output Go

When you submit a batch SAS job, usually the log and output files are stored in the SAS current folder. Normally, this is the folder that contains the SAS.EXE file. The log and output files have the same filename as the SAS program, with different extensions. The log file has an extension of .LOG, and the output file has an extension of .LST.

For example, if the SAS program you submit is C:\MYPROG.SAS, the log file is C:\MYPROG.LOG and the output file is C:\MYPROG.LST.

Accept these default filenames and locations, or add system options to either the **Target** field in the Properties dialog box or the SAS configuration file to control where the log and output files are stored. The PRINTTO procedure is also useful when routing the log and output files elsewhere.

Note

> Although the SAS System as a general rule accepts long filenames, the batch log and output filenames are truncated to eight characters. For example, if you submit a file named BATCHHTML.SAS, the log file is named BATCHH~1.LOG and the listing is named BATCHH~1.LST. For more information on truncated filenames, see "Understanding Truncated Filenames" in Chapter 1.

Exceptions to the Rule: When you drop a program file icon onto the SAS.EXE icon in the Windows Explorer, the log and output files are created in C:\Program Files\Common Files\System\Mapi\1033\NT for Windows 2000. The location may differ for the Windows NT and Windows XP environments.

Creating Two Copies of the Log and Output: To create copies of the log and output files, use the ALTLOG and ALTPRINT system options. This technique creates two copies of the log and output files—one in the default place and one in the place you specify. For example, add the following options to your SAS configuration file:

```
-ALTLOG C:\SASLOGS
-ALTPRINT C:\SASOUT
```

These options tell the SAS System to place one copy of the log and output files in the SAS current folder and one copy in the folders C:\SASLOGS and C:\SASOUT, respectively. The filenames are the same as the SAS program filename, with extensions of .LOG and .LST.

Creating Only One Copy of the Log and Output: If you want only one copy of your log and output files, use the LOG and PRINT system options. For example, adding the following options to your SAS configuration file causes the batch logs and output to be stored in the specified folders:

```
-LOG C:\SASLOGS
-PRINT C:\SASOUT
```

In this case, no copies of the log and output are stored in the SAS current folder.

Combining Windowing and Batch Modes

There may be times when the choice between batch mode and a windowing session is a hard one to call—you like to edit your code using the Enhanced Editor, but you like submitting your code in batch. Or, the majority of your program is noninteractive, but you'd really like to view the data with the FSVIEW procedure.

One of the nice features of using the SAS System under Windows is that it allows you this flexibility. The next two sections describe two methods you can use to mix and match windowing and batch sessions.

Submitting Batch Jobs from a Windowing Session: Because Windows supports multiple SAS sessions, you can edit your programs using a windowing session and then submit the finalized code in a separate batch job. Here are the basic steps for this approach:

1. Start a SAS session. Open your file into the Enhanced Editor window, and edit it.
2. When the code is finalized, save it.
3. Submit an X statement:

   ```
   x '"c:\path\sas.exe saved-code"';
   ```

In the X statement, *path* is the path to the SAS.EXE file and *saved-code* is the full pathname of the file that contains the program you saved. This X statement starts a separate SAS session, running in batch mode. When the batch job is finished, you can examine the log and output from the batch job using your windowing session. (If the pathnames do not contain spaces, you can eliminate the outer pair of single quotation marks.)

Calling a Windowing Session from a Batch Job: Sometimes, you want to do the opposite of the previous scenario—that is, start a windowing session from a batch job. This is possible in certain situations. For example, suppose your program first does a lot of number crunching and statistics generating—no windows needed for that. So you save system resources by starting your program in batch mode. But you want to see your data in tabular form, using PROC FSVIEW. When your program calls PROC FSVIEW, it switches to windowing mode.

While you can look at and scroll through your data, you cannot issue any windowing commands. When you close the FSVIEW window, your program returns to batch mode.

Interrupting a Batch Job

To stop a batch SAS job, make the BATCH SAS window active and click **Cancel**.

Alternatively, press CTRL-BREAK. Make sure the BATCH SAS window or the SAS icon (representing the minimized batch job) is active. It may take a few seconds for the BREAK dialog box to appear; do not press CTRL-BREAK more than once.

Of course, if something goes terribly wrong and your display is frozen, try pressing CTRL-ALT-DEL to end the batch SAS task or to reboot, as described in "Canceling the Entire SAS Session" in Chapter 4. If the worst has happened, turn off your computer. However, this technique can result in lost or corrupted data, so use it only when absolutely necessary.

13 Using SAS to Execute System Commands and Applications

Introduction

What's New: The SYSTASK statement offers a powerful alternative to the X statement.

Sometimes you may want to issue a command to the Windows environment (such as copying a file) or start another Windows application without leaving your SAS session. You can now either use the X statement and X command or use the SYSTASK statement. The following sections describe the details of using each technique, as well as some SAS system options that affect operating system commands issued from your SAS session. This chapter also discusses how to add an application name to the SAS System **Tools** menu.

Understanding How Operating System Commands Are Executed by SAS

Although the days of the command-driven DOS operating system are long gone, Windows still allows you to open a command-prompt window (akin to the UNIX "terminal window"). When issued from the SAS System, all Windows operating system commands are executed by default in the SAS current folder, unless the command contains a different folder specification. In most cases in the Windows 2000 environment, the current folder is C:\Documents and Settings*Windows-user-name*.

Note

The method you use to start the SAS System can affect the folder used as the current folder. See Chapter 11 for more details.

For example, if you wanted to start Microsoft Word, SAS looks for the winword.exe file in the SAS current folder unless you specify the entire pathname of the winword.exe file.

Note

To change the current folder, double-click the current folder icon in the SAS System status bar. For more details, see "Changing the SAS System Current Folder" in Chapter 3.

Using the X Statement and X Command

What's New The X statement and X command default to a windowed (not a full-screen) command-prompt environment.

The X statement is a SAS programming statement that can be submitted in any SAS program under Windows. The X command is a windowing command that serves the same purpose as the X statement. You can use the X statement and the X command to issue Windows operating system commands and to start other Windows applications. The following discussion uses the X statement in the examples; however, the syntax and examples are identical for the X command (except that windowing commands are not followed by a semicolon).

The syntax of the X statement to issue a Windows operating system command is as follows:

X '*system-command*';

When you submit the X statement, the screen displays the results of the DOS command (such as a folder listing). You must type EXIT at the command prompt and press ENTER to return to your SAS session. If the X statement invokes another Windows application, that application appears on top of your SAS session, ready for input.

Using Spaces in the X Statement: The Windows command prompt program interprets spaces as the end of a command and the beginning of a command argument. Therefore, if pathnames contain spaces, you must enclose them in double quotation marks. For example, if you try to submit

```
/*  This does NOT work... */
x 'C:\Program Files\Microsoft Office\Office\winword.exe';
```

you get an error about C:\Program not being a valid Windows operating system command. Instead, add double quotation marks around the pathname:

```
/* But this does work. */
x '"C:\Program Files\Microsoft Office\Office\winword.exe"';
```

The first pair of quotation marks (the single ones) are for the X statement; the second pair of quotation marks (the double ones) are for Windows itself.

Alternatively, you can use the truncated version of the names, to eliminate the spaces. The equivalent of the previous command, using truncated names, is

```
x 'c:\Progra~1\Micros~2\Office\winword.exe';
```

(In this example, there are two folders, named Microsoft Office and Microsoft Frontpage on the system. Therefore, the truncated version of Microsoft Office is Micros~2.)

If the Windows operating system command contains no spaces at all, you can omit the single quotation marks, as in

```
x dir;
```

This command displays the contents of the SAS current folder.

Using the X Statement and X Command with No Parameters: You can execute the X statement or X command without any parameters. That is, submit

```
X;
```

When you submit this statement, a Windows command-prompt window appears. You can work as long as you like in the command-prompt environment, issuing Windows operating system commands. To return to your SAS session, type EXIT at the command prompt and press ENTER.

Note

> While the default behavior is to display a small window with a command-prompt, you can change to a full-screen command-prompt environment by pressing ALT-ENTER. Pressing ALT-ENTER again toggles the session back to a small window. You can also use the mouse to increase the height of the command-prompt window and to move the window. You cannot increase the width of the command-prompt window.

By default, you cannot use your SAS session until you close the command-prompt session. However, you can use ALT-ESC, ALT-TAB, or CTRL-ESC, or use the Windows Taskbar to work in other applications while the command-prompt window that you started from your SAS session is still active. To return to the command-prompt window, click the command-prompt window's button in the Windows Taskbar.

Controlling How the X Statement and X Command Work: These SAS system options affect how the X statement and X command work: XCMD, XWAIT, XSYNC, and XMIN. (These system options also affect the CALL SYSTEM routine and the %SYSEXEC statement.)

- *Enabling the X statement and X command.* The XCMD system option must be in effect before you can use the X command or X statement in your SAS session. If NOXCMD is in effect and you issue an X command or submit an X statement, you receive the following warning in your SAS log:

  ```
  Shell escape is not valid in this SAS session.
  ```

The XCMD option is valid only at invocation of the SAS System. Therefore, you must specify it, for example, in your SAS configuration file, as a parameter of the **Target** field of the Properties dialog box for the SAS System icon, or as a parameter in the Run dialog box. XCMD is the default value.

- *Keeping or closing the command-prompt window.* The XWAIT option controls whether you have to close the command-prompt window before you can return to your SAS session. By default, if you issue the X statement or X command, you have to close the resulting command-prompt window or application before you can continue using your SAS session. If you want to be able to immediately return to your SAS session, set this option to NOXWAIT. The default value is XWAIT.

  To set the XWAIT option, issue an OPTIONS statement. Here is a sample OPTIONS statement:

  ```
  options noxwait;
  ```

  Note

  > You can also change the setting for the XWAIT option using the SAS System Options window. See "Customizing SAS System Options during Your SAS Session" in Chapter 11. However, setting the XWAIT system option with the OPTIONS statement or the SAS System Options window affects only the current SAS session. If you want to permanently set the XWAIT system option, edit your SAS configuration file, as described in Chapter 11.

  If you start a command-prompt window with an "empty" X statement, although you can continue to use your SAS session if you set this option to NOXWAIT, the SAS System still displays a dialog box, reminding you that the command-prompt window is in effect.

  If you execute a command (such as DIR) with the X statement, with XWAIT in effect, the command-prompt window will flash by too fast for you to read the results of your command.

  Note

  > The XWAIT system option does not affect Windows applications, such as Word or Excel. It applies only to applications that execute in a command-prompt window.

- *Starting an asynchronous command-prompt window or application.* The XSYNC option controls whether you can use your SAS session while the command-prompt window or other Windows application is active. By default, you cannot do anything in your SAS session until you type EXIT at the command prompt or close the Windows application that you started with the X statement or X command. If you want to be able to use your SAS session while the command-prompt window or Windows application is still active, set this option to NOXSYNC. The default value is XSYNC.

Note

> If your SAS program needs the results of an X statement or X command before continuing, do not use NOXSYNC; if you do, your program continues to run before the results of the X statement or command are available. This may generate error messages or incorrect results.

To set the XSYNC option, issue an OPTIONS statement. Here is a sample OPTIONS statement:

```
options noxsync;
```

Note

> You can also change the setting for the XSYNC option using the SAS System Options window. See "Customizing SAS System Options during Your SAS Session" in Chapter 11. However, setting the XSYNC system option with the OPTIONS statement or the SAS System Options window affects only the current SAS session. If you want to set the XSYNC system option permanently, edit your SAS configuration file, as described in Chapter 11.

If NOXSYNC is in effect, any time you execute a Windows operating system command or start another Windows application using the X statement or X command, your SAS session is still active.

- *Minimizing the applications that you start with the X statement and X command.* The XMIN system option controls how the applications that you start with the X statement and X command appear when they start up. By default, the XMIN system option is off, and an application starts up in its default active state (for example, Word starts up as a non-maximized window). If you prefer the applications to start up as minimized (visible only in the Windows Taskbar), specify XMIN. This option is valid both at SAS invocation (for example, in your SAS configuration file, in the **Target** field of the Properties dialog box for the SAS System icon, or in the Run dialog box), or in an OPTIONS statement. You can also change its value in the SAS System Options window, as described in "Customizing SAS System Options during Your SAS Session" in Chapter 11. The default value is NOXMIN.

Using the X Statement to Start Another SAS Session: One handy application of the X statement is to use it to submit other batch SAS jobs, or even to start a second (or third) interactive SAS session. Use the same syntax as you would to start a batch or interactive SAS session from the Windows Run dialog box. (See "Starting Your Batch Job from the Run Dialog Box" in Chapter 12 for more information on using the Run dialog box.)

Using the DLGRUN Command

If you prefer a more interactive method of executing commands and applications, issue the DLGRUN command from the command bar. This command opens the Run dialog box (similar to the Windows Run dialog box), as shown in Figure 13.1.

Figure 13.1 Run Dialog Box Opened by the DLGRUN Command

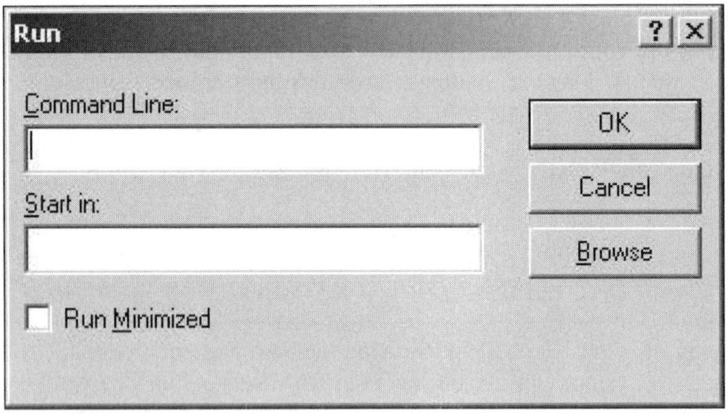

Enter the command (such as DIR) or the application pathname in the **Command Line** field. Remember to use quotation marks if the pathname contains spaces. Use the **Browse** button to navigate to the application if you are unsure of the pathname.

If the application requires a working folder, enter the appropriate folder name in the **Start in** field.

Clicking the **Run Minimized** option causes the application to show only as an icon in the Windows Taskbar.

The XSYNC and XWAIT system options control the operating system command or application started by the Run dialog box, just as they control commands or applications started with the X statement or X command.

Using the SYSTASK Statement

The SYSTASK statement offers an alternative to the X statement and X command. There are several differences.

- The default execution mode of the SYSTASK is asynchronous, whereas the default execution mode of the X statement and X command is synchronous.
- The XWAIT, XSYNC, XMIN, and XCMD system options have no effect on the SYSTASK statement.
- Commands executed with the SYSTASK statement do not use a command-prompt window.
- The SYSTASK statement offers much more programmatic flexibility than the X statement. For example, you can assign unique names to each spawned task, store the status of a particular task, list all active tasks, and stop (kill) a specified task.

- The SYSTASK statement can also be used to spawn SAS/CONNECT processes. This application of the SYSTASK statement is beyond the scope of this book, but for a brief description of the possibilities, see Chapter 15, "Using SAS/CONNECT Software to Connect Your PC to Other Systems."

The following paragraphs get you started with using the SYSTASK statement. For more details, see SAS Help and Documentation.

The SYSTASK statement has three basic forms: one to start tasks, one to list tasks, and one to stop tasks. Each of these forms is described briefly here.

Starting a Task: The basic syntax of using the SYSTASK statement to start a task is as follows:

> SYSTASK COMMAND '*operating-system-command*' WAIT|NOWAIT TASKNAME=*task-name* MNAME=*macro-var-name* STATUS=*status-var-name*;

Here is a explanation of the various components of this version of the SYSTASK statement:

COMMAND	is a keyword, indicating you want to start a task.
operating-system-command	is the operating system command, such as an application name, along with any parameters used by that command.
WAIT|NOWAIT	controls whether execution of the current SAS session is suspended until the task completes. NOWAIT is the default value.
task-name	is a unique identifier for the task you are starting. Task names that contain spaces must be enclosed in quotation marks. If you omit TASKNAME=, the SAS System generates a name automatically, in the form task*n*, where *n* starts at 0.
macro-var-name	specifies a unique macro variable that will store the task name (either the one you specify with TASKNAME= or, if you omit TASKNAME=, the automatically generated task name). Macro variables can be up to 32 characters long.
status-var-name	specifies a unique macro variable that will store the return code from the operating system command.

Here is an example of using the SYSTASK statement to start a task. The following statement starts an instance of Microsoft Word and names the task "Word for Taking Notes." This name is stored in a macro variable named "WordNotes1," and the status is stored in a macro variable named "WordNotesStatus."

Note

> The SAS System creates the macro variables for you, and initializes them to NULL.

```
SYSTASK COMMAND '"c:\program files\microsoft
office\office\winword.exe"'
   TASKNAME="Word for Taking Notes" MNAME=WordNotes1
   STATUS=WordNotesStatus;
```

Detecting Errors: To ensure a submitted SYSTASK COMMAND statement has executed successfully, you should monitor two separate return codes:

- The return code from the entire SYSTASK statement is stored in the automatic macro variable, SYSRC. A SYSRC value of 0 indicates successful completion; a non-zero value indicates there was a problem (perhaps a syntax error, or there weren't enough system resources to complete the task).
- The macro variable you specify in the STATUS= option stores the return code from the operating system command.

You can examine the values stored in the macro variables, using the %PUT statement, as in the following code:

```
%put &sysrc;
```

Figure 13.2 shows the resulting SAS log from submitting the Microsoft Word task example.

Figure 13.2 Sample SAS Log, Showing Contents of SYSRC Macro Variable

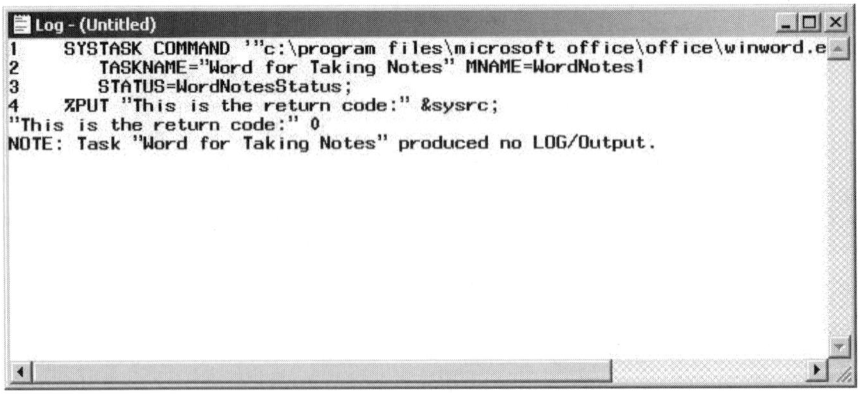

```
Log - (Untitled)
1     SYSTASK COMMAND '"c:\program files\microsoft office\office\winword.e
2        TASKNAME="Word for Taking Notes" MNAME=WordNotes1
3        STATUS=WordNotesStatus;
4     %PUT "This is the return code:" &sysrc;
"This is the return code:" 0
NOTE: Task "Word for Taking Notes" produced no LOG/Output.
```

After you close the Word application opened in this example, you can examine the result of the status macro variable using the %PUT statement. Figure 13.3 shows the resulting SAS log.

Figure 13.3 Sample SAS Log, Showing Contents of Task Status Macro Variable

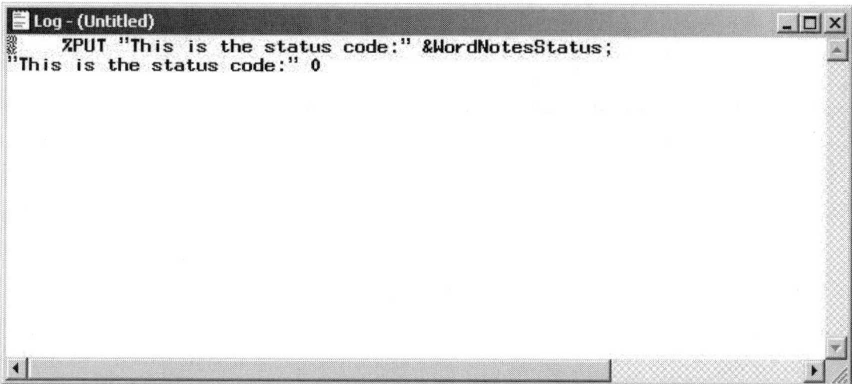
Log - (Untitled)
%PUT "This is the status code:" &WordNotesStatus;
"This is the status code:" 0

Proofread your operating system commands carefully; the SAS log may give no indication of an error when you submit a command that contains an error (such as a pathname that contains spaces). Also, some tasks are still considered running, even though the task may not really have executed. For example, if you submit the operating system command "DUR c:\" (instead of "DIR c:\"), the SAS log contains no errors, even though DUR is not a valid Windows operating system command. However, if you list the active tasks (see the next section), the task is still considered RUNNING.

Seeing Which Tasks Are Active: It may be helpful to see which tasks are still active, and what each task's status is. For this, use the following syntax of the SYSTASK statement:

SYSTASK LIST _ALL_ | *task-name*;

If you specify _ALL_, all active tasks are listed in the SAS log. If you specify just a task name, only that task's information is listed in the log. Figure 13.4 shows a sample SAS log with some task information.

Figure 13.4 Sample SAS Log Showing Task Information

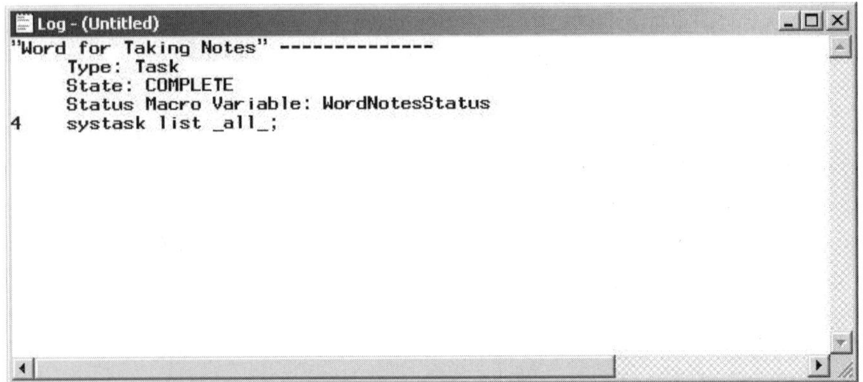

Note

> As an alternative to submitting a SYSTASK LIST statement, you can use the LISTTASK statement.

Stopping a Task: Tasks remain active (either RUNNING or COMPLETE) until you stop them. Use the following version of the SYSTASK statement to stop a task:

SYSTASK KILL _ALL_ | *task-name*;

If you specify _ALL_, all active tasks are terminated. If you specify just a task name, only that task is terminated. There is no dialog box that asks for confirmation, so use this statement carefully.

Note

> As an alternative to submitting a SYSTASK KILL statement, you can use the KILLTASK statement.

Adding Applications to the SAS Tools Menu

If you find yourself consistently needing to start another Windows application (such as Microsoft Word or Windows Notepad) from your SAS session, you may want to add the application's name to the **Tools** menu in the SAS System so that all you have to do is click **Tools** and then click the application's name to start it.

To add an application to the **Tools** menu, use the REGISTER system option in your SAS configuration file. (See Chapter 11 for information on editing the SAS configuration file.)

The syntax of the REGISTER system option is as follows:

REGISTER '*menu-text*' '*command*' < '*working-folder*'>

- *menu-text* is the text you want displayed in the **Tools** menu.
- *command* is the command that starts the application.
- *working-folder* is optional and specifies a working folder for the application. (Some applications require a working folder specification, while others do not; read your application documentation for more information.)

For example, to start Microsoft Word, you might add the following to your SAS configuration file:

```
-REGISTER 'Start MS Word' 'C:\WINWORD\WINWORD.EXE'
```

The Windows command-prompt program interprets spaces as the end of a command and the beginning of a command argument. Therefore, pathnames cannot contain spaces. For example, if you try

```
    /* This does NOT work... */
-register 'Start MS Word' 'C:\Program Files\Microsoft
Office\Office\winword.exe'
```

you get an error about C:\Program not being a valid Windows operating system command. For pathnames that contain spaces, you must use the truncated version of the names. The equivalent of the previous command, using truncated names, is

```
    /* This DOES work... */
-register 'Start MS Word'
'c:\Progra~1\Micros~2\Office\winword.exe'
```

(In this example, there are two folders, named Microsoft Office and Microsoft Frontpage on the system. Therefore, the truncated version of Microsoft Office is Micros~2.)

Figure 13.5 shows the resulting **Tools** menu.

Figure 13.5 Adding an Application Name to the Tools Menu

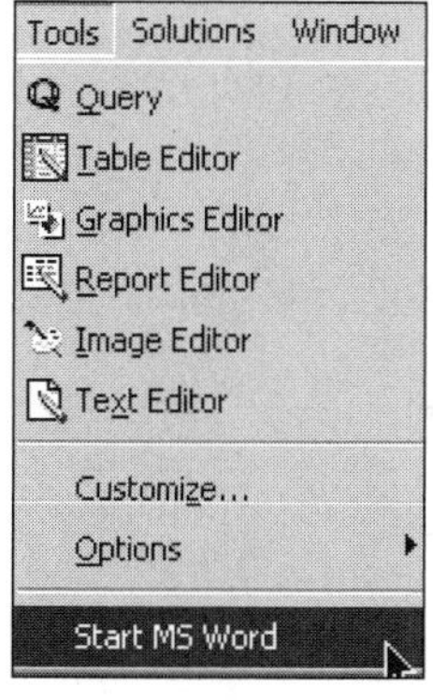

You can add up to eight applications to the SAS System **Tools** menu.

Note

The syntax of the command you specify in the REGISTER option is not tested until you click the menu choice. Therefore, if there is a mistake in the pathname for an application, you cannot tell just from looking at the SAS System menu.

14 Sharing Data between SAS and Windows Applications

Introduction

One of the biggest advantages of working under Windows is that many different applications can share data. For example, you can transfer PROC TABULATE output to a Microsoft Word file or bring spreadsheet data into a SAS table.

There are many ways of sharing data between the SAS System and other Windows applications; this chapter demonstrates the fundamental aspects of data sharing using four methods:

- cut-and-paste
- SAS Import/Export Wizard
- Dynamic Data Exchange (DDE)
- Object Linking and Embedding (OLE).

More information is available in some of the books listed in the "Welcome to SAS 9.1 for Windows" section at the beginning of this book. The discussions and examples in this chapter use the following software:

- Excel
- Microsoft Word97 for Windows
- Microsoft Paint
- Corel Gallery 2
- Visio 5.

Data sharing works with many software packages. So, if you do not have the software used in the examples, you can still use the examples as a starting point, but you may not be able to use them exactly as written.

Deciding Which Information-Sharing Method to Use

Each data-sharing technique discussed in this chapter has its advantages and disadvantages, times when it is useful and times when it is not. To begin, here are some brief definitions of each technique:

- Cut-and-paste lets you use the Windows Clipboard to transfer data between two applications. It preserves rich text formatting (RTF); you can use this method to transfer text and graphics. This is a manual method, in that you must mark and copy the object in the source application, then paste the object into the target application. Cut-and-paste is a static method—after the data are pasted in, any changes in the original file do not affect the pasted copy.
- The SAS Import/Export Wizard helps you import files (such as a spreadsheet) into the SAS System or export a SAS table to another format (such as a database or comma-delimited file). Like cut-and-paste, the data transfer is not dynamic (if the original data change, the change is not reflected in the imported or exported copy).
- Dynamic Data Exchange (DDE) lets Windows applications programmatically share text-based data (for example, between the SAS System and a spreadsheet). For the SAS System, this method usually uses the FILENAME statement and DATA steps. This method is fairly automatic, and you can create a dynamic link between the SAS System and the other application.
- Object Linking and Embedding (OLE) lets Windows applications share "objects," which are a combination of data (including graphics, sound files, videos, and so on) and the functionality needed to work with those data. The examples in this chapter use OLE with SAS/AF software FRAME entries. SAS/EIS software also supports OLE.

Consider the following when choosing a data-sharing method:

- All Windows applications support cut-and-paste.
- The SAS Import/Export Wizard supports many file types, including comma-delimited files, tab-delimited files, or user-formatted files.
- For you to use either DDE or OLE, both applications—the "sender" and "receiver" (or, in computer terms, the server and the client)—must support the data-sharing method.

When designing your data-sharing applications, check your other applications' documentation to see if they support the data-sharing technique you want to use. Also, use Table 14.1 to choose a method that meets your needs.

Table 14.1 Summary of Data-Sharing Methods

Method	Supports Textual Data	Supports Graphics	Can Be Dynamic
cut-and-paste	X	X	
Import/Export Wizard	X		
DDE	X		X
OLE	X	X	X

Using Cut-and-Paste

Cut-and-paste is probably the simplest data-sharing method.

To copy text or graphics, mark the text or graphic in the source application (such as Microsoft Word or Excel). In the source application's menu, click **Edit** → **Copy** (or press CTRL-C). If you want to delete the text or graphic from the source application, use **Cut** instead of **Copy** (or press CTRL-X). This transfers the data to the Windows Clipboard.

Now click in the SAS window into which you want to paste the text or graphic (such as the Enhanced Editor, Program Editor, SOURCE, or GRAPH window). Click **Edit** → **Paste** in the SAS System main menu (or press CTRL-V).

Of course, you can also cut or copy text and graphics in the SAS System and paste them into other applications.

Note

In order to paste graphics into the SAS System (such as into the GRAPH window or into a Graphic entry in a SAS/AF application), you must have access to SAS/GRAPH software.

In cutting and pasting text, RTF attributes (such as font, type size, and highlighting attributes such as underlining) are preserved when you copy from the SAS System to another application, provided the target application supports RTF. When you copy text from another application to the SAS System, such formatting is lost.

Note

You can paste text only into SAS windows that support text input, such as the Enhanced Editor, Program Editor, NOTEPAD, and SOURCE windows.

For more information on cut-and-paste, as well as drag-and-drop (which is another method of cutting and pasting), see Chapter 3.

Using the SAS Import/Export Wizard

What's New: Many changes and enhancements have been made to the Import/Export Wizard.

FasTip: Select **File** → **Import** or **File** → **Export**.

The SAS Import/Export Wizard is a handy method of converting data from one format to another. For example, using the Import Wizard, you can bring a tab-delimited set of data from a Word document into the SAS System as a SAS table. Or, using the Export Wizard, you can convert a SAS table into an Excel spreadsheet or a PC File Formats file (a database file).

To access the Import/Export Wizard, click **File** in the SAS System main menu, then click **Import Data** or **Export Data**. The Import/Export Wizard is also available from other portions of the SAS System, such as the SQL Query window and SAS/ASSIST software.

Note

To use the Import/Export Wizard with database files, including Microsoft Excel 2002 and Microsoft Access 2002 files, you must license SAS/ACCESS software. If you are an Excel user, the SAS 9.1 Import/Export Wizard allows you to export to a specific sheet in a workbook, or to multiple sheets.

Suppose you have a set of data about vegetables in a file where the data are separated by commas:

```
Vegetable,Germination,Zone
corn,1 week,all
eggplant,2 weeks,7 and above
beans,4 days,all
carrots,10 days,all
```

To convert these data into a SAS table using the Import Wizard, follow these steps:

1. Click **File** → **Import Data**. The Import Wizard appears, as shown in Figure 14.1.

Figure 14.1 Import Wizard – Select Import Type Window

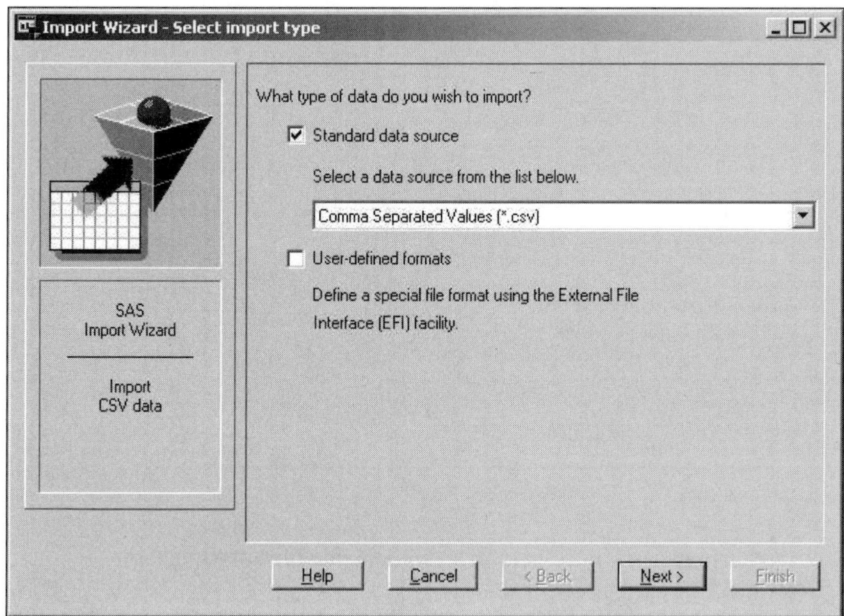

Note

> Depending on your screen size and resolution, you may have to close all docked windows and maximize the main SAS window to see all of the Import Wizard window.

2. Because your file is comma-delimited, click the down arrow next to the text-entry field under **Standard data source**, and click **Comma Separated Values (*.csv)**. Now click **Next**, to display the window shown in Figure 14.2.

Figure 14.2 Import Wizard - Select File Window

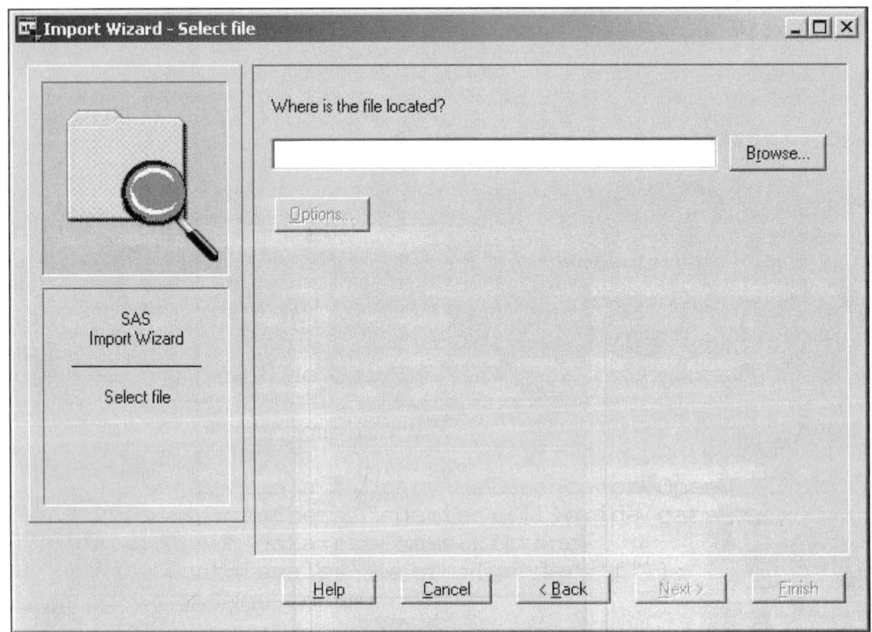

3. Type the name of the file in the text-entry field. For example, the filename might be C:\SASBOOK\MyData.CSV.

4. After you type the filename into the text-entry field, you can click the **Options** button to set the import options. Figure 14.3 shows a sample Delimited File Options dialog box.

Figure 14.3 Delimited File Options Dialog Box for the Import Wizard

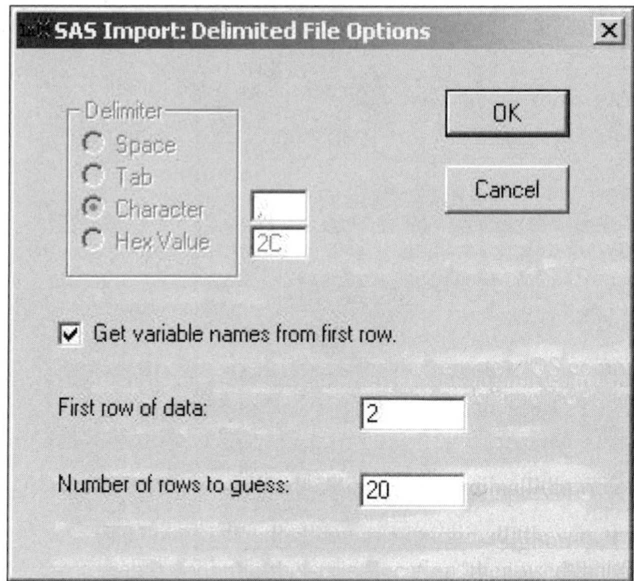

5. After you've set the options, click **OK**, then click **Next** in the Select file window to progress to the window shown in Figure 14.4.

Figure 14.4 Import Wizard – Select Library and Member Window

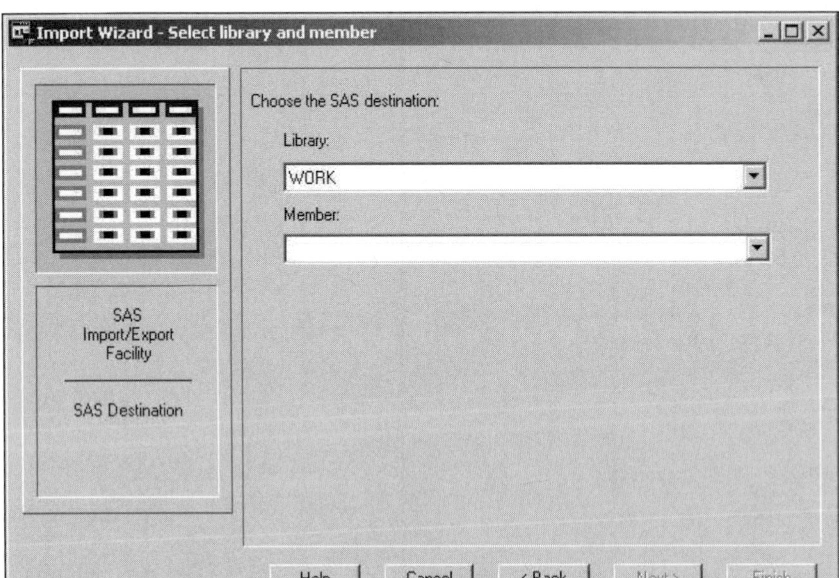

6. Click the down arrow next to the **Library** field, and click the SAS data library in which you want to store the new SAS table. Then type the name of the new member in the **Member** field. For example, you might select SASUSER as the data library, and give the table a member name of VEGGIES.

7. After you've selected the library and member name, click **Next**. This displays the Create SAS Statements window, shown in Figure 14.5.

Figure 14.5 Import Wizard – Create SAS Statements Window

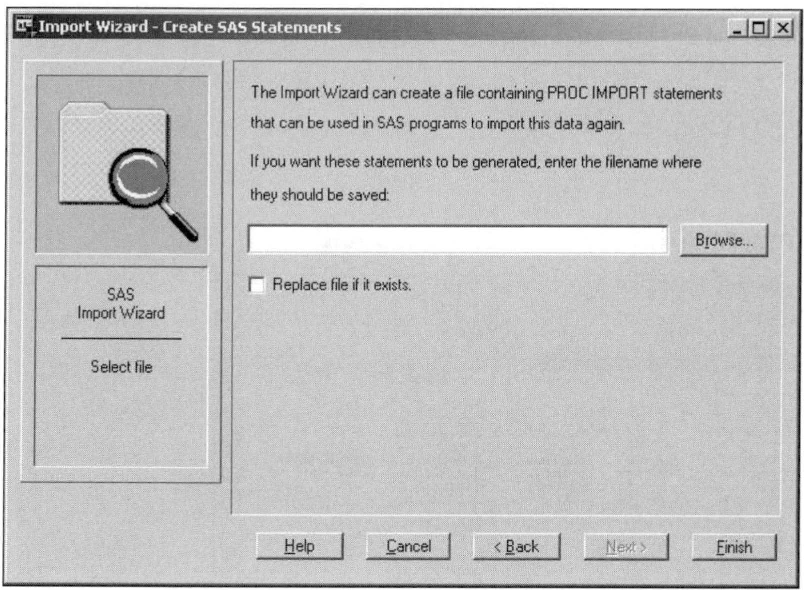

If you would like the SAS System to automatically generate a program that you can later run (in batch mode, for example) to import this data, enter a filename. You must supply both the filename and the extension (.SAS). If you do not specify a pathname, the file is by default stored in the SAS current folder. For details on the current folder, see "Determining the SAS System Current Folder" in Chapter 11.

8. Now click **Finish**. The new table is created, and the SAS log indicates where and how the data were saved. For example, here is a portion of the log that appears after importing the Vegetable data:

```
NOTE: 5 records were read from the infile
'C:\SASBOOK\MYDATA.CSV'.
      The minimum record length was 15.
      The maximum record length was 28.
NOTE: The data set SASUSER.VEGGIES has 5 observations and 3
variables.
NOTE: DATA statement used (Total process time):
      real time           0.06 seconds
      cpu time            0.03 seconds

5 rows created in SASUSER.VEGGIES from
C:\SASBOOK\MYDATA.CSV.

NOTE: SASUSER.VEGGIES was successfully created.
```

You might want to scan the SAS log after the Import Wizard is finished, to see if the table creation went as you expected. Also, you may want to print the table to see if it was created properly. For example, Figure 14.6 shows the PROC PRINT output for the table created in this example, using the following code:

```
proc print data=sasuser.veggies;
run;
```

Figure 14.6 PROC PRINT Output for the New SAS Table

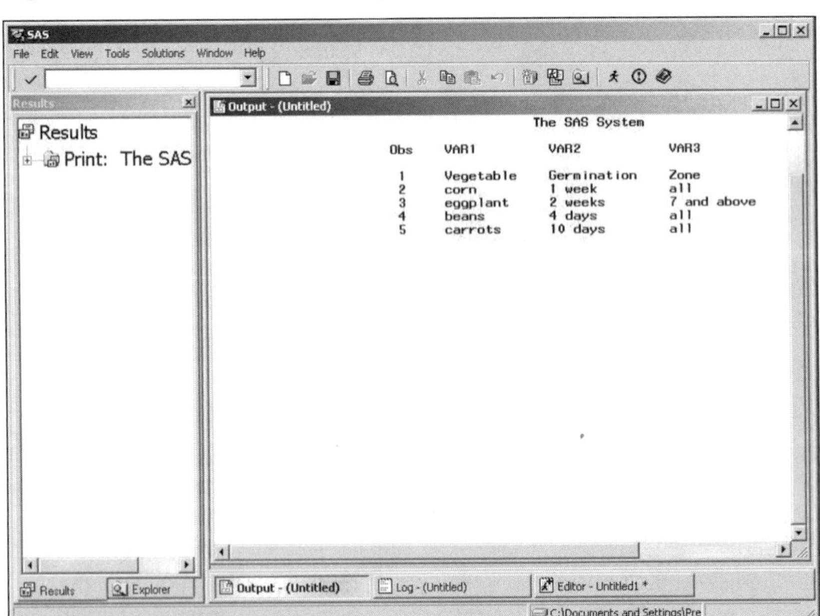

The SAS Export Wizard works similarly to the Import Wizard—simply follow the instructions in the window, and use the **Help** button if you need help on a particular window.

Understanding Dynamic Data Exchange (DDE)

What's New: Changes to ODS offer an alternative to DDE; new examples.

Using DDE with the SAS System requires a FILENAME statement that sets up a file shortcut for the specific data that you want to transfer (either from the SAS System to the other application or from the other application to the SAS System). For DDE, the syntax of the FILENAME statement has two forms, depending on whether you are transferring raw data or application-specific commands.

DDE Syntax for Transferring Raw Data: To transfer data between the SAS System and another application, use the following form of the FILENAME statement to set up the DDE connection:

```
FILENAME file-shortcut DDE 'DDE-triplet|CLIPBOARD' <DDE-
options>;
```

Here is an explanation of the components of this form of the FILENAME statement:

- `file-shortcut` can be any valid file shortcut for the SAS System.
- DDE is a required keyword that tells the SAS System you are using DDE.
- *DDE-triplet* or CLIPBOARD tells the SAS System exactly which data you want to transfer. Think of the DDE triplet as the ID for the data. Each unique set of data has a unique ID.
- `DDE-options` are one or more options that control how the data exchange is handled. For example, the NOTAB option is useful when you want to transfer data that do not contain tabs between values.

When you specify CLIPBOARD in the FILENAME statement, the SAS System looks at the data stored in the Clipboard and determines the DDE triplet for you. The only thing that you have to do is to copy the data you want to transfer to the Clipboard. To do this, highlight the data in the other Windows application. In the application's menu, click **Edit** → **Copy**. Now return to your SAS session to submit the FILENAME statement.

But sometimes the SAS System cannot find the DDE triplet using the Clipboard; in these cases (for example, with Microsoft Word), you must specify the DDE triplet directly.

To specify the DDE triplet directly, you must know three things about the application that you are writing data to or reading data from:

- the name of the executable file for the application. Although many applications support DDE, Microsoft Word, Excel, and Access are some of the most popular applications. The following table shows the executable filename to use in the DDE triplet for these three applications.

Application	Executable Filename
Word	winword
Excel	excel
Access	msaccess

- the name of the file that you want to access (worksheet, document, and so on)
- how to refer to the access point in the file (rows/columns, bookmarks, and so on).

This information is separated by special characters, as follows:

executable-file|data-file!access-point

The executable file is always followed by a vertical bar, and the name of the data file is always followed by an exclamation point.

Here are three examples of DDE triplets and an explanation of each:

- `123w|august.wk4!a:a1..a:f5`
  - `123w` is the name of the Lotus 1-2-3 executable file.
  - `august.wk4` is the name of the Lotus 1-2-3 file that you want to access.
  - `a:a1..a:f5` refers to worksheet A and the row/column range A1 through F5.
- `winword|august.doc!bookmk1`
  - `winword` is the name of the Microsoft Word executable file.
  - `august.doc` is the name of the Word document that you want to access.
  - `bookmk1` is the name of the bookmark in the Word file that marks the place in the document that you want to access.
- `excel|sheet1!r5c1:r27c3`
  - `excel` is the name of the Excel executable file.
  - `sheet1` refers to the Excel file that contains the data that you want to access.
  - `r5c1:r27c3` refers to rows 5 to 27, columns 1 to 3.

If you want to use DDE with another application, you must figure out how files are named and how you reference the exact place in the file you want to access. But after you determine how one type of DDE triplet is formed (for example, for spreadsheets or word processing documents), you can almost guess the triplet for another application of the same type.

Example 2 later in this chapter illustrates using the DDE triplet to transfer data between SAS and other applications.

DDE Syntax for Sending Commands to an Application: When you want to send commands to another application from your SAS session, you use a slightly different form of the FILENAME statement (sometimes called the DDE doublet):

```
FILENAME file-shortcut DDE 'executable-file|SYSTEM' <DDE-options>;
```

In this form of the FILENAME statement, you substitute the keyword SYSTEM for the file and access point. Examples 3 through 7 illustrate using the SYSTEM keyword.

The following seven examples will get you started using DDE with SAS. Although all these examples use Microsoft Word and Microsoft Excel as the DDE server, the principles apply equally as well to any application that supports DDE. SAS Help and Documentation contains many other examples, and the "DDE Resource List" that follows the examples points you to further reading.

Example 1: Starting Word from Your SAS Session: Before you can send DDE statements from SAS to another application, that application must be up and running. You can start the application manually (using the **Start** button, for example), or you can use the X statement in SAS to start it. The X statement is not part of DDE but is useful in DDE programs.

Before using the X statement to start another Windows application, submit an OPTIONS statement to specify NOXSYNC and NOXWAIT. Otherwise, your SAS session is unusable until you close the other Windows application. Also, because it takes a while for the other Windows application to start up, you may want to submit a null DATA step and the SLEEP function after the X statement to pause your SAS program long enough for the application to get ready.

The following code sets the NOXSYNC and NOXWAIT system options, starts Word, and pauses the SAS System for 15 seconds:

```
options noxsync noxwait;
x 'c:\winword\winword.exe';
data _null_;
   x=sleep(15);
run;
```

Refer to Chapter 13 for more information on using the X statement.

Example 2: Reading Data from Microsoft Word: Here is an example of reading data from Microsoft Word using DDE. For DDE to work between the SAS System and Microsoft Word, you must define bookmarks in your Word document at each place where you want to read or write data. Then, you submit a FILENAME statement for each bookmark. Also, Word must be running and the document must be open when you access it via DDE from your SAS session.

Note

> In general, you can have only one Word document open at a time to use DDE successfully.

This example uses a Word document named AUGUST.DOC. It contains data about a company's billing for August. In the document, a bookmark named NUMBER marks the invoice number, and a bookmark named CLIENT marks the client's name. The SAS program reads the information at each of these bookmarks and prints them in the Output window.

Here is the code for this example:

```
   /* Define the file shortcuts for the two bookmarks. */
   /* The NOTAB option is necessary so the */
   /* SAS System does not expect tabs */
   /* between columns. */
filename number dde 'winword|august.doc!number'
         notab;
filename client dde 'winword|august.doc!client'
         notab;
   /* Associate the library reference INVOICE with */
   /* the folder C:\SAS\INVOICES. */
libname invoice 'c:\sas\invoices';

   /* Create the table INVOICE.AUGUST, */
   /* read the information at the two */
   /* bookmarks, and store the data in columns. */
data invoice.august;
      /* Set the column length to an */
      /* arbitrary number. */
    length invnum $45 invclnt $45;
      /* Get ready to read the first bookmark. */
    infile number;
      /* Read the invoice number as a */
      /* character column. */
    input invnum $;
      /* Get ready to read the second bookmark. */
      /* Because the data include spaces, use some */
      /* other arbitrary character as the */
      /* delimiter. */
    infile client dlm='@';
      /* Read the client as a character column. */
    input invclnt $;
run;

   /* Print the output. */
proc print;
run;
```

Example 3: Opening and Closing a Word Document: Because you must have all of the documents open before submitting your DDE code, you may want to have your SAS program open the documents for you. You accomplish this using the special keyword SYSTEM in the DDE triplet, which enables you to send commands to another application.

In this example, the null DATA step sends the appropriate File Open command to Word. Word must be running before you submit this code.

```
filename mycmds dde 'winword|system';
data _null_;
   file mycmds;
   put '[FileOpen.Name="c:\invoices\august.doc"]';
run;
```

Commands sent via DDE are enclosed in square brackets.

When your program is finished, you may want to close the document and close Word. The following code accomplishes this (assuming that the file shortcut MYCMDS is still active):

```
data _null_;
   file mycmds;
      /* Close the active Word document. */
   put '[FileClose]';
   put '[FileExit]'; /* Close Word. */
run;
```

Example 4: Inserting a File into a Word Document: SAS ODS (see Chapter 8) creates very nice looking HTML files. But how to get that output into Word? One way is to use DDE to insert the HTML file directly into your Word document, as in the following example:

```
filename mycmds dde 'winword|system' notab lrecl=850;
data _null_;
   file mycmds;
   put '[EditBookmark.Name="MyMark1", .Goto]';
   put '[StartOfLine]';
   put '[InsertFile.Name="C:\MyHTML1.htm",
          .ConfirmConversions=0]';
run;
```

In this example, the PUT statements send commands to Word that locate the cursor at the beginning of a particular bookmark (MyMark1), then insert a file called MyHTML1.htm. Done this way, the output is inserted into the Word document and the data are completely editable. If you would prefer the SAS output to be inserted as a graphic, see Example 6.

Note

The LRECL=850 option in the FILENAME statement is not strictly necessary in this example, as the commands are fairly short. But the default of 255 may not be long enough for some commands you send with the PUT statement.

Example 5: Combining the SAS Macro Language and DDE: DDE by itself is powerful; it becomes even more powerful when combined with the SAS macro language. In Example 4, the PUT statements had the bookmarks and filename hard-coded into them. But if you want to insert many files at many different bookmarks, this hard-coded approach results in long and unwieldy code. A better approach is to write a SAS macro that takes the file to insert and the target bookmark as parameters. Here is such a macro:

```
%macro InsertFile(filename,markname);
   put "[EditBookmark.Name=""&markname"", .Goto]";
   put "[StartOfLine]";
   put "[InsertFile.Name=""&filename"",
        .ConfirmConversions=0]";
%mend;
```

Now, inserting different files at different bookmarks is as simple as calling the macro several times, with different parameter values, as in the following code segment:

```
filename mycmds dde 'winword|system' notab lrecl=850;

data _null_;
   file mycmds;
   %InsertFile(C:\testing1.htm,MyMark1);
   %InsertFile(C:\testing2.htm,MyMark2);
run;
```

Although this book does not address using the SAS macro language, there are plenty of good books about it available. Start with SAS Help and Documentation; you may also want to obtain *Carpenter's Complete Guide to the SAS Macro Language*, by Art Carpenter (available from SAS).

Example 6: Inserting an Object into a Word Document, via a Word Macro: You can record (or write) a macro in Word, then call that macro from SAS via DDE. The following code calls a Word macro named InsertTestingObjectAtBookmark(). This Word macro inserts an HTML object (possibly created with SAS ODS) at a bookmark named MyMark2.

For reference, the macro contains the following commands:

```
Sub InsertTestingObjectAtBookmark()
    Selection.GoTo What:=wdGoToBookmark, Name:="MyMark2"
    Selection.Find.ClearFormatting
    With Selection.Find
        .Text = ""
        .Replacement.Text = ""
        .Forward = True
        .Wrap = wdFindContinue
        .Format = False
        .MatchCase = False
        .MatchWholeWord = False
        .MatchWildcards = False
        .MatchSoundsLike = False
        .MatchAllWordForms = False
    End With
    Selection.HomeKey Unit:=wdLine
```

```
    Selection.InlineShapes.AddOLEObject
ClassType:="NetscapeMarkup", FileName _
        :="C:\testing.htm", LinkToFile:=False,
DisplayAsIcon:=False
End Sub
```

Now, you can simply call the macro from SAS:

```
filename mycmds dde 'winword|system' notab;
data _null_;
   file mycmds;
   put '[InsertTestingObjectAtBookmark()]';
run;
```

For information on creating and saving macros in Word, see your Microsoft Word documentation and help files. The Word macro illustrated here does not take any arguments. Using DDE to call Word macros that take arguments is not so simple, and is beyond the scope of this introductory chapter.

Example 7: Using DDE to Send HTML-Formatted PROC TABULATE Output to an Excel File: This example uses the SASHELP.CLASS data set, installed with every copy of the SAS System, to send some nicely formatted PROC TABULATE output to Microsoft Excel. The comments explain each step of the code.

```
   /* Turn off the XWAIT and XSYNC system options, so Excel
      will run independently of SAS. */
options nodate noxwait noxsync;

   /* Turn off listing output and turn on HTML output. */
ods listing close;
ods html file="c:\Table1.html" style=minimal;

   /* Use the SASHELP.CLASS data set (installed with SAS) to
      create a new data set. */
data mydata;
   set sashelp.class;
   obsno=_n_;
run;

   /* Increase the linesize to accommodate the data and Excel
      commands. */
options linesize=150;
```

```
title "Sending PROC TABULATE Output to Excel";
proc tabulate data=mydata format=12.;
   class sex age;
   table (age all='All Ages')
          *(n='Number of students'*f=9.
          pctn='Percent of total'),
   sex='Gender' all='All Students'/ rts=50;
run;

   /* Close the HTML destination. */
ods html close;

   /* Start Excel. Your pathname may differ. */
x '"c:\program files\microsoft office\office\excel.exe"';

   /* Cause the SAS System to wait 5 seconds, for Excel to
      finish starting up. */
data _null_;
   x=sleep(5);
run;
quit;

   /* Define the CMDS fileref for sending commands to Excel. */
filename cmds dde 'excel|system';

data _null_;
   file cmds;
      /* Pull the TABULATE HTML output into Excel. */
   put '[open("c:\table1.html")]';
      /* Save the Excel file. */
   put '[save.as("c:\NewTable.xls")]';
      /* Wait for a half-second for the save to be completed. */
   x=sleep(.5);
      /* Close the file and close Excel. */
   put '[close("false")]';
   put '[quit()]';
run;
quit;
```

Figure 14.7 shows how the data look in Excel, before Excel closes.

Figure 14.7 PROC TABULATE Output in Excel

Sending PROC TABULATE Output to Excel

Age		Gender F	Gender M	All Students
11	Number of students	1	1	2
	Percent of total	5	5	11
12	Number of students	2	3	5
	Percent of total	11	16	26
13	Number of students	2	1	3
	Percent of total	11	5	16
14	Number of students	2	2	4
	Percent of total	11	11	21
15	Number of students	2	2	4
	Percent of total	11	11	21
16	Number of students	.	1	1
	Percent of total	.	5	5
All Ages	Number of students	9	10	19
	Percent of total	47	53	100

Helpful Hints, Dos, and Don'ts for DDE Users: This section compiles a few useful tips for beginning DDE users.

- **Finding Out What Commands to Send:** The syntax of the commands passed via the SYSTEM keyword is totally application-dependent. For example, Excel has different commands to open a file than Word does. A good way to determine the commands that your application accepts is to use the application's macro recorder. Then look at the text of the macro that you generated.

- **Using the Correct Syntax of Word Commands:** For current versions of Microsoft Word and Microsoft Excel, recording a macro generates Visual Basic (VB) commands. Although you can call VB macros with a PUT statement (as in Example 6), you cannot use the PUT statement to send individual VB commands. The commands you include in a PUT statement must be Word Basic or Excel v4.0 Macro Language commands. For example, the commands sent in Example 4 are WordBasic commands. And if you wanted to send the individual commands to insert an object (as is done in Example 6), instead of calling a macro, the syntax of the commands would be different. Here is the WordBasic equivalent of the Insert Object code used in Example 6:

```
put '[EditBookmark.Name="MyMark2", .Goto]';
put '[StartOfLine]';
put '[InsertObject.FileName="C:\Testing.htm", .Link=0,
    .Tab=1, .Class="NetscapeMarkup"]';
```

Word and Excel no longer include references for these older languages in the help files shipped with newer versions of the applications. However, you can download the old help files from the Web. Search the Microsoft Web site for the files macrofun.exe (for Excel) and wrdbasic.exe (for Word). Or, use Google or a similar search engine to find these files. You may also want to obtain a copy of the *Word Developer's Kit, Third Edition*, and the Excel v4.0 *Function Reference*. These books are long out of print, but may be available from used book stores or Web sites.

- **Use the Proper Spacing:** Do not insert a space between portions of commands. For example, there should be no space between the "`FileOpen`" and the "`.Name`" portions of the WordBasic `FileOpen` command. Although Word accepts spaces when you run a macro from within Word, the spaces are not accepted when passed through the DDE connection and cause error messages to appear in your SAS log.
- **Use Care If You Have More Than One File Open at a Time:** The results of using DDE when you have more than one file open at a time can be surprising. Sometimes you will get an error message in the SAS log about the DDE session not being ready. Other times, the active document may not be the one you think it is, and you will insert text or read data from the wrong file. A good idea is to either have only one document open at a time, or specify the active document using the WordBasic command `WindowList x`, where *x* represents the number of the document in Word's window list (under the **Window** menu choice).

DDE Resource List: Although SAS Help and Documentation contains many examples of DDE, the following alphabetical list of papers and Web sites also may be useful as you develop your DDE programs. As you will see from some of the papers, complex and powerful combinations of macros (both SAS and other applications') and DDE are possible. Trial and error and perseverance are also usually necessary. Most of these papers are from SUGI and SEUGI proceedings and are available from the SAS Web site.

- "Getting Started with Dynamic Data Exchange" (H. Schreier, SESUG 6)
- Technical Support Document #325 – "The SAS System and DDE" (SAS Institute, available from http://ftp.sas.com/techsup/download/technote/ts325.pdf)
- "Using Dynamic Data Exchange to Pour SAS Data into Microsoft Excel" (Koen Vyverman, SEUGI 18)
- "Switching from Microsoft WordBasic to Microsoft Visual Basic for Applications" (Microsoft Corp., available at msdn.microsoft.com/library/en-us/dnword97/html/wbtovba.asp)

- "Using SAS and DDE to Execute VBA Macros in Microsoft Excel" (Christopher Roper, SUGI 25)
- "Using Dynamic Data Exchange to Export Your SAS Data to MS Excel—Against All ODS, Part I" (Koen Vyverman, SUGI 26)
- "Creating Custom Excel Workbooks from Base SAS with Dynamic Data Exchange: A Complete Walkthrough" (Koen Vyverman, SUGI 27)
- "Using Dynamic Data Exchange with Microsoft Word" (Jodie Gilmore, SUGI 22)

Understanding Object Linking and Embedding (OLE)

What's New: Using the menus (**Tools → Development and Programming → Frame Builder**) to create a new FRAME entry now allows you to create the FRAME entry in any existing SAS data library and catalog; you are not constricted to creating the FRAME entry in the WORK library.

Like DDE, Object Linking and Embedding (OLE) is a way of sharing data between Windows applications. But OLE is more flexible and powerful than DDE. While this chapter does not explain or illustrate all aspects of using OLE with the SAS System, it does provide enough information to get you started.

Note

OLE is not simple to use. By the time you understand OLE and have followed the examples, you will no longer be a "Windows neophyte."

Using OLE with the SAS System requires SAS/AF or SAS/EIS software. However, after you've created the application, it can be run by users who do not have SAS/AF or SAS/EIS software installed. This chapter illustrates creating a SAS/AF application; the procedures are similar for creating SAS/EIS applications.

With OLE, you store "objects" in your SAS/AF application. Each object represents not only data but also how to work with that data. For example, if you place a Word document in your SAS/AF application, the SAS/AF application does not store the text—it stores information about the Word document and about how to retrieve that document. With OLE, you can share anything that is "data" in its widest sense: graphics, sound files, text files, video clips, spreadsheets, and so on.

In OLE parlance, your SAS/AF application is the client (or "container") application—it stores the object. The application that created the object is called the OLE server.

Understanding Linked Objects: "Linking" refers to creating a dynamic connection between an object in your SAS/AF application and that object's OLE server.

An example helps demonstrate this. Suppose you want to display a Microsoft Word text file in your SAS/AF application. You could cut and paste the text into the application. But that is a one-way process—if you change the text in your SAS/AF application after you cut and paste the text, the changes are not reflected in the original Word document. Or, if you edit the original file, the changes are not visible in the SAS/AF application.

But if you use OLE to link the text file to your application, you can edit the file by clicking its image in your SAS/AF application, or you can edit the file by bringing up Word and editing the file from there. In either case, the changes are visible on the other end of the link.

In technical terms, the Word file is a "linked object," and the location and size of the object are stored with your SAS/AF application. (This information is called metadata and is like a map.) The actual data (the text) are not stored in the SAS/AF application.

Understanding Embedded Objects: "Embedding" an object differs from linking, in that the connection between an embedded object and the object's OLE server is not dynamic. You can edit the object only from your SAS/AF application. If you change the original file, the changes are not visible in the SAS/AF application. With embedding, both the object and its data are stored with the SAS/AF application.

Embedded objects come in two types: static and nonstatic.

- Static objects appear in the SAS/AF application, but you cannot edit them. These objects are useful in applications where you are providing information that you do not want people to change (for example, a picture).
- Nonstatic objects can be edited by the SAS/AF application user, usually by double-clicking the object's representation in the FRAME entry. This type of object is useful in applications where you want the user to either be able to edit the object or at least have access to the application that created the object.

Understanding OLE Verbs: Every OLE object (except static embedded objects, which are really pictures) supports one or more actions, called OLE verbs. For example, a Word OLE object supports the Edit verb, while a sound file supports two verbs, Play and Edit. These verbs are defined by the OLE server application. There is always a default verb for an object—to activate the object with the default verb, double-click the object's icon in your SAS/AF application.

Understanding Visual versus Open Editing: Another OLE concept you need to understand is "visual editing" versus "open editing." Visual editing is available only with applications that support OLE 2.0. Visual editing means that when you edit an OLE object in your SAS/AF application, you edit that object from the SAS window—another window does not need to open. All the tools from the application that created the OLE object are available to you in the SAS window (menus, tool bars, and so on). Only the **File** and **Window** menus are maintained by the client application (in this case, the SAS/AF application).

Open editing means that when you edit an OLE object, the object's server is launched in its own window instead of sharing the client's window.

Adding OLE Objects to Your SAS/AF Application—An Overview: The first step to using OLE in your SAS/AF applications is to create a SAS catalog. Then, within this catalog, create entries—in particular, FRAME entries to hold OLE objects. Next, add OLE objects to the FRAME entry. Remember, to create FRAME entries, you must have SAS/AF software.

The following two examples walk you through creating two SAS/AF applications using OLE. The examples assume that you know a little bit about SAS/AF software, but you do not need to be an expert.

Note

There are two levels of OLE—OLE 1.0 and OLE 2.0. The SAS System supports both levels; other applications you may be using may support only OLE 1.0 (check your application's documentation). If this is the case, you may be able to use only a subset of the OLE capabilities of the SAS System. Both of these examples use only features supported by OLE 1.0. More complicated examples illustrating OLE 2.0 features are included in SAS Institute documentation.

Example 1: Using Embedded Objects: You teach driver's education, and you are creating an online study application for students. The application displays road signs and their meanings. The students look at each screen to learn the sign, then progress to the next screen. This example uses only embedded objects.

1. To begin, use the BUILD command to create a new SAS catalog and invoke a new instance of the SAS Explorer window. You can use any existing SAS data library; this example uses the SASUSER library and creates a catalog named TRAFFIC. Here is the command:

   ```
   BUILD SASUSER.TRAFFIC
   ```

   A new SAS Explorer window appears with the new catalog highlighted, as shown in Figure 14.8.

Figure 14.8 Results of the BUILD Command

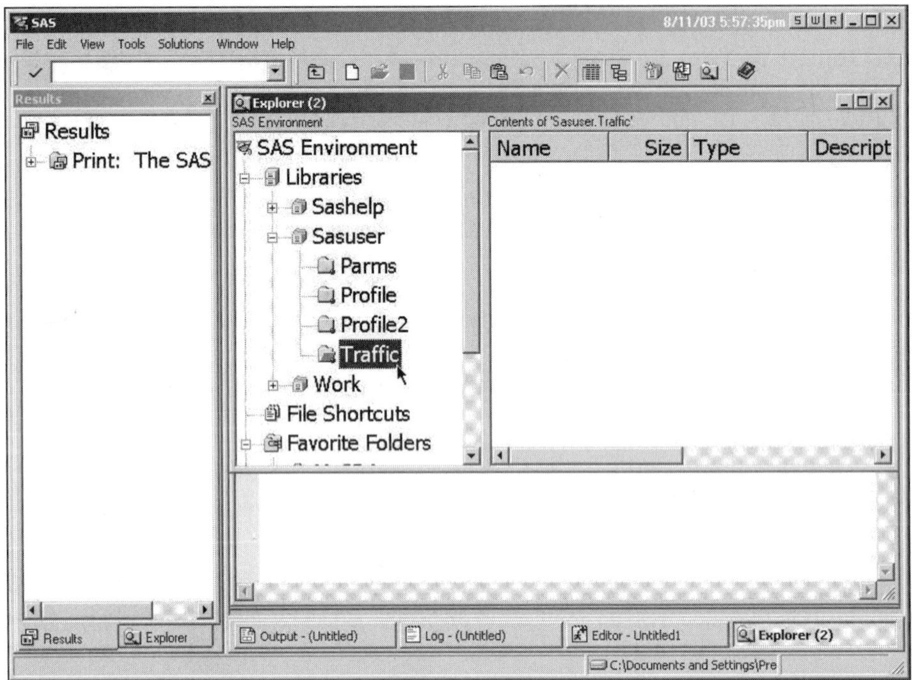

2. Right-click the TRAFFIC catalog, and click **New** in the resulting popup menu. This opens the New Entry dialog box, as shown in Figure 14.9.

Figure 14.9 New Entry Dialog Box

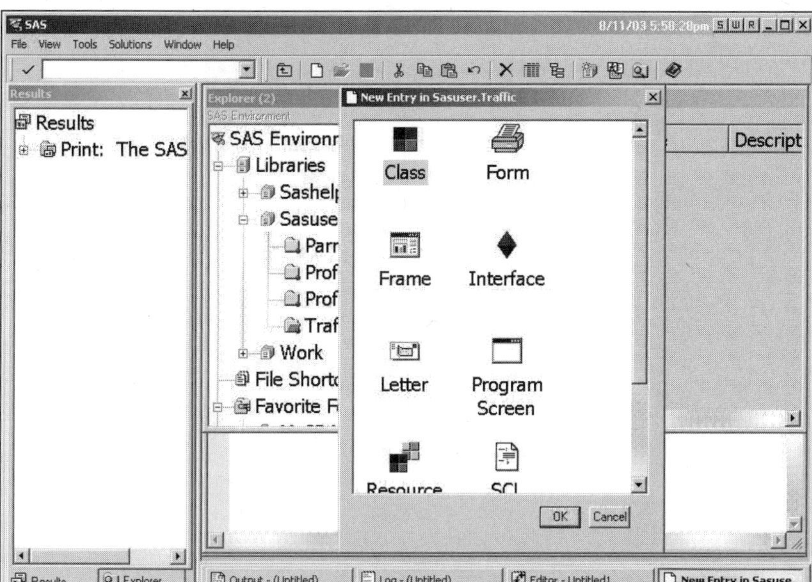

3. Double-click **Frame** in the New Entry dialog box. This opens the BUILD: DISPLAY window for an untitled FRAME entry, as well as the Components window, as shown in Figure 14.10.

   Note

   In the figure, the BUILD: DISPLAY window has been maximized. It is recommended that you do the same when you are working with FRAME entries, as objects pasted into the FRAME entries will not appear unless they fit within the visible part of the FRAME window.

Figure 14.10 BUILD: DISPLAY and Components Windows

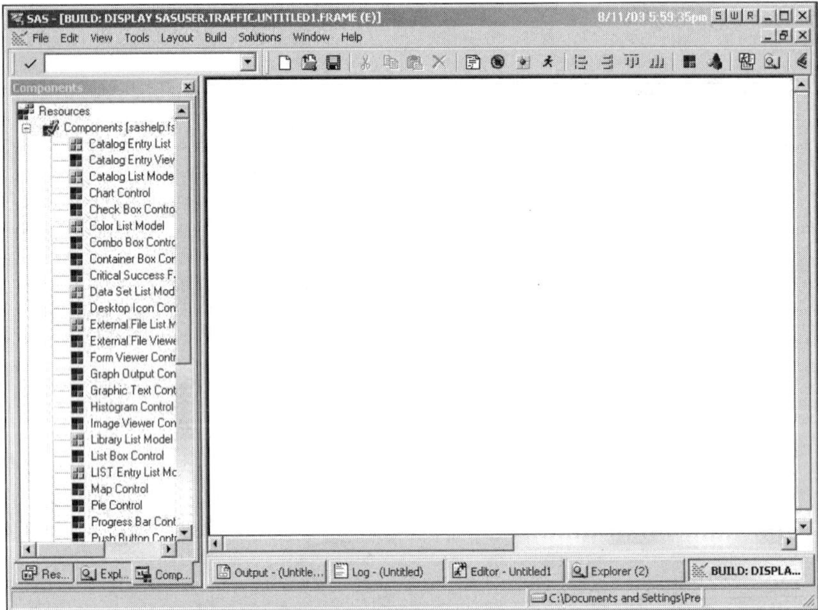

4. Place the picture of the road sign in the Clipboard. Do this by opening your graphics package, opening the sign's file, then copying it to the Clipboard. (This is usually done by clicking **Edit**, then clicking **Copy** in the graphics package's main menu.) After the Clipboard contains the sign's image, you're ready to paste it into the FRAME entry.

5. In the Components window, scroll to the bottom of the list and click the plus sign next to **Version 6 objects**. The list should look similar to the one in Figure 14.11.

Figure 14.11 Expanded Version 6 Objects Components List

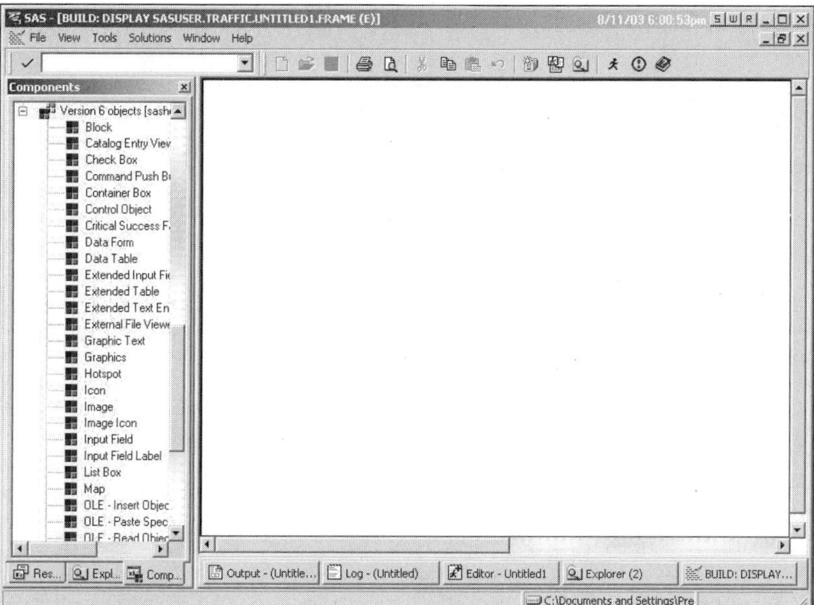

6. Scroll through the **Version 6 Objects** list until you see **OLE - Paste Special**. Click this line, then drag the component into the BUILD: DISPLAY window. When you release the mouse button, the Paste Special dialog box appears, as shown in Figure 14.12. Depending on what graphics program you used to open the file, the selections in the dialog box might be slightly different.

Figure 14.12 Paste Special Dialog Box

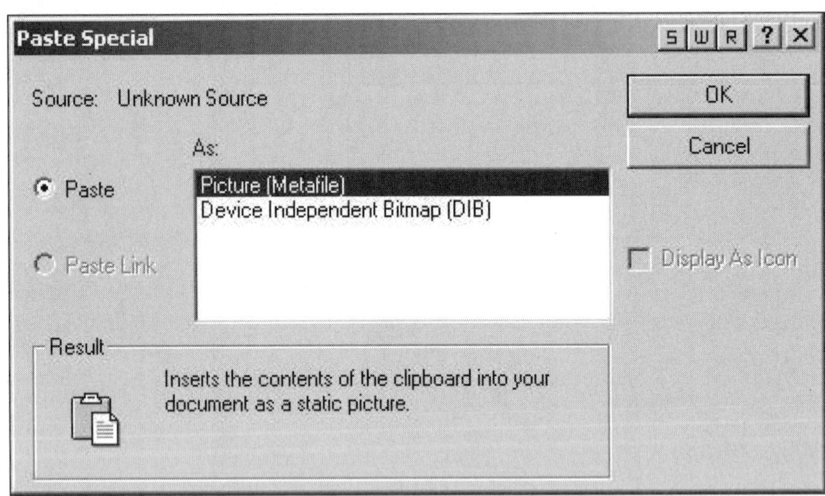

7. To create an embedded object, make sure the **Paste** option is selected, not **Paste Link**. In Figure 14.12, the **Paste Link** option is grayed out because the source of the graphic (Corel Gallery 2, Version 2.0 in this case) does not support OLE.

   Choose the format of the graphic in the **As** field. In Figure 14.12, the **Picture (Metafile)** format is chosen.

8. After the options are set to your satisfaction, click **OK**. The sign appears in the FRAME entry, as shown in Figure 14.13.

Figure 14.13 The Sign Object in the BUILD: DISPLAY Window

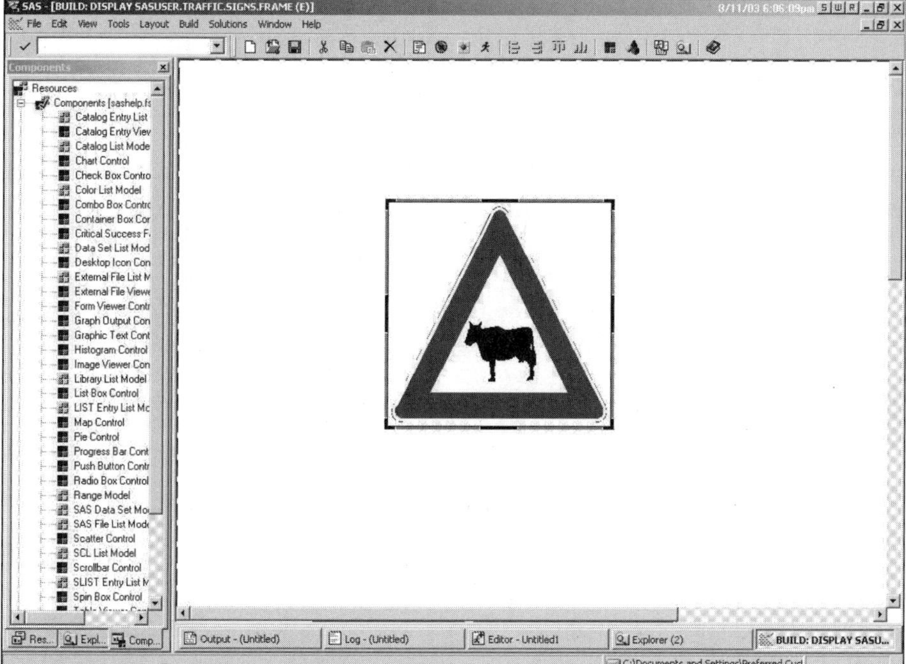

Don't worry if the sign is not exactly where you want it in the window—you can move it (see step 9). Also, the object is given a default name, which you can change (see step 10).

Depending on your graphic's source, you may see another dialog box before the graphic appears in the BUILD: DISPLAY window. For example, Corel Gallery displays a Paste Graphic dialog box that enables you to set the size of the graphic. Some graphics packages do not display this type of dialog box.

9. If the sign is not the right size or in the right place, resize it and move it. Click once inside the region to select it. Now place the mouse pointer over the corners or sides and resize it as you would a window. When the mouse pointer is over a corner, it turns into a four-headed arrow. When the mouse pointer is over a vertical or horizontal resize area, it turns into a two-headed arrow. To move the graphic, place the mouse pointer over a side where the pointer turns into a hand. Now drag the region to where you want it.

10. If you do not want to use the default name for the object, you can rename it. Right-click the object, then click **Object Attributes** in the resulting popup menu. The OLE - Paste Special Attributes dialog box appears, as shown in Figure 14.14.

Figure 14.14 OLE - Paste Special Attributes Dialog Box

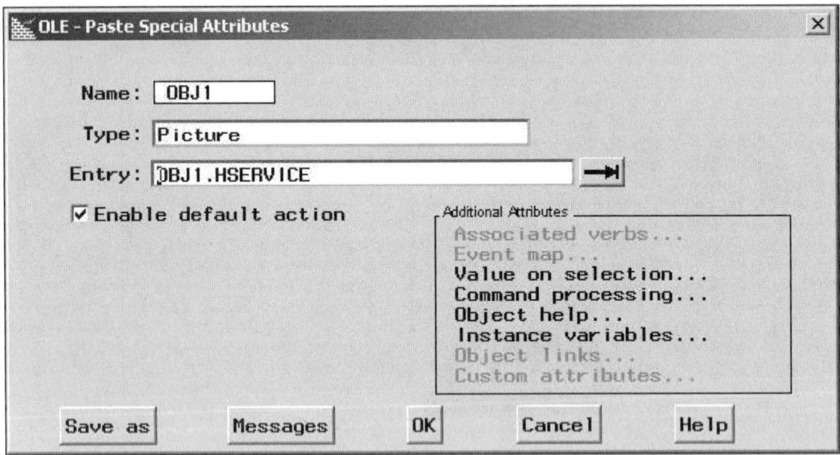

11. To change the object's name, edit the **Entry** field, which currently reads OBJ1.HSERVICE. Use the arrow and Backspace keys to delete the OBJ1 part of the name, and type in the name of the object that you want to use, such as SIGN1. Do not change the entry type (.HSERVICE). Also edit the **Name** field (in this case, to SIGN1). When you are finished, click **OK**.

Caution

> You can rename objects ONLY before you save a FRAME entry. You cannot rename objects with the OLE – Paste Special Attributes dialog box after the FRAME entry is saved.

12. To describe the sign, you need to create an object that displays text. There are several ways to do this, but one way is to create a text box in Microsoft Word, then copy that to the Clipboard.
13. Return to the BUILD: DISPLAY window, and drag another **OLE - Paste Special** component into the BUILD: DISPLAY window (as you did in step 6). In the Paste Special dialog box, choose **Paste**, and click the appropriate object type. Now click **OK**.
14. Rename the object if you want, using the OLE - Paste Special Attributes dialog box (as you did in steps 10 and 11), then click **OK**. The text appears in the object; if it is not positioned correctly, move and resize it to your satisfaction (as you did in step 9). Figure 14.15 shows how your screen might look after you have added the sign's description.

Figure 14.15 The First Sign and Its Description

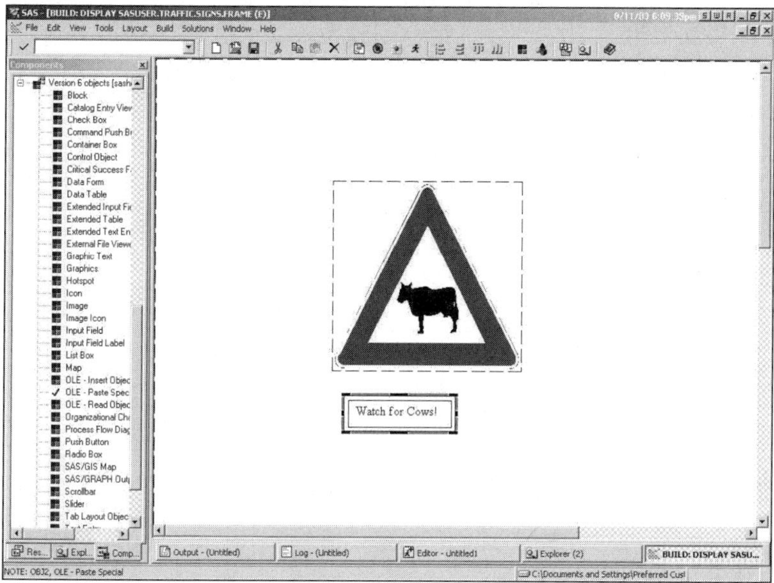

This method of inserting a text object ensures a static object—that is, one that cannot be edited by users of your SAS/AF application (you do not want people changing the sign's description).

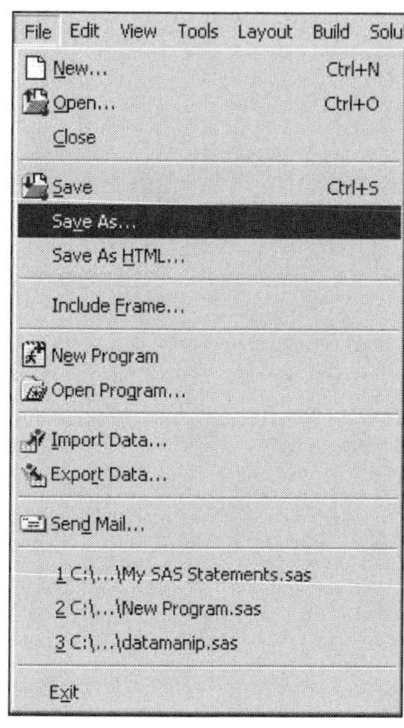

15. You must save your work before the OLE objects become permanent parts of your FRAME entry. To save your work, click **File** in the SAS System main menu, then click **Save As**. The Save As dialog box appears, as shown in Figure 14.16.

Figure 14.16 Save As Object Dialog Box for Saving Catalog Entries

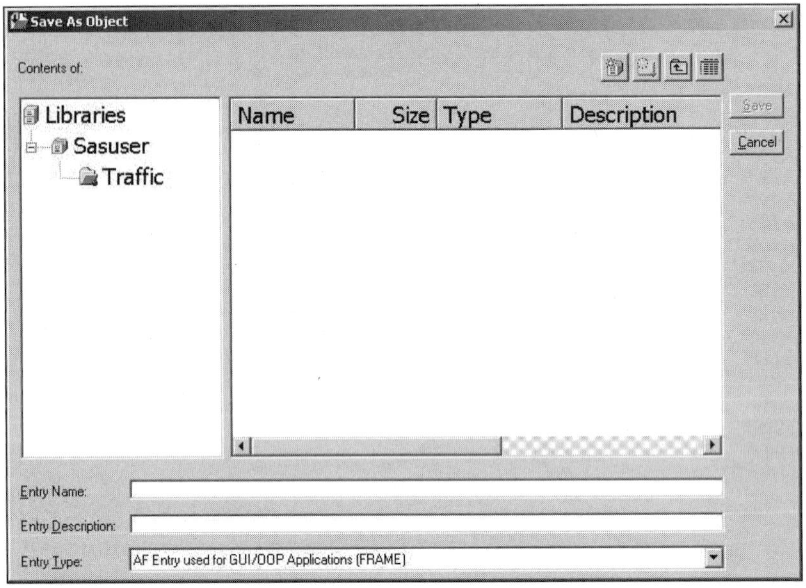

Enter an entry name, such as SIGNS, in the **Entry Name** field, and enter an entry description, such as Traffic Sign Information, in the **Entry Description** field. Now click **Save**.

16. For some signs, you may need to provide more information than the small description can hold. For these signs, add a "Text Document" icon. First, create the text file that contains the detailed information about the sign. Create this file with a word processing program that supports OLE, such as Microsoft Word, Windows Notepad, or the Windows WordPad editor. Save the file.

17. Now return to the BUILD: DISPLAY window. Drag an **OLE - Insert Object** component from the Components window into the BUILD: DISPLAY window. The Insert Object dialog box appears, as shown in Figure 14.17.

Figure 14.17 Insert Object Dialog Box

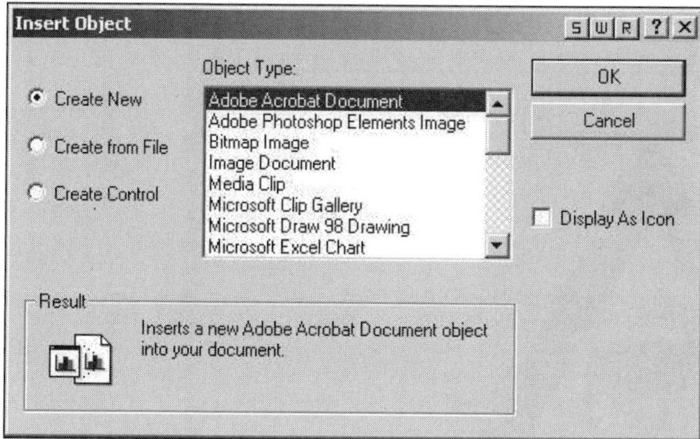

18. Click the **Create from File** option, and type the full pathname of the text file in the **File** field. Also click **Display As Icon** so that the entire text does not appear in the FRAME entry. When you click this option, the default icon for the file you've selected appears, as does a **Change Icon** button. For this example, we'll use the default icon; it is possible to create your own icons and use them instead.

    Note

    You can change the default label displayed with the default icon by clicking **Change Icon**, typing new text in the **Label** field in the Change Icon dialog box, and then clicking **OK**.

19. Click **OK** to close the Insert Object dialog box. The icon is added to your FRAME entry, as shown in Figure 14.18.

Figure 14.18 FRAME Entry with the Text Document Icon Added

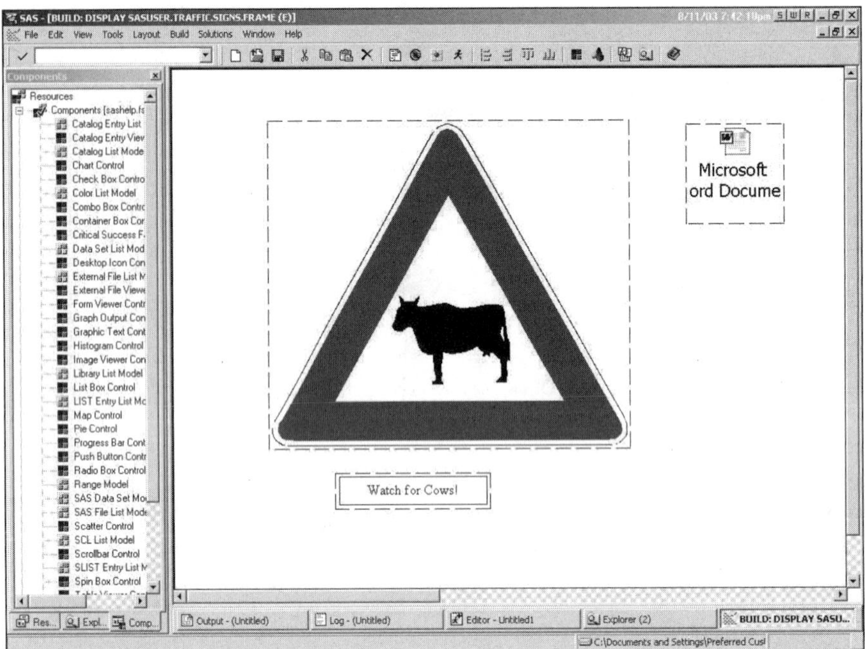

You can move and rename the object as previously described in steps 9, 10 and 11. For example, you might want to rename this object to INFO1. While the sign and the sign description are static embedded objects, the INFO1 object is a nonstatic embedded object.

20. Save the catalog entry by clicking **File** → **Save** in the SAS System main menu.

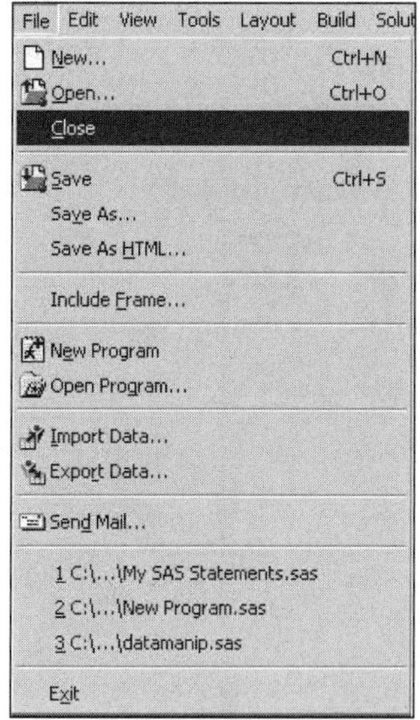

21. Close the BUILD: DISPLAY window by clicking **File → Close** in the SAS System main menu. When you are prompted whether you want to save the changes, click **Yes**. The FRAME entry is saved and the BUILD: DISPLAY window closes.

Note

Be sure that the BUILD: DISPLAY window is active before clicking **Close**; otherwise, you could end up closing your entire SAS session.

When the driver's education student runs the SAS/AF application and double-clicks the Text Document icon, the additional information is displayed, as shown in Figure 14.19.

Figure 14.19 Viewing the Text Represented by the Word Document Icon

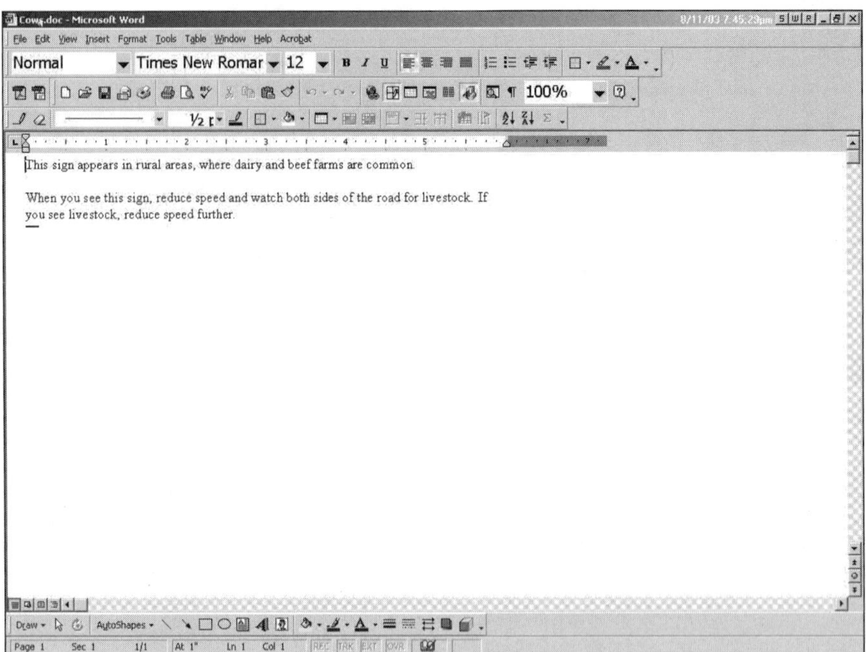

Obviously this is a small piece of the entire application; you need to add SCL code and other objects to your FRAME entries to enable students to progress from one sign to the next, do error checking, and so on.

Managing HSERVICE Objects: It may be tempting to rename HSERVICE objects using the SAS Explorer—but DO NOT DO SO. Always use the OLE – Paste Special Attributes dialog box *before saving the FRAME* to rename the components in your FRAME entry. Trying to rename them using the SAS Explorer prevents the FRAME entry from finding the components. You can, however, use the Properties dialog box to add informative descriptions to HSERVICE objects. For example, right-click the SIGN1 component, then click **Properties**. Figure 14.20 shows the resulting dialog box.

Figure 14.20 Properties Dialog Box for HSERVICE Entries

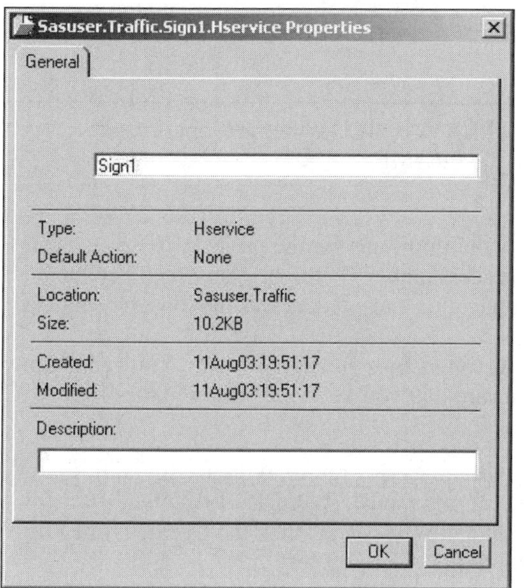

Do not edit any field except the **Description** field. After entering a description, click **OK** to close the Properties dialog box.

Example 2: Using Linked Objects: Example 1 used embedded objects, both static and nonstatic. Embedded objects were useful in that example because the information did not change—the signs would always look the same, and the descriptions were finalized. In this example, you use linked objects. Linked objects are useful in applications where the information changes often, and you want your SAS/AF application user to have access to the latest changes or to be able to make changes to the information.

In this example, the SAS/AF application provides information about a company's construction project overseas. The application lets the user view the latest cost figures for the project, shows up-to-date floor plans, and even provides photos (updated weekly) of various parts of the project. While only a portion of the application is shown here, you get a good idea of how to create the other portions using the illustrated techniques.

1. As with Example 1, the first step is to create a catalog and a FRAME entry. In Example 1, you used the BUILD command. For this example, you'll use the menus. Click **Solutions** in the SAS System main menu, then click **Development and Programming**, and then click **Frame Builder**. In SAS 9.1, this opens a SAS Explorer window, just as the BUILD command does.
2. Double-click the SAS data library in which you want to store your new application.

3. Right-click the SAS catalog in which you want to create the new FRAME entry. In the resulting popup menu, click **New**, then double-click **Frame** in the New Entry dialog box. This opens a new DISPLAY: BUILD window.

   Note

   > It is recommended that you maximize the DISPLAY: BUILD window for best results while pasting and inserting OLE objects into the FRAME.

4. The first piece of the application we'll create is the floor plan for the project. These plans are updated periodically to reflect changes the engineers make. Therefore, you need to create a linked object so that each time the SAS/AF application runs, it accesses the most recent data.

   For this example, the floor plans are stored in graphics files created by Visio. You can use any other graphics program that supports OLE. Be sure that you've saved your graphics file before continuing.

5. After you've created and saved your floor plan graphics file, return to the BUILD: DISPLAY window. Drag an OLE - Insert Object component into the BUILD: DISPLAY window from the Components window. The Insert Object dialog box appears. Click the **Create from File** tab, and type the graphic's filename in the **File** field.

   Also click both the **Link** and **Display As Icon** options. Figure 14.21 shows the Insert Object dialog box with these changes.

Figure 14.21 Insert Object Dialog Box

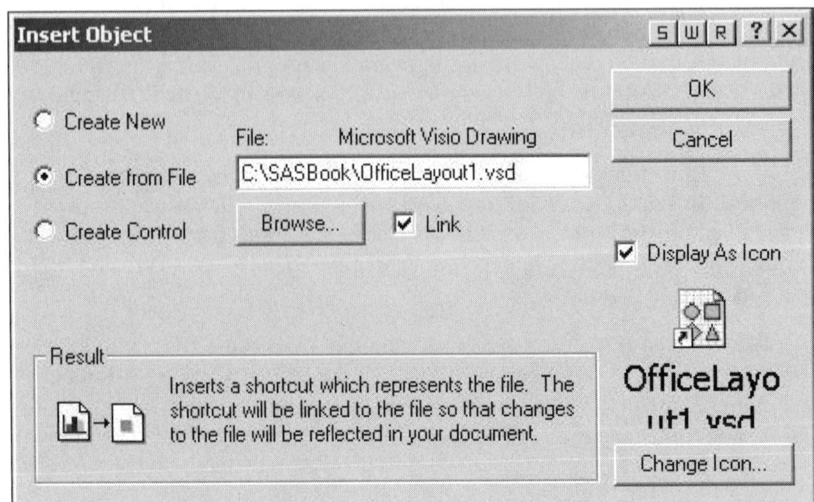

If you do not want to use the default icon, you must create your own icon using a bitmap editor, and use the **Change Icon** button to specify this new icon. Remember that you can change the label used with the default icon as well by clicking **Change Icon** and editing the **Label** field.

6. When you've finished with the Insert Object dialog box, click **OK**. Now you see the object's icon, as shown in Figure 14.22.

Figure 14.22 Floor Plan Icon Added to the FRAME Entry

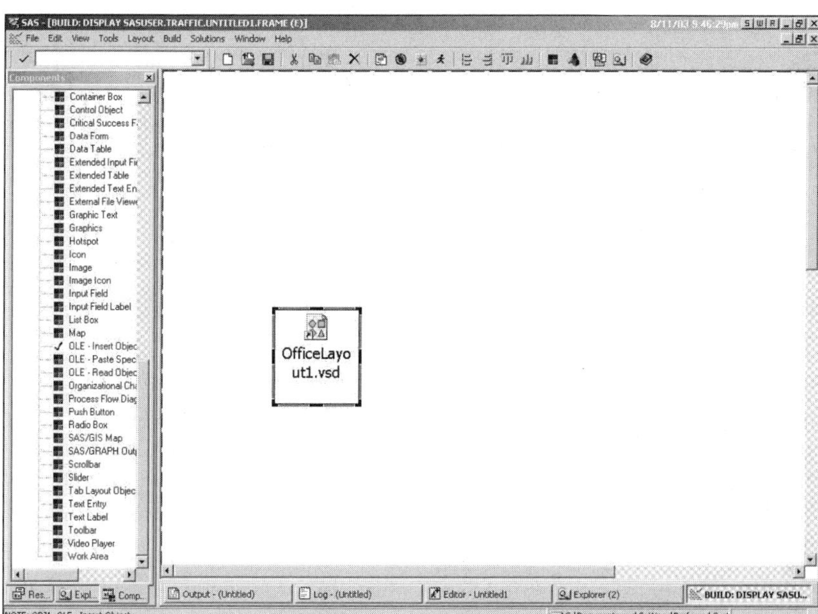

7. Rename and move the object as necessary. (For details on renaming and moving objects, see steps 9, 10, and 11 in Example 1.)

Note

> Some graphic file types do not support being used in this manner. You may need to experiment a bit with your graphics package to find a file type that works for you.

By default, the link between your SAS/AF application and the data source (the graphics file) is automatic. That is, whenever the source is updated, the changes are reflected in the SAS/AF application. To view the object, the user of the SAS/AF application double-clicks on the object's icon. If the engineers have added a new wing to the existing plan, your SAS/AF application shows that wing.

8. To add a photo to your application, repeat steps 1–7, except that you may not want the photo shown as an icon—you may prefer to display the actual photo. It may be small, but the SAS/AF application user can double-click the photo to open the graphics application, where the photo can be examined in detail.

   Note

   > Some photo file types work better in certain situations than others. For example, while JPEG files are detailed, they are also large and may use up too much RAM. The BMP and TIFF file formats are good choices for OLE because they preserve detail well, are supported by many programs, and create smaller files than some other formats.

9. When you finish adding objects to the FRAME entry, click **File** → **Save** in the SAS System main menu.

10. Close the BUILD: DISPLAY window by clicking **File** → **Close** in the SAS System main menu.

You can use similar techniques to add a spreadsheet object to your FRAME entry (possibly using Excel or Lotus 1-2-3) that shows the current expenditures for the project. Another possible component of the application could be a timeline, created with a project management package. You could also add more FRAME entries if necessary, and add SCL code to let the user move from one FRAME entry to the next. Using OLE and linked objects, your SAS/AF application users always have access to the latest data and information.

Running a SAS/AF Application: To run your SAS/AF application, you can use either the SAS Explorer window or the AF command.

To run a SAS/AF application using the SAS Explorer, right-click the entry you want to start with. In the resulting popup menu, click **Run**.

To use the command bar to run a SAS/AF application, issue a command in the following form:

AF C=*library-reference.catalog.entry.type*

library-reference.catalog.entry.type is the first entry of the application (the starting point). For example, to run the application created in Example 1, the command is

```
AF C=SASUSER.TRAFFIC.SIGNS.FRAME
```

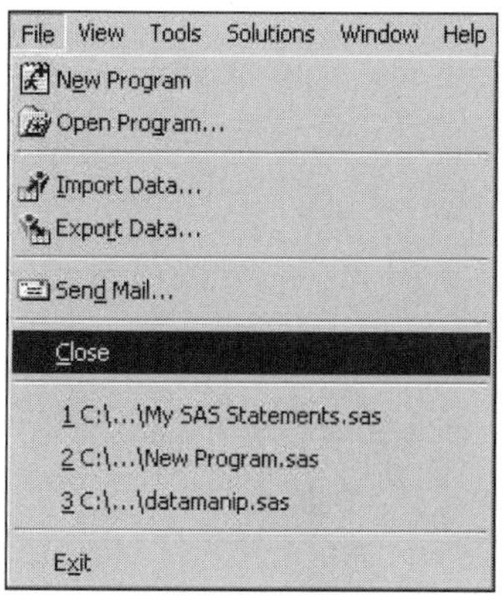

To close the SAS/AF application, click **File** → **Close** in the SAS System main menu.

15 Using SAS/CONNECT Software to Connect Your PC to Other Systems

Introduction

What's New: Multiprocessing capabilities, spawners, increased security, SAS/CONNECT Monitor window, and many more enhancements have been added to SAS/CONNECT software.

Except for Chapter 14, which discussed using SAS/AF software, this book has confined itself to discussing features of Base SAS software. However, this chapter also discusses a separate product, SAS/CONNECT software. SAS/CONNECT software enables you to connect your Windows SAS session to SAS sessions running on other systems—perhaps a z/OS mainframe, a UNIX workstation, or even another PC on your network—as well as connect from these systems back to your Windows SAS session. SAS/CONNECT also lets you take advantage of multiple processors on the same PC.

The beauty of SAS/CONNECT software is that it enables you to access data stored on other computers and also to use more powerful computers to do "number crunching" or other CPU-intensive programming tasks. All this activity can be controlled through a single client SAS session. This chapter shows, by example, the basics of using SAS/CONNECT software.

To use SAS/CONNECT software, you need some sort of connection between your computer and the other system and also some communications software. TCP/IP is the most commonly used communications access method in the Windows environment.

This chapter does not teach you how to install your communications software. Nor does this chapter discuss all of the features and considerations of SAS/CONNECT software; it is intended only to get you started. If you plan to use SAS/CONNECT software extensively, read the latest edition of SAS/CONNECT documentation.

As with most computer topics, communications between computers has its own jargon. So, this chapter first acquaints you with the terms that you encounter while using SAS/CONNECT software. Then, the chapter helps you conceptualize how SAS/CONNECT software works and how it can help you. Finally, five examples give you concrete experience using SAS/CONNECT software.

Learning Client/Server Terminology

What's New: Spawners and multiprocessing (MP).

The APPC communications access method is no longer supported.

SAS/CONNECT software is called "client/server" software. That is, it provides a bridge between your computer (the client), which requests data and services, and another computer (the server), which provides these data and services. Your computer is also referred to as the local computer or local host, whereas the server computer is referred to as the remote computer or remote host. You need the SAS System installed on both the local and remote computer in order to use SAS/CONNECT software. After you have SAS/CONNECT software installed, you can send data in both directions between the local and remote computer.

As an example, suppose you have data stored on z/OS, but you want to analyze that data from your Windows SAS session. With SAS/CONNECT software, you connect your Windows SAS session to a SAS session on z/OS. You then remote submit program statements (such as DATA and PROC steps) to the z/OS session. The z/OS SAS session analyzes the data and passes the results to the Output window on your PC. Or, the z/OS SAS session can pass data from z/OS to your PC for analysis there. When you move data from the remote computer to your PC, you "download" the data. When you move data in the opposite direction, from your PC to the remote computer, you "upload" the data.

To connect your PC to the remote computer, you use a "communications access method." A communications access method is a protocol for how two computers talk to each other. TCP/IP is the only applicable communications access method for use in the Windows environment.

If you are connected to the Internet under Windows, you probably already have some TCP/IP software installed. TCP/IP supports all remote connections.

Using Spawners: A spawner is a service that corresponds to a single port on the remote computer that "listens" for requests for connections to the remote computer. The spawner starts a remote SAS session on the remote computer on behalf of the connecting client. A spawner encrypts the data exchanged to establish the connection so that the user ID and password are not transmitted as clear text. A spawner also allows multiple clients to connect to a remote computer through a single port (which facilitates security and saves resources).

Note

Spawners must be installed and configured by a system manager, using the SPAWNER SAS command. See your SAS/CONNECT documentation for details.

Using Multiprocessing: MP CONNECT, which debuted in Version 8 of the SAS System, enables even further economization of computing resources by letting you divide time-consuming tasks into multiple independent units of work and execute them in parallel on different servers or computers. You can then coordinate all the results into your original SAS session, thereby reducing the total elapsed time necessary to execute a particular application. For example, suppose an application needs to sort two SAS data sets, then merge them into a final data set. The two PROC SORTs can be run in parallel, and when they both finish, the merge can take place. MP CONNECT provides this type of parallelism.

In SAS 9.1, MP CONNECT supports some new features, such as library reference inheritance and "piping" the output of one SAS process as input into another SAS process. Other SAS/CONNECT enhancements for SAS 9.1 include improved security and enhanced data compression and file transfer performance. For more details, see your SAS/CONNECT documentation.

Understanding How SAS/CONNECT Software Works

SAS/CONNECT software often uses a "script file" that invokes the SAS System on the remote computer and defines the parameters of the connection between the local and remote SAS sessions. These script files are plain text files that are shipped with SAS/CONNECT software. You can use these files as is, or you can modify them to meet your particular needs. There is a sample script file for using TCP/IP to connect from Windows to every other operating system that SAS supports.

When you set up a connection between the local and remote SAS sessions using a script file, you can specify the following information from the local SAS session:

- the script file
- the communications access method to use
- an identification code for the remote SAS session (the remote session name).

On the remote side, the SAS System must be configured properly for the connection. The configuration differs, depending on what operating system you are connecting to. For example, if you are connecting to z/OS, several SAS system options need to be set in the remote SAS session. For more information, refer to *Communications Access Methods for SAS/CONNECT and SAS/SHARE Software*.

It is possible to connect to several different remote SAS sessions at the same time, using different remote session names. And while beginning SAS/CONNECT software users may prefer to specify the connection information using dialog boxes, it is also possible to specify this information programmatically, using SAS statements and system options. This enables you to use

SAS/CONNECT software in batch mode. The last example in this chapter is a batch mode example.

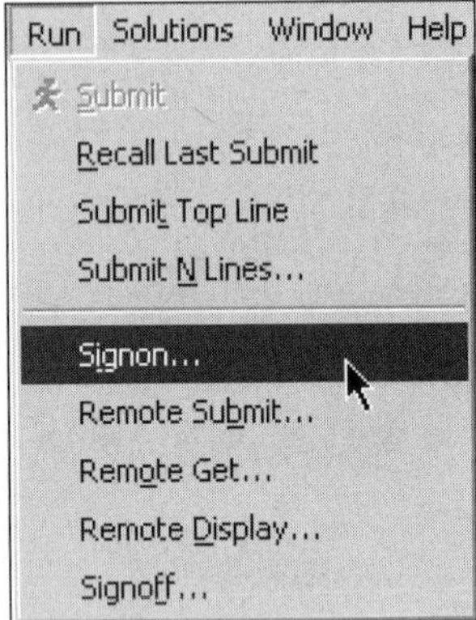

Initiating the Connection: To initiate the connection, make the Enhanced Editor (or Program Editor) window active. Click **Run** in the SAS System main menu, then click **Signon**. The Signon dialog box appears, as shown in Figure 15.1.

Figure 15.1 Signon Dialog Box

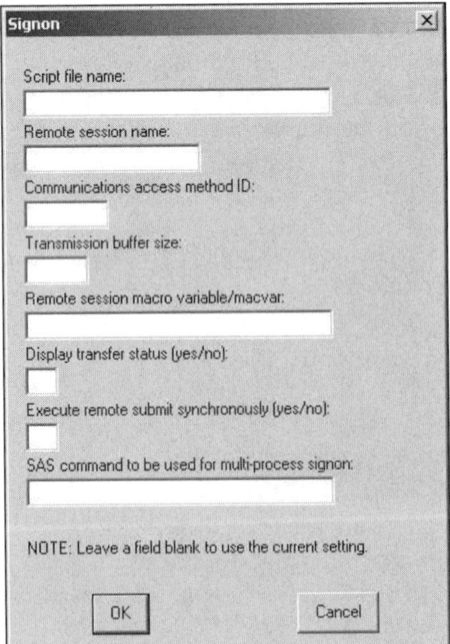

In the top field in the Signon dialog box, type the script file you want to use. By default, the SAS System looks for script files in !SASROOT\CONNECT\SASLINK. If your script file is located in another folder, be sure to type in the full pathname.

In the next field, type the remote session name you want to use. For the TCP access method, this is usually a machine name defined in the services file on your PC. It can be a one- or two-level name, with each level limited to eight characters or less.

In the next field, enter the communications access method ID. When you've typed the values, click **OK**. The default values for the other fields are sufficient for many users; a more detailed discussion of these values is beyond the scope of this book. For more information, refer to *Communications Access Methods for SAS/CONNECT and SAS/SHARE Software*.

Note

Completing the connection may take a few minutes, depending on the speed of your networks and the response time of the computer you are connecting to.

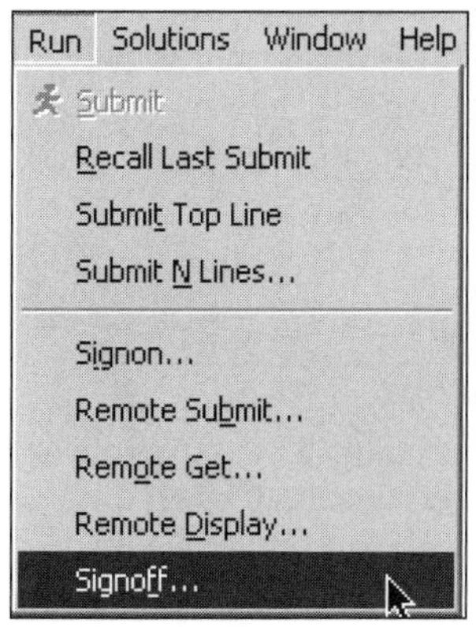

Terminating the Connection: To end the connection to a remote computer, make the Enhanced Editor (or Program Editor) window active. Click **Run** → **Signoff** in the SAS System main menu. The Signoff dialog box appears, which is similar to the Signon dialog box. Specify the script file, remote session name, and communications access method ID for the connection you want to terminate, and click **OK**.

Deciding How to Use SAS/CONNECT Software

When you submit SAS statements that execute on a remote computer, you are using "compute services." When you access data stored on a remote computer, you can choose between using "data transfer services" and "remote library services." Which services you should use depends on your particular needs and how your computers are set up.

For example, if you have a PC that has minimum RAM and a slow processor and your data are stored on a mainframe, you probably want to use a combination of compute services and data transfer services so that all the processing and number crunching occurs on the mainframe, and only the results get passed back to your PC. On the other hand, if your PC is a fast machine, you need to do lengthy data analysis, and your remote server is overworked, then you may want to use only data transfer services to download a copy of the data to your PC and do the computing there.

Data transfer services involve uploading and downloading data between remote and local computers. In contrast, "remote library services" (RLS) let you access the data directly on the remote system via the network. For RLS, you submit a LIBNAME statement on your local computer that defines the SAS data library on the remote computer. Then, you can use this library reference in any of your programming statements. Think of data transfer services as a moving van—the physical data are moved from one system to the other. RLS, on the other hand, is like a periscope from your PC to the remote system—you can see and use the data, but the data are not permanently relocated. Only the requested records are moved between the remote and local computers, and these records are not written to disk.

Understanding SAS/CONNECT Software's Compute Services

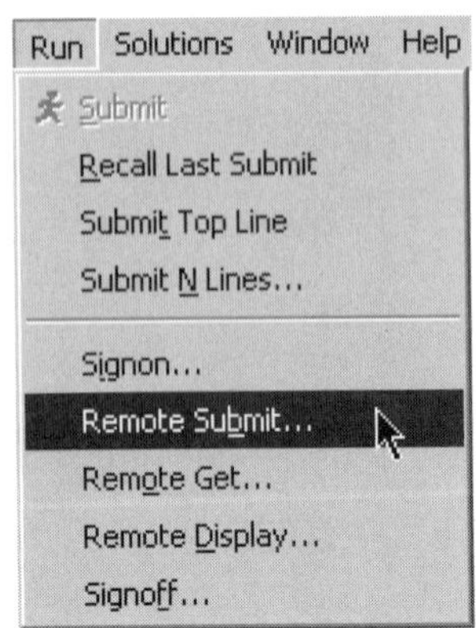

Submitting code that executes on a remote computer is as simple as submitting code on your own PC, after you have established the connection to the remote computer. Type the code into the editor. Then, click **Run → Remote Submit** in the SAS System main menu. This opens the Remote Submit dialog box, as shown in Figure 15.2.

Figure 15.2 Remote Submit Dialog Box

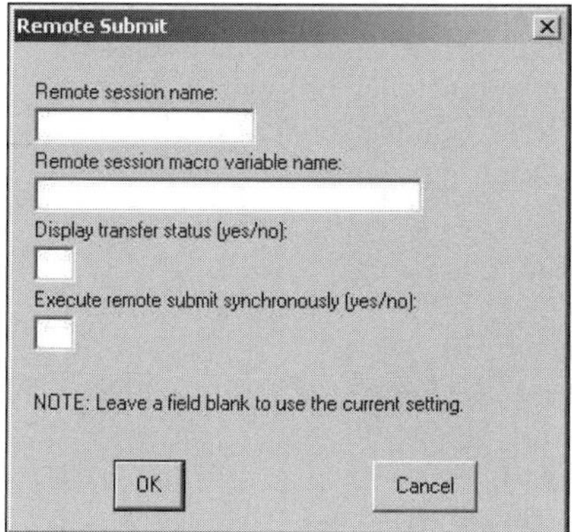

Because it is possible to have several remote connections active at once, you must enter the remote session name in the top field of the Remote Submit dialog box. Otherwise, the statements are submitted to the most recently referenced remote session.

Fill in the other fields as necessary; usually the default values are sufficient. When you are ready to remote submit the code, click **OK**.

Note

Any library references, file shortcuts, and tables that you reference in code that you remote submit exist on the remote computer—not on your PC.

If you prefer to use SAS statements instead of menus, use the RSUBMIT and ENDRSUBMIT statements to remote submit your code. Example 1 later in this chapter gives an example of using compute services, and Example 5 illustrates how to use the RSUBMIT and ENDRSUBMIT statements.

Deciding When to Use Compute Services: In general, use compute services when the remote computer has better, faster hardware resources than your PC. Also, use compute services to execute the application on the computer where the data reside. When you use compute services, you can use SAS components on the remote computer that are not installed on your PC (such as SAS/STAT or SAS/INSIGHT software). Figure 15.3 shows how compute services work.

Figure 15.3 Compute Services

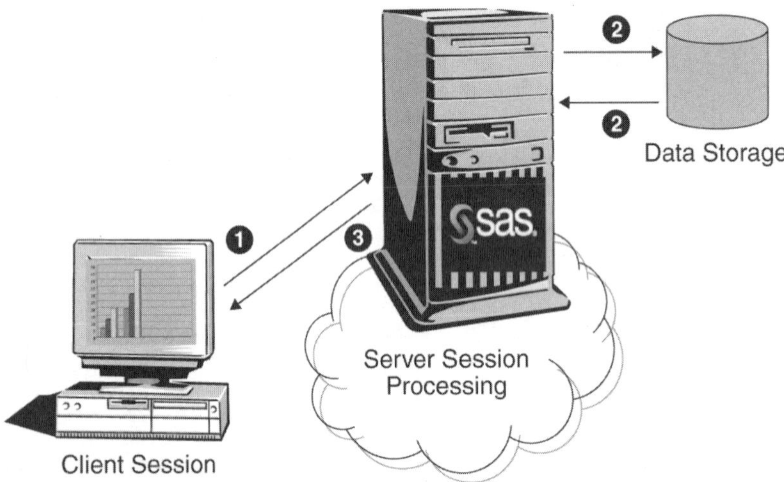

❶ Send SAS statements to the server session for processing

❷ Utilize server data in the server session

❸ Receive results at the client

Understanding SAS/CONNECT Software's Data Transfer Services

To copy data from the remote computer to your PC and vice versa, use the DOWNLOAD and UPLOAD procedures.

The DOWNLOAD procedure copies data from the remote computer to your PC; the UPLOAD procedure sends data from your PC to the remote computer. Both of these procedures can transfer SAS tables, SAS catalogs, SQL views, and MDDB files, as well as external files (for example, executable files and text files). You can even use these procedures to transfer an entire SAS data library using a single statement. By using subsetting features of the SAS System, such as the WHERE statement, you can move only the data you need.

Both the DOWNLOAD and UPLOAD procedures execute on the remote computer and must be submitted with the RSUBMIT statement or the **Remote submit** menu item. Any library references or file shortcuts used with these procedures must be defined to the remote computer prior to the execution of the UPLOAD or DOWNLOAD, using LIBNAME and FILENAME statements that you remote submit.

Example 2 later in this chapter illustrates using the DOWNLOAD and UPLOAD procedures.

Deciding When to Use Data Transfer Services: In general, use data transfer services when you are processing large amounts of data or developing an application that repeatedly accesses data. If you do not download the data, you tie up the network every time you access the data. By downloading the data, you use the network only once. Also, use data transfer services to make a backup copy of data. Figure 15.4 shows how data transfer services work.

Figure 15.4 Data Transfer Services

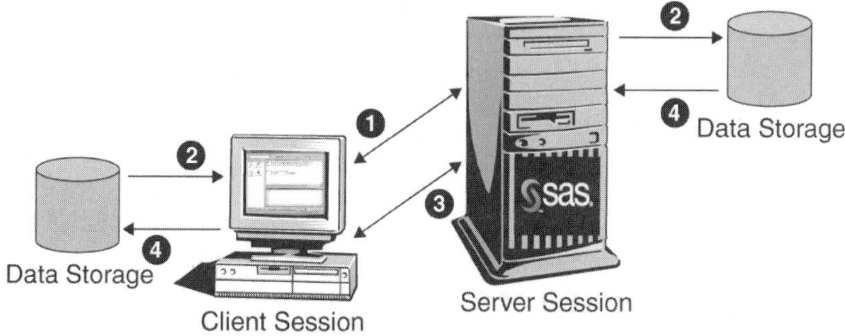

❶ Request upload of data records from client to server

❷ Data is copied from client and written to disk on the server

❸ Request download of data records from server to client

❹ Data is copied from server and written to disk on the client

Understanding SAS/CONNECT Software's Remote Library Services

What's New: RLS now supports cross-architectural read-only access to most catalog entry types.

Instead of using PROC DOWNLOAD to move a disk copy of the data from the remote computer to your PC, you can use SAS/CONNECT software's Remote Library Services (RLS) to directly access data on the remote computer. What makes RLS unique is that it enables you to execute your SAS program on your PC, but transparently access data that reside on the remote computer, without explicitly downloading them and creating a local disk copy.

To use RLS, you submit a special LIBNAME statement from your PC, which defines a library reference on the remote computer. This LIBNAME statement uses several keywords not used in a regular LIBNAME statement. Example 3 later in this chapter shows you how this LIBNAME statement and RLS work.

Using RLS with SAS Tables: RLS can access all types of SAS tables (including data defined by SAS data views and SAS/ACCESS access descriptors).

Using RLS with SAS Catalogs: RLS can update SAS catalogs only if both the local and remote computers use the same internal representations of data. This means that the local and remote operating systems must store both character and numeric data in the same way. However, starting with Version 8, RLS does allow read-only support across architectures for all catalog entry types supported by the CPORT and CIMPORT procedures.

For example, Windows NT uses the ASCII character set and stores numbers in byte order, so you can use RLS to access SAS catalogs between Windows NT computers. But z/OS uses the EBCDIC character set and stores numbers in byte-reversed order, so you cannot update z/OS SAS catalogs using RLS from your Windows SAS session.

Using RLS with SAS Stored Programs: RLS cannot access SAS PROGRAM files from any remote computer.

Deciding When to Use Remote Library Services: In general, use RLS when you need to execute your SAS program on your local computer but you need access to data on the remote computer and do not want to download a disk copy of the data. Remember that RLS requires use of the network every time you access the data, so if your network is slow or crowded, you may not want to use RLS. In general, use RLS only when processing small to medium amounts of data. Figure 15.5 shows how remote library services work.

Figure 15.5 Remote Library Services

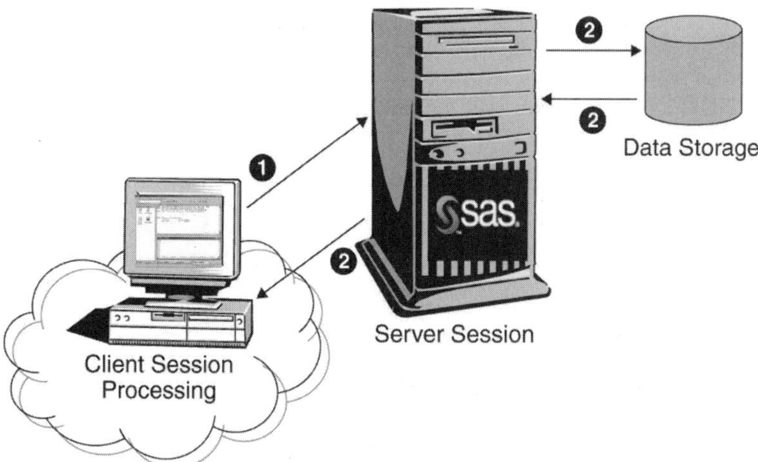

❶ Client processing requests records from server or requests records to be written to server

❷ Data records written to server or sent to client for processing

Note

> SAS 9.1 RLS does not permit a SAS 9.1 client or server to connect to a Version 6 client or server. One alternative method is to use PROC UPLOAD and PROC DOWNLOAD, which allow connections between clients and servers that run SAS 9.1 and Version 6.

Example 1: Using Compute Services

Your PC is directly connected to OpenVMS Alpha via the TCP/IP access method. You want to execute your code on the OpenVMS Alpha system, which you access via the OpenVMS Alpha spawner. You choose to remote submit the statements because the program requires a large table to be sorted. In this example, the OpenVMS node is named WALKER and the spawner service's name on OpenVMS is MKTSPAWN. (The details of setting up the spawner on OpenVMS are not shown.)

Here are the steps to work this example:

1. Submit a FILENAME statement that points to the TCPVMS script, such as the one here:

```
filename tcpvms "C:\Program Files\SAS\
   SAS 9.1\connect\saslink\tcpvms.scr";
```

2. Initiate the connection: click **Run** → **Signon**.

   Type TCPVMS in the **Script file name** field. If you omit the FILENAME statement in step 1, you must specify the full pathname for the script, such as C:\PROGRAM FILES\SAS\SAS 9.1\CONNECT\SASLINK\TCPVMS.SCR.

3. In the second field, type a two-level name that specifies the OpenVMS node name and the spawner name (in this example, WALKER.MKTSPAWN). In the **Communications access method ID** field, type TCP.

4. Click **OK** to initiate the connection.

5. Now you're ready to type into the Enhanced Editor window the program you want to run under OpenVMS. Here is the program:

```
   /* Tell the OpenVMS SAS session to use */
   /* the HOST sort utility. /*
options sortpgm=host;

   /* Define a library reference on OpenVMS. */
libname panthers 'species::[florida.cats]';
proc sort data=panthers.kittens
     out=females (where=(gender='f'));
     by age idnum;
run;

proc print data=females;
     title='Female Florida Panther Kittens';
     by age;
run;
```

6. When the program is ready to submit, click **Run** → **Remote Submit**. Type the two-level remote session name in the top field (WALKER.MKTSPAWN). Now click **OK**. The code is submitted to the SAS session on OpenVMS, and when it is finished, the Output window on your PC displays the results of the program.

7. When you are finished with the OpenVMS SAS session, terminate the connection by clicking **Run** → **Signoff**. Type the same values you typed in the Signon dialog box, and click **OK**.

For steps 6 and 7, if the OpenVMS session is the active SAS/CONNECT session, you can leave the session name field blank.

Note

Although this example uses a spawner with a script file, some spawners are set up for scriptless access. See Example 4, later in this chapter. Also, if you have only one remote session defined, the default will be that session name. So, if you want, you can skip entering the session name in the Remote Submit and Signoff dialog boxes.

Example 2: Using Data Transfer Services

Your PC is directly connected to z/OS through the TCP/IP access method. You need to access some car emission data on z/OS. The table is not large, and you need only about half of it, but you do need to do repetitive analysis on it. So, you decide to download the table to your PC using PROC DOWNLOAD. Then you use PROC UPLOAD to send the results back to z/OS.

Here are the steps to work this example:

1. Determine your remote session name. For TCP/IP access, the remote session name is the remote computer's Internet address. However, the remote session name must be eight characters or fewer. So, you may need to use a SAS macro to define a nickname for the remote session name.

   Suppose the Internet address for the remote z/OS computer is tiger@company.com. The following SAS statement assigns the nickname to390 to this address:

   ```
   %let to390=tiger@company.com;
   ```

   Submit this statement locally (for example, press F3).

2. Now initiate the connection: click **Run** → **Signon**. In Example 1, we used a FILENAME statement to point to the script location, then used that file shortcut to point to the script. An alternative method is to type the full pathname for the appropriate script in the **Script file name** field. For example, you might specify

   ```
   C:\PROGRAM FILES\SAS\SAS 9.1\CONNECT\SASLINK\TCPTSO.SCR
   ```

   For the second field, type the remote session name (in this example, to390). In the **Communications access method ID** field, type TCP. Now click **OK** to initiate the connection.

3. Now you're ready to type into the Enhanced Editor window the DOWNLOAD procedure statements. Here is the program. The WHERE statement pulls out only the data for vehicles made from 1975 to 1977 whose weight is larger than 6000 pounds and whose hydrocarbon emissions are greater than 750 parts per million.

   ```
       /* Define a library reference on z/OS. */
   libname pollute 'vehicle.test.results';
   proc download data=pollute.large out=large;
      where year between 1975 and 1977
         and weight > 6000
         and hydcarb >= 750;
   run;
   ```

4. When the program is ready to submit, click **Run** → **Remote Submit**. Type the remote session name in the top field (it is the same name you typed into the Signon dialog box). Now click **OK**. The code is submitted to the SAS session on z/OS. When it is finished, the temporary table LARGE is created on your PC in the WORK data library. You can now analyze this data repeatedly, without tying up the network with further traffic. If the z/OS session is the active

SAS/CONNECT session, you can leave the session name field blank in the Remote Submit dialog box.

5. After you have finished analyzing the data, send the results back to z/OS. Suppose the results of your analysis are in the temporary table HYDCARB. Type the following program into the editor:

```
proc upload data=hydcarb
            out=pollute.hydcarb;
run;
```

   Click **Run** → **Remote Submit**. Type the remote session name in the top field (the same name you typed into the Signon dialog box). Now click **OK** to submit the PROC UPLOAD step to z/OS. If the z/OS session is the active SAS/CONNECT session, you can leave the session name field blank.

6. When you are finished with the z/OS SAS session, terminate the connection by clicking **Run** → **Signoff**. Enter the same values that you typed in the Signon dialog box, and click **OK**. If the z/OS session is the active SAS/CONNECT session, you can leave the session name field blank.

Example 3: Using Remote Library Services

Your PC is directly connected to a UNIX workstation via the TCP/IP access method. A table containing vehicle emissions data is stored on the UNIX computer. You need to access a small portion of this table to plot which vehicles had high carbon monoxide emissions. Because you need only a small portion of the data and you do not plan to repeatedly analyze the data, RLS is an efficient method of accessing the data.

Here are the steps to work this example:

1. Determine your remote session name. For TCP/IP access, the remote session name is the remote computer's Internet address. However, the remote session name must be eight characters or less. So, you may need to use a SAS macro to define a nickname for the remote session name.

   Suppose the Internet address for the remote UNIX computer is 1.20.327.45. The following SAS statement assigns the nickname tounix to this address:

```
%let tounix=1.20.327.45;
```

   Submit this statement locally (for example, press F3).

2. Now initiate the connection: click **Run** → **Signon**. Type the full pathname for the appropriate script in the script file field. For example, you might specify

```
C:\PROGRAM FILES\SAS\SAS 9.1\CONNECT\SASLINK\TCPUNIX.SCR
```

in the **Script file name** field. For the second field, enter the remote session name (in this example, tounix). In the **Communications access method ID** field, type TCP. Click **OK** to initiate the connection.

3. To use Remote Library Services, you submit a LIBNAME statement to your PC that identifies the remote SAS session. For example, the LIBNAME statement in the following program defines the library reference CO. The REMOTE option tells the local SAS session this is an RLS LIBNAME statement, and the SERVER option specifies the remote session name for the UNIX SAS session, where the SAS data library resides. Submit this program locally (for example, press F3).

```
libname co
     '/home/user/smith/vehicles/light/tests'
     server=tounix;
data co.high_co;
   set co.year81;
   where carbmono > 1.2;
run;

proc plot data=co.high_co nolegend;
   title1 '1981 Vehicles Weighing Less than
      6,000 Pounds';
   title2 'with High Carbon Monoxide Emissions';
   title3 '(Measured in Percentage)';
   plot vin*carbmono='*';
run;
```

The Output window on your PC displays the plot.

Note

While the above code uses RLS, it is not a particularly efficient use because data are first read from server to client, then written back to the server. It would be more efficient to either remote submit the DATA step, or download the HIGH_CO data set to the local computer and then use PROC PLOT on the local copy.

4. When you are finished with the UNIX SAS session, terminate the connection by clicking **Run → Signoff**. Type the same values you typed in the Signon dialog box, and click **OK**. If the UNIX session is the active SAS/CONNECT session, you can leave the session name field blank.

Example 4: Combining Compute, Data Transfer, and Remote Library Services along with Parallel Processing

Your PC is connected without a script to a z/OS computer via the TCP/IP access method, using a spawner. Your application uses a combination of compute, data transfer, and remote library services. This application uses RLS to merge two tables (one on z/OS, one on the PC) into a new one, then uses data transfer services to upload the new table to the z/OS computer. Two sorts are necessary (one on the PC, one on z/OS), which are run in parallel using MP CONNECT technology. Then, the program uses compute services to do some tabulation, using z/OS. The output of the TABULATE procedure appears on the local PC. In this example, the z/OS spawner is named TSOSPAWN. (The details of setting up the spawner on z/OS are not shown.)

Here are the steps to work this example:

1. Determine the remote session name for the z/OS session. For TCP access, the remote session name is the remote computer's Internet address. However, the remote session name must be eight characters or less. So, you may need to use a SAS macro to define a nickname for the remote session name.

   Suppose the Internet address for the remote z/OS computer is tiger@company.com. The following SAS statement assigns the nickname to390 to this address:

   ```
   %let to390=tiger@company.com tsospawn;
   ```

   Submit this statement locally (for example, press F3).

2. Because the z/OS spawner is set up to run without a script, you must specify a user name and password when you initiate the connection. The Signon dialog box does not allow you to specify this information, so instead, use the OPTIONS and SIGNON statements to set the appropriate values. The _PROMPT_ value for the PASSWORD= option causes SAS to prompt you for your password.

   ```
   options comamid=tcp remote=to390;
   signon user=sasexpert password=_prompt_;
   ```

3. The next step is to submit an RLS-type LIBNAME statement that refers to a SAS data library on z/OS and a regular LIBNAME statement to define a library reference for a local SAS data library. Note the use of the two-level identifier in the SERVER= option.

   ```
   libname os390 remote 'joeuser.data' server=to390;
   libname win 'c:\wildcat\info';
   ```

   Submit these two statements locally (for example, press F3).

4. Now you are ready to merge the two tables (one remote, one local) together, to form a new, local table that contains both vital statistics (like weight and age) and location information for the various species of wild cats in the United States. Again, these statements are submitted locally and create a temporary table, CATINFO, on the PC.

The first step in the match-merge is to sort each of the tables by ID. Because the two tables are on different systems, this is a perfect example of when MP CONNECT technology can save processing time. For the table stored on z/OS, remote submit the PROC SORT (using RLS with the SORT procedure is usually inefficient).

```
proc sort data=os390.vital;
   by id;
run;
```

Submit these statements remotely by clicking **Run** → **Remote Submit** in the SAS System main menu, then typing the remote session name (to390.TSOSPAWN) in the top field. To activate parallel processing, type **NO** in the **Execute remote submit synchronously** field. Click **OK** to start the sort.

Now sort the local table and create the merged table:

```
proc sort data=win.region;
   by id;
run;

   /* Issue a waitfor statement so the merge doesn't start
      until the remotely submitted sort is complete. */
waitfor _all_ to390;

   /* Create the merged table. */
data catinfo;
   merge os390.vital win.region;
   by id;
run;
```

Submit these statements locally (for example, press F3).

5. Now you want to move the CATINFO table to z/OS, using the UPLOAD procedure. Note that a new LIBNAME statement is necessary because this portion of the program is not using RLS. Submit these statements remotely by clicking **Run** → **Remote Submit** in the SAS System main menu, then typing the remote session name (to390) in the top field, then clicking **OK**.

```
libname cat 'joeuser.data';
proc upload data=catinfo
     out=cat.catinfo;
run;
```

6. Because you want to do the tabulation on z/OS, the PROC TABULATE step is also remote submitted. Click **Run → Remote Submit**, and specify to390 as the remote session name.

```
proc tabulate data=cat.catinfo
             format=comma8.;
   title 'Tabulation of Wild Cat Information
         Organized by Species and Region';
   class species region;
   var weight age;
   table species*region,
   age*mean*f=8.2 weight*mean*f=8.2 age*n;
run;
```

   This program tabulates the mean weight and age of each species of cat, organized by region. It also tells you how many cats are in each region. Even though the program was submitted remotely, the results of the TABULATE procedure appear in the Output window on your PC.

7. When you are finished with the z/OS SAS session, terminate the connection by clicking **Run → Signoff**. Type the remote session name (to390) in the remote session name field; leave the other fields blank. Now click **OK**.

Example 5: Using SAS/CONNECT Software in Batch Mode

Your PC is connected to UNIX via the TCP/IP access method. You have a batch program that uses SAS/CONNECT software to process some data and download a resulting table to your PC. The processing occurs on the UNIX computer. In this example, the remote session name is tounix.

SAS/CONNECT software works equally well in windowing or batch mode, and you can use compute, data transfer, and remote library services as well as MP CONNECT in both modes. The only difference between using SAS/CONNECT software in batch mode and in windowing mode is that in batch mode you do not have dialog boxes available to perform signon, remote submit, and signoff, so you must use the corresponding statements.

Note

> The programmatic approach is not limited to batch mode only; you can also use these techniques in the interactive environment if you prefer them to dialog boxes.

Specifying the Script File in Batch Mode: Instead of typing the script file in the Signon dialog box, in batch mode use the special file shortcut RLINK by submitting a FILENAME statement that associates RLINK with the script file. Here is an example for the TCP/IP access between Windows and UNIX:

```
filename rlink '!SASROOT\connect\saslink\tcpunix.scr';
```

Submit this statement locally before you sign on to the remote computer.

Specifying the Remote Session Name in Batch Mode: In batch mode, use the %LET statement to define the remote session name. Begin by determining the remote session name for the UNIX session. For example, for TCP/IP access, the remote session name is the remote computer's Internet address. However, the remote session name must be eight characters or less. So, you may need to use a SAS macro to define a nickname for the remote session name.

Suppose the Internet address for the remote UNIX computer is 1.45.735.26. The following SAS statement assigns the nickname tounix to this address:

```
%let tounix=1.45.735.26;
```

Submit this statement locally before you initiate the connection to the remote computer.

Specifying the Communications Access Method in Batch Mode: Instead of typing the communications access method in the Signon dialog box, in batch mode use the COMAMID SAS system option. Put this option in your SAS configuration file or in an OPTIONS statement. This example uses an OPTIONS statement.

For example, for the TCP/IP communications access method, the value for the COMAMID option is TCP. Here is a sample COMAMID option specification:

```
options comamid=tcp;
```

Put the OPTIONS statement in your AUTOEXEC.SAS file if you use SAS/CONNECT software regularly.

Note

> The TCP access method is the default in the Windows environment, so it is possible to omit the above OPTIONS statement.

Initiating the Connection in Batch Mode: Instead of clicking **OK** in the Signon dialog box, in batch mode use the SIGNON statement. The SIGNON statement takes the remote session name as an argument. Here is an example:

```
signon tounix;
```

Submit this statement locally.

Note

> If you set the REMOTE= option to the tounix value, you could use the SIGNON statement without any parameters.

Remote Submitting SAS Statements in Batch Mode: Instead of using the **Remote submit** menu item, in batch mode use the RSUBMIT and ENDRSUBMIT statements in your code. Place the RSUBMIT statement before the first statement in the remote program; place the ENDRSUBMIT statement after the last statement in the remote program, as in the following example:

```
rsubmit tounix;
   libname unixdata 'janeuser/tempdata/july';
   proc sort data=unixdata.hightemps;
      by date;
   run;
endrsubmit;
```

This example defines a library reference for a UNIX SAS data library and performs an in-place sort on a table in that library.

Note

> Because by default the RSUBMIT statement submits the code to the last remote session you have established, you could omit the remote session name in the RSUBMIT statement. To submit the code to a different remote session, be sure to specify the remote session name in the RSUBMIT statement.

Terminating the Connection in Batch Mode: Instead of clicking **OK** in the Signoff dialog box, in batch mode use the SIGNOFF statement with the remote session name as the argument, as in the following example:

```
signoff tounix;
```

Submit this statement locally (for example, press F3).

Batch Example Code: Here is an entire sample batch program, with comments.

```
   /* Define a nickname for the remote session ID. */
%let tounix=1.45.735.26;
   /* Set the communications access method. */
options comamid=tcp;
.   /* Assign the RLINK file shortcut to the
       appropriate script file. */
filename rlink '!SASROOT\connect\saslink\tcpunix.scr';
   /* Define a library reference on the local PC, where
      the downloaded table is stored. */
libname windata 'c:\temp\july';
signon; /* Initiate the connection. */

   /* Begin the remote submitted block of code. */
rsubmit;
   /* Define a library reference for a UNIX data library. */
libname unixdata 'janeuser/tempdata/july';
```

```
   /* Create a temporary table that contains the high and
      low temperatures for July. */
data hilo;
       merge unixdata.hi (drop=date place
                 rename=(time=hitime))
             unixdata.lo
                 (rename=(time=lotime));
run;

   /* Download the merged table. */
proc download data=hilo out=windata.hilo;
run;

   /* End the remote submitted block of code. */
endrsubmit;
   /* Terminate the most recently referenced connection. */
signoff;
```

Monitoring Your SAS/CONNECT Tasks

With the advent of MP CONNECT, asynchronous RSUBMIT blocks, and other new features, it is possible to have several SAS/CONNECT tasks running at once. The SAS Explorer offers a handy way to keep track of which tasks are asynchronous or synchronous and which tasks are completed. You can also display Log and Output windows for specific tasks and delete tasks.

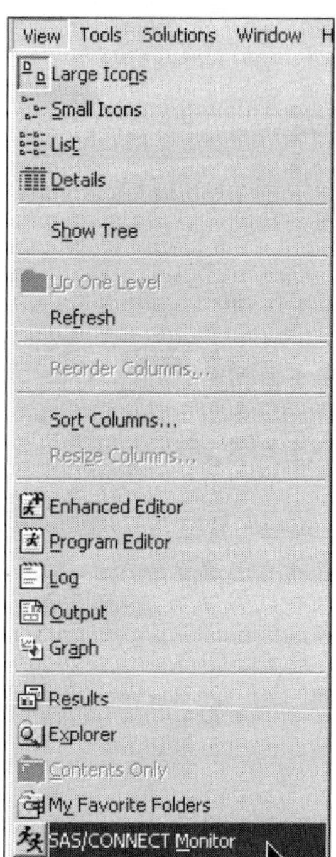

To access the SAS/CONNECT Monitor, make the SAS Explorer the active window. Now click **View → SAS/CONNECT Monitor**. Figure 15.6 shows a sample SAS/CONNECT Monitor window, listing three tasks.

Figure 15.6 Sample SAS/CONNECT Monitor Window

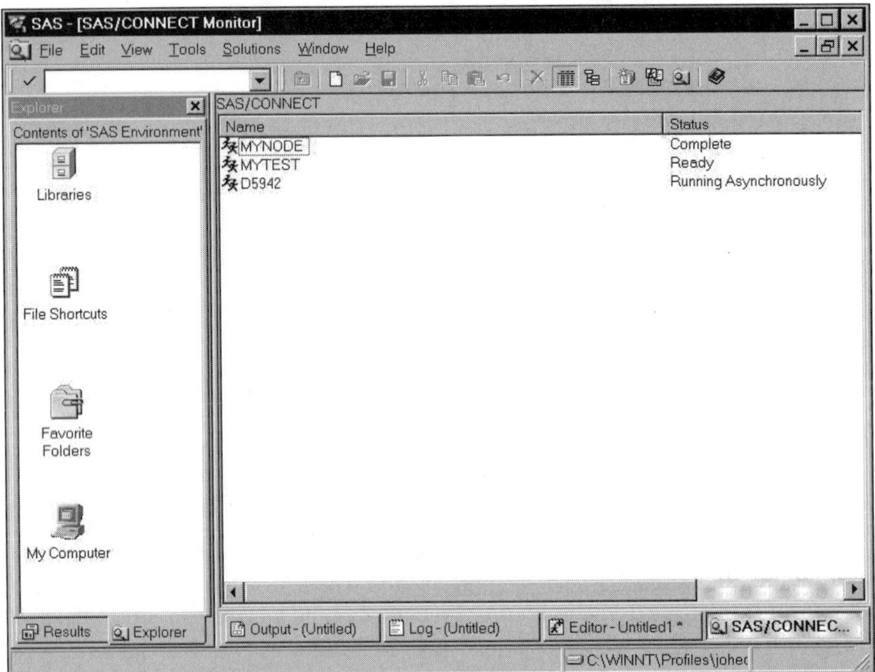

The SAS/CONNECT Monitor is automatically updated as tasks start, run, and complete.

Deleting a Task: When you sign off from a remote session (using the Signoff dialog box or the SIGNOFF statement), the task is automatically removed from the SAS/CONNECT Monitor window. If you want to remove a task from the SAS/CONNECT Monitor because it appears to be hung up or in a problematic state, right-click the task in the SAS/CONNECT Monitor window. In the resulting popup menu, click **Kill**. This action kills the entire remote session immediately; you cannot sign off or perform any further communication within that remote session.

Viewing the SAS Log and Output for Asynchronous Tasks: To open a Log and Output window for a specific task listed in the SAS/CONNECT Monitor window as running asynchronously, right-click the task in the SAS/CONNECT Monitor window. In the resulting popup menu, click **RDisplay**.

Appendix 1 Troubleshooting

Introduction

This appendix provides some hints for solving commonly encountered problems. The problems are organized into groups that match the chapters, such as printing, batch programming, and using SAS/CONNECT software.

If your problem is not addressed in this appendix, you may want to visit the Knowledge Base on the SAS Institute Web site (support.sas.com).

Learning to Do Windows and Performing the Basic SAS Software Tasks under Windows

Problem: The SAS System has caused a General Protection Fault (GPF).

Solution: Press CTRL-ALT-DEL. From the dialog box that appears, select **Task Manager**, where you can end any applications that are not responding, or select **Shut Down** to reboot your computer. The latter causes you to lose any unsaved tables and catalogs you created in your SAS session and in other applications as well.

Problem: Your keyboard has locked up and you cannot type or use the mouse.

Solution: First, press CTRL-ALT-DEL. If that does not work, turn off your computer, then turn it back on. This causes you to lose all unsaved data in all Windows applications.

Problem: Your mouse buttons do not work the way you expect.

Solution: Someone may have changed the mouse from a right-handed to a left-handed mouse or vice versa. Click **Start** → **Settings** → **Control Panel**. In the Control Panel window, double-click the Mouse icon, and use the resulting dialog box to reset your mouse's properties.

Problem: The Windows application you want to use is hidden behind several other open windows.

Solution: Click the application's name in the Windows Taskbar.

Problem: The SAS window you want to use is hidden behind several other open SAS windows.

Solution: Click the window's name in the window bar at the bottom of the main SAS window. Alternatively, click **Window** in the SAS System main menu, then click the name of the window you want to see. If you have more than nine SAS windows open, click **Window** → **More Windows** to see a complete list of open SAS windows; double-click the name of the window you want to see.

Problem: The SAS window bar does not appear at the bottom of the main SAS window.

Solution: Issue the WWINDOWBAR command from the command bar to toggle the window bar back on. Alternatively, right-click the status area at the bottom of the main SAS window, and click **Window Bar** in the resulting popup menu.

Problem: You cannot see the entire SAS window or dialog box—it seems to extend off the screen and buttons or fields are hidden.

Solution: Undock or close all docked SAS windows. This frees up more space for the window or dialog box. If you still cannot see all of the buttons or features of the window or dialog box, try making the entire main SAS window bigger, then resize the window or dialog box; this should enable you to see the entire window or dialog box. If the problem persists, you may have to increase your screen resolution.

Problem: You cannot see all the tools on the SAS System tool bar.

Solution: Resize the tool bar by dragging the separator between it and the command bar to the left. This makes the command bar smaller and the tool bar bigger. Also deselect **Large icons** on the **Toolbars** tab of the Customize Toolbars dialog box. Click **Tools → Customize** in the SAS System main menu to access the Customize Toolbars dialog box.

Editing and Working with Files

Problem: You cannot click in the Enhanced Editor or Program Editor window. Every time you do, your computer beeps, and the mouse pointer is an hourglass.

Solution: You may have a synchronous command-prompt session active or have a dialog box open waiting for input (either in the SAS session or in another Windows application).

Look at the Windows Taskbar. If **Command Prompt** is listed, click that task. Type EXIT at the command prompt to close the command-prompt session. To keep this from happening again, submit an OPTIONS statement in your SAS session with the NOXWAIT option.

If the Windows Taskbar does not list any active command-prompt sessions, press ALT-ESC to toggle through all open windows to see if you have an open dialog box that needs input. If neither CTRL-ESC nor ALT-ESC works, your Windows session may be hung up—see the second problem under "Learning to Do Windows and Performing the Basic SAS Software Tasks under Windows," earlier in this appendix.

Problem: You want to customize your editing options but don't see the **Enhanced Editor** or **Program Editor** choice in the **Tools → Options** menu.

Solution: Make the appropriate window active (Enhanced Editor or Program Editor) before opening the **Tools → Options** menu.

Submitting SAS Code

Problem: Your program is in an infinite loop.

Solution: Click the Attention icon on the SAS tool bar or press CTRL-BREAK. When the Tasking Manager appears, click on the appropriate line, then click **OK**. Now the BREAK dialog box appears. Click **Y to halt data step/proc**, then click **OK**.

Problem: The **Recall Last Submit** menu item does not work.

Solution: You have probably cleared the window. Try using the UNDO command repeatedly to back through your actions. If this does not work, you must retype your text or reopen the file. Also, you may experience difficulty in recalling code to the Enhanced Editor that was submitted from the Program Editor.

Printing

Problem: Your printer output does not look like you expect it to look.

Solution: Be sure you have selected the correct printer for your output. Also check the font and typesize settings, and check your SAS configuration file for LINESIZE, PAGESIZE, SYSPRINT, SYSPRINTFONT, and other system options that affect printer output.

Problem: Your SAS output looks funny and things do not align.

Solution: You may have chosen a proportional font for your printer output. Change the font to a monospace font such as Courier or SAS Monospace.

Problem: You cannot access the print preview feature.

Solution: The print preview feature is not available if you have **Use Forms** selected in the Print Setup dialog box.

Problem: You get an error message when you try to print a bitmap file.

Solution: Check your free disk space—printing large files requires some free disk space for temporary files. Delete unnecessary files to free up more disk space.

Problem: You have a color printer and have selected the **Color** option in the Print dialog box, but still get black-and-white output.

Solution: Check the value of the COLORPRINTING system option. If this option is set to NOCOLORPRINTING, you will not get color output. Also, the Enhanced Editor does not support color printing.

Adjusting Your Windows Environment

Problem: You cannot resize or move the main SAS window.

Solution: The main SAS window is probably maximized. Check the Maximize/Restore button in the upper-right corner of the main SAS window. If it is a single box, click on it once. Now you can resize or move the main SAS window.

Problem: You cannot see all the tools on the SAS System tool bar.

Solution: Resize the command bar by dragging the separator (to the right of the command bar) to the left. Now you will be able to see more tools. Also deselect **Large icons** on the **Toolbars** tab of the Customize Toolbars dialog box. Click **Tools** → **Customize** in the SAS System main menu to access the Customize Toolbars dialog box.

Problem: You set colors in some SAS windows, but the next time you start the SAS System, the colors did not stick.

Solution: You may have forgotten to issue a WSAVE command from each window you changed. Make the changes again, and this time issue the WSAVE command from each window you change, or select the **Save settings on exit** option in the Preferences dialog box on the **General** tab. Also try issuing the WSAVE ALL command from the command bar.

Problem: You've closed one of the main SAS System windows, such as the Log or Output window, and want it back—but it's not listed in the **Window** menu.

Solution: Click the SAS Programming Windows icon on the SAS System tool bar. This icon is not available if the Enhanced Editor window is active.

Problem: You try to move or resize the SAS Explorer or Results window, but cannot.

Solution: The SAS Explorer and Results windows are docked. To undock these windows, select **Window** → **Docked**, so the check mark next to **Docked** disappears. You can now move and resize the SAS Explorer and Results windows.

Problem: You want to customize your SAS Explorer options but don't see the **Explorer** choice in the **Tools** → **Options** menu.

Solution: Make sure the SAS Explorer window is active before selecting **Tools** → **Options** → **Explorer**.

Problem: You issue the TOOLLOAD command from the Enhanced Editor, but nothing happens.

Solution: To load a new set of tools into the Enhanced Editor, use the following syntax:

```
TOOLLOAD WINDOW BAR tool-set
```

Using Advanced Features of the Enhanced Editor

Problem: The Enhanced Editor is not available.

Solution: Check your SAS configuration file(s) for the NOENHANCEDEDITOR system option. If this option is present, remove it. Also check the **Edit** tab of the Preferences dialog box, to see if the **Use Enhanced Editor** choice is disabled. If so, click this choice to turn the Enhanced Editor on.

Using the SAS Output Delivery System

Problem: You cannot find your HTML output.

Solution: Check in the temporary directory for your SAS session, which by default in the Windows 2000 environment is located as a subfolder of C:\Documents and Settings*Windows-user-name*\Local Settings\Temp\SAS Temporary Files. Also check the **Results** tab of the Preferences dialog box to see which filename is specified there.

Problem: You are using the ODS statement to generate HTML or PDF output, but the output doesn't appear when you expect it to.

Solution: Before you can view your HTML or PDF output, you must use the ODS HTML CLOSE or ODS PDF CLOSE statement to close the output destination.

Managing SAS Files

Problem: You have accidentally deleted a file.

Solution: If the file was deleted using the Windows Explorer, look in the **Recycle Bin** on the Windows desktop to recover the file, as described in "Restoring Deleted Files" in Appendix 3. If the file was deleted using the SAS System (from the SAS Explorer, for example), the file cannot easily be restored without a third-party file restoration utility such as Norton Utilities.

Problem: You know a file exists, but you cannot remember where you stored it.

Solution: Use the Windows Explorer to find the file, either by navigating through various folders or using the **Search** capability. Alternatively, many dialog boxes in the SAS System (such as the Open dialog box) contain a **Browse** button. Click this button to search through your computer's drives and folders until you find the file.

Problem: You cannot perform a file operation, such as rename, move, or delete, because you get a SAS error message about "insufficient authorization."

Solution: The file is protected by either the SAS System, Windows, or both. If the file is protected by the SAS System, you must specify the READ=, WRITE=, and ALTER= data set options and their respective passwords when you access the file. If the file is protected by Windows, use the Windows Explorer to display and change the file attributes. To do this, right-click the file's icon in Windows Explorer, then click **Properties**. The Properties dialog box appears, showing the file attributes.

Another possibility is that the file is being used by another Windows application. For example, you may be trying to access a text file that is already open in Word. If this is the case, close the file in the other application, then try accessing it with the SAS System again.

Problem: You can't remember which library reference points to which SAS data library.

Solution: Issue the LIBNAME command from the command bar. The resulting window lists all active library references and the SAS data libraries they point to, along with the library references' associated engines.

Problem: You can't remember which file shortcut points to which external file.

Solution: Issue the FILENAME command from the command bar. The resulting window lists all active file shortcuts and the external files or folders they point to.

Customizing Your Start-up Files and SAS System Options

Problem: The SAS System displays a message during initialization that it cannot find the SAS configuration file.

Solution: Add the CONFIG system option to your SAS command (for example, at the end of the **Target** field in the Properties dialog box). Be sure to specify the full pathname for the SASV9.CFG file.

Problem: The SAS System does not execute the AUTOEXEC.SAS file.

Solution: Add the AUTOEXEC system option to your SAS command (for example, at the end of the **Target** field in the Properties dialog box). Be sure to specify the full pathname for the AUTOEXEC.SAS file.

Problem: The SAS System cannot read the SASV9.CFG or AUTOEXEC.SAS files.

Solution: You may have syntax errors in these files. In the SASV9.CFG file, precede each option name with a hyphen, and do not use equal signs between the system option name and the value.

Check your AUTOEXEC.SAS file for missing semicolons, missing comment delimiters, and mismatched quotation marks.

Another possible cause of this problem is that you may have inadvertently saved the SASV9.CFG or AUTOEXEC.SAS file in a non-ASCII format. If you have recently edited these files with a word processing program, check to see if you saved the files in a proprietary format. If so, this adds formatting characters to the file that the SAS System cannot interpret. Re-edit the files and save them as plain text (ASCII) files.

Using Batch Mode

Problem: You cannot start your SAS batch job; double-clicking on a SAS program file icon starts a windowing session.

Solution: Use the Options dialog box in the Windows Explorer to edit the default action for .SAS, .SAS7BPGM, and .SS2 files. See "Double-Clicking on a File Icon in the Windows Explorer" in Chapter 12 for more details.

Problem: You get the error message "PATHDLL not found" or "CONFIG file not found" when you start your batch SAS job.

Solution: Try specifying the CONFIG system option in the SAS command (such as in the **Target** field in the Properties dialog box or in the **Open** field in the Run dialog box). If you already have the CONFIG option specified, be sure it references the correct pathname.

Problem: The LOG and LST files from your batch job are not where you expect them to be.

Solution: Check your program for PROC PRINTTO statements. Also, check your SAS configuration file for LOG, ALTLOG, PRINT, and ALTPRINT system options. Look in the SAS current folder and in the folder containing the batch SAS program to see if the log and list files ended up there. Also look in the folder C:\Program Files\Common Files\System\Mapi\1033\NT for Windows 2000. (The location may differ for the Windows NT and Windows XP environments.)

Problem: You are using PROC PRINTTO to send the SAS procedure output or log to a printer, but the print queue seems to be stuck.

Solution: You must include an empty (no options) PROC PRINTTO step at the end of your program to close the printer file.

Using SAS to Execute System Commands and Applications

Problem: When you submit an X statement or X command, the SAS log displays this message:

```
Shell escape is not valid in this SAS session.
```

Solution: The XCMD system option is turned off. Start SAS again, this time specifying the XCMD system option. (This option is not valid in the OPTIONS statement.)

Problem: The result of the operating system command that you executed via an X statement or X command flashes by so fast that you cannot read it.

Solution: Submit the following OPTIONS statement:

```
options xwait;
```

Now resubmit your X statement or X command. To return to your SAS session, press any key.

Problem: You started a Windows application via the X statement or X command but now cannot use your SAS session while the application is open.

Solution: Close the application. Now submit the following OPTIONS statement:

```
options noxsync;
```

The next time you start an application with the X statement or X command, it runs independently of your SAS session.

Problem: You used the X statement or X command to start a Windows application but get an error message about being out of memory.

Solution: Each application you run takes up RAM. If your machine has a small amount of RAM available, you may be able to run only a few Windows applications at a time. Close unnecessary applications, and try the X statement or X command again.

Problem: Your program uses the X statement but generates error messages or incorrect results. You are sure your programming statements are correct.

Solution: If the results of the X statement are not available before your program continues, it will not generate correct results. Specify XWAIT in your SASV9.CFG file, so your SAS program will not continue without your permission. Also, if you are starting another application such as Word, use the SLEEP function to pause your program long enough for the other application to start.

Sharing Data between SAS and Windows Applications

Problem: When using DDE, your data do not look like they should. All the data are in one cell, there are tabs where you do not expect them, or the data are truncated.

Solution: Remember that the SAS System expects tabs between columns. By default, it writes columns to separate cells when the data contain spaces. Use the NOTAB option in the FILENAME statement when you define the DDE file shortcut to suppress this default behavior. If the data contain spaces but are truncated, use the DLM statement option to define another delimiter.

Problem: When you submit your SAS DDE program, an error message says the SAS System cannot communicate with the other application.

Solution: Remember that the application must be open before you submit your DDE SAS program. Either manually start the application, or use the X statement or X command to start it. You may need to use the SLEEP function to pause your SAS program long enough for the application to start.

Problem: The macro you recorded with the Microsoft Word macro recorder does not work in your SAS DDE program.

Solution: If you are using a newer version of Word, such as Word97 or Word 2000, the macros recorded by the Word macro recorder are in Visual Basic. However, you must use Word Basic syntax in DDE programs. To get help with Word Basic syntax, obtain a copy of the *Word Developer's Kit, Third Edition.*

Problem: When you paste an object into a FRAME window, the object does not appear.

Solution: If the object is too big to fit entirely inside the FRAME window, it does not appear immediately. Save the FRAME entry, then reopen it; the object should now appear, so you can resize it.

Problem: The OLE objects in your SAS/AF applications do not reflect changes.

Solution: You may have forgotten to select the **Paste Link** option in the Paste Special dialog box or the **Link** option in the Insert Object dialog box, thereby creating an embedded object instead. Re-create the object, ensuring that this time you select the **Paste Link** option.

Problem: When you open a FRAME entry containing linked objects, you get a message that the link is unavailable.

Solution: Someone may have moved the source file for the object. Right-click on the object in the BUILD: DISPLAY window, then click **Linked *xyz* Object** in the resulting popup menu (where ***xyz*** represents the object type, such as Visio or Document). In the second-level popup menu, click **Links**, which opens the Links dialog box. Click the link you want to modify, then click **Change Source**. Type the new pathname in the **File name** field, then click **OK**. Now click **Update Now** in the Links dialog box to update the link. Finally, close the Links dialog box by clicking **Close**.

Using SAS/CONNECT Software to Connect Your PC to Other Systems

Problem: You receive errors when you try to initiate a remote connection.

Solution: Check the syntax of your script file. If your network is busy, the connection may time out before it is complete. In the script file, look for a PAUSE or similar command and increase the time.

Problem: You try to access a SAS catalog using Remote Library Services (RLS) but receive error messages.

Solution: Because of how characters and numbers are internally represented by operating systems, you can access SAS catalogs through RLS from the following operating systems only: Windows 3.1 (Win32s), Windows NT, Windows 95, Windows 98, Windows 2000, Windows XP, and subsequent releases of Windows.

Problem: You want to transfer an external file without the automatic conversion from one operating system format to another.

Solution: Use the BINARY option in the PROC DOWNLOAD or PROC UPLOAD statement, which prevents these procedures from converting the file format.

Problem: You need to transfer a text file whose record length is more than 132 bytes.

Solution: Use the LRECL option to set the record length in both the local and remote FILENAME statements.

Problem: You try to download or upload some data, but you receive errors in the SAS log.

Solution: The DOWNLOAD and UPLOAD procedures must be remote submitted. Use either the **Remote submit** item in the **Run** menu, or use the RSUBMIT and ENDRSUBMIT statements to remote submit your upload and download steps.

Note

> Refer to the SAS/CONNECT documentation for a more comprehensive list of troubleshooting advice.

Appendix 2 Using the SAS System Viewer

Introduction

The SAS System Viewer is not by default installed with the SAS System. However, unless your site administrator has created an install image that does not include the SAS System Viewer, it is part of the software shipped with SAS 9.1.

Note

> You may find the more full-featured Enterprise Guide, described in Chapter 10, a better "thin client" solution than the SAS System Viewer. Also, since the SAS System Viewer is a free product, it may not receive enhancements as often as you would like.

Installing the SAS System Viewer

Insert the SAS Client Side Components, Volume 1 CD-ROM (The SAS Software Navigator) into your CD-ROM drive. If Autorun is enabled, you'll see a screen similar to the one shown in Figure A2.1.

Figure A2.1 Preparing to Install the SAS System Viewer

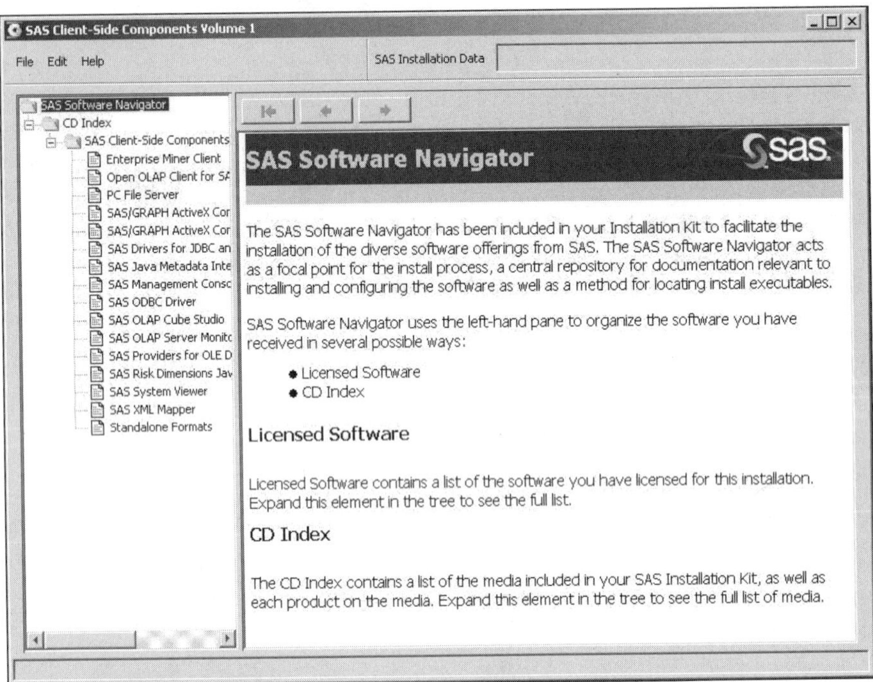

Click **SAS System Viewer** in the left-hand frame. Now a window similar to the one in Figure A2.2 appears.

Figure A2.2 Installing the SAS System Viewer

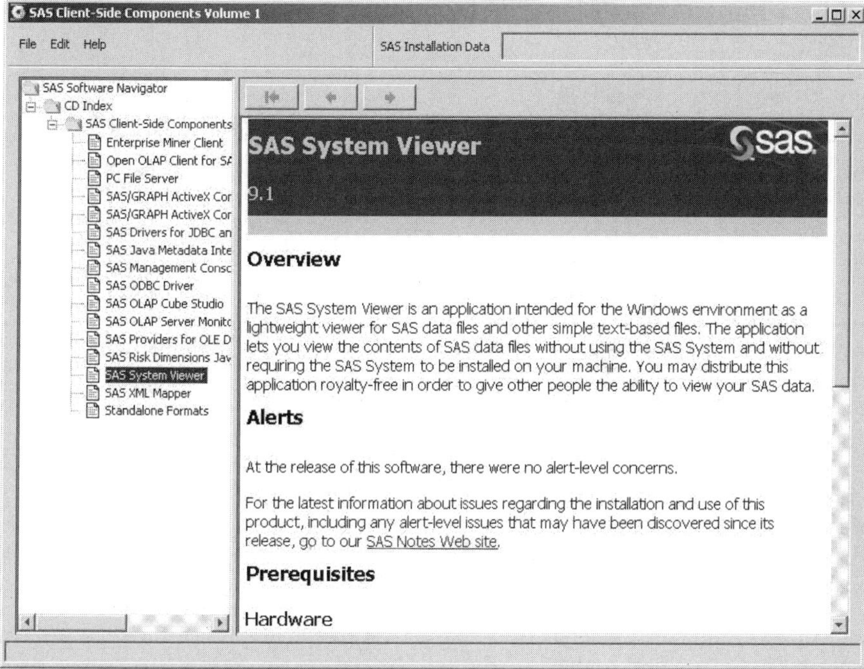

Scroll down the right-hand frame until you see the heading “Installation.” Click the **Install** link under this heading, then follow the instructions on your screen to complete the installation.

Starting the SAS System Viewer

What’s New: You can now drop SAS data sets (tables) onto the SAS System Viewer icon to start the Viewer and open the data set.

Once the SAS System Viewer is installed, you can start it in several ways.

Starting the SAS System Viewer from the Desktop: To start the SAS System Viewer from the Windows desktop, click the **Start** button, then click **Programs** → **SAS** → **SAS System Viewer 9.1**.

Starting the SAS System Viewer from the **Start** menu opens the SAS System Viewer but does not open any particular file. Use the SAS System Viewer’s **File** menu to open the file you want to see.

Starting the SAS System Viewer from a Command-Prompt Window: Use the following syntax to start the SAS System Viewer from a command prompt:

sv <*SAS-file*> </p | /pt *printer-name*>

- *SAS-file* is the name of one of the supported types of SAS files (such as a SAS program or a SAS table). If you do not provide a filename, the SAS System Viewer starts but does not open any SAS file.
- /p prints the SAS file to the default printer.
- /pt *printer-name* prints the SAS file to the specific printer named by *printer-name*. See "Discovering What Printers Are Available" in Chapter 5 for more information. Use quotation marks around a printer name that contains spaces or special characters.

The /p and /pt options are mutually exclusive.

Note

> Unless you have added the folder that contains the SV.EXE program to your Windows system variable PATH, you must specify the full pathname for the SV program at the command prompt.

Using Drag-and-Drop with the SAS System Viewer: You can start the SAS System Viewer by dragging a file icon that represents a text-based file (such as an .htm or .sas file) or a SAS data set (.sas7bdat or .sd2) and dropping it on an icon that represents the SAS System Viewer. The Viewer starts up and shows the contents of the file you dropped.

If the SAS System Viewer is already open, you can drag and drop both text-based files and SAS files (such as SAS tables and catalogs) to the SAS System Viewer.

Note

> Drag-and-drop with the SAS System Viewer is available only from the Windows Explorer; you cannot drag and drop file icons from the SAS Explorer onto the SAS System Viewer.

SAS System Viewer Capabilities

The SAS System Viewer enables you to

- view files created with the SAS System (such as SAS tables) without starting the SAS System—you can even use the SAS System Viewer without having the SAS System installed on your computer.
- edit and save text-based files (such as .sas and .txt files).
- submit SAS code in batch or interactive mode.
- print many different kinds of files (including SAS tables and text-based files such as SAS programs).

File Types Supported by the Viewer: The SAS System Viewer can show you the contents of many file types from both the Windows environment and the OpenVMS environment, including:

- SAS programs (.sas) and other text-based files (.dat, .cfg, .htm, .html)
- PC SAS tables (.sas7bdat, .sd7, .sd2, .ssd, and .ssd0X) as well as VMS SAS tables
- SAS output (.lst and .lis)
- SAS logs (.log)
- JMP data files (.jmp)
- directory information for PC Version 6 SAS catalogs (.sc2, .sct, and .sct0x)—but not SAS 7 or SAS 9.1 SAS catalogs—as well as for VMS catalogs
- SAS transport files (.stx and .xpt)
- SAS configuration files (.cfg)
- comma-delimited (.csv), space-delimited (.prn), and tab-delimited files (.txt).

Once you have a file open in the SAS System Viewer, you can edit it (if the file is a text-based file), print it, search for text, subset your data, format your data, sort your data, and do many other useful tasks. If the file is a SAS program, you can submit the code from the SAS System Viewer.

Also, you can have several files open at once. Figure A2.3 shows the SAS System Viewer with two files open—a table and a SAS program.

Figure A2.3 SAS System Viewer

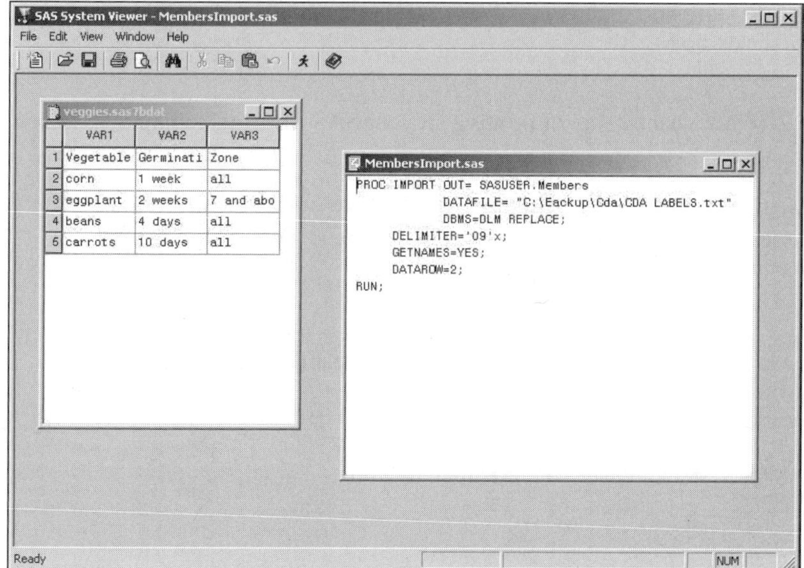

Getting Help

For further information on the SAS System Viewer, start the Viewer and click **Help** in the SAS System Viewer menu. Now click **Help Topics** and select a topic that interests you.

Submitting Code from the SAS System Viewer

One handy way of submitting code is from the SAS System Viewer. When you have a file that contains SAS code open in the Viewer, you can choose between submitting the code in batch mode and submitting it interactively.

To submit a batch SAS job from the SAS System Viewer, click the Run icon on the SAS System Viewer tool bar.

Alternatively, click **File** → **Batch Submit** in the SAS System Viewer main menu to submit the job in batch mode. To submit an interactive SAS job from the SAS System Viewer, click **File** → **Submit** in the SAS System Viewer main menu. A new instance of SAS is opened (even if one is already running), and the code is submitted.

Note

If you already have a SAS session running, your SASUSER profile will not be available to the session opened by the SAS System Viewer.

Printing from the SAS System Viewer

What's New: Page Setup is now one menu-level deeper, and grid options are now set in a separate dialog box.

The SAS System Viewer offers a handy way of printing all your SAS files—including SAS tables and SAS programs.

Defining the Page Setup: You have a lot of control over how the SAS System Viewer presents your data. To access these features, click **File** → **Printing Options** → **Page Setup** in the SAS System Viewer main menu.

Note

The SAS System Viewer Page Setup dialog box is completely separate from the Page Setup dialog box accessed from the SAS System.

Figure A2.4 shows the SAS System Viewer Page Setup dialog box.

Figure A2.4 SAS System Viewer Page Setup Dialog Box

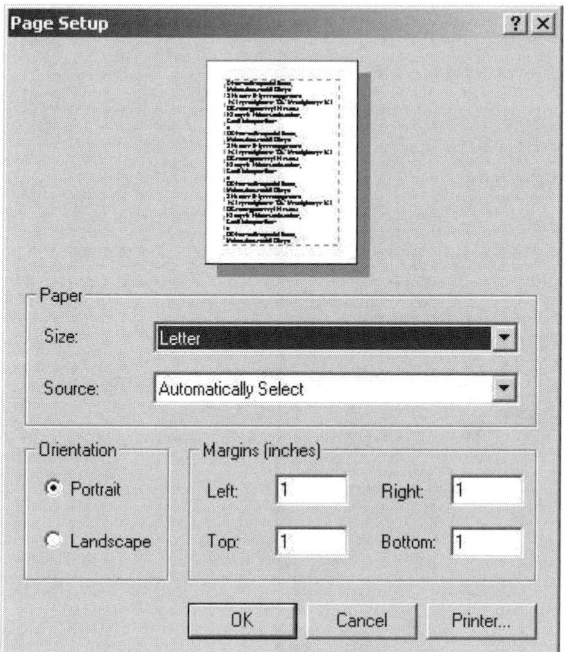

The various fields enable you to alter settings associated with how your data are presented on the page, as described in the following list:

Paper	sets paper size and source.
Orientation	controls whether output is landscape or portrait.
Margins	sets top, bottom, left, and right margins.

When you have adjusted the settings to your satisfaction, click **OK** in the Page Setup dialog box. The choices you have made will be reflected in all subsequent print jobs from the SAS System Viewer, until you change the settings again.

Defining the Grid Setup: You can also control how your SAS tables are printed, such as modifying the font used for headers and specifying where lines are to be drawn (between columns, between rows, and so on). To access these features, click **File → Printing Options → Grid Setup** in the SAS System Viewer main menu.

Figure A2.5 shows the SAS System Viewer Page Setup dialog box.

Figure A2.5 SAS System Viewer Grid Setup Dialog Box

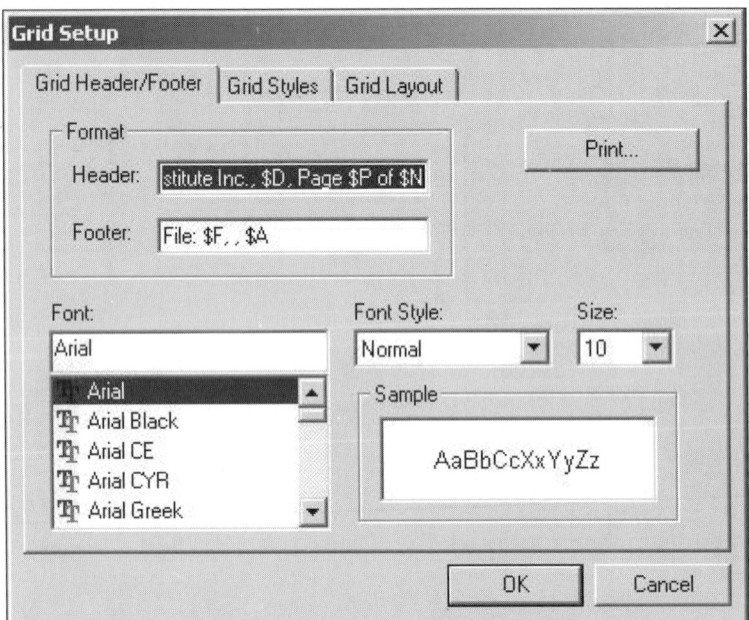

The various tabs enable you to alter settings associated with how your data are presented on the page, as described in the following list:

Grid Header/Footer	customizes the grid header and footer format.
Grid Styles	defines how the grid is displayed, such as using lines.
Grid Layout	controls whether rows or columns are ordered first and how the page is centered (vertically or horizontally).

When you have adjusted the settings to your satisfaction, click **OK** in the Grid Setup dialog box. The choices you have made will be reflected in all subsequent print jobs from the SAS System Viewer, until you change the settings again.

Previewing Your Print Job: If you want to see how the file will look when printed, click **File → Print Preview** in the SAS System Viewer main menu. Figure A2.6 shows a sample of how your screen might look.

Figure A2.6 SAS System Viewer Print Preview Feature

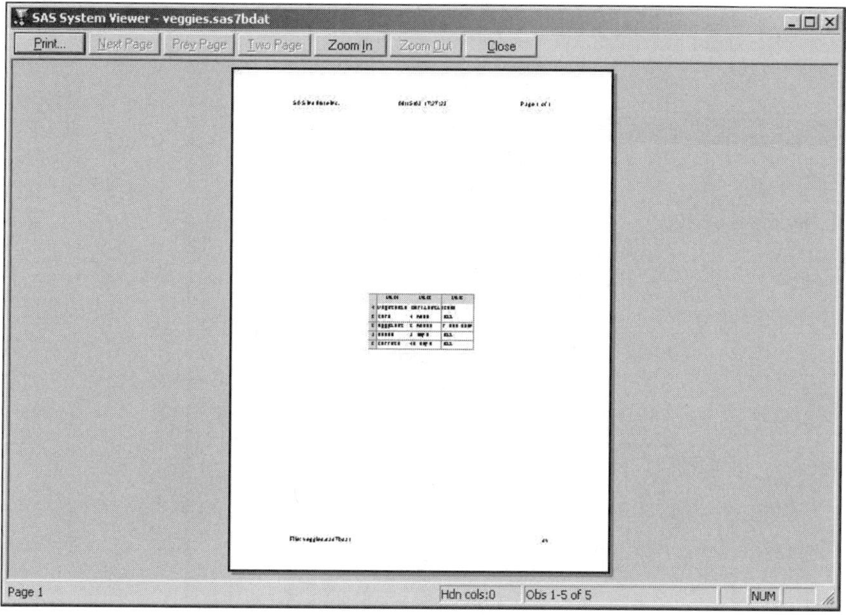

Use the tool bar buttons to change the view and perform other view-related tasks:

- Use the **Two Page** (toggles to **One Page**), **Zoom In** and **Zoom Out**, and **Next Page** and **Prev Page** buttons to adjust and navigate the view.
- Click **Close** to close the print preview and return to the normal view of the file.
- Click **Print** to open the Print dialog box (described in the next section).

Note

If all these buttons are not visible on your display, resize the SAS System Viewer and individual windows to make them larger.

Using the SAS System Viewer Print Dialog Box: The SAS System Viewer's Print dialog box is a standard Windows Print dialog box, and works like the Print dialog box in the SAS System—you can choose the printer, what pages to print, how many copies to print, and whether to print to a file. Figure A2.7 shows the SAS System Viewer Print dialog box.

Figure A2.7 SAS System Viewer Print Dialog Box

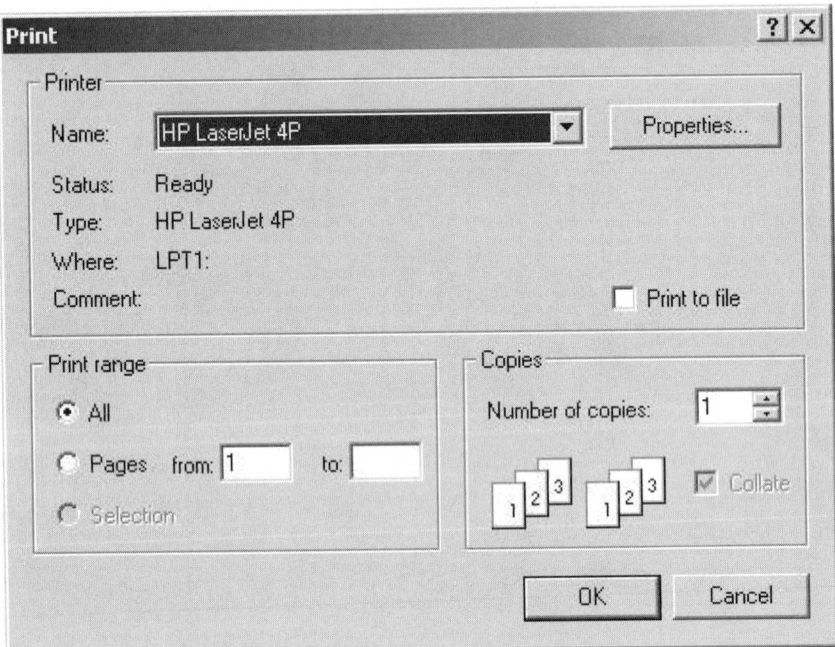

Viewing HTML Output with the SAS System Viewer

Viewing HTML files with the SAS System Viewer is similar to viewing any other type of file. Click **File → Open** in the SAS System Viewer main menu. When the Open dialog box appears, scroll the **Files of type** field until **HTML Document** is visible. Click this file type, then double-click the file you want to view in the list of files.

The file is displayed, just as it would appear in the Results Viewer window or in a Web browser.

Appendix 3 Becoming Familiar with the Windows Explorer

Note

> The descriptions and screen shots in this appendix are for Windows 2000. Users of Windows NT and Windows XP may experience slightly different behavior or see slightly different screens.

While you can use the SAS System to rename, delete, copy, and move files, you may also want to use the Windows Explorer, which is a Windows application for managing files. Figure A3.1 shows the Windows Explorer displaying the SAS folder with its files and subfolders.

Figure A3.1 The Windows Explorer Listing the Contents of the SAS Folder

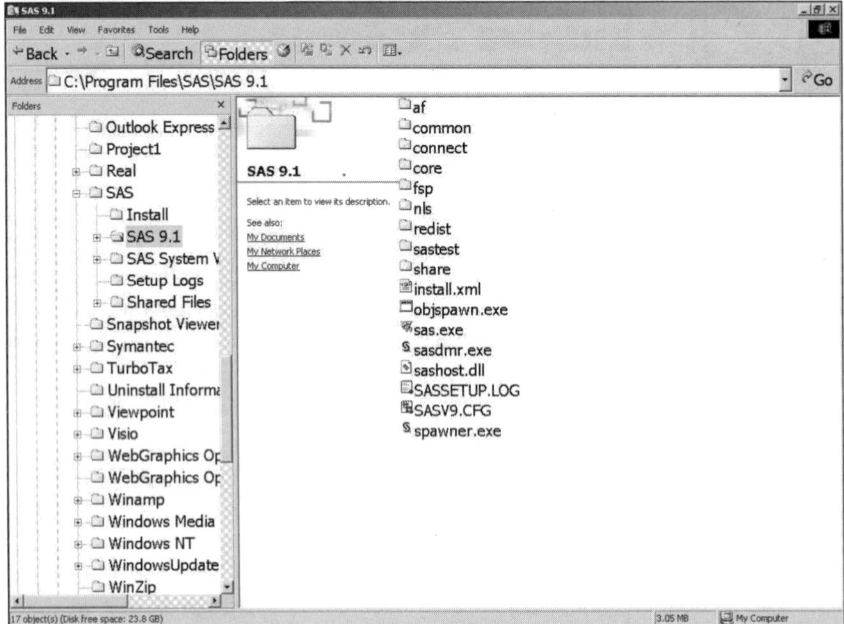

Your display may look different from this, depending on which SAS products you have installed.

Note

By default, the Windows Explorer does not show file extensions in the file list. See "Displaying Hidden Files and File Extensions" later in this chapter for information on how to get the Windows Explorer file list to show these items.

Starting the Windows Explorer

To start the Windows Explorer, right-click the **Start** button, then click **Explore**. The Windows Explorer is divided into two panes (left and right). The left pane displays folders and subfolders; the right pane displays the contents of those folders and subfolders. (Your right-click **Start** menu may look a bit different, depending on what software you have installed on your system.)

To see the contents of a particular folder, use the scroll bar in the left pane to get to the folder you want to see. Click the folder name—the contents of that folder are displayed in the right pane.

If you double-click a folder in the left pane, any subfolders in that folder are displayed below the folder. This is called "expanding" the folder. Double-clicking the folder again "collapses" the folder so that the subfolders are not shown.

The Windows Explorer uses different icons to indicate various file types. Some executable files have rectangular icons with a bar across the top; other executable files use a special icon associated with the program. If the file can be edited (such as a text file), the icon looks like a tiny page with text on it. Folders and subfolders are indicated by little file folders.

To see the contents of a subfolder in the right pane, double-click the subfolder name. The view changes accordingly. To change drives, scroll to the top of the left pane and click the drive you want to see.

Copying and Moving Files

You can use the Windows Explorer menus to copy and move files. For example, see Figure A3.2.

Figure A3.2 Preparing to Copy a File Using the Windows Explorer

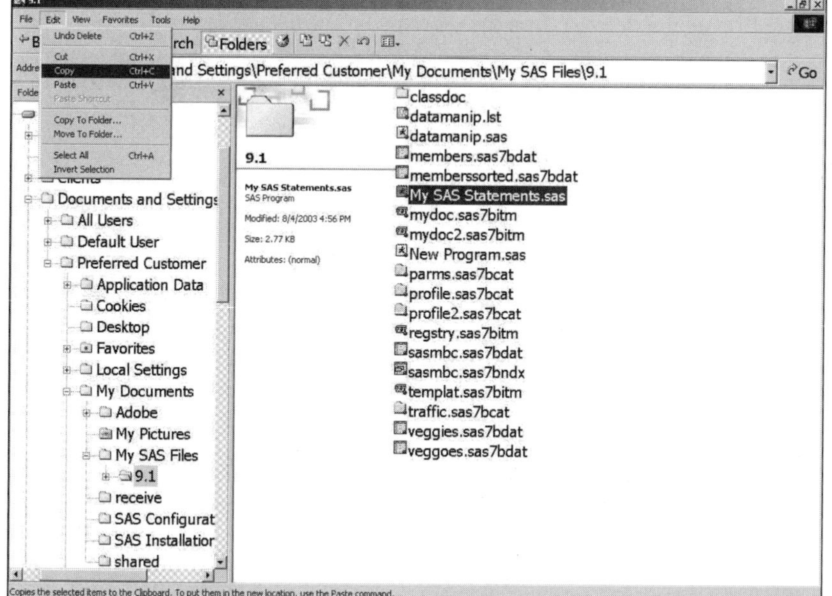

The file MY SAS Statements.sas is highlighted. Remember, to highlight a file, click its name. To copy this file to a different folder, click **Edit** → **Copy** in the Windows Explorer menu. The file is copied to the Windows Clipboard. Now display the folder where the copied file is to go, and highlight the folder name by clicking it. After the target folder is highlighted, click **Edit** → **Paste** in the Windows Explorer menu. The file is copied to the target folder.

Moving a file works exactly the same except that you click **Cut** in the Windows Explorer **Edit** menu instead of clicking **Copy**.

Renaming Files

To rename a file using the Windows Explorer, highlight the file by clicking it. Click **File** → **Rename** in the Windows Explorer menu. A box appears around the filename. Type the new name, and press ENTER.

Deleting Files

To delete a file using the Windows Explorer, highlight the file by clicking its name. Click **File** → **Delete** in the Windows Explorer menu. A dialog box asks if you are sure that you want to send the file to the Recycle Bin. Click **Yes** to complete the file deletion.

Note

Files sent to the Recycle Bin are not deleted from the system. To completely delete a file, double-click the Recycle Bin icon on the desktop, highlight the file in the file list, and press DELETE. A dialog box asks if you are sure that you want to delete the items. Click **Yes** to complete the deletion.

Warning

Be careful when you move, rename, or delete files—some files, such as the SASUSER.PROFILE catalog, must have a particular name in order to work. In general, it is safe to move, rename, or delete catalogs and other files that you have created; do not move, rename, or delete files created automatically by the SAS System. Nor is it a good idea to rename SAS tables using the Windows Explorer, because the table name is also stored in the table's header information.

Restoring Deleted Files

You can use the Recycle Bin to restore a file that you have recently deleted from a Windows Explorer window.

Here are the steps for restoring a deleted file:

1.  Double-click the Recycle Bin icon on the Windows desktop.
2. When the Recycle Bin opens, click the name of the file that you want to restore.
3. Click **File** → **Restore** in the Recycle Bin menu. The file is restored to whatever folder it was originally stored in.

Warning

Files deleted from within the SAS System are not sent to the Recycle Bin—they are deleted completely from the hard disk. To recover these files, you must have a third-party file restoration utility, such as Norton Utilities.

Creating Folders

You may want to create new folders and subfolders to store the files associated with your work with the SAS System. For example, you might need separate folders for SAS programs, SAS logs, SAS output, and miscellaneous files.

To use the Windows Explorer to create a folder or subfolder, click **File** → **New** in the Windows Explorer menu. When a list of choices appears, click **Folder**. A new folder icon appears in the right pane, ready for a new name. Type the name and press ENTER. The folder is now ready to store files.

Displaying Hidden Files and File Extensions

By default, the Windows Explorer does not show hidden files in its file lists, nor does it show file extensions for "known file types." If you want to see hidden files and/or file extensions in the Windows Explorer folder listings, follow the appropriate steps for your operating system.

Warning

Hidden files are usually hidden for a purpose—they are rarely files that you need to manage in any way. You do not need to change the properties of a hidden file.

Windows 2000 and Windows XP:

1. Click **Start** → **Settings** → **Control Panel**.
2. Double-click **Folder Options**.
3. Click the **View** tab.

4. Click **Show hidden files and folders** to display hidden files. Deselect **Hide file extensions for known file types** to display file extensions for all files.
5. Click **OK** to close the dialog box, then close the Control Panel.

Windows NT:

1. Open the Windows Explorer.
2. Click **View** → **Options**.
3. Select **Show all files** to display hidden files. Deselect **Hide file extensions for known file types** to display file extensions for all files.

Closing the Windows Explorer

To close the Windows Explorer, click its Close button.

Appendix 4 Accessibility and the SAS System

Introduction

Even if you do not consider yourself "disabled," you may be surprised at how your productivity and comfort can be increased by taking advantage of some of the accessibility options available in both the SAS System and Windows itself.

The SAS System accessibility features help bring SAS into compliance with the accessibility standards for electronic information technology adopted by the U.S. Government under Section 508 of the U.S. Rehabilitation Act of 1973 (as amended).* The great majority of SAS windows and dialog boxes are compliant with Section 508. These include (there are many more) the main SAS window, Enhanced Editor, tool bar customization dialog boxes and windows, SAS Explorer, and Results Viewer.

The following sections address how you can customize the SAS windowing environment so that it is more accessible to people with disabilities. Taking advantage of some of these features can benefit many people who need larger fonts, need keyboard-only (as opposed to mouse) access to portions of the SAS System, or use screen readers and other assistive technology.

Microsoft Windows also offers many accessibility features. The final two sections in this appendix address many of these, as well.

Choosing between the Standard and Fully Accessible SAS User Interface

Use the ACCESSIBILITY system option to choose the level of accessibility offered by the user interface. While the standard user interface enables you to use accessibility aids to read

---

* For more information on Section 508, see www.section508.gov.

components of many SAS windows and dialog boxes, the fully accessible user interface adds accessibility aids to even more SAS windows and dialog boxes.

In particular, the fully accessible user interface adds buttons to these dialog boxes so that all commands and tabbed pages are accessible using the keyboard:

- the **Customize** tab of the Customize Tools dialog box
- some SAS Properties dialog boxes.

For example, Figure A4.1 shows the standard version of the **Customize** tab side-by-side with the accessible version.

Figure A4.1 Comparison of Standard and Accessible Versions of a SAS Dialog Box

Standard Interface

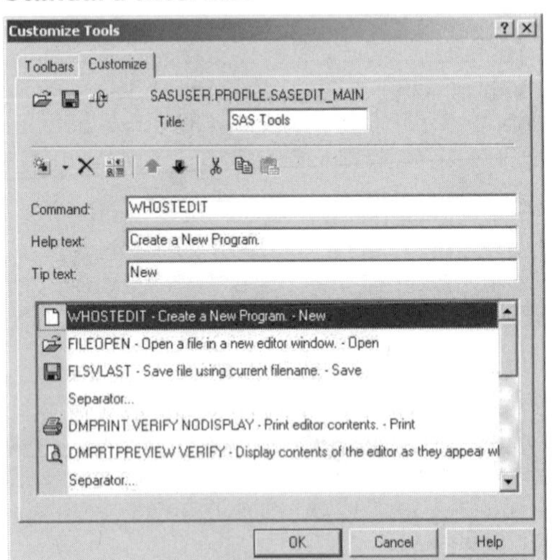

Accessible Interface

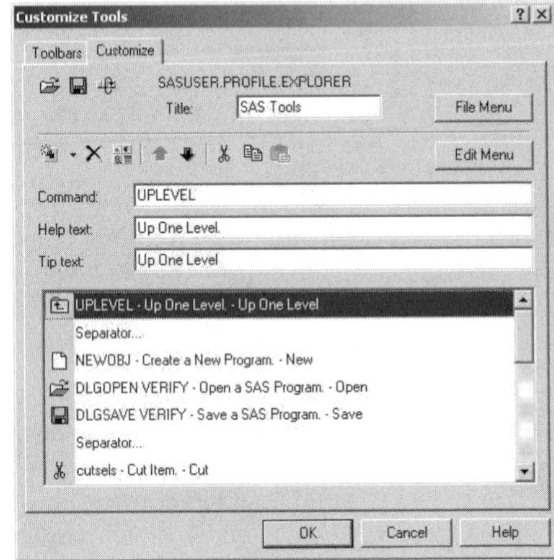

The ACCESSIBILITY system option is valid only at SAS start-up. For example, you can specify it in the SAS command or in your SAS configuration file. The syntax of the ACCESSIBILITY option is as follows:

```
-ACCESSIBILITY STANDARD | EXTENDED
```

Note

> If you set the ACCESSIBILITY system option to EXTENDED, you cannot use the overstrike cursor (such as in the Enhanced Editor or Program Editor).

Enterprise Guide and Accessibility: Enterprise Guide also supports some accessibility features. To enable them, click **Tools** → **Options** in the Enterprise Guide main menu, then click the **General** tab. On this tab, click **Enable accessibility features**.

Accessing the SAS Menus with Only Keyboard Input

The SAS System recognizes hot keys for all menu choices. This allows you to access the menus without using the mouse. To move input focus to the menu bar, press the ALT key (but don't hold it). When you do so, underlines appear in each of the main menu choices. Typing the letter that is underlined opens that particular menu. Each submenu choice also has an underline. Typing that letter either executes a command (action) or opens yet another submenu, depending on what the menu choice is.

Pressing ALT again removes input focus from the menu bar (and removes the underlines from the menu choice names).

Other keys are useful when interacting with the SAS System using the keyboard:

arrow keys	move the menu choice up and down and between menus.
TAB key	moves the cursor from field to field in dialog boxes.
SHIFT-TAB	moves the cursor backward through fields in dialog boxes.

Enlarging the Fonts Used in SAS Windows

Many people may find the SAS System's default type difficult to read. You can enlarge the font used in many portions of the SAS System. However, the technique differs, depending on which portion of the SAS System you want to change.

Only monospace fonts work well with the SAS System; proportional fonts do not produce satisfactory results. By default, the SAS System uses the Sasfont font in windows. Other monospace fonts that are common include Courier and IBMPCDOS.

Table A4.1 gives a quick reference to the various font areas you can affect and how they are modified. The subsequent sections provide more detail.

Table A4.1 Techniques for Increasing Font Size in Your SAS Session

Area Affected	Method to Access
"standard" SAS windows (such as the Program Editor, Log, Output, and NOTEPAD)	**Tools → Options → Fonts** or FONT system option
Enhanced Editor	**Tools → Options → Enhanced Editor**
Descriptive text in the SAS Explorer and command bar text	SYSGUIFONT system option
Font used in the Results Viewer window	Cycle Font tool on SAS System tool bar

Note

When you enlarge the font size, less information is visible at one time in a window. You may need to maximize the SAS window in order to allow space for large fonts to be readable, and it is possible that some dialog boxes will extend off the edge of the screen.

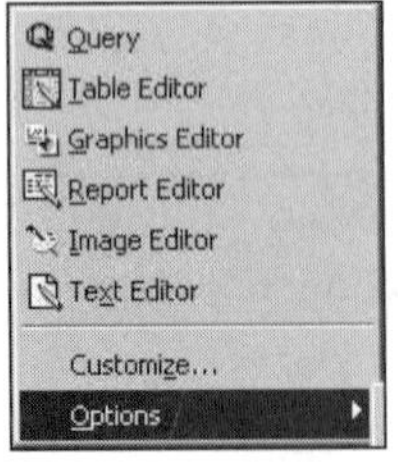

Enlarging the Font in "Standard" SAS Windows: Change the font in windows such as the Program Editor, Log, Output, and NOTEPAD windows by using the Font dialog box. To open the Font dialog box, type DLGFONT in the command bar or select **Tools → Options → Fonts**.

Note

The **Fonts** menu choice is not available from the **Options** submenu if the Enhanced Editor is the active window.

Figure A4.2 shows a sample Font dialog box.

Figure A4.2 Font Dialog Box

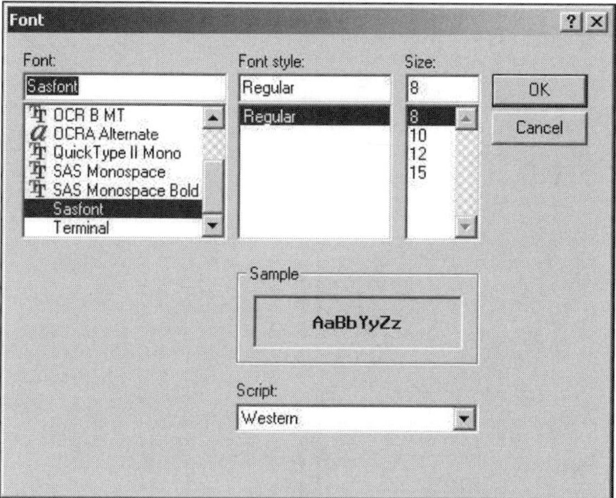

You can choose a monospace font name in the **Font** field and a font size in the **Size** box. The maximum font size you can choose is 15 points.

When the settings are satisfactory, click **OK**. The font you choose in the Font dialog box accessed through the **Tools → Options** menu affects only the font used in SAS windows. To affect the font used for printer output, use the **Font** button in the Print Setup dialog box.

The font setting you choose from the Font dialog box is retained from one SAS session to the next only if you have selected **Save settings on exit** in the Preferences dialog box. Otherwise, the setting is temporary (unless you issue a WSAVE command from the command bar).

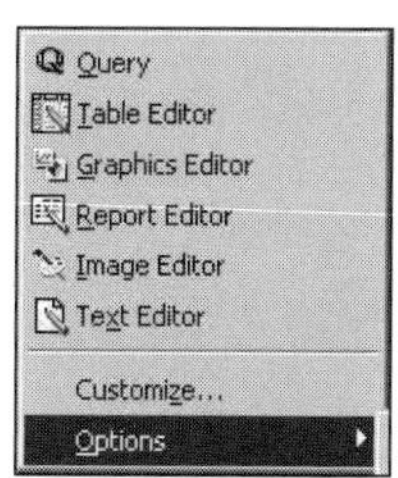

Enlarging the Font in the Enhanced Editor: The Enhanced Editor does not recognize the font setting in the Font dialog box. To change the font in the Enhanced Editor, first make sure it is the active window. Next, click **Tools → Options → Enhanced Editor**. Figure A4.3 shows the resulting dialog box.

Figure A4.3 Enhanced Editor Options Dialog Box

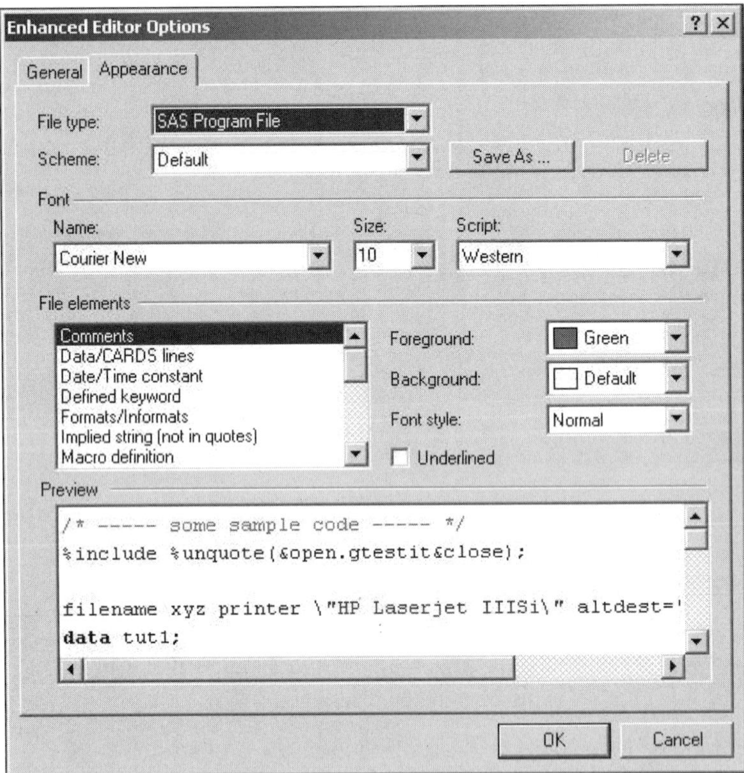

Use the **Name** and **Size** fields in the **Font** area to adjust the font to something you are comfortable reading. The maximum font size you can choose is 72 points.

When you are satisfied, click **OK**.

Note

> The Enhanced Editor remembers your font settings from one SAS session to the next, so you do not have to reset them every time you run the SAS System.

Enlarging the Fonts Used in the Descriptive Text of the SAS Explorer: To enlarge the font used in descriptive text (such as the tab labels) that appears in the SAS Explorer as well as the text that appears in the command bar, use the SYSGUIFONT system option.

This system option is valid only at SAS start-up (such as in the SAS command or in your SAS configuration file). The syntax of the SYSGUIFONT system option is as follows:

-SYSGUIFONT *"font-name" <font-size>*

Here is an explanation of the components of the SYSGUIFONT system option:

- *"font-name"* is a required option that specifies the name of a valid Windows font that matches the name of the font as it is installed on your system. Quotation marks are necessary.
- *font-size* specifies the font size to use for the window text. If you omit *font-size*, SAS uses the default size of 8 points.

Enlarging the Fonts Used in the Results Viewer Window: When viewing HTML files in the Results Viewer window, you can temporarily enlarge the fonts displayed by clicking the Cycle Font tool on the SAS System tool bar. Be sure the Results Viewer window is the active window.

The font size you choose by clicking Cycle Font is permanent, even from one SAS session to the next, until you change it again. The Cycle Fonts tool has no effect on any type of output except HTML. For example, it has no effect on PDF or RTF output.

Customizing Icons Used by the SAS System

The SAS GUI uses icons in several places—in the SAS Explorer, on the SAS System tool bar, and in some menus. You can customize these icons to some extent.

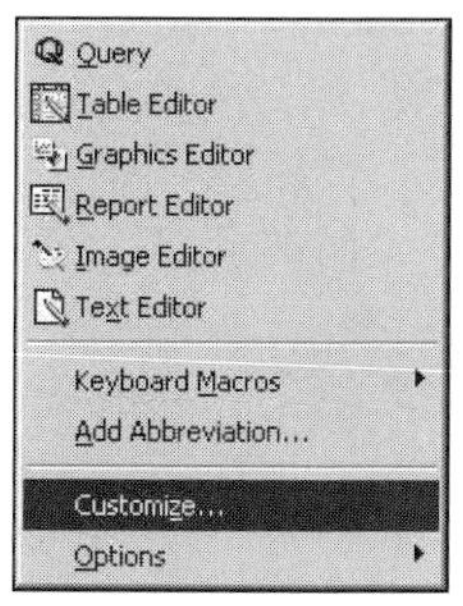

Enlarging Tool Bar Icons: You can make the SAS System tool bar icons larger, if you want. To do so, click **Tools** → **Customize**. This opens the Customize Tools dialog box, as shown in Figure A4.4.

Figure A4.4 Using the Customize Tools Dialog Box to Show Large Icons

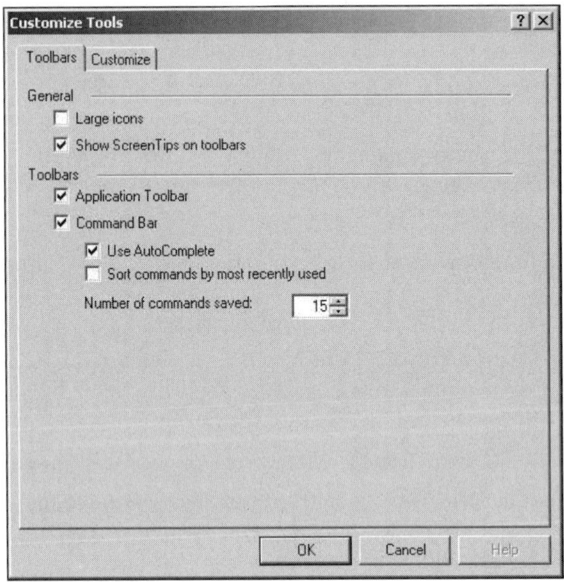

On the **Toolbars** tab, click **Large icons**. Figure A4.5 shows a comparison of the SAS System tool bar using the default icon size versus the large icons.

Figure A4.5 Comparison of Small and Large Tool Bar Icons

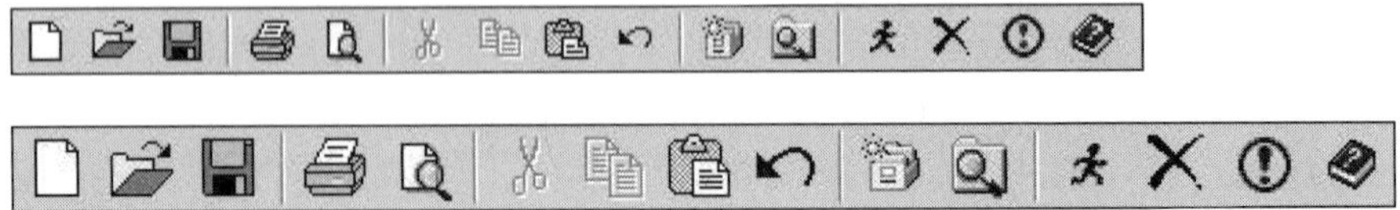

The **Large icons** option affects only the tool bar; it does not affect the tool box.

Note

> Depending on your screen resolution, using large icons may make some tool icons disappear off the edge of your screen. To use large icons, it is recommended that you have a high-resolution display.

Enlarging SAS Explorer Icons: You can also enlarge the icons used in the SAS Explorer window (as well as the My Favorite Folders window). By default, the SAS System uses small icons to represent libraries, data sets, and so on. To use large icons, make the SAS Explorer window active, then click **View** → **Large Icons**. The view adjusts accordingly. Figure A4.6 shows a comparison of the large and small icons used by the SAS Explorer.

Figure A4.6 Comparison of Large and Small Icons in the SAS Explorer

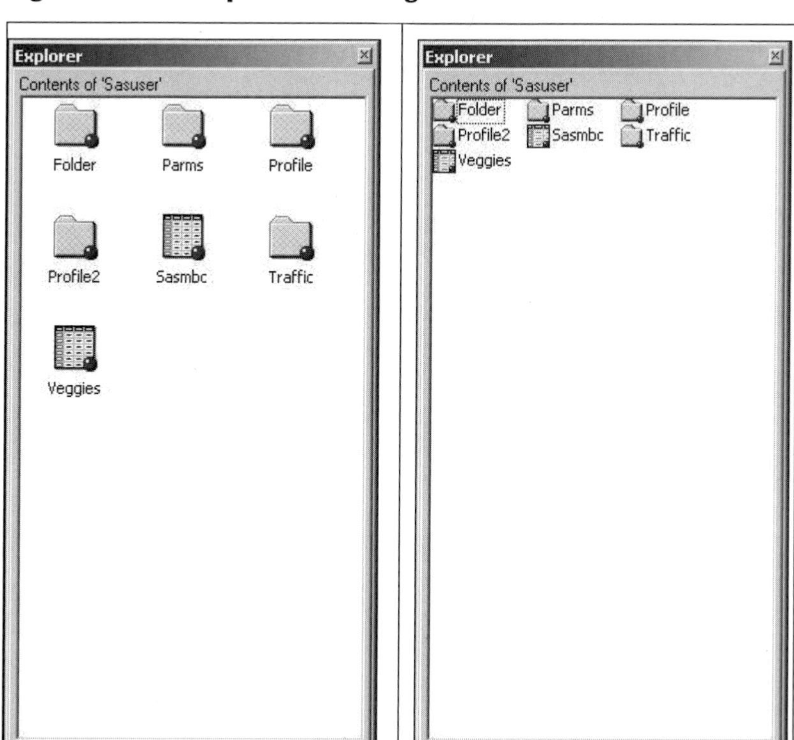

Note

> The large icon view is mutually exclusive with the list or details view. Nor does this technique affect the size of the icons used in the Results window.

Turning Off Icons in Menus: Some screen readers do not work well when reading menus that contain icons. If you encounter this problem, you can turn off the icons in the SAS menus. To turn the menu icons off, use the NOMENUICONS system option. This system option is valid both at SAS System start-up and in an OPTIONS statement, and has the following syntax:

MENUICONS | NOMENUICONS

(Use a hyphen in front of the menu name if you are using it at SAS System start-up, as with all system options.) By default, this option is set to MENUICONS. Figure A4.7 shows the View menu with and without menu icons.

Figure A4.7 Comparison of View Menu, Depending on the Setting of the MENUICONS System Option

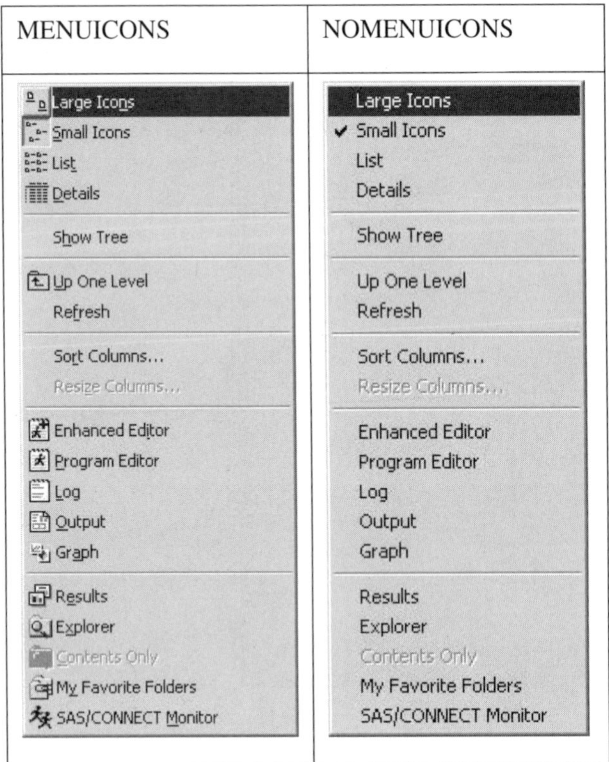

Note

For more ways to customize icons, see the first two bulleted items in "A Few More Useful Tips," later in this appendix.

Resizing the SAS Docking View

You can use your mouse to resize the area used to dock the SAS Explorer, Results window, and so on, just as you resize any other window. However, there are also other methods to accomplish this task.

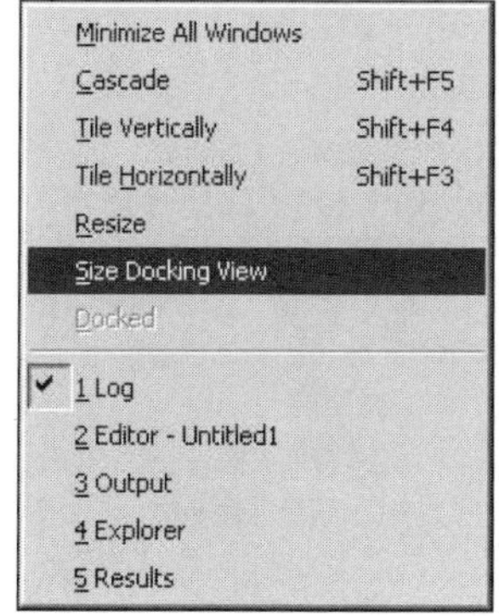

1. Use the hotkeys to access the menu choice **Window → Size Docking View** (press ALT, W, S in that order, but don't hold down the ALT key), or issue the WDOCKVIEWRESIZE command. This causes the mouse pointer to be positioned over the right margin of the docking area and turn into a double-headed arrow.

2. Now use your arrow keys to move the margin right or left. Holding the Control key down while using the arrow keys will move the margin a larger amount to the right or left. Here are two other useful keys:
   - HOME moves the docking area margin all the way to the left.
   - END moves the docking area margin all the way to the right.

3. Press ENTER to end resize mode and accept the change you made.

Note

To cancel out of resize mode, press ESC. This has an effect only if you have not already pressed ENTER to accept the change. You cannot undo a docking area resize except by resizing the area again.

When you end resize mode by pressing ENTER, the mouse pointer remains a double arrow until you move it.

The changes to the docking area size are not retained from one SAS session to the next by default. To make them permanent, select **Save settings on exit** on the **General** tab of the Preferences dialog box (see Chapter 6), and/or issue a WSAVE ALL command from the command bar.

Customizing How List Views Are Sorted in the SAS System

By default, the SAS Explorer and other windows that display a list view of files sort the entries by name. You can change how list views are sorted without using the mouse.

1. Make sure a window that uses columns is active (such as the SAS Explorer or My Favorite Folders window).

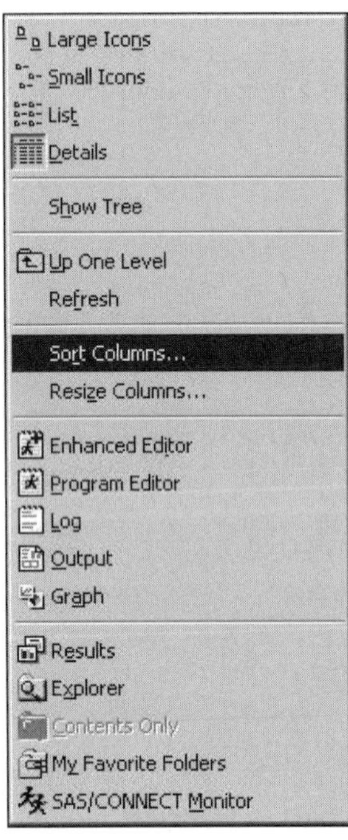

2. Use the hotkeys to access the menu choice **View → Sort Columns** (press ALT, V, R in that order, but don't hold down the ALT key), or issue the DLGCOLUMNSORT command. This causes the Sort Columns dialog box to appear, as shown in Figure A4.8.

Figure A4.8 Sort Columns Dialog Box

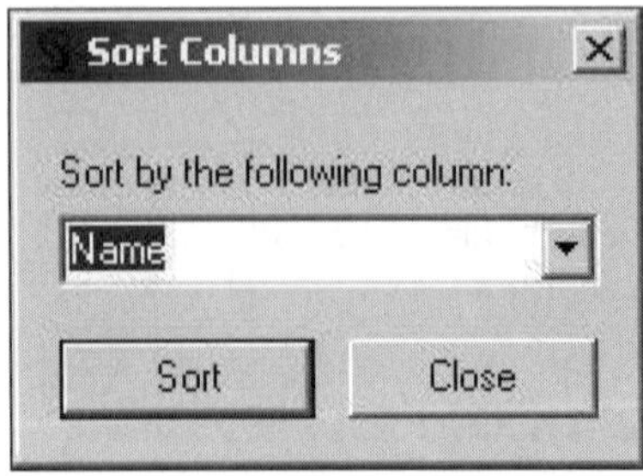

3. Choose a column name, then click **Sort**. The names of the columns to sort by vary, depending on what is in the list view. For example, if the SAS Explorer is showing the contents of the Libraries item, columns include Engine and Host Path Name. If you are examining the contents of a particular SAS library, columns include Size and Description.

   To close the Sort Columns dialog box, click **Close**.

Note

> You do not need to have list view or details turned on to use either the **Sort Columns** menu choice or the DLGCOLUMNSORT command. They work with both the small icon and large icon views, as well. You cannot save the column sort settings from one SAS session to the next.

Reversing the Sort Order: By default, the first time you select a column to sort by in the Sort Columns dialog box and click **Sort**, the sort is performed in ascending order. To reverse the sort order, click **Sort** again. The sort order is reversed. (This works even if you close the Sort Columns dialog box then open it again.)

Customizing the Width of List View Detail Columns in the SAS System

You can change column widths without using the mouse.

1. Make sure a window that uses columns is active (such as the SAS Explorer or My Favorite Folders window).
2. Use the hotkeys to access the menu choice **View → Resize Columns** (press ALT, V, Z in that order, but don't hold down the ALT key), or issue the DLGCOLUMNSIZE command. This causes the Column Settings dialog box to appear, as shown in Figure A4.9.

Figure A4.9 Column Settings Dialog Box

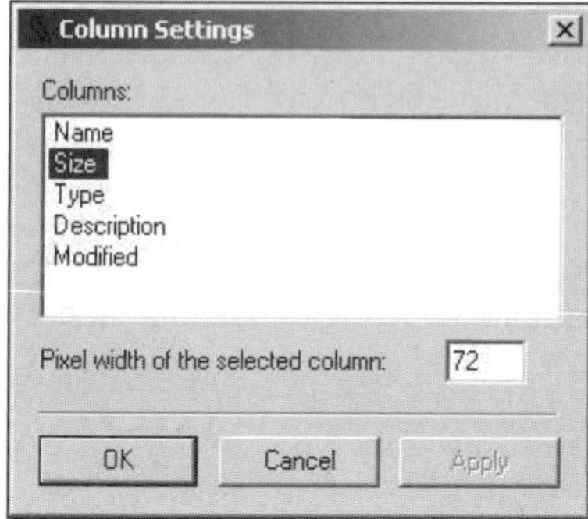

3. Select a column name (they vary, depending on the contents of the SAS Explorer), then type a pixel width in the width entry field. To apply the new width without closing the Column Settings dialog box, click **Apply**. To close the dialog box, click **OK**.

Note

> Although you do not need to have details turned on to use the DLGCOLUMNSIZE command, you do need to have the list view active (instead of large icons or small icons). You can access the **Resize Columns** menu choice only if details are turned on.

The column width settings are not retained from one SAS session to the next.

Windows 2000 Accessibility Features

Windows 2000 offers several accessibility features.* These features can make using the SAS System (and Windows in general) easier to use for people with sight, hearing, and mobility impairments. The subsequent sections will get you started exploring the accessibility features of Windows. For more detailed instructions, refer to the Windows online help.

Overview of Windows 2000 Accessibility Features: Windows 2000 offers the following accessibility programs:

- **Magnifier** — enlarges a portion of the screen.
- **Narrator** — uses text-to-speech technology to read the contents of the screen aloud.
- **On-Screen Keyboard** — lets you use a pointing device to type on screen.
- **Utility Manager** — lets users control accessibility programs, check on such programs' status, and automate the start-up of such programs.

In addition to these four programs, Windows 2000 also offers the following accessibility tools, via the Control Panel's **Accessibility Options**:

- **StickyKeys** — alters the behavior of certain control keys, such as SHIFT, ALT, and CTRL, so that multi-key commands (such as SHIFT-ALT-F5) can be executed one keystroke at a time.
- **FilterKeys** — adjusts the response of the keyboard, so that, for example, a key held down for a long period of time does not represent several instances of that key being pressed but rather only one instance. You can also select to ignore brief keystrokes, and adjust the repeat rate of keys.
- **ToggleKeys** — causes the computer to beep when certain control keys are pressed, such as Num Lock or Caps Lock.
- **SoundSentry** — accompanies system sounds (like error beeps) with a visual cue, such as a blinking program window.

---

* The features described here are standard in versions of Windows 2000 Professional and Windows 2000 Server purchased in the United States. If you purchased your copy outside the U.S., contact your subsidiary to discover whether these products and services are available in your area.

- **ShowSounds** — causes programs to display icons or captions for program speech and sounds.
- **Sound Schemes** — allows you to customize the sounds associated with a variety of "events" (such as errors and warnings).
- **High Contrast** — improves the contrast of the screen by using alternative colors and font sizes.
- **MouseKeys** — enables the numeric keypad on your keyboard to perform mouse functions.
- **SerialKeys** — enables you to use alternative input devices in place of a keyboard and mouse.
- **Dvorak keyboard layouts** — offer an alternative to the standard QWERTY keyboard layout.

The Windows 2000 Accessibility Wizard helps you set up the various accessibility features and programs to suit your particular needs.

Starting the Accessibility Wizard: To begin customizing your computer for your needs, click **Start → Programs → Accessories → Accessibility → Accessibility Wizard**. Figure A4.10 shows the first screen of the Accessibility Wizard.

Figure A4.10 Sample Accessibility Wizard Screens

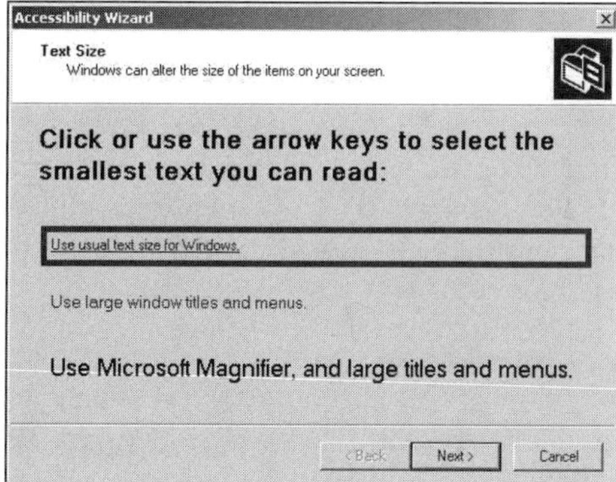

Follow the instructions on each screen, clicking **Next** to progress to the next step. When the wizard is finished, your computer will be tuned to your special needs and will allow you to be more productive while you use the SAS System. You can now use the Control Panel to further adjust the accessibility features, if necessary.

Using the Control Panel to Adjust Windows 2000 Accessibility Features: Begin by clicking **Start → Settings → Control Panel**. Now double-click **Accessibility Options**. Figure A4.11 shows the resulting window.

Figure A4.11 Control Panel Accessibility Options

Each tab in the Accessibility Options window lets you customize settings for that part of your computer. For example, FilterKeys is located on the **Keyboard** tab; SoundSentry is located on the **Sound** tab, and High Contrast is located on the **Display** tab. Explore the various tabs and settings until you find a combination that suits you.

Setting a Sound Scheme: If you have trouble hearing tones in a certain range (or if you can't stand the annoying beep that occurs every time you get a new e-mail message) you can adjust the sound scheme. To begin, click **Start** → **Settings** → **Control Panel**, then double-click **Sounds and Multimedia**. Now click the **Sounds** tab, which is shown in Figure A4.12.

Figure A4.12 Sound Panel

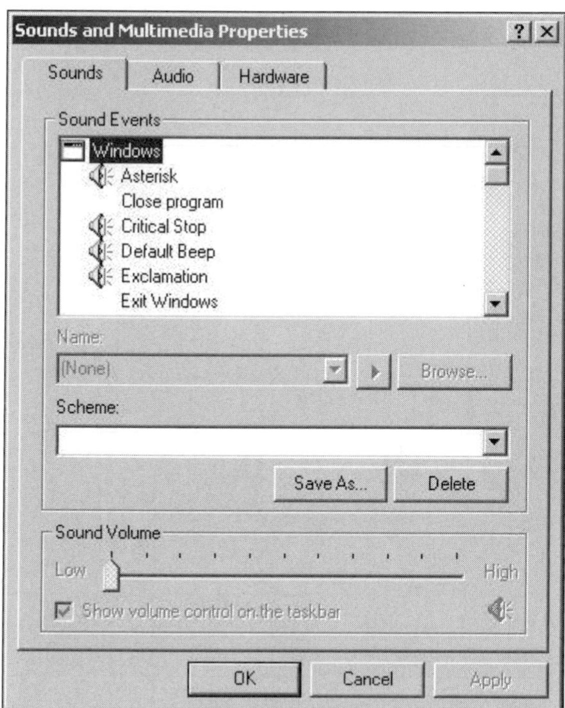

Scroll through the **Sound Events** list until you see the event you want to affect (such as **New Mail Notification**), then click the event name. Now click the down arrow next to the **Name** field, and select the sound you want to associate with the event (such as **None** or **ding.wav**). Click **OK** to make the change permanent. You can also adjust the sound volume, or save a collection of settings to a new scheme name.

Introducing the Utility Manager: The Utility Manager provides you with an efficient way to keep track of accessibility programs, such as Narrator and Magnifier. You can use the Utility Manager to start and stop accessibility programs, check on the status of an accessibility program, or program an accessibility program to start at a specified time (such as when your computer starts).

To start the Utility Manager, click **Start** → **Programs** → **Accessories** → **Accessibility** → **Utility Manager**. Figure A4.13 shows the Utility Manager window.

Figure A4.13 Utility Manager

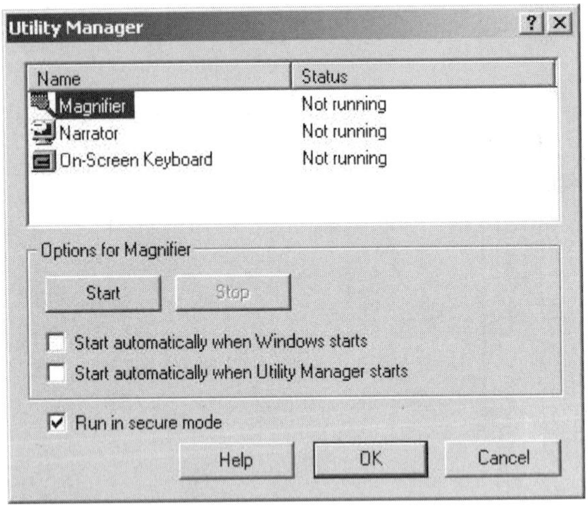

Note

> You must be part of the Windows Administrator group in order to specify that an accessibility program start automatically when Windows starts.

Introducing the Magnifier: The Magnifier ships with Windows 2000, and can help make the screen more readable if your vision is less than perfect. It does not magnify the entire screen, but uses a separate window that displays a magnified portion of the screen. To start the Magnifier, open the Utility Manager (see “Introducing the Utility Manager” on the previous page), select **Magnifier** in the list of programs, and click the **Start** button in the Utility Manager window. Figure A4.14 shows a sample desktop with the SAS System open, with the Magnifier window showing a portion of the SAS Explorer.

Figure A4.14 Using the Magnifier

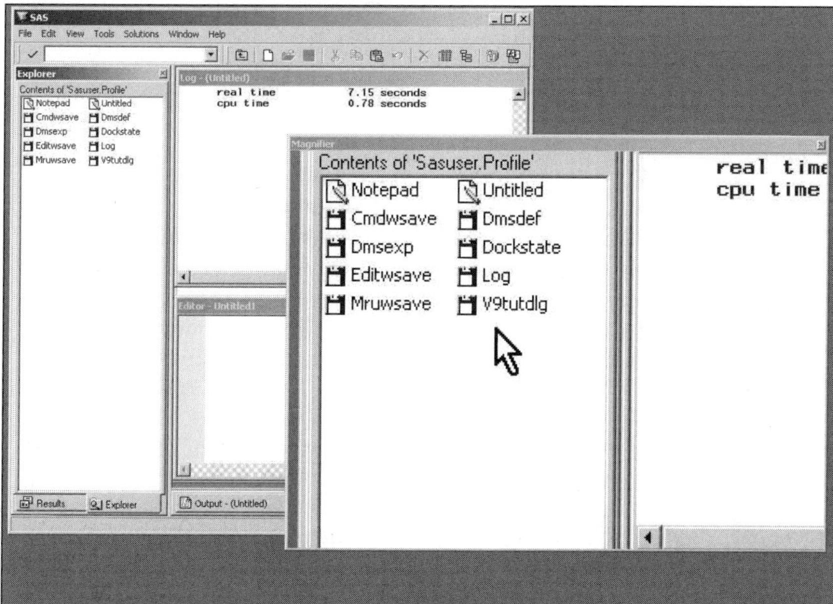

Note

> An alternative way to start the Magnifier program is to type `Magnifier` in the Run dialog box accessible from **Start** → **Run**.

Introducing the Narrator: The Narrator ships with Windows 2000, and is a text-to-speech utility. The Narrator reads what is displayed on the screen (for example, the contents of the active window, menu options, or the text you have typed). To start the Narrator, open the Utility Manager (see "Introducing the Utility Manager" earlier in this appendix), select **Narrator** in the list of programs, and click the **Start** button in the Utility Manager window.

Note

> You cannot use the Narrator without a sound card. Also, the Narrator is not available in all languages.

A Few More Useful Tips: The Windows Control Panel also offers some accessibility customizations through its **Display** and **Mouse** options.

- To increase the size of the icons on the Windows desktop and in the first-level **Start** button menu, click **Start** → **Settings** → **Control Panel**, then double-click **Display**. Click the **Effects** tab, then select the **Use large icons** option and click **OK**. This makes the icons on the Windows desktop much more visible. Unfortunately, the descriptive text below the icons stays the same size, as do the icons and text associated with deeper levels of the **Start** button menu.

- To increase the size of icons and/or text in Windows Explorer and SAS Explorer, and elsewhere in your system, click **Start** → **Settings** → **Control Panel**, then double-click **Display**. Click the **Appearance** tab. Now click the down arrow next to the **Item** field, and click **Icon** (you may need to scroll through the **Item** list). Finally, select a font name and size in the **Font** and **Size** fields, then close the dialog box by clicking **OK**. Not only does the descriptive text of icons increase in the SAS Explorer and SAS Results window, but so do fields such as the font and paragraph names in Microsoft Word and other programs.

  Note

  You can experiment with other selections in the **Item** list to further customize your display.

- To increase the size of the mouse pointer, click **Start** → **Settings** → **Control Panel**, then double-click **Mouse**. Click the **Pointers** tab; in the **Scheme** area, scroll through the list of available pointer schemes. Look for one called "Extra Large" or "Magnified." The exact schemes available depend on the mouse you have connected to your system. After choosing a scheme, click **OK**. The mouse pointer now exhibits the new scheme. (If you don't like the new one, you can always use the Mouse dialog box to choose a different one. Try various schemes until you find one you like.)

  Note

  "Taking Control of Your Mouse" in Chapter 1 gives more information on customizing your mouse.

If These Are Not Enough... Many more powerful accessibility tools are available, if the minimal level of accessibility offered by the standard Windows 2000 accessibility features is not enough. For example, programs exist that

- read information that is displayed on the screen in Braille or synthesized speech
- enable you to type or use the mouse by speaking
- modify how the keyboard and mouse behave.

Here are a few Web sites and other resources to get you started on your search for tools and programs that will help you be a more productive SAS user:

- **Microsoft Accessibility Web site** — www.microsoft.com/enable — a catalog of accessibility aids as well as a lot of other information.

- **STC AccessAbility Interest Group (SIG) Web site** — www.stcsig.org/sn — an exhaustive list of resources, articles, publications, and so on for a wide variety of disabilities. Although this site is maintained by a Society for Technical Communication SIG, it is of interest to many people outside the field of technical communication.
- **Trace R&D Center** — www.trace.wisc.edu — a database of over 18,000 products and other information for people with special needs.
- **Recording for the Blind and Dyslexic Web site** — www.rfbd.org — digital and audio versions of Microsoft product documentation and other printed matter.

Windows XP Accessibility Features

Windows XP builds on the accessibility features available in Windows 2000. New options include more cursor options, fast user switching (so you can switch user profiles without logging off and on again), and a simplified visual design. See Microsoft's Web site for more information (www.microsoft.com/enable).

Appendix 5 Exporting and Importing Information from the SAS Registry

Introduction

The SAS registry, like the Windows registry, is a complex but powerful tool for storing personal preferences, configuration settings, and so on. Typically, most SAS users do not need to worry about the SAS registry. Also, editing the SAS registry improperly can harm your SAS configuration settings, and could even prevent the SAS System from starting.

However, there are certain times when editing the SAS registry information can be useful. One such time is when you need to edit the attributes of a library reference. Perhaps you defined a library reference with the read-only V6 engine, but for some reason now need it to use the V9 engine. Or, maybe you need to change the physical path associated with the library reference. For example, a reorganization of the file structure on your system might require you to change hundreds of library references' physical paths.

While there are several ways to approach this problem (see "Editing Attributes of a Library Reference" in Chapter 9), one method is to use the SAS registry.

Note

There are many other things you can do with the SAS registry—this appendix barely scratches the surface of the SAS registry topic. See SAS Help and Documentation for more information about the SAS registry.

Getting Library References into the SAS Registry

Before you can use the SAS registry to manage your library references, you must ensure they are stored in the SAS registry. To accomplish this, select the **Enable at Startup** check box in the New Library dialog box when you create each library reference that you want stored in the SAS registry. (See "Creating a New Library Reference" in Chapter 9 for more information on using the New Library dialog box.)

Exporting the SAS Registry

Once you have used the New Library dialog box and the **Enable at Startup** check box to define your library references, the next step is to export the SAS registry information to a text file. To do so, submit the following code:

```
proc registry export = "c:\myreg.txt";
run;
```

Note

> You can use any filename in the EXPORT= option specification. C:\MYREG.TXT is just an example. The file extension must be .TXT, however.

Editing the Exported Registry File

Now that the SAS registry information is stored in a text file, you can examine it and edit it. Open the text file you specified in the EXPORT= option with a plain text editor, such as Windows Notepad.

Warning

> To edit your exported SAS registry information, you must use a text editor that saves the file as plain text. (If you use a word processing application, be sure to save the file as a plain ASCII text file without formatting codes.)

Figure A5.1 shows a sample SAS registry file open in the Windows Notepad editor.

Figure A5.1 Sample Exported SAS Registry File

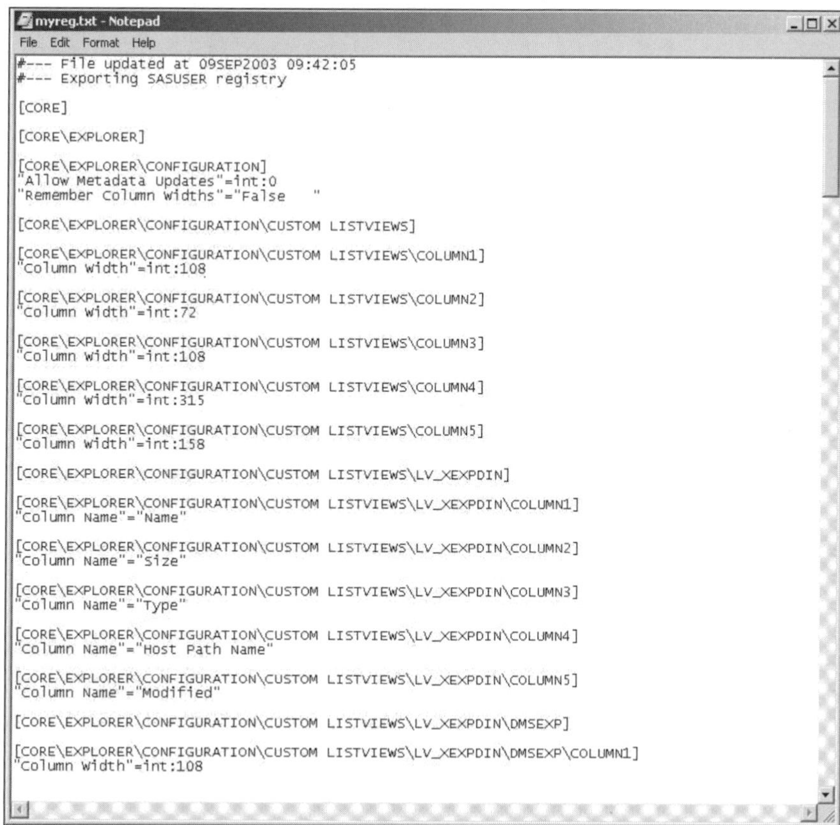


```
#--- File updated at 09SEP2003 09:42:05
#--- Exporting SASUSER registry

[CORE]

[CORE\EXPLORER]

[CORE\EXPLORER\CONFIGURATION]
"Allow Metadata Updates"=int:0
"Remember Column Widths"="False    "

[CORE\EXPLORER\CONFIGURATION\CUSTOM LISTVIEWS]

[CORE\EXPLORER\CONFIGURATION\CUSTOM LISTVIEWS\COLUMN1]
"Column Width"=int:108

[CORE\EXPLORER\CONFIGURATION\CUSTOM LISTVIEWS\COLUMN2]
"Column Width"=int:72

[CORE\EXPLORER\CONFIGURATION\CUSTOM LISTVIEWS\COLUMN3]
"Column Width"=int:108

[CORE\EXPLORER\CONFIGURATION\CUSTOM LISTVIEWS\COLUMN4]
"Column Width"=int:315

[CORE\EXPLORER\CONFIGURATION\CUSTOM LISTVIEWS\COLUMN5]
"Column Width"=int:158

[CORE\EXPLORER\CONFIGURATION\CUSTOM LISTVIEWS\LV_XEXPDIN]

[CORE\EXPLORER\CONFIGURATION\CUSTOM LISTVIEWS\LV_XEXPDIN\COLUMN1]
"Column Name"="Name"

[CORE\EXPLORER\CONFIGURATION\CUSTOM LISTVIEWS\LV_XEXPDIN\COLUMN2]
"Column Name"="Size"

[CORE\EXPLORER\CONFIGURATION\CUSTOM LISTVIEWS\LV_XEXPDIN\COLUMN3]
"Column Name"="Type"

[CORE\EXPLORER\CONFIGURATION\CUSTOM LISTVIEWS\LV_XEXPDIN\COLUMN4]
"Column Name"="Host Path Name"

[CORE\EXPLORER\CONFIGURATION\CUSTOM LISTVIEWS\LV_XEXPDIN\COLUMN5]
"Column Name"="Modified"

[CORE\EXPLORER\CONFIGURATION\CUSTOM LISTVIEWS\LV_XEXPDIN\DMSEXP]

[CORE\EXPLORER\CONFIGURATION\CUSTOM LISTVIEWS\LV_XEXPDIN\DMSEXP\COLUMN1]
"Column Width"=int:108
```

Use Notepad's Find dialog box (CTRL-F) to search for the beginning of the library reference section of the exported file. This section is marked by the text

[CORE\OPTIONS\LIBNAMES]

You can see from Figure A5.2 that the sample exported file contains definitions for two library references, MYLIB and MYLIB2.

Figure A5.2 Sample Exported SAS Registry File

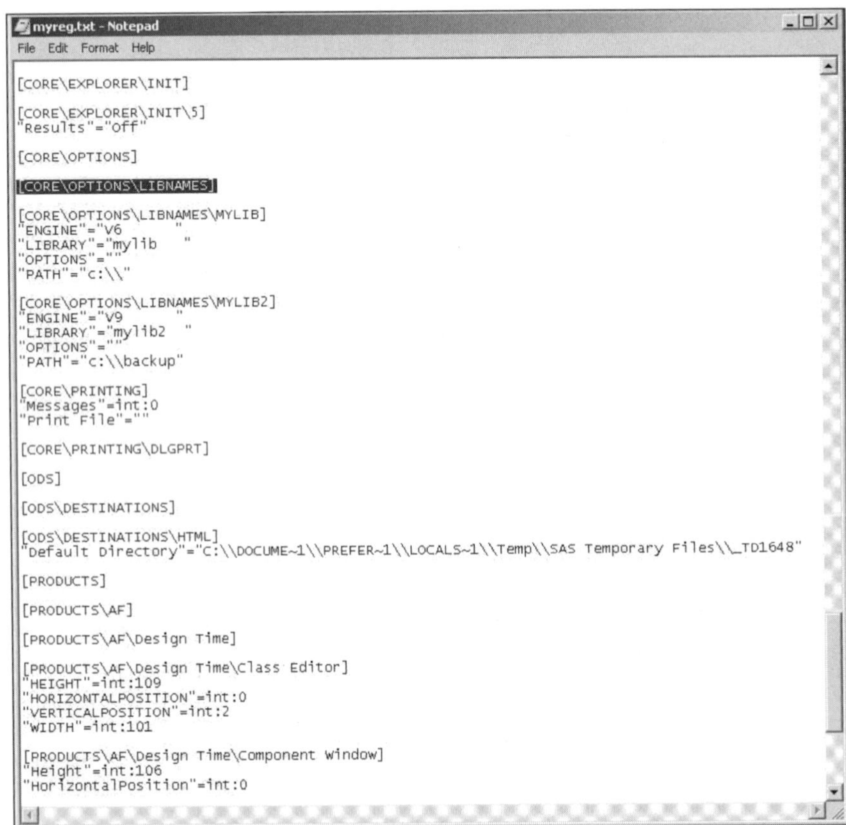

myreg.txt - Notepad

File Edit Format Help

```
[CORE\EXPLORER\INIT]

[CORE\EXPLORER\INIT\5]
"Results"="Off"

[CORE\OPTIONS]

[CORE\OPTIONS\LIBNAMES]

[CORE\OPTIONS\LIBNAMES\MYLIB]
"ENGINE"="V6      "
"LIBRARY"="mylib   "
"OPTIONS"=""
"PATH"="c:\\"

[CORE\OPTIONS\LIBNAMES\MYLIB2]
"ENGINE"="V9      "
"LIBRARY"="mylib2  "
"OPTIONS"=""
"PATH"="c:\\backup"

[CORE\PRINTING]
"Messages"=int:0
"Print File"=""

[CORE\PRINTING\DLGPRT]

[ODS]

[ODS\DESTINATIONS]

[ODS\DESTINATIONS\HTML]
"Default Directory"="C:\\DOCUME~1\\PREFER~1\\LOCALS~1\\Temp\\SAS Temporary Files\\_TD1648"

[PRODUCTS]

[PRODUCTS\AF]

[PRODUCTS\AF\Design Time]

[PRODUCTS\AF\Design Time\Class Editor]
"HEIGHT"=int:109
"HORIZONTALPOSITION"=int:0
"VERTICALPOSITION"=int:2
"WIDTH"=int:101

[PRODUCTS\AF\Design Time\Component Window]
"Height"=int:106
"HorizontalPosition"=int:0
```

You can edit the information associated with each library reference by editing the appropriate lines in the exported file. For example, you could change the physical path for MYLIB from C:\ to C:\MySASFiles by changing the line that reads

```
"PATH"="c:\\"
```

to

```
"PATH"="c:\\MySASFiles"
```

Note

Because of the syntax of the exported SAS registry file, the backslash (\) character must be followed by an additional backslash.

Once you have made the changes you need to make, save the file. Be sure you save it in text-only format.

Importing the Edited Registry Information

The final step is to import the edited SAS registry file into your SAS session. Use the following code to perform this step:

```
proc registry import = "myreg.txt";
run;
```

Use the same filename in the IMPORT= option that you used in the EXPORT= option when you exported the SAS registry information.

Glossary

active window: the application or part of an application that is ready to accept input.

application: a program with its attendant windows. Examples include programs such as the SAS System, Microsoft Word, and Netscape Navigator.

click: to press a mouse button once. Unless otherwise specified, click refers to the left mouse button.

client: an application that requests data or information from another application. For example, in OLE, the SAS System is the OLE client.

Clipboard: a Windows component that is like a pegboard—a place to store something until you need it again. Typically, the Clipboard is used to store text or graphics that you want to copy somewhere else.

close: to shut down an individual window or an entire application.

Close button: an X in the top-right corner of an application's main window. Clicking on the Close button closes the application. Every Windows application has a Close button, as do most windows within an application.

Compute Services: the process of submitting SAS statements that execute on a remote computer, in the context of SAS/CONNECT software.

Control Panel: a Windows application that manages various aspects of your desktop, such as printers, colors, device drivers, the keyboard and mouse, and so on. The Control Panel is part of the **Settings** program group that is accessed through the **Start** button.

Data Transfer Services: the process of uploading and downloading data between remote and local computers, in the context of SAS/CONNECT software.

DDE: *See* Dynamic Data Exchange (DDE).

DDE triplet: used in a FILENAME statement when you are using DDE (Dynamic Data Exchange).The DDE triplet tells the SAS System how to access data at a particular point in a file.

desktop: your screen, where all applications appear and where you do all of your work with Windows.

dialog box: a type of window that solicits information from you. Usually, you must supply this information before you can continue using an application.

directory: *See* folder.

double-click: to press the left mouse button twice quickly.

download: to move data from a remote computer to a local computer.

drag-and-drop: a method of using the mouse to move an object on your desktop from one place to another. You can drag and drop text, file icons, and graphics. Usually, when you drop the object, some action is taken, such as copying text or submitting a file.

Dynamic Data Exchange (DDE): a method of sharing text-based data between Windows applications.

embedded object: an OLE object that is not linked to the server application. The object and its data are stored in the client application. Embedded objects can be static or non-static. *Contrast with* linked object.

fileref: *See* file shortcut.

file shortcut: a nickname the SAS System uses for an external file or folder. You define file shortcuts with the FILENAME statement or using the SAS Explorer. In Version 6 of the SAS System, a file shortcut was called a fileref.

folder: a collection of files.

full pathname: the complete name of the physical file, including the drive, folder, subfolder, filename, and extension. An example of a full pathname is C:\SAS\SASUSER\APPEND.SAS.

icon: a pictorial representation of a Windows object. Examples of objects that can be represented by icons include entire applications, individual windows, and files.

library reference: a nickname the SAS System uses for a SAS data library. You define library references with the LIBNAME statement, the SAS Explorer, or the Active Libraries dialog box. In Version 6 of the SAS System, a library reference was called a libref.

libref: *See* library reference.

linked object: an OLE object that is dynamically connected to its OLE server. When you paste a linked object into an OLE client application, only the object—not the data—is stored in the client application. The data remain independent of the client. *Contrast with* embedded object.

main SAS window: the borders within which most SAS activities operate. A notable exception is SAS Help and Documentation, which opens in its own main window.

maximize: to cause an application or a window that is represented by an icon to return to full size and take up the whole display.

menu: a visual method of executing commands in an application. To use the menu, click on a menu choice.

minimize: to cause an application or a window to become an icon.

mouse: the handheld device you use to select and manipulate applications and text. The mouse activates the mouse pointer on the screen.

MP CONNECT: a feature of SAS/CONNECT software that lets you divide time-consuming tasks into multiple independent units of work and execute them in parallel on different servers or machines.

non-static embedded object: an OLE object that, when activated, can start its server application. *Contrast with* static embedded object.

object: something created by an OLE server that can be pasted into an OLE client application. Examples of objects are graphics, pieces of text, video clips, and sound files.

Object Linking and Embedding (OLE): a graphical method of sharing data between Windows applications.

ODS: *See* Output Delivery System (ODS).

OLE: *See* Object Linking and Embedding (OLE).

open editing: an OLE concept in which, when you edit an OLE object, the OLE server application starts in its own window, with its own menus and tool bars. *Contrast with* visual editing.

Output Delivery System (ODS): the portion of the SAS System that enables you to create different forms of output, such as SAS listing, HTML, and PDF output.

point: to move the mouse pointer over a particular item on the screen, such as a menu item, a word, or an icon.

popup menu: a menu that appears when you click the right mouse button.

program group: a collection of application icons in the **Start** button menu.

Remote Library Services (RLS): a method of data access used with SAS/CONNECT software. RLS accesses data directly on the remote computer without permanently transferring the data to the local computer.

right-click: to click the right mouse button once. Usually, this opens a popup menu.

RLS: *See* Remote Library Services (RLS).

SAS Explorer: a SAS window that lets you move, copy, rename, delete, and otherwise manage your SAS files (such as tables and catalog entries).

SAS table: a term synonymous with SAS data set.

SAS workspace: *See* main SAS window.

screen tip: an explanation of an application feature (such as a tool or a field in a dialog box) that appears when you hold the mouse pointer over the area for a few seconds.

scroll bar: a method of moving vertically or horizontally in a document. Scroll bars have arrows that you click to move the file view.

server: an application that provides data or services to another application. For example, in OLE, the application Word, Excel, or Lotus 1-2-3 can be an OLE server.

shortcut: a pointer or link to any object, such as a file, program, network folder, Control Panel tool, or disk drive.

spawner: a service that corresponds to a single port on the remote computer that listens for requests for remote connections to the remote computer. The spawner starts a remote SAS session on the remote computer on behalf of the connecting client.

StartUp folder: a Windows program group that contains programs that start immediately when Windows boots up.

static embedded object: an OLE object that is a picture. You cannot activate a static embedded object (that is, open its server application). *Contrast with* non-static embedded object.

style attribute: a specific aspect of the data presentation. For instance, the BACKGROUND= attribute controls the color for the background of an HTML table, and the FONT_STYLE= attribute specifies whether to use a roman, a slant, or an italic font. Used in ODS.

style definition: a collection of style elements that controls the overall appearance (color, font face, font size, and so on) of your output. Used in ODS.

style element: a collection of style attributes that apply to the presentation of a particular aspect of the output, such as column headers or cell data. Examples of style elements may also specify default colors and fonts for output that uses the style definition. Used in ODS.

subfolder: a collection of files that is part of a folder.

table: *See* SAS table.

table definition: a collection of table elements that describes how to render the output for a tabular output object. A table definition determines the order of table headers and footers, the order of columns, and the overall appearance of the output object that uses it. Each table definition contains or references table elements. Used in ODS.

table element: a collection of attributes that apply to a particular table column, header, or footer. Typically, these attributes specify something about the data rather than about their presentation. For instance, FORMAT= specifies the SAS format to use in a column. However, some attributes describe presentation aspects of the data. Used in ODS.

Taskbar: a portion of the Windows desktop that lists by name all of the open Windows applications. To access an application, click on its name in the Taskbar.

template store: a SAS file that stores the template (for ODS) definitions (style, table, and so on) that SAS provides, and definitions that you create using the TEMPLATE procedure. Definitions that SAS provides are in the template store SASHELP.TMPLMST. You can store your definitions in any template store where you have write access.

title bar: the horizontal element at the top of a Windows application's main window that tells you which application you are running. Individual windows inside an application also have title bars.

tool bar: a visual method of executing commands in a Windows application. Each command is represented by an icon. To execute the command, click on the appropriate icon.

upload: to move data from a local computer to a remote computer.

visual editing: an OLE concept in which, when you edit an OLE object, the OLE server application menus and tool bars meld with the OLE client's menus and tool bars. *Contrast with* open editing.

window bar: a portion of the main SAS window that lists all of the open SAS windows. To access a window, click on its name in the Window Bar.

Windows Explorer: a Windows application that lets you move, copy, delete, rename, and otherwise manage your files. The Windows Explorer can be accessed by right-clicking on the **Start** button and then clicking **Explore**.

wizard: a Windows tool that guides you through a process, such as adding a printer to your system, installing new software, or importing data into a SAS table.

Index

D

E

F

M

N

O

Q

S

T

U

V

X

Symbols

Call your local SAS office to order these books from Books by Users Press

Advanced Log-Linear Models Using SAS®
by **Daniel Zelterman** . . . . Order No. A57496

Analysis of Clinical Trials Using SAS®: A Practical Guide
by **Alex Dmitrienko, Walter Offen, Christy Chuang-Stein,**
and **Geert Molenbergs** . . . . Order No. A59390

Annotate: Simply the Basics
by **Art Carpenter** . . . . Order No. A57320

Applied Multivariate Statistics with SAS® Software, Second Edition
by **Ravindra Khattree**
and **Dayanand N. Naik** . . . . Order No. A56903

Applied Statistics and the SAS® Programming Language, Fourth Edition
by **Ronald P. Cody**
and **Jeffrey K. Smith** . . . . Order No. A55984

An Array of Challenges — Test Your SAS® Skills
by **Robert Virgile** . . . . Order No. A55625

Carpenter's Complete Guide to the SAS® Macro Language, Second Edition
by **Art Carpenter** . . . . Order No. A59224

The Cartoon Guide to Statistics
by **Larry Gonick**
and **Woollcott Smith** . . . . Order No. A5515

Categorical Data Analysis Using the SAS® System, Second Edition
by **Maura E. Stokes, Charles S. Davis,**
and **Gary G. Koch** . . . . Order No. A57998

Cody's Data Cleaning Techniques Using SAS® Software
by **Ron Cody** . . . . Order No. A57198

Common Statistical Methods for Clinical Research with SAS® Examples, Second Edition
by **Glenn A. Walker** . . . . Order No. A58086

Debugging SAS® Programs: A Handbook of Tools and Techniques
by **Michele M. Burlew** . . . . Order No. A57743

Efficiency: Improving the Performance of Your SAS® Applications
by **Robert Virgile** . . . . Order No. A55960

The Essential PROC SQL Handbook for SAS® Users
by **Katherine Prairie** . . . . Order No. A58546

Fixed Effects Regression Methods for Longitudinal Data Using SAS®
by **Paul D. Allison** . . . . Order No. A58348

Genetic Analysis of Complex Traits Using SAS®
Edited by **Arnold M. Saxton** . . . . Order No. A59454

A Handbook of Statistical Analyses Using SAS®, Second Edition
by **B.S. Everitt**
and **G. Der** . . . . Order No. A58679

Health Care Data and the SAS® System
by **Marge Scerbo, Craig Dickstein,**
and **Alan Wilson** . . . . Order No. A57638

The How-To Book for SAS/GRAPH® Software
by **Thomas Miron** . . . . Order No. A55203

support.sas.com/pubs

Instant ODS: Style Templates for the Output Delivery System
by **Bernadette Johnson** . . . . Order No. A58824

In the Know... SAS® Tips and Techniques From Around the Globe
by **Phil Mason** . . . . Order No. A55513

Integrating Results through Meta-Analytic Review Using SAS® Software
by **Morgan C. Wang**
and **Brad J. Bushman** . . . . Order No. A55810

Learning SAS® in the Computer Lab, Second Edition
by **Rebecca J. Elliott**. . . . . Order No. A57739

The Little SAS® Book: A Primer
by **Lora D. Delwiche**
and **Susan J. Slaughter** . . . . Order No. A55200

The Little SAS® Book: A Primer, Second Edition
by **Lora D. Delwiche**
and **Susan J. Slaughter** . . . . Order No. A56649
(updated to include Version 7 features)

The Little SAS® Book: A Primer, Third Edition
by **Lora D. Delwiche**
and **Susan J. Slaughter** . . . . Order No. A59216
(updated to include SAS 9.1 features)

Logistic Regression Using the SAS® System: Theory and Application
by **Paul D. Allison** . . . . Order No. A55770

Longitudinal Data and SAS®: A Programmer's Guide
by **Ron Cody** . . . . Order No. A58176

Maps Made Easy Using SAS®
by **Mike Zdeb**. . . . . Order No. A57495

Models for Discrete Data
by **Daniel Zelterman** . . . . Order No. A57521

Multiple Comparisons and Multiple Tests Using SAS® Text and Workbook Set
(*books in this set also sold separately*)
by **Peter H. Westfall, Randall D. Tobias, Dror Rom, Russell D. Wolfinger,**
and **Yosef Hochberg** . . . . Order No. A55770

Multiple-Plot Displays: Simplified with Macros
by **Perry Watts** . . . . Order No. A58314

Multivariate Data Reduction and Discrimination with SAS® Software
by **Ravindra Khattree,**
and **Dayanand N. Naik** . . . . Order No. A56902

Output Delivery System: The Basics
by **Lauren E. Haworth** . . . . Order No. A58087

Painless Windows: A Handbook for SAS® Users, Third Edition
by **Jodie Gilmore** . . . . Order No. A58783
(*updated to include Version 8 and SAS 9.1 features*)

PROC TABULATE by Example
by **Lauren E. Haworth** . . . . Order No. A56514

Professional SAS® Programming Shortcuts
by **Rick Aster** . . . . Order No. A59353

Quick Results with SAS/GRAPH® Software
by **Arthur L. Carpenter**
and **Charles E. Shipp**. . . . . Order No. A55127

Quick Results with the Output Delivery System
by **Sunil Gupta** . . . . Order No. A58458

Quick Start to Data Analysis with SAS®
by **Frank C. DiIorio**
and **Kenneth A. Hardy** . . . . Order No. A55550

Reading External Data Files Using SAS®: Examples Handbook
by **Michele M. Burlew** . . . . Order No. A58369

Regression and ANOVA: An Integrated Approach Using SAS® Software
by **Keith E. Muller**
and **Bethel A. Fetterman** . . . . Order No. A57559

SAS® Applications Programming: A Gentle Introduction
by **Frank C. DiIorio** . . . . Order No. A56193

SAS® for Forecasting Time Series, Second Edition
by **John C. Brocklebank**
and **David A. Dickey** . . . . Order No. A57275

SAS® for Linear Models, Fourth Edition
by **Ramon C. Littell, Walter W. Stroup,**
and **Rudolf Freund** . . . . Order No. A56655

SAS® for Monte Carlo Studies: A Guide for Quantitative Researchers
by **Xitao Fan, Ákos Felsővályi, Stephen A. Sivo,**
and **Sean C. Keenan** . . . . Order No. A57323

SAS® Functions by Example
by **Ron Cody** . . . . Order No. A59343

SAS® Macro Programming Made Easy
by **Michele M. Burlew** . . . . Order No. A56516

SAS® Programming by Example
by **Ron Cody**
and **Ray Pass** . . . . Order No. A55126

SAS® Programming for Researchers and Social Scientists, Second Edition
by **Paul E. Spector** . . . . Order No. A58784

SAS® Survival Analysis Techniques for Medical Research, Second Edition
by **Alan B. Cantor** . . . . Order No. A58416

SAS® System for Elementary Statistical Analysis, Second Edition
by **Sandra D. Schlotzhauer**
and **Ramon C. Littell**. . . . . Order No. A55172

SAS® System for Mixed Models
by **Ramon C. Littell, George A. Milliken, Walter W. Stroup,** and **Russell D. Wolfinger** . . Order No. A55235

SAS® System for Regression, Second Edition
by **Rudolf J. Freund**
and **Ramon C. Littell**. . . . . Order No. A56141

SAS® System for Statistical Graphics, First Edition
by **Michael Friendly** . . . . Order No. A56143

The SAS® Workbook and Solutions Set
(*books in this set also sold separately*)
by **Ron Cody** . . . . Order No. A55594

Selecting Statistical Techniques for Social Science Data: A Guide for SAS® Users
by **Frank M. Andrews, Laura Klem, Patrick M. O'Malley, Willard L. Rodgers, Kathleen B. Welch,**
and **Terrence N. Davidson** . . . . Order No. A55854

Statistical Quality Control Using the SAS® System
by **Dennis W. King**. . . . . Order No. A55232

A Step-by-Step Approach to Using the SAS® System for Factor Analysis and Structural Equation Modeling
by **Larry Hatcher**. . . . . Order No. A55129

A Step-by-Step Approach to Using the SAS® System for Univariate and Multivariate Statistics, Second Edition
by **Larry Hatcher, Norm O'Rourke,**
and **Edward Stepanski** . . . . Order No. A55072

Step-by-Step Basic Statistics Using SAS®: Student Guide and Exercises
(*books in this set also sold separately*)
by **Larry Hatcher**. . . . . Order No. A57541

Survival Analysis Using the SAS® System: A Practical Guide
by **Paul D. Allison** . . . . Order No. A55233

Tuning SAS® Applications in the OS/390 and z/OS Environments, Second Edition
by **Michael A. Raithel** . . . . Order No. A58172

Univariate and Multivariate General Linear Models: Theory and Applications Using SAS® Software
by **Neil H. Timm**
and **Tammy A. Mieczkowski**. . . . . . . Order No. A55809

Using SAS® in Financial Research
by **Ekkehart Boehmer, John Paul Broussard,**
and **Juha-Pekka Kallunki** . . . . Order No. A57601

Using the SAS® Windowing Environment: A Quick Tutorial
by **Larry Hatcher**. . . . . Order No. A57201

Visualizing Categorical Data
by **Michael Friendly** . . . . Order No. A56571

Web Development with SAS® by Example
by **Frederick Pratter** . . . . Order No. A58694

Your Guide to Survey Research Using the SAS® System
by **Archer Gravely**. . . . . Order No. A55688

JMP® Books

JMP® for Basic Univariate and Multivariate Statistics: A Step-by-Step Guide
by **Ann Lehman, Norm O'Rourke, Larry Hatcher,**
and **Edward Stepanski** . . . . Order No. A59814

JMP® Start Statistics, Third Edition
by **John Sall, Ann Lehman,**
and **Lee Creighton** . . . . Order No. A58166

Regression Using JMP®
by **Rudolf J. Freund, Ramon C. Littell,**
and **Lee Creighton** . . . . Order No. A58789

support.sas.com/pubs